AF649529

Nine Dimensions of Scaffolding for Multilingual Learners

For Dr. Rita Dunn, a dear mentor we all shared and from whom we learned so much!
We are forever grateful for her guidance.
Her legacy lives on in all we do.

Nine Dimensions of Scaffolding for Multilingual Learners

Maria G. Dove
Andrea Honigsfeld
Carrie McDermott Goldman

CORWIN

CORWIN

For information:

Corwin
A Sage Company
2455 Teller Road
Thousand Oaks, California 91320
(800) 233-9936
www.corwin.com

Sage Publications Ltd.
1 Oliver's Yard
55 City Road
London EC1Y 1SP
United Kingdom

Sage Publications India Pvt. Ltd.
Unit No 323-333, Third Floor, F-Block
International Trade Tower Nehru Place
New Delhi 110 019
India

Sage Publications Asia-Pacific Pte. Ltd.
18 Cross Street #10-10/11/12
China Square Central
Singapore 048423

Copyright © 2026 by Corwin Press, Inc.

All rights reserved. Except as permitted by U.S. copyright law, no part of this work may be reproduced or distributed in any form or by any means, or stored in a database or retrieval system, without permission in writing from the publisher.

When forms and sample documents appearing in this work are intended for reproduction, they will be marked as such. Reproduction of their use is authorized for educational use by educators, local school sites, and/or noncommercial or nonprofit entities that have purchased the book.

All third-party trademarks referenced or depicted herein are included solely for the purpose of illustration and are the property of their respective owners. Reference to these trademarks in no way indicates any relationship with, or endorsement by, the trademark owner.

No AI training. Without in any way limiting the author's and publisher's exclusive rights under copyright, any use of this publication to "train" generative artificial intelligence (AI) or for other AI uses is expressly prohibited. The publisher reserves all rights to license uses of this publication for generative AI training or other AI uses.

ISBN 978-1-0719-1998-9

Library of Congress Control Number: 2025027187

Vice President and Editorial Director: Monica Eckman
Senior Acquisitions Editor: Megan Bedell
Senior Content Development Editor: Mia Rodriguez
Senior Editorial Assistant: Natalie Delpino
Production Editor: Vijayakumar
Copy Editor: Tammy Giesmann
Typesetter: TNQ Tech Pvt. Ltd.
Proofreader: Girish Sharma
Indexer: TNQ Tech Pvt. Ltd.
Cover Designer: Candice Harman
Marketing Manager: Melissa Duclos

DISCLAIMER: This book may direct you to access third-party content via web links, QR codes, or other scannable technologies, which are provided for your reference by the author(s). Corwin makes no guarantee that such third-party content will be available for your use and encourages you to review the terms and conditions of such third-party content. Corwin takes no responsibility and assumes no liability for your use of any third-party content, nor does Corwin approve, sponsor, endorse, verify, or certify such third-party content.

Contents

Companion Website Resources

CHAPTER 1

FIGURE 1.4: SCAFFOLDING IMPLEMENTATION
TABLE 1.1: THE CARES LENS

CHAPTER 2

TABLE 2.1: QUESTION STEMS AND PROMPTS VIA BLOOM'S TAXONOMY
TABLE 2.2: QUESTION AND PROMPT EXAMPLES IN AN EARTH SCIENCE CLASS USING STAGES OF LANGUAGE ACQUISITION AND BLOOM'S TAXONOMY
TABLE 2.5: PEER WRITING ANALYSIS GUIDE

CHAPTER 3

TABLE 3.1: ACADEMIC LANGUAGE DIMENSIONS, FEATURES, CHALLENGES, AND ESSENTIAL SCAFFOLDING PRACTICES
FIGURE 3.6: PWIM SCAFFOLDS FOR FIRST GRADERS ON PLAYGROUNDS
FIGURE 3.9: ACCOUNTABLE TALK PLANNING TOOL

CHAPTER 4

TABLE 4.3: STORYBOARD TEMPLATE
TABLE 4.4: SELF-ASSESSMENT OF MULTIMODAL LEARNING CHOICES

CHAPTER 5

TABLE 5.2: MULTISENSORY STRATEGY REFLECTION CHART
TABLE 5.3: VIDEO VIEWING TEMPLATE
FIGURE 5.10: GALLERY WALK RESPONSE SHEET

CHAPTER 6

TABLE 6.2: "LIFT A LINE" METACOGNITIVE TOOL
TABLE 6.5: DIFFERENTIATING GRAPHIC SCAFFOLDS BASED ON THE 3MS

CHAPTER 7

CHAPTER 8

CHAPTER 9

CHAPTER 10

online resources

These resources are available for download at
https://companion.corwin.com/courses/NineDimensionsofScaffoldingforMLs

Acknowledgments

We would like to offer our heartfelt gratitude to our brilliant former editor, Dan Alpert, now enjoying a well-earned retirement. Dan, you believed in two unknown authors, Maria and Andrea, many years ago, taking us under your wing with unwavering faith in our potential. Your mentorship, wisdom, and keen awareness of what the field needed to hear propelled our work forward and gave us the courage to believe in ourselves. You championed our voices, guided us with care, and left an indelible mark on both our journey and the field of teaching multilingual learners. We are forever grateful for your counsel and your ability to see what was possible. We miss our frequent emails and phone calls and carry your lessons with us always.

We wish to thank Megan Bedell, our acquisitions editor, Mia Rodriguez, our content development editor, Lucas Schleicher, content development manager, and the entire Corwin team for their support and guidance throughout this process. Your efforts have helped shape and refine our work, ensuring this book is positioned to make the greatest possible impact. We appreciate your professionalism, collaboration, and patience in bringing this project to completion, and we are grateful for the role each of you has played in making it a reality.

We would like to extend our sincere thanks to Sherry Liptak for her invaluable assistance with the final readthrough of the page proofs. Your meticulous attention to detail and thoughtful input have helped us ensure the clarity and quality of our work, and we are truly grateful for your support during this critical stage of the process.

We extend our deepest gratitude to all the educators who contributed to this work. Your insights, experiences, and dedication to the profession have enriched this project in countless ways. Your willingness to share your practices and perspectives with us has been instrumental in shaping the ideas presented here, and we are deeply inspired by your commitment to making a difference in the lives of multilingual learners:

Brianna Adachi, Kandice Adams, Yonique Benn, Andrea Bitner, Kristie Budich, Grace Campbell-Sheran, Dr. Hyonsuk Cho, Elizabeth Choi, Kristin Chouinard, Kelly Cray, Tamara Coburn, Rachel Cutter, Melissa Dinelli, Melissa Dishart, Dr. Elena Dokshansky, Dominique Donnelly, Dr. Amy Eckelmann, Jennifer Edwards, Sarah Elia, Holly Ellis, Sasha Engelsman, Sarah Forbes, Michelle Gill, Courtney Gilpin, Mariel Gómez de la Torre–Cerfontaine,

Claribel González, Yulissa Gutierrez, Crystal Hafner, Amanda Haleiko, Louise Herington, Erin Holtkamp, Tan Huynh, Kristina Jackson, Adile Jones, Sarah Kawzenuk, Dr. Nadia Khan-Roopnarine, Cierra LaBounty, Claudia Leon, Katie Leven, Sherry Liptak, Christine Lopez, Jenna Maneri, Migdalia Marco, Samantha Marengo, Hannah McGoff, Maria Neckonoff, Alycia Owen, Selvi Oyola, Amy Peabody-Chieffo, Natalie Pecoraro, Dr. Sinelia Espindola Peixoto, Lani Perez-Santana, Mary Sue Ragsdale, Jason Raymond, James Ridgely, Heather Rubin, Mary Sandoval, Holly Sawyer, Adeline Scibelli, Dr. Victoria Seelinger, Pushpanjali Sengupta, Kimberly Shorey, Nicole Sibiski, Holly Siggins, Marni Smith, Emily Smyth, Kanako Suwa, Dr. Katie Toppel, Alexis Tucker, Jessica Vest, Nick Villani, Nancy Weng, and Rosemary Zavaglia Rutigliano.

Finally, to our families, friends, and colleagues who have supported us through the years, we cannot thank you enough for your patience, encouragement, and belief in us. Your unwavering support has been a source of strength. To everyone who played a part in bringing this project to life, we are profoundly grateful.

About the Authors

Maria G. Dove, EdD, is professor in the School of Education and Human Services at Molloy University, Rockville Centre, New York. She teaches preservice and inservice teachers about the research and best practices for implementing effective instruction for English learners, and she supports doctoral students in the EdD program in Educational Leadership for Diverse Learning Communities. Before entering the field of higher education, she worked for over thirty years as an English-as-a-second-language teacher in public school settings (Grades K–12) and in adult English language programs in the greater New York City area. She frequently provides professional development for educators throughout the United States on the teaching of multilingual learners. She also serves as a mentor for new ESOL teachers as well as an instructional coach for general-education teachers and literacy specialists.

With Andrea Honigsfeld, she has coauthored multiple best-selling Corwin books, including *Collaboration and Co-Teaching: Strategies for English Learners* (2010), *Common Core for the Not-So-Common Learner, Grades K–5: English Language Arts Strategies* (2013), and *Common Core for the Not-So-Common Learner, Grades 6–12: English Language Arts Strategies* (2013), *Collaboration and Co-Teaching: A Leader's Guide* (2015), *Co-Teaching for English Learners: A Guide to Collaborative Planning, Instruction, Assessment, and Reflection* (2018). Along with other Corwin top-named authors, she coauthored *Breaking Down the Wall: Essential Shifts for English Learner Success* (2020). In addition, she coedited, *Coteaching and Other Collaborative Practices in the EFL/ESL Classroom: Rationale, Research, Reflections, and Recommendations* (2012) and *Co-Teaching for English Learners: Evidence-Based Practices and Research-Informed Outcomes* (2020) published by Information Age. With Audrey Cohan and Andrea Honigsfeld, she coauthored *Beyond Core Expectations: A Schoolwide Framework for Serving the Not-So-Common Learner* (2014) published by Corwin and *Team Up, Speak Up, Fire Up: Educators, Students, and the Community Working Together to Support English Learners* (2020) published by ASCD.

Andrea Honigsfeld, EdD, is professor in the School of Education and Human Services at Molloy University, Rockville Centre, New York. Before entering the field of teacher education, she was an English-as-a-foreign-language teacher in Hungary (Grades 5–8 and adult) and an English-as-a-second-language teacher in New York City (Grades K–3 and adult). She also taught Hungarian at New York University. She was the recipient of a doctoral fellowship at St. John's University, New York, where she conducted research on individualized instruction. She has published extensively on working with multilingual learners and teacher collaboration. She received a Fulbright Award to lecture in Iceland in the fall of 2002. In the past 22 years, she has been presenting at conferences across the United States, China, Denmark, Japan, the Philippines, Sweden, Thailand, the United Kingdom, and the United Arab Emirates.

She coauthored *Differentiated Instruction for At-Risk Students* (2009) and coedited the five-volume *Breaking the Mold of Education* series (2010–2013), published by Rowman and Littlefield. She is also the coauthor of *Core Instructional Routines: Go-To Structures for Effective Literacy Teaching, K–5 and 6–12* (2014), *Growing Language and Literacy* (K-8 and 6–12, 2019, 2024 respectively) published by Heinemann. With Maria G. Dove, she coedited *Coteaching and Other Collaborative Practices in the EFL/ESL Classroom: Rationale, Research, Reflections, and Recommendations* (2012), *Co-Teaching for English Learners: Evidence-Based Practices and Research-Informed Outcomes* (2020), *Portraits of Collaboration: Educators Working Together to Support Multilingual Learners* (2022), and coauthored *Collaboration and Co-Teaching: Strategies for English Learners* (2010), *Common Core for the Not-So-Common Learner, Grades K–5: English Language Arts Strategies* (2013), *Common Core for the Not-So-Common Learner, Grades 6–12: English Language Arts Strategies* (2013), *Beyond Core Expectations: A Schoolwide Framework for Serving the Not-So-Common Learner* (2014), *Collaboration and Co-Teaching: A Leader's Guide* (2015), *Co-Teaching for English Learners: A Guide to Collaborative Planning, Instruction, Assessment, and Reflection* (2018), *Collaborating for English Learners: A Foundational Guide to Integrated Practices* (2019), and *Co-Planning: 5 Essential Practices to Integrate Curriculum and Instruction for English Learners* (2022). She is a contributing author of *Breaking Down the Wall: Essential Shifts for English Learner Success* (2020), *From Equity Insights to Action* (2021), *Digital-Age Teaching for English Learners* (2022), *Collaboration and Co-Teaching for Dual Language Learners: Transforming Programs for Multilingualism and Equity* (2023), *Breaking Down the Monolingual Wall: Essential Shifts for Multilingual Learners' Success* (2024). *Collaboration for Multilingual Learners With Exceptionalities: We Share the Students* (2024), and *Collaborative Assessment for Multilingual Learners and Teachers: Pathways to Partnerships* (2025). Ten of her Corwin books are bestsellers.

Dr. Carrie McDermott Goldman, an associate professor at Molloy University's School of Education and Human Services (Rockville Centre, NY), brings over two decades of experience to her role teaching preservice and inservice teachers. Her career demonstrates a commitment to transforming education through innovative teaching, mentorship, and promoting equitable learning opportunities for all students. Her areas of expertise include culturally responsive-sustaining pedagogies, teaching English to students of other languages (grades PK–12 and adults); elementary, middle, and secondary education; curriculum development, program development and restructuring, co-teaching, multi-tiered systems of support; and teacher mentoring. Dr. McDermott Goldman works with school district administrators to strengthen instructional programming as well as supervise and evaluate these practices through customizable coaching and mentorship protocols. She is also involved in several research projects involving culturally responsive-sustaining pedagogies, integrated instruction and assessment for multilingual learners, co-teaching practices, and graduate education program impact. Dr. McDermott Goldman coauthored the best-selling book *From Equity Insights to Action: Critical Strategies for Teaching Multilingual Learners* (2021). In addition, she has published textbook chapters in (2021) *Effective Teacher Collaboration for English Language Learners: Cross-Curricular Insights From K–12 Classrooms, Approaches to Classroom Management for Diverse and Inclusive Schools, Teaching Science to English Language Learners: Preparing Pre-Service and In-Service Teachers*, and *Teaching History and Social Studies to English Language Learners*, written articles in the *Journal of Leadership and Instruction, New York State ASCD Impact Journal,* and IDIOM, as well as presented at various conferences including TESOL International, NYS TESOL, LIESOL, and The Teachers' Institute.

CHAPTER 1

Why Scaffolding?

"We reject the idea that English language learners have less promise than others. What is true, however, is that they have much more to learn than do their English-proficient peers . . ."
Aída Walqui & Leo van Lier, 2010, p. 24

Scaffolding instruction is not just another teaching approach to learning—it is a critical nonnegotiable for multilingual learners. It is a lifeline to language development, academic achievement, and a profound sense of belonging. Without it, multilingual learners are at risk of being left behind, caught in a cycle of limited success and marginalized in classrooms due to a lack of opportunities that foster their full engagement and expression.

Becoming proficient in another language is no small feat, but scaffolded instruction for multilingual learners can transform this journey into a pathway of steady progress with exciting discoveries and manageable steps along the way. Imagine being surrounded by a language you do not understand and cannot yet grasp—what would you need to gain function and facility in that language to learn new academic content? Scaffolding bridges the gap between a learner's current language abilities and the proficiency required to more fully access and engage with it. To this end, providing support through targeted strategies and rich educational environments makes learning accessible. When scaffolded strategies are incorporated as essential supports for multilingual learners, they sustain their progress and drive their success. They provide the structure and guidance that makes language and content learning attainable.

Scaffolding cracks open the door to general education curricula. Without it, grade-level content can feel insurmountable. However, through thoughtful instructional planning, multilingual learners can be provided with the footholds they need. These practices do not just assist students in keeping up; they help them truly demonstrate their abilities through hands-on learning, engaging with peers, and showcasing their strengths—including their cultural and linguistic assets—in meaningful, interactive ways. Scaffolded instruction ensures multilingual learners do not just sit on the sidelines but take their rightful place front and center with their classmates, ready to assume the academic rigor of grade-level study.

Most critically, scaffolding fosters belonging. By enabling multilingual learners to work significantly alongside their peers—whether through group projects, technology integration, discussions, or peer work—scaffolding dismantles barriers to learning. It empowers all students to contribute, connect, and take pride in their progress and personal growth. Without scaffolding, multilingual learners are denied the opportunities they deserve, but with it, they can soar! For these reasons, scaffolding instruction is not an option. It is a practice that transforms classrooms into spaces of equity, possibility, and hope, beautifully captured by Claribel González's sketchnote (see Figure 1.1).

FIGURE 1.1 ● What is Scaffolding for Multilingual Learners?

Source: Claribel Gonzalez. Used with permission.

WHAT IS SCAFFOLDING?

Creating learning environments that effectively support all students is a significant challenge for today's educators. While most students enter school expecting to engage in meaningful experiences that lead to academic success, their learning needs are diverse and complex. How can schools ensure that grade-appropriate curricula are accessible and purposeful for every student? Moreover, how can curricula, instruction, and assessment be thoughtfully designed to address the unique and varied needs of multilingual learners? Scaffolding instruction addresses these challenges.

Scaffolding is commonly defined as a temporary support system designed to help students acquire new knowledge and skills, enabling them to engage fully in age- or grade-appropriate instruction. It involves identifying the skills and knowledge students need, assessing what they already know and can do independently, and providing the necessary support. In one of the earliest definitions available, Bruner (1978) described scaffolding as "the steps taken to reduce the degrees of freedom in carrying out some task[s] so that the child can concentrate on the difficult skill she is in the process of acquiring" (p. 19). We do not quite view scaffolding instruction as limiting a child's freedom; in fact, we believe scaffolding offers enhanced guidance and support that increases students' choices, options, and possible ways for learning, particularly when scaffolding approaches are co-constructed with the learner. All in all, the goal of scaffolding learning is to foster independent learners who can:

- Internalize essential skills and strategies
- Select the approaches to learning they need
- Achieve through a gradual transfer of responsibility
- Complete tasks on their own

We believe scaffolded instruction should be viewed as a mindset—a particular way of thinking about how planning instruction begins with the student in mind and not the subject matter. When teachers consistently focus on the unique needs of individual learners, scaffolding instruction—providing students with the support they need to acquire new information, develop a new skill, work as a team, use oral and written language effectively, complete an assigned task, and so on—becomes second nature. By adopting a mindset built on scaffolding, teachers embrace the idea of providing learners with the right amount of support at the right time.

WHAT TEACHERS SAY ABOUT SCAFFOLDING STUDENT LEARNING

When scaffolds as temporary supports are put in place, we bridge the gap between where students are currently and where we want them to go. The decision on how much scaffolding will be used depends on their current level of language skills and knowledge of the content area, but the ultimate goal is for students to feel that success is attainable. To me, it's applying the growth mindset to my teaching every day. So, I tell my students:

I know you can get there successfully. Here's this extra guidance and/or support to help you get there easier. With practice, you'll be able to get there on your own in the future!

You can do this! I know you can, but as you're learning language and content, let me support you by making this into a manageable chunk. Later on, you're going to amaze me, your other teachers, and ultimately yourself at what you can do on your own!

—Katie Leven, itinerant English as a new language (ENL) teacher, Orleans/Niagara BOCES, New York

THE PRICE OF ONE-SIZE-FITS ALL INSTRUCTION

A single-track teaching method, in which all students are taught in the same way, often leads to an overreliance on remedial programs for multilingual learners that pull them from general education classrooms for instruction. This practice, though well-intentioned, fragments students' schedules, isolates them from their English-proficient peers, and reinforces a deficit view of their abilities. Instead of addressing the diverse needs of multilingual learners within the classroom, this approach places the burden on students to adapt to disjointed schedules for their learning rather than empowering teachers through instructional methods to meet students where they are.

When multilingual learners are frequently pulled out for separate instruction, they may miss valuable opportunities to access grade-level material, engage in peer learning, build meaningful relationships within their general education classrooms, and learn from the content-area expert. This fragmented approach to instruction for multilingual learners can leave them feeling marginalized and disconnected from their classroom community. Furthermore, the emphasis on remediation often focuses narrowly on language skills, sidelining students' strengths, prior knowledge and experience, and potential to contribute meaningfully within their grade-level classes. Being caught in a cycle of remediation limits the academic growth of students and hinders their development of social-emotional skills alongside peers.

Teachers who rely on one-size-fits-all instruction fail to create equitable learning environments. Scaffolding allows multilingual learners access to grade-level content by providing tailored support. Without these supports, these students are often left to struggle through content that assumes prior knowledge and linguistic proficiency they have not yet acquired. By providing scaffolded instruction, multilingual learners can remain engaged in meaningful, grade-level work while learning alongside their peers and developing content-specific language and disciplinary literacy skills. See Figures 1.2 and 1.3 for how Kimberly Shorey, a third-grade

FIGURE 1.2 • Anchor Chart to Build Foundational Understanding of Key Concepts

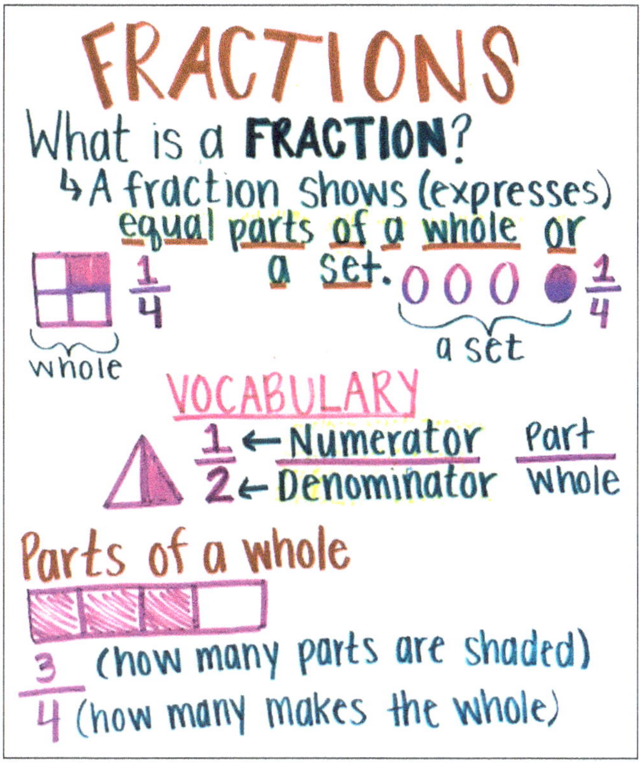

Source: Kimberly Shorey. Used with permission.

FIGURE 1.3 • Anchor Chart to Advance Mathematical Thinking and Disciplinary Language Use

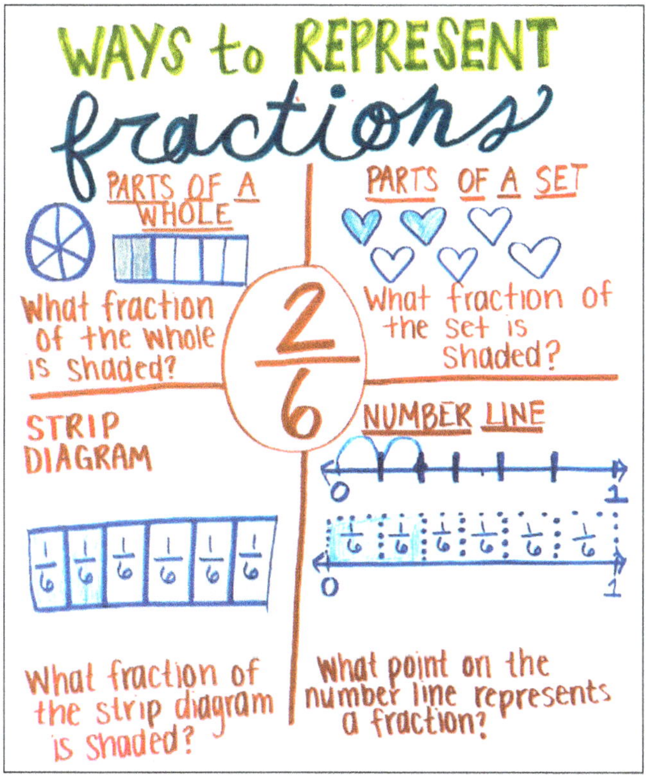

Source: Kimberly Shorey. Used with permission.

teacher in Framingham, Massachusetts, effectively utilizes rotating anchor charts to provide visual support for all students while enhancing multilingual learners' understanding of content and precise academic language use and fostering an inclusive classroom environment at the same time. This approach not only addresses academic needs but also fosters a sense of belonging, equity, and collaboration. The cost of neglecting scaffolding is great—it perpetuates inequities that hinder student success.

IS IT A SCAFFOLD OR IS IT A STRATEGY?

We are often asked how to differentiate between when a strategy serves as a scaffold and when a strategy itself requires scaffolding for multilingual learners. The simple answer is that sometimes a strategy is a scaffold, and sometimes a strategy needs to be scaffolded. The relationship between strategies and scaffolding instruction is nuanced, as strategies can function as scaffolds or may themselves require scaffolding to be effective. Understanding this distinction is critical for designing instruction that meets diverse student needs.

Sometimes, a strategy is a scaffold. In this case, the strategy serves as a support between what students currently know and what they are expected to learn or do. For example, using graphic organizers to help students establish their thoughts before writing is a scaffold. The organizer provides structure and guidance, enabling students to focus on generating ideas and developing their writing skills. Over time, as students gain confidence and proficiency, the need for the organizer may diminish, or they might incorporate and apply it independently as a tool they regularly use to organize ideas for writing.

Other times, a strategy needs to be scaffolded, meaning the strategy itself is complex or unfamiliar and must be broken down into manageable steps for students to use effectively. For instance, teaching students to write an argumentative essay may involve introducing mentor texts—examples or exemplars of student writing—as a strategy for teaching evidence-based claims. Using mentor texts requires scaffolding through think-alouds, guided practice in analyzing evidence, and collaborative discussions to help students effectively link the evidence in the text to what is claimed. Without such scaffolding, students may struggle to understand or apply what is being taught, especially if it demands higher-order thinking or language skills they are still developing.

The distinction between these roles highlights the importance of tailoring instruction to meet students where they are. Teachers must assess whether a strategy can serve as an immediate scaffold or whether it requires scaffolding itself to ensure accessibility. By recognizing this dynamic, more effective learning experiences can be planned, equipping students with the tools they need to succeed while gradually fostering their independence.

WHAT ARE SOME REQUIREMENTS FOR IMPLEMENTING SCAFFOLDED APPROACHES TO LEARNING?

Purposeful instruction requires intentional planning and a deep understanding of students' needs. Scaffolding is *not* a one-size-fits-all strategy; it demands flexibility and adaptability to provide the right level and kind of support at the right time. Educators must consider factors such as students' prior knowledge, cultural backgrounds, and linguistic abilities to design scaffolds that are both effective and meaningful. Additionally, scaffolding involves a commitment to fostering independence, ensuring that support empowers students to take ownership of their learning. By thoughtfully applying scaffolding strategies, teachers can create inclusive and rigorous learning environments that enable all students to succeed.

Providing learning support for multilingual learners requires five basic elements. They are:

1. understanding the strengths and needs of multilingual learners,
2. scaffolding content and language integration,
3. flexibility and adaptability with scaffolding approaches,
4. ongoing assessment and feedback, and
5. fostering independence and student agency through scaffolded instruction.

Figure 1.4 illustrates how each of these elements is essentially interconnected and builds on one another to create a comprehensive system of support. Attending to students' needs is at the framework's core, whereas ensuring student independence and autonomy occupies the outermost layer, suggesting that everything we do begins and ends with our students.

UNDERSTANDING THE STRENGTHS AND NEEDS OF MULTILINGUAL LEARNERS

Let's agree to always start with an asset-based approach. Fully understanding the many gifts, talents, funds of knowledge, and richly lived experiences students bring from home is essential when working with multilingual learners. At the same time, we must also take a comprehensive approach to mapping out strategies and responses to their unique needs. We frequently ask the in-service teachers and practicing educators we work with in our graduate courses and workshops what they perceive multilingual learners need to be successful. Here are the results of their typical answers captured as a Mentimeter word cloud (see Figure 1.5).

FIGURE 1.4 ● Scaffolding Implementation

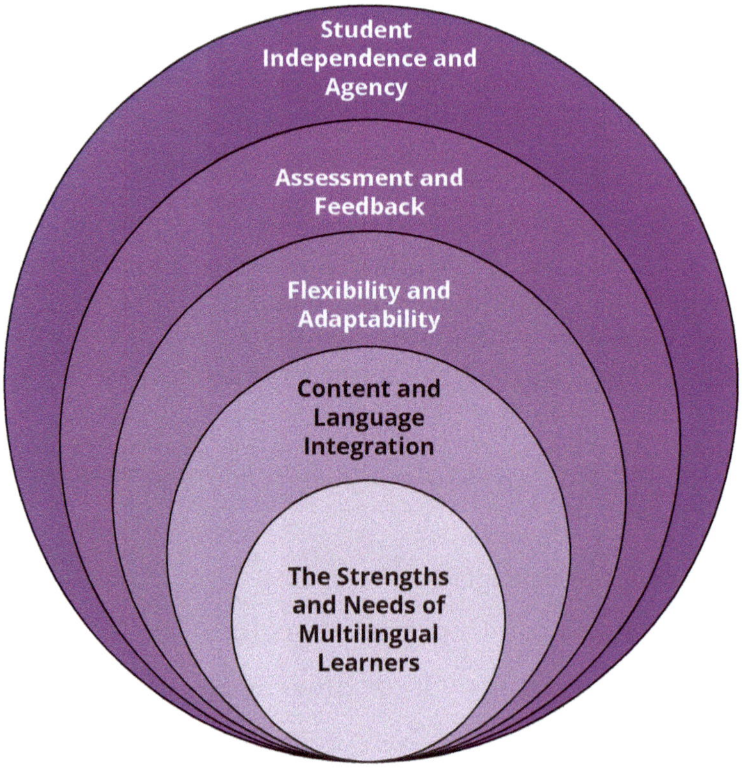

online resources Available for download at https://companion.corwin.com/courses/NineDimensionsofScaffoldingforMLs

FIGURE 1.5 ● Teacher Responses to What Multilingual Learners Need to Be Successful

Although multilingual learners need patient and caring teachers, they also need teachers who are equipped with the knowledge and skills to plan accessible, effective instruction tailored to their unique needs. Masoumi, Bourbour, and Lindqvist (2024) determined that ". . . strengthening teachers' pedagogical, technological, and content knowledge can further support teachers in their skills to scaffold children's learning" (p. 1220). While a welcoming and supportive classroom environment is essential, it must be paired with intentional teaching practices grounded in understanding how multilingual learners acquire language, develop literacy, and learn content concepts and skills simultaneously.

To succeed, multilingual learners need instruction that builds on their existing strengths and backgrounds while addressing the challenges of navigating academic content, cultural norms, and school expectations in a new language. This type of instruction requires teachers who value their students' diverse linguistic and cultural experiences and possess the expertise to design scaffolds that make complex learning attainable. Multilingual learners benefit from varied strategies—images, realia, sentence frames, word walls, and so on—as well as opportunities to engage in meaningful dialogue with peers. These approaches require careful planning and a genuine understanding of how language and literacy are developed alongside content learning.

Additionally, multilingual learners thrive when their teachers recognize that they are not just learning English but also learning through English. This dual focus demands that teachers integrate language objectives with content objectives, ensuring students develop both the academic language and subject-specific knowledge necessary for success.

All in all, multilingual learners need teachers who combine patience and care with the ability to plan, implement, and adapt research-based strategies. This pairing of support and expertise empowers students to access grade-level content, build their persistence to learn, and fully participate in their class communities. When teachers are both compassionate and skilled, multilingual learners are better positioned to achieve their potential and thrive in school and beyond.

SCAFFOLDING FOR LANGUAGE AND CONTENT INTEGRATION

Integrating content and language learning is a cornerstone for instruction in inclusive classrooms for multilingual learners, and scaffolding offers the support they need to engage with grade-level material while simultaneously developing their language skills. Without scaffolding, the complexity of academic content and the demands of learning a new language can create significant barriers, leaving many students overwhelmed and unable to fully participate in their education.

By breaking tasks into manageable steps and providing a range of targeted supports, scaffolding offers multifaceted guidance for students to connect what they already know with what they are expected to learn. These strategies help students access challenging content while building the language skills necessary to express their understanding. Scaffolding enables multilingual learners to build on prior knowledge and internalize new information and ensures that they can actively engage in classroom activities.

Moreover, scaffolding promotes equity by enabling multilingual learners to participate alongside their peers in meaningful, grade-level learning experiences. It shifts the focus from remediation to empowerment, from struggling to striving, from deficits to assets, emphasizing that students can achieve high standards with appropriate support.

FLEXIBILITY AND ADAPTABILITY WITH SCAFFOLDING APPROACHES

Fundamental to the effective use of scaffolding for instruction are flexibility and adaptability. Scaffolds should not be static, predetermined instruments for learning; rather, they must respond to the individual and changing needs of students. These dynamic approaches allow teachers to provide the right level of support at the right time, ensuring that scaffolds remain effective, practical, and relevant. For example, multilingual learners may initially need sentence frames or starters to complete writing tasks, but as their confidence and skills grow, the scaffold can shift to open-ended prompts and word banks that encourage independent selection of the shape and structure of a piece of writing as well as the words and phrases used. Similarly, scaffolds in math might begin with students using visual aids or manipulatives to problem solve and later evolve into their consideration of a series of strategic questions to support their completion of a task.

Flexibility also means being attuned to students' emotional and social needs, which can impact their readiness to engage with learning. By observing, assessing, and responding in real time, teachers can maintain the delicate balance of challenge and support that scaffolding requires. This responsiveness ensures that scaffolding not only helps students overcome immediate challenges but also builds their long-term endurance to take risks and capacity to tackle complex tasks independently.

ONGOING ASSESSMENT AND FEEDBACK

Two critical components of effective scaffolding are ongoing assessment and feedback to ensure that support strategies remain responsive to students' needs. Scaffolding requires continuous monitoring to understand where students excel and where they may need additional assistance. Teachers can use formative assessments, such as observations, student reflections, class discussions, anecdotal notes, or nonverbal techniques, e.g., thumb up/down, to gauge student understanding and gather real time feedback. This data helps identify when to adjust supports by adding or reducing assistance.

Constructive feedback plays a vital role in this process, as it not only highlights areas for improvement but also reinforces what students are doing well. Effective feedback is:

- *Specific* – it focuses on a particular skill, concept, or part of the task instead of being vague or general. For example:
    - General: "Good job!"
    - Specific: "You used strong evidence from the text to support your argument in the second paragraph."
- *Actionable* – it provides students with clear, specific steps they can take to improve their performance. For example:
    - Not Actionable: "Your essay needs more detail."
    - Actionable: "Add a specific example from the text to support your main argument in paragraph three."
- *Aligned with the learning objectives and success criteria* – it directly addresses the specific skills, knowledge, or behaviors that students are expected to demonstrate. For example:
    - Success Criterion: "Use at least two pieces of textual evidence to support your argument."
    - Feedback: "You used one piece of textual evidence effectively in paragraph four. To meet the criteria, add another quote or paraphrase from the text to strengthen your argument."

For multilingual learners, feedback might include tailored guidance on language usage, content understanding, and strategies for applying learning across contexts. Teachers should also reflect on their own practices, analyzing whether their scaffolding approaches meet students' needs and make adjustments accordingly.

WHAT TEACHERS SAY ABOUT SCAFFOLDING

Kelly Cray, secondary cultural and language support educator has the following take on "removing" scaffolds:

As a student, it feels like you are running behind the pack in a race and then you get a boost so you can finally just keep up, and it is ripped away. Instead of removing scaffolds, I teach my students how to replicate them independently. For example, how to build their own word banks. Since this is an extra step, it is more work. This means when they don't need them anymore, they stop using them. However, they have built the skill so when a challenging assignment comes along, they can build their own scaffolds to help themselves be successful.

FOSTERING INDEPENDENCE AND STUDENT AGENCY THROUGH SCAFFOLDED INSTRUCTION

A commitment to fostering independence is central to effective scaffolding. The main goal of scaffolding is to empower students to take ownership of their learning by gradually transferring responsibility from the teacher to the student. This process requires intentional planning and thoughtful instructional delivery to ensure students build the skills and confidence needed.

The gradual release of responsibility framework (Pearson & Gallagher, 1983, Fisher & Frey, 2021) "suggests that the cognitive load should shift purposefully from teacher-as-model, to joint responsibility, to independent practice, and application by the learner" (Fisher et al., 2020, p. 12). It involves setting clear goals, providing appropriate levels of support, and gradually removing those supports as students gain confidence and competence. Through this intentionality, scaffolding addresses immediate learning needs and equips students with the skills and strategies to succeed independently. Ultimately, fostering independence through scaffolding equips students with the tools and mindset to face challenges, adapt to new learning contexts, and thrive beyond the classroom.

Students can independently leverage scaffolding strategies to deepen their understanding and effectively apply concepts, enabling them to break down complex topics into manageable parts. Through scaffolding approaches, multilingual learners can gradually develop the skills needed to become self-directed learners and act with agency. See how independence evolves using scaffolding, viewed through our CARES lens (see Table 1.1).

TABLE 1.1 ● The CARES Lens

ELEMENTS OF THE CARES LENS	WHAT STUDENTS ARE ABLE TO DO
***C**hoice*	Students identify and choose tools that best represent their preferences and goals, understanding their scope and purpose as well as how to use them effectively for specific activities.
***A**utonomy*	Scaffolds help teachers gradually transfer responsibility for knowledge and language

	development to students. Students learn to use tools, practice collaboratively, and eventually apply them independently, with opportunities for teacher support, and guidance as needed.
***R**outines*	Multilingual learners develop routines with clear roles and responsibilities, helping them understand expectations and achieve success. Over time, they internalize these routines and navigate the classroom with confidence.
***E**ngagement*	Students view scaffolds as engaging tools that amplify their voice, foster agency, and help them connect to learning in manageable steps.
***S**elf-Regulation*	Scaffolds empower students to take control of their learning, setting achievable but ambitious goals and monitoring their progress while building tolerance for ambiguity and adaptability to new situations.

online resources — Available for download at https://companion.corwin.com/courses/NineDimensionsofScaffoldingforMLs

WHAT ARE THE UNIQUE GOALS OF THIS BOOK?

In this text, we offer practical ideas based on research-informed instructional practices to scaffold the learning of content, language, and literacy for multilingual learners. Our intention with this work is to support teachers to offer multilingual learners greater and consistent access to grade-level content as they build mastery in English. We want to dispel the belief that multilingual learners, particularly those students who are at an entering or emerging level of English proficiency, need to place their academic schooling on hold and master a certain level of English before they can engage with grade-appropriate subject matter. In our view, this type of thinking fails to recognize the immense abilities, strengths, talents, and potential that multilingual learners bring to school.

First and foremost, we believe multilingual learners deserve rigorous, age-appropriate curricula that challenge their intellect, stimulate critical thinking, deepen their understanding of the subject matter, and support the application or transfer of their learning to new contexts. They need to study relevant topics in which they can see their own lives reflected as well as deepen their awareness of the greater world. To this end, our goal with this book is to support teachers to use research-informed and evidence-based teaching practices that provide multilingual learners with the help they need to overcome their unique challenges. In addition, we further advocate for a focus on building relationships between multilingual learners, their teachers, and their peers to foster acceptance and belonging. Curricula design, relevancy of subject matter, targeted instructional practices, and social and emotional stability are critical to not only the academic success of these students but also serve to dispel the misconceptions about the ability of multilingual learners to learn.

BOOK OVERVIEW

In this volume, we offer a nine-point framework for scaffolding instruction that supports the linguistic and academic development of multilingual learners in grades K-12. This book focuses on nine approaches to scaffolding—instructional, linguistic, multimodal, multisensory, graphic, digital, interactive, social-emotional, and environmental—that were introduced in our Corwin book, *Co-Planning: Five Essential Practices to Integrate Curriculum and Instruction for English Learners* (Honigsfeld & Dove, 2022) (see Figure 1.6). We expound on each of the nine approaches, detailing instructional and assessment strategies and techniques based on research-informed and evidence-based best practices.

FIGURE 1.6 ● The Nine Dimensions of Scaffolding

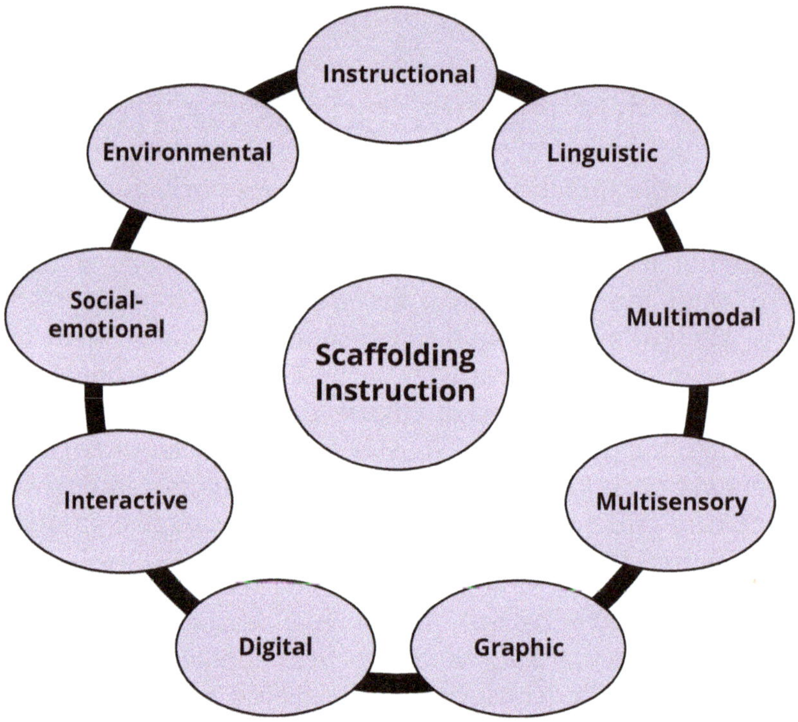

The inspiration for this book arose from conversations with teachers and school leaders about planning instruction for multilingual learners and addressing the challenge of supporting all students in meeting grade-level standards. This book is designed to help educators understand scaffolded instruction for multilingual learners and guide them in developing and adapting strategies to meet their students' needs within their unique contexts. Our goal was to create a practical, user-friendly, and richly illustrated resource featuring authentic examples from numerous educators in the field to demonstrate the effective application of scaffolding strategies as well as to celebrate successful practices.

As we visit classrooms and observe teachers in the field, we notice there are some who—at times with the best of intentions—persistently maintain low expectations for multilingual learners, failing to engage these students in grade-level work. Even more disturbing are situations when English language development curricula or online learning apps are used that promote skill-and-drill frameworks devoid of opportunities for students to think critically, engage in genuine inquiry, or incorporate their personal frames of knowledge. Generally speaking, some teachers might feel underprepared to support multilingual learners, particularly those at the earlier stages of English language proficiency. This book aims to address the use of effective approaches, techniques, and strategies for these students so that they are better able to participate in grade-appropriate learning alongside their English-proficient peers with carefully planned scaffolds and supports.

Our main purpose is to guide teachers in supporting multilingual learners so that they can participate in standards-based general education curricula. We invite our readers to consider each type of scaffolded support, how particular strategies provide targeted assistance for various purposes, and how to make instructional decisions and develop strategies to support all learners. We foster the practice of collaboration among teachers so that together, they may determine what types of scaffolds will afford students equitable access to the core curriculum, the development of English language and literacy, and the appropriate assessments that accurately measure their knowledge, skills, and abilities. To illustrate these points, we share authentic stories and examples from successful teachers whom we met in schools and districts across the United States.

We are confident that the contents of this book will help our readers better understand how to scaffold instruction for multilingual learners so that they may have greater access to and engagement with grade-level, standards-based general education curricula. By applying the approaches outlined in this book, readers can expect to see increased student participation and improved comprehension among multilingual learners, enabling them to successfully complete tasks and experience a stronger sense of inclusion and belonging in the classroom. Interactive features, such as periodic stop-and-process probes connected to research-informed and evidence-based recommendations, are designed to keep readers actively engaged. Additionally, end-of-chapter reflection questions provide valuable opportunities for both individual reflection and collaborative discussions within professional learning communities.

CHAPTER CONTENTS

The following provides a summary of the key insights and focus areas each chapter will explore. Each chapter targets one of the nine dimensions of scaffolding instruction for multilingual learners, creating a comprehensive journey through each scaffolding approach. Here is what each chapter will uncover following this introductory chapter.

CHAPTER 2: INSTRUCTIONAL SCAFFOLDING

In this chapter, we carefully outline the practice of instructional scaffolding, structuring lessons in ways that are accessible for learners at all levels of academic and language readiness. We highlight how instructional scaffolding helps multilingual learners engage in learning by breaking complex tasks into manageable steps and providing tailored support, such as questioning, modeling, and guided practice.

CHAPTER 3: LINGUISTIC SCAFFOLDING

This chapter focuses on linguistic scaffolds that support the use of language that is necessary to communicate and attain academic growth, work with complex concepts, and develop new academic skills across content areas. Through linguistic scaffolding, the full range of multilingual repertoires students and teachers possess are leveraged, and multiple techniques are used to offer language-specific support.

CHAPTER 4: MULTIMODAL SCAFFOLDING

In this chapter, multimodal scaffolding is featured. We describe how multimodalities are critical to students having access to the same information. Multimodal scaffolding is also inherent to and essential for how students retrieve, make meaning from and respond to new information, and engage in disciplinary practices.

CHAPTER 5: MULTISENSORY SCAFFOLDING

This chapter focuses on approaches to multisensory scaffolding—visual, auditory, tactile, and kinesthetic. Readers will develop an understanding of how learners can use multiple senses to process and retain information and engage in academic, language learning, and literacy practices.

CHAPTER 6: GRAPHIC SCAFFOLDING

This chapter addresses graphic scaffolding, a commonly used technique that provides easier access to new learning for multilingual learners. Graphic representations generally offer quick and organized visual access to complex concepts while also helping to synthesize key information.

CHAPTER 7: DIGITAL SCAFFOLDING

This chapter explores using digital tools for learning, such as watching and listening to videos, simulations, or animations; taking virtual tours of national parks, monuments, and museums; using educational applications, and so on, to develop targeted content and language skills. Additionally, it highlights how students can take a more active role and create digital content.

CHAPTER 8: SCAFFOLDING SOCIAL-EMOTIONAL LEARNING

In this chapter, we explore scaffolding social-emotional learning—the purposeful, pedagogical use of linguistic and nonlinguistic communication tools that help students build relationships. It supports the social development as well as emotional response to learning for multilingual learners.

CHAPTER 9: INTERACTIVE SCAFFOLDING

In this chapter, we focus on interactive scaffolding as a process where meaning-making, language and literacy development, and engagement happen in the company of others. When students interact with their peers, time is allotted for them to formulate their own ideas about the content and practice using academic language both in authentic and structured ways.

CHAPTER 10: ENVIRONMENTAL SCAFFOLDING

In this final chapter, we discuss environmental scaffolding and how its practices can provide a safe and secure physical or virtual setting for learning to take place. It focuses on how to best provide a supportive environment for multilingual learners to enhance their academic, linguistic, and social-emotional growth and development.

FROM INSTRUCTIONAL TO ENVIRONMENTAL SCAFFOLDING: HOW SCAFFOLDING STRATEGIES INTERSECT

Different types of scaffolding strategies often overlap, as they share the common goal of providing students with the support needed to access learning. While each type of scaffolding addresses a specific area, their interconnectedness enhances their overall effectiveness in fostering student engagement and understanding.

For instance, linguistic scaffolding, such as providing sentence frames or word banks, often overlaps with multisensory scaffolding—using visuals such as charts, diagrams, or images. Both strategies aim to make abstract concepts concrete and accessible by reducing cognitive load and clarifying meaning. Similarly, tactile scaffolding, which involves hands-on learning tools like manipulatives, can complement linguistic scaffolding by providing a physical connection to abstract ideas. For example, students learning geometry might use manipulatives alongside labeled diagrams and descriptive language.

Multimodal strategies—using multiple formats such as text, audio, video, and interactive elements—align closely with multisensory strategies, which engage sight, hearing, touch, and sometimes smell or taste. Both approaches address diverse learning needs and ensure students have multiple pathways to grasp concepts.

Environmental scaffolding, such as creating print-rich classrooms or strategically designed seating arrangements, often supports social-emotional learning scaffolding by creating spaces where students feel safe and valued. A welcoming classroom environment with accessible resources fosters collaboration, confidence, and a sense of belonging, which are critical for learning, especially for multilingual learners.

These overlaps are intentional, as they create layers of support that reinforce one another. A teacher might combine multiple types of scaffolding in a single lesson—for example, using a word wall (environmental and linguistic scaffolding) alongside group discussions (social-emotional scaffolding) and hands-on experiments (multisensory scaffolding). This integration ensures that all students, regardless of their strengths or challenges, have equitable opportunities to engage with and master the content. The interconnected nature of scaffolding strategies enhances learning by addressing the whole student cognitively, emotionally, and socially. See Figure 1.7 for what may be a powerful example of multiple-dimensional scaffolding. Sarah Elia, a secondary ENL teacher at Saugerties High School, New York, and her students were practicing key vocabulary related to enduring issues for global history class (such as scarcity, conflict, population growth, etc.). She would show a word, and the ball would be passed around for students to say something about it—it could be a simple definition, a word in their home language (use a translator if needed), a description of the term, and example of the term, and so on. Through this game-like activity, Sarah utilized multiple scaffolding approaches as she invited her students to co-construct meaning about key concepts, review key vocabulary in an engaging way that lowers their affective filter (Krashen, 1982), interact with each other and use tactile and kinesthetic approaches to learning.

PROGRAM MODELS: WHERE SCAFFOLDING IS IMPLEMENTED

Within each chapter, we emphasize how scaffolded instruction can be applied across various program models, including general education classes, integrated co-taught classes for multilingual learners, standalone or pullout English language development classes, and special education classes. Additional settings where these strategies are highly relevant include bilingual classes and dual-language programs.

FIGURE 1.7 ● Incorporating Multiple Scaffolding Strategies

Source: Adile Jones. Used with permission.

In *general education classrooms* with diverse student populations, scaffolded instruction ensures multilingual learners can access grade-level content.

In *integrated co-taught settings*, scaffolding involves collaboration between the content teacher and the language learning specialist. Together, they design supports that balance language acquisition with literacy learning and academic content.

In *standalone or pullout English language development (ELD) classes*, targeted language development support is offered. Scaffolding is tailored to build foundational language skills through varied instructional approaches.

In special education classes with multilingual learners, scaffolding is essential to instruction and accommodate individual learning profiles in order to break tasks into smaller steps and provide consistent routines to support both language and content learning.

In *bilingual settings*, scaffolding supports language development in both the students' home language and English. Teachers strategically use translanguaging techniques to build a strong foundation for learning.

In *dual-language programs*, scaffolding involves balancing the use of two languages while ensuring comprehension and participation in academic tasks.

While not every chapter explicitly addresses all program models, the scaffolding techniques described are universally applicable across these settings. The strategies outlined in this book are designed to be adaptable, ensuring that educators in any instructional context can implement them effectively to meet the diverse needs of their students.

INFLUENTIAL VOICES ON SCAFFOLDING INSTRUCTION

We would like to acknowledge the foundational work of scholars and educators who have shaped our understanding of scaffolding instruction. Their research and writings have provided valuable insights into how scaffolding supports student learning and continue to influence classroom practices.

Aída Walqui and Leo van Lier (2010) named scaffolding the *pedagogy of success* and noted that scaffolds "should be constantly changed, dismantled, extended, and adapted in accordance with the needs" of the students (p. 24).

Pauline Gibbons (2015) highlights the three major characteristics of scaffolding as follows:

- It is *temporary* help that assists a learner to move toward new concepts, levels of understanding, and new language.
- It enables learners to know *how to do something* (not just what to do) so that they will be better able to complete similar tasks alone.
- It is *future oriented:* in Vygotsky's words, what a learner can do with support today, he or she will be able to do alone tomorrow. (p. 15)

Gibbons (2015) calls for high-challenge, high support instruction that is integrated and carefully planned. She challenges the notion that multilingual learners "need to first 'learn English' before they can learn subject content. As we have seen, in a well-planned integrated curriculum where there is a dual focus on both content and language, students have many opportunities to develop subject knowledge and relevant academic language simultaneously." (p. 93)

There is a newly rekindled interest in scaffolding in the professional literature and in classrooms across the United States alike. Nancy Frey and colleagues (2023) identify three key characteristics of scaffolding such as being (a) only needed when the task is too difficult to complete; otherwise, (b) responsive to individual needs and adjustable; and (c) temporary.

Similarly, in the introductory chapter to their edited volume, Luciana C. de Oliveira and Ruslana Westerlund (2023) name some consistent features of scaffolding with multilingual learners in mind, including it being (a) dynamic and contingent upon student needs, (b) customized and adaptive, rather than routine and generic, (c) connected to student learning and growing autonomy; and (d) either planned or spontaneous. All the chapters are aligned to these basic premises whether the participating author or author team offers a theoretical framework, a case study, or a teacher education perspective. In the introductory chapter, de Oliveira and Westerlund suggest that "considering scaffolding as help or routine support does not see scaffolding as adaptive and tailored as students gain responsibility and gain autonomy over their thinking" (p. 2). Later in the same volume, Aída Walqui and Mary Schmida (2023) offer a three-level approach to conceptualizing scaffolding—micro, meso, and macro, indicating scaffolding may occur within the context of a task, a lesson, and/or a unit.

Barbara Blackburn (2025) also cautions that scaffolding is connected to rigorous instruction for any student, and it should never be considered discriminatory or punitive. She believes rigor involves more than assigning difficult tasks to students; it requires thoughtfully supporting and scaffolding their learning to help them achieve high levels of challenge successfully (Blackburn, 2008).

By building on these contributions, we further explore and expand the conversation around scaffolding in this book. We provide practical insights and strategies that teachers can implement to meet the needs of multilingual learners. Through this work, we hope to inspire a deeper understanding of how scaffolding can foster equity, engagement, and academic success for all students.

BEYOND TEMPORARY SUPPORT: SCAFFOLDS THAT EMPOWER

There tends to be much agreement among educators that scaffolding is a process of contingent support. In this book, we will challenge the notion that scaffolds go up, and scaffolds always come down because they cannot always come down! They might move sideways or further up to elevate learning to the next level and maintain rigor. For multilingual learners, scaffolds may not come down because:

- They may become the learners' permanent tool kit.
- They may help maximize student independence and self-reliance.
- They may travel across content areas and contexts, also referred to as recurrence, and are applied to new contexts.
- They may respond to students' multiple complex learning needs.
- They may be necessary to sustain learning.

Rethinking the traditional metaphor of scaffolding is essential, particularly when considering the needs of multilingual learners. Rather than viewing scaffolds as temporary structures that must be removed, we should recognize their potential to evolve into enduring tools that empower students. By responding to the diverse needs of students, scaffolds not only sustain learning but also elevate it to higher levels of rigor. Embracing this broader perspective ensures that all students, especially multilingual learners, are equipped to succeed and thrive. Further, we acknowledge that students must be given the opportunity to ask questions about their own learning and make decisions about what works best for them. The questions in Table 1.2 help educators reflect on their decision-making process and invite students to think critically about their own learning and decide which tools make the most sense for them. To further strengthen autonomy, encourage students to ask themselves: *What am I learning? What is this scaffolding approach or tool typically used for? When do I use this approach or tool? Is it a good fit for the assignment? What am I ultimately responsible for?*

TABLE 1.2 ● Aligning Teacher's and Student's Reflection Questions for Scaffolding

TEACHER	STUDENTS
What do my students need to know? How will they evidence this?	What do I need to know? How do I show it?
How do students know the critical parts? What do they need to know about them?	How do I know the important parts and what I need to know about them? What scaffold would work best?
What is not essential?	What can I skim through?
How do ideas connect to what students already know? How do they show this?	What connections can I make? How do I show that I can make connections?
What new ideas have students learned?	What new ideas did I learn?
What are students confused about? Where are they stuck? What resources can I provide to make the information more clear?	What confuses me? What am I unsure of? How do I get more information to learn more?

WHAT TEACHERS SAY ABOUT SCAFFOLDING

Scaffolding is not just an important teaching tool, but it is also a form of self-advocacy. As students are able to interact with the content on their level, they are able to participate more in group discussions. Receptive comes before productive language, therefore it is important for students to hear and see content in meaningful ways, such as through images, body movements, realia, or videos. I often use leveled or thematic texts for students. For productive language, sentence frames and stems can be essential to lessening the cognitive load so we can better assess their understanding of content. Consistent graphic organizers are key to scaffolding because the information they need is presented in a way that is easily accessible. The most important aspect of scaffolding is that students should never feel like they're out of their zone of proximal development. It is up to us to ensure that they feel positive about their school work; self-eficacy is essential to promoting intrinsic motivation, self-confidence, and a love of learning!

—Amy Eckelmann, EdD, ENL teacher, Rockville Centre, New York, adjunct teacher education professor, Molloy University

KEEP THIS IN MIND

When implementing scaffolding approaches, teachers should focus on understanding their multilingual learners' language proficiency levels, cultural backgrounds, and prior knowledge to tailor supports effectively. Scaffolds should align with clear learning objectives and success criteria, gradually building independence by starting with maximum support and progressively reducing intensity as students gain more skills. Students should be guided in making decisions about when and whether to reduce scaffolding approaches.

Scaffolding instruction can be challenging and demanding, especially when addressing students' varied proficiency levels and grade-level readiness. Remember to carefully manage time constraints that may limit opportunities for individualized support and avoid over-scaffolding, which can discourage students from taking risks or developing independence.

By maintaining a learner-centered approach, scaffolding can better promote both academic and language learning with multilingual learners.

SUMMARY

Scaffolding is essential for multilingual learners, supporting language mastery, academic success, and a sense of belonging. Without it, these students may not be able to engage fully in learning or access grade-level content. Scaffolding provides targeted approaches that help students to make gains given their current language skills and the proficiency needed to understand grade-level material. Providing focused support, scaffolding helps students build essential skills, actively participate in learning, and gain independence. It enables multilingual learners to engage in general education curricula, showcase their abilities, and collaborate meaningfully with peers. More than a strategy, scaffolding is a mindset. By centering planning instruction for multilingual learners with these approaches, teachers can create inclusive, equitable classrooms where multilingual learners can grow, succeed, and meaningfully contribute to their own learning.

Questions

1. How can scaffolding instruction help multilingual learners overcome barriers to accessing grade-level content and fully engaging in classroom activities?
2. What strategies would you use to balance providing support with fostering independence in multilingual learners?
3. In what ways does adopting a "scaffolding mindset" change how teachers approach lesson planning and instruction?
4. How can scaffolding techniques be tailored to address multilingual learners' diverse needs and language proficiency levels in inclusive classrooms?

CHAPTER 2

Instructional Scaffolding

"Successful learning depends on customization, and scaffolding is essential to making it work for each child. However, scaffolding can limit growth and actually cause students to disengage if it is too constraining or if there is no progression toward increasing independence."
Bridget Dalton, 2012, p. 337

Instructional scaffolding involves teaching routines and techniques that break down complex tasks into manageable steps and provide specific guidance for students to fully participate and engage in the learning process. Through this type of scaffolding, teachers design lessons to make language and literacy development as well as content learning accessible for multilingual learners no matter what their level of English language proficiency might be. Using questioning techniques, guided practice, modeling, demonstration, and chunking information, teachers provide their students with the means for task completion and overall learning success. In turn, these supports are gradually reduced as students become more confident, independent learners and gain mastery.

WHO IS IT FOR?

Instructional scaffolding can be used with any student who needs direction and support to understand and apply new concepts, learn grade-appropriate skills, complete multi-step tasks, or comprehend complex texts in various academic domains. In particular, instructional scaffolding helps multilingual learners navigate complex and challenging content and learning experiences by introducing new material in incremental steps, thereby reducing the amount of language students must discern at any given time. It provides opportunities to break down complex written and spoken language in that the lesson is delivered in more manageable parts. It also encourages peer support using certain strategies that incorporate collaborative student work. Finally, it prepares students for independent work while also offering them multiple occasions to gather and integrate feedback from teachers or peers. This type of scaffolding can be implemented for students of all ages with little to no alteration in the technique selected. Overall, instructional scaffolding is a valuable tool for integrating content and language learning for multilingual learners.

HOW IS INSTRUCTIONAL SCAFFOLDING USED ACROSS PROGRAM MODELS?

Instructional scaffolding is widely used in classroom settings, including general education, co-taught, and integrated English language development (ELD) classes as follows:

- In general education classes, teachers respond to individual needs by structuring lesson routines in ways that incorporate a variety of strategies to help students grasp new concepts or complete tasks. These strategies include modeling, demonstration, step-by-step instructions, guided questions, and group work.
- In co-taught classes, grade-level or content-area teachers collaborate and co-plan with ELD teachers to design lessons with instructional scaffolding in mind and provide targeted support for multilingual learners. Some instructional activities to accommodate diverse learning needs include breaking down complex tasks into smaller steps, using realia to model or demonstrate skills and concepts, and strategically grouping students for instruction.
- In standalone ELD classes, instructional scaffolding is fundamental to how teachers work with multilingual learners. Teachers tailor their approach to support language acquisition and engagement with the target content; thereby, instructional scaffolding provides students with a manageable path to developing foundational language and literacy skills and accessing the curriculum.

WHAT TEACHERS SAY ABOUT INSTRUCTIONAL SCAFFOLDING

There is no "one size fits all" approach for supporting English Learners (ELs) in the classroom. However, finding the right size to fit their academic language proficiency level, content readiness, and social/emotional needs is the key to promoting their growth. This is why providing multiple access points to content and networking opportunities is an essential part of the English Learner Plan. Every time we schedule courses and plan instruction for students, we think about how they will access information and people. We review the WIDA "Can do" descriptors. We provide the student with academic choices to demonstrate learning of material in each assignment. We connect them with mentors and classmates. And most of all, we increase, decrease, revisit, and adjust the size of the academic and language load as they grow.

—Andrea Bitner, EL educator, author, Philadelphia, Pennsylvania

WHY IS INSTRUCTIONAL SCAFFOLDING AN IMPORTANT APPROACH TO STUDENT LEARNING?

Students cannot learn if they do not understand the material being presented. In order to support students to make logical connections between what they already know and what is being taught, students need support to develop the cognitive pathways to remain focused, internalize new information, make comparisons, problem solve, and form unique ideas to accomplish a range of learning tasks. In order to support these cognitive functions, teachers need to scaffold instruction, particularly for culturally and linguistically diverse learners, so they can get from point A to point B and beyond.

Instructional scaffolding provides students with access points into the learning process and ensures their steady progress to mastery. Its main focus is on lesson design and how instruction is delivered so that content and language learning are more readily attained. It supports students to aim their attention on learning targets by providing clear goals as well as gradual, carefully moderated bits of information that guide students throughout the learning arc of the lesson and the unit. Instructional scaffolding also offers students many opportunities to be exposed to new information as well as meaningful practice with tasks alongside the teacher and peers before students are expected to work on their own.

HOW DOES INSTRUCTIONAL SCAFFOLDING SPECIFICALLY RELATE TO MULTILINGUAL LEARNERS' NEEDS?

Instructional scaffolding is a learner-centered approach that recognizes and addresses the individual needs of the learner; it provides tailor-made support, adjusts to students' facility with content and language learning, and ultimately fosters independence. Instructional scaffolding meets multilingual learners' individual needs by incrementally shifting the tasks students accomplish with teacher or peer support to students internalizing and applying learning strategies independently to complete tasks on their own. Teachers begin by modeling, then providing explicit, step-by-step guidance. As students become more confident and proficient, the support will become more moderate—also referred to as fading—so that multilingual learners may tackle tasks with less direct support and may work more independently. Instructional scaffolding is responsive to multilingual learners by allowing for appropriate adjustments as students make progress academically, linguistically, and with their social-emotional development. This approach ensures that the level of overall instructional support provided remains germane to students' current abilities and skills while also considering setting incrementally higher yet achievable goals for them.

FROM RESEARCH TO PRACTICE

In a seminal work, Jamie McKenzie (1999) identified eight characteristics of scaffolded instruction as follows:

1. It provides clear, step-by-step directions.
2. It clarifies purpose and keeps motivation at the forefront.
3. It helps students remain on task.
4. It offers expectations and feedback.
5. It directs students to appropriate sources.
6. It eliminates uncertainty and surprise.
7. It streamlines the work effort.
8. It builds and sustains momentum.

Reflect on the following:

- Consider building a lesson with the above eight characteristics of scaffolded instruction in mind. *How do they translate into specific instructional practices for the sake of multilingual learners? How would you provide step-by-step directions, and what might you do to maintain students' motivation to remain engaged with the task?*
- Consider carefully the type of feedback and feed-forward that would be most useful to your multilingual learners at different levels of language proficiency. *How might you use these eight characteristics of scaffolded instruction as a checklist for planning accessible lessons for multilingual learners?*

WHAT TEACHERS SAY ABOUT INSTRUCTIONAL SCAFFOLDING

Most of the scaffolding that I use in class comes from the instructional scaffolding approach. Although I use other methods, such as graphic and digital [scaffolding], most of the planning on my part includes elements of instructional scaffolding.

—Dominique Donnelly, bilingual special education teacher, Brentwood UFSD, New York

GETTING STARTED WITH INSTRUCTIONAL SCAFFOLDING

Instructional scaffolding provides students with the means to access, navigate, comprehend, and respond to academic content as well as develop language and literacy skills. Before selecting appropriate scaffolding strategies to support student learning, teachers must know their multilingual learners—their proficiency levels and academic backgrounds as well as their specific strengths and needs. Learning standards and lesson objectives should also be carefully considered when designing scaffolded instruction and step-by-step procedures for lesson delivery. With instructional scaffolding, here are some things to consider:

- Each part of the lesson should provide support for learning.
- Exemplary models must be student-friendly and accessible to all.
- Effective scaffolded support is achieved when students do not remain together as a single group for the entire lesson.
- Practical demonstrations are indispensable.
- Questions foster critical thinking, language use, and retention of new material.
- Instructional routines and scaffolding go hand in hand.
- Above all, teacher clarity is most critical for student success.

In the next section, we explore instructional scaffolding in detail and offer specific examples of strategies that can be readily used with multilingual learners.

TEACHING PRACTICES

Instructional scaffolding is a diverse set of strategies that provide students with support and guidance to reach improved levels of understanding and increased facility with language and literacy. They serve as a critical foundation for the effective teaching of multilingual learners and empower all students to become increasingly independent learners. In this chapter, we present a range of instructional scaffolding methods, from providing clear explanations and modeling tasks to offering opportunities for practice and feedback. These scaffolding techniques are invaluable tools that can be applied across subject areas and grade levels, ultimately fostering a deeper and more meaningful learning experience for students. We also wish to recognize that there are numerous other ways that day-to-day instruction can and should be scaffolded based on the nature of the curriculum, the unique needs of the students, and teachers' own evidence-based practices.

The instructional scaffolding strategies that are featured here include (a) questioning techniques, (b) guided instruction, and (c) teacher clarity. Following the description of each instructional scaffolding technique, we provide concrete examples along with ready-to-use or easily adaptable tools and real-life practices from K-12 classrooms to illustrate their use.

INSTRUCTIONAL SCAFFOLDING PRACTICE #1: QUESTIONING TECHNIQUES

Using questioning techniques strategically creates opportunities for learning to be interactive and engaging by prompting students' thoughts and ideas. When coupled with dialogue and feedback, incorporating carefully developed questions into lessons creates purposeful and meaningful ways in which students not only engage with content but also develop critical academic language learning. Asking questions may seem to be something that teachers do naturally and intuitively as a part of the typical flow of any lesson. However, most of the questions teachers spontaneously ask may not match the cognitive abilities of multilingual learners and may focus on simple recall, illustration of ideas, or summary of the topic at hand. In order to fully involve all students in learning, it is important to preplan and carefully craft before, during, and after-lesson questions to guide students' thinking and engage them cognitively, regardless of their language proficiency levels.

Scaffolded questions encourage all students to engage with the lesson and collaborate with one another. They are essential for multilingual learners to promote critical thinking, check for understanding, and set class discussions into motion with their full engagement. When you use these strategies inclusively, you create an environment where every student, regardless of language proficiency, can actively participate in learning. When working with multilingual learners, your challenge (and opportunity) is to adapt your questions to provide additional support while the questions remain cognitively stimulating and demanding. Start with simpler, more direct questions to help multilingual learners grasp fundamental concepts; next, increasingly ask more cognitively demanding questions, promoting higher-order thinking. Although the cognitive demands may be rigorous, the language used in the questions might be adjusted according to the language proficiency level of the students.

ADVANTAGES OF THIS PRACTICE

Questioning techniques are versatile tools that can be adapted to suit the needs of individual learners in inclusive and interactive learning environments. They encourage multilingual learners to actively engage with the lesson and provide opportunities to practice and enhance language skills. Questioning techniques can build students' confidence in their ability to participate fully in class activities, and in turn, they can foster a sense of belonging for multilingual learners. This type of scaffolding also can ensure that all students are challenged to think critically despite their level of language proficiency. Using these strategies effectively, empowers students to explore challenging content, work with peers, share their thoughts, and develop more effective communication.

EXAMPLE #1: WAIT TIME AND RESPONSE STRATEGIES

When teachers conduct questioning and discussion with multilingual learners in mind, they offer extended time for students to process questions, retrieve information, and formulate responses. This technique, known as "wait time" (Rowe, 1972), is an important scaffold for teachers to incorporate when asking questions because it allows additional time for students to respond. It can have a significant impact on the participation and learning of multilingual learners as they are better able to participate in meaningful, in-depth discussions using their full linguistic repertoires and overcome perceived language barriers.

An example of the use of wait time is Numbered Heads Together (Kagan & Kagan, 2015), a collaborative activity in which all students are engaged in responding to questions. With this response structure, students work in teams of four, with each team member assigned a number (1–4). When the teacher presents the class with a question or prompt, students collaboratively work in their teams to formulate a collective response. After a designated time, the teacher randomly calls out a number, and all students with that corresponding number must raise their hands, from which one is selected to provide an answer. This strategy for providing wait time ensures that all students can consider plausible answers with the support of their team before being called on to respond. Other ways you can use productive wait time are by inviting students to gather thoughts on sticky notes or index cards in the language of their choice and/or the modality of their choice; as their names suggest, a *Quick Write* or a *Quick Draw* provides time for students to jot down a few preliminary thoughts using words or images.

Question responses should allow for all students to have opportunities to answer, benefit from interaction with peers, and be accountable for their learning. Jackie Acree Walsh (2022) identifies what teachers might consider when selecting ways for students to engage with questions. There are multiple techniques for teachers to use to enhance wait time through response structures including:

- *Think-Pair-Share* – after a question is posed, students have an opportunity to think of a response; after a short amount of time, they turn to a partner and share their answer.
- *Think-Jot-Pair-Share* – similar to Think-Pair-Share with an added step, students think about a response to a question, jot down their ideas, and then turn and talk with a partner
- *Four-Square Share* – in teams of four, students jot down their individual answers to a question and then share their ideas, one at a time, while others take notes; students individually write their final response to the question from the notes taken.
- *Response Chaining* – each student has an agree/disagree card; after a question is posed, student #1 answers, and all other students hold up their cards to agree or disagree. Student #1 then calls on another student to elaborate on the same question. All students hold up their cards again to agree or disagree. The process continues until the class decides the conversation is complete.
- *Tech Support Response* – students respond to questions using technology on tablets or laptops using Poll Everywhere, AnswerGarden, Kahoot, Quizlet, and so on.

EXAMPLE #2: BLOOM'S TAXONOMY WITH QUESTION STEMS AND PROMPTS

The original version of Bloom's taxonomy (1956) is a seminal framework for categorizing educational objectives with six levels of cognitive complexity—knowledge, comprehension, application, analysis, synthesis, and evaluation. It can be used to develop questions that promote higher-order thinking with more open-ended questions that require students to think critically, consider different perspectives and viewpoints, tap into their prior knowledge and learning, and support their arguments with evidence.

It is time consuming for teachers to prepare all their questions in advance of their lessons, so they tend to rely on spontaneous questioning during class time, leading to varying levels of effectiveness. At other times, they may use questions provided in curriculum guides or teacher guidebooks that are rarely designed to address the unique contexts of classrooms with multilingual learners. Impromptu questioning usually focuses on surface-level information including simple recall of facts, yes/no questions, or closed-ended questions with single correct responses. At times, teachers may even pose questions that, in turn, they end up answering themselves. While all teachers create questions on the spot as part of effective teaching, it is critical for every lesson to be developed with a well-prepared set of questions that lead students to a deeper understanding of the topic at hand.

To facilitate planning various types of questions, start by using question stems and prompts based on Bloom's taxonomy. These stems and prompts guide the designing of questions for students to better engage with content at multiple cognitive levels. They also ensure instruction is well-aligned with goals for learning as students are challenged to analyze, synthesize, and evaluate information. Table 2.1 identifies possible question stems and prompts at each level of cognitive complexity. Notice how knowledge, comprehension, and application questions and prompts focus on closed-ended, surface-level questions/prompts requiring basic recall and use of information and how they become more complex as the cognitive demand increases. The revised terminology for Bloom's Taxonomy, updated in 2001 by Anderson and Krathwohl, is included in each level in parenthesis.

TABLE 2.1 ● Question Stems and Prompts via Bloom's Taxonomy

COGNITIVE LEVELS	QUESTION AND PROMPT STEMS
Knowledge (Remembering): Recall of information	Who ______________? Where____________? What ______________? Why____________? When______________? How____________? Describe what happens when_______________.
Comprehension (Understanding): Organizing and stating facts and ideas	Summarize/Retell _______________. Identify the main idea of _____________. Explain what is meant by _____________. What is the meaning of _____________? How would you rephrase ___________? Which statement supports __________?
Application (Applying): Using knowledge in new situations	How would you apply this information to ______? What examples can you find to _________? Using what you know, how would you solve _______?

(Continued)

(Continued)

COGNITIVE LEVELS	QUESTION AND PROMPT STEMS
	How might you make use of these facts to________? Which of these approaches would you use to _____? Why is _________ an example of _________?
Analysis (Analyzing): Separating a whole into parts	What conclusions can you draw from_________? How would you classify ________________? How does _________compare/contrast with ________? What evidence supports_____________? How is ____________ related to _________? What information justifies the idea of ___________?
Synthesis (Evaluating) Combining ideas to form new ones	What might you infer from_____________? What solutions would you suggest for ________? Why do you agree/disagree with _____________? How might you prove/disprove_____________? How valuable is the importance of __________? What choice would you have made if____________?
Evaluation (Creating): Making decisions, judgements, and creating opinions	Identify the most valuable idea__________. Prioritize from greatest to least important__________. What criteria would you use to assess______ and why? What changes would you make to___________? What would have happened if _____________? How would you design _________in order to ________?

online resources Available for download at https://companion.corwin.com/courses/NineDimensionsofScaffoldingforMLs

In a seminal article, "Asking the Right Questions," Jane Hill and Kathleen Flynn (2008) emphasize incorporating effective questioning techniques into classroom instruction, especially in the context of multilingual learners. The authors advocate for tiered questions combining a comprehensive understanding of the stages of language acquisition—preproduction, early production, speech emergence, intermediate fluency—and their defining characteristics and suggested prompts for questioning students effectively in alignment with the cognitive levels of Bloom's taxonomy. Hill and Flynn stress that multilingual learners can respond to higher-level questions when teachers appropriately develop them with language acquisition stages in mind as well as the use of scaffolding techniques to promote the progress of multilingual learners. Examples of higher order thinking questions, using the first three levels of language proficiency, are aligned with Hill and Flynn's work and illustrated in Table 2.2.

TABLE 2.2 ● Question and Prompt Examples in an Earth Science Class Using Stages of Language Acquisition and Bloom's Taxonomy

HIGHER-ORDER COGNITIVE LEVELS OF BLOOM'S TAXONOMY	LEVELS OF LANGUAGE ACQUISITION		
	PREPRODUCTION (ENTERING): STUDENTS ARE NONVERBAL IN THE TARGET LANGUAGE	EARLY PRODUCTION (EMERGING): STUDENTS PRODUCE PHRASES AND SHORT SENTENCES	SPEECH EMERGENCE (DEVELOPING): STUDENTS PRODUCE SENTENCES AND BRIEF PARAGRAPHS
Analysis	Identify an environmental issue in your community and its impact by selecting the appropriate photographs.	Compare the effects of a hurricane and a tsunami. How are they similar?	Study a fossil and a rock. How are they similar, and how are they different?
Synthesis	What causes earthquakes? Select the correct pictures and share with the class.	Create a diagram that shows the relationship between Earth's tilt and the seasons. Tell what happens using the diagram and the words "fall" and "winter."	Explain how the water cycle works. Use the words evaporation, condensation, and precipitation.
Evaluation	Which of these is not a natural disaster? Point to the correct picture.	Which layer of the Earth is closest to the surface, where we find land and oceans?	How can people minimize the damage caused by earthquakes?

online resources Available for download at https://companion.corwin.com/courses/NineDimensionsofScaffoldingforMLs

EXAMPLE #3: THICK AND THIN QUESTIONS

Students' ability to ask and answer questions is foundational for reading comprehension and critical thinking. The ability to ask questions is integral for comprehension, problem solving, and active learning. Student-generated questions clarify information; they engage students in academic dialogue and support them to become self-directed learners. However, it has been our experience that most teachers support students to answer questions but not to ask them. Although proficient readers automatically ask questions while they read, less proficient readers need extra support and practice to ask critical questions.

Thick and Thin Questions is an activity that allows students to practice asking questions about text. Students must discern between and create "thick" questions, which require deeper thinking and analysis, and "thin" questions, which are more readily answerable as they focus more on details right on the surface of the text. The following is an overview of the characteristics of each type of question:

Thick questions:

- Focus on broad themes,
- Promote deep discussion,
- Are often complex and need interpretation,
- Require different pieces of evidence from the text to answer, and
- Often begin with "Why?" or "How come?"

Thin questions:

- Most often request straight-forward information,
- Focus on details explicitly expressed in the text,
- Support students to figure out word meaning, and
- Clarify specific information in the text.

Begin this activity with a mini lesson on each type of question. Have teams or pairs of students examine samples of both types of questions to determine whether they are thick or thin. Enhance this activity with a game-like sorting task. Discuss each question in a debrief. Next, preview the text students are about to read by activating prior knowledge, reviewing key vocabulary, explaining unfamiliar concepts, and so on. After the preview, ask students to work individually to read and annotate the assigned text by jotting down questions on sticky notes, one question per note. To support multilingual learners with this activity, consider how some students might work together in pairs, use their full linguistic repertoires, or collaborate on the task in a small group with the teacher. In addition, multilingual learners might be asked to annotate a reduced amount of text. After reading, students take turns sharing their questions with the class, and through discussion, determine whether their questions are thick or thin. Each note is then placed on a divided chart, one side for thick questions and the other for thin questions. Table 2.3 identifies some examples of thick and thin questions.

TABLE 2.3 • Thick and Thin Question Examples

THICK QUESTIONS	THIN QUESTIONS
• How can small changes in our daily lives protect our environment from pollution?	• What common gas released by vehicles contributes to air pollution? • Which type of waste contributes to land pollution?

• How can community members work together to implement a plan to reduce pollution? • What policies should be developed to address plastic pollution in our oceans?	• What is one major source of water pollution in urban areas?

Teaching students how to ask thick and thin questions supports their comprehension by actively engaging with the text. Generating thick questions, in particular, challenges students to analyze, interpret, and infer while reading. It is especially important for multilingual learners because it promotes practice with productive language skills, requiring students to develop questions and formulate responses at different levels of complexity. This strategy can be successfully used with most grade levels, but it can require extensive modeling and guided practice for it to be most effective.

KEEP THIS IN MIND

There are several challenges that can arise when using questioning techniques with multilingual learners. Questions are often spoken, which provides students with a reduced number of clues as to the meaning of unfamiliar words or complex terminology. Depending on their age or grade level, some students may hesitate to answer questions due to fear of mispronouncing words or making grammatical missteps, which might lead to feelings of embarrassment. Additionally, abstract questions may present difficulties for multilingual learners. Teachers need to be aware of these challenges and mitigate them by adjusting the complexity of the questions or providing support in the home language when needed, using visual aids, and, most of all, sustaining a supportive and inclusive learning environment. Another challenge with using questioning techniques is that they take time to prepare. Some questioning strategies are labor intensive and time consuming, but they are well worth the effort.

Consider what Kanako Suwa, a secondary English as an additional language (EAL) teacher, does to foster independence in students by scaffolding their reading. See Figure 2.1 for an example of how Kanako scaffolds Kafka's (1915, 2010) *Metamorphosis* by leaving brief prompting questions in their books. Students continue to be supported even when they read at home on their own or read ahead in class without having a teacher sitting next to them to ask the same questions. It also helps students figure out how often they should annotate because the prompts act as a reading break.

FIGURE 2.1 ● Scaffolding Independent Reading With Carefully Placed Questions and Prompts

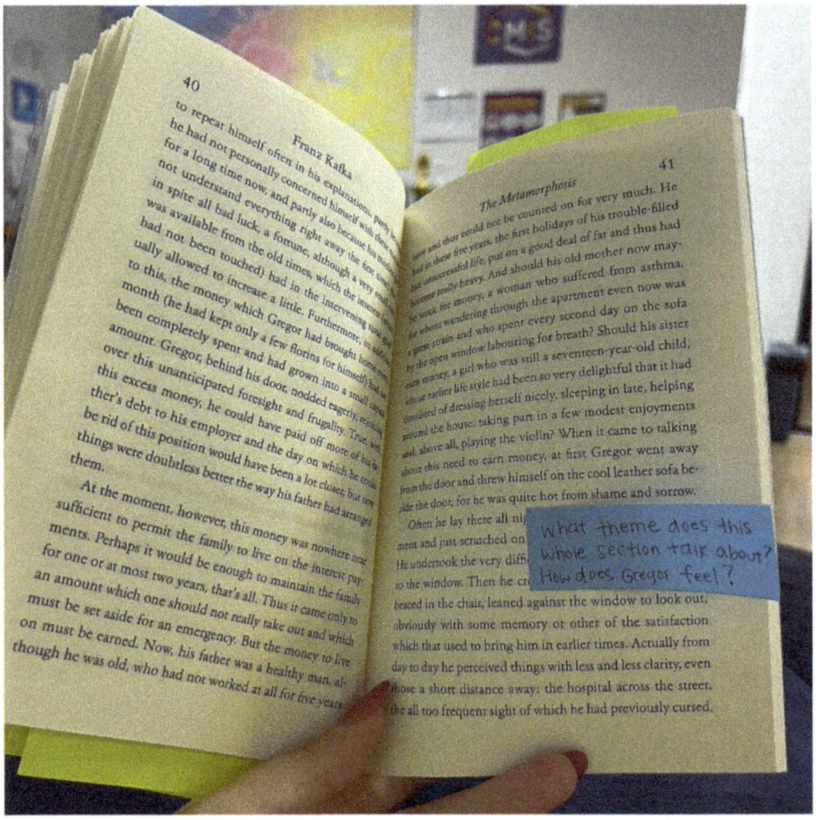

Source: Kanako Suwa. Used with permission.

INSTRUCTIONAL SCAFFOLDING PRACTICE #2: GUIDED INSTRUCTION

Guided instruction is an effective teaching strategy that offers the right amount of support and direction for students to consolidate their understanding of new concepts, develop or internalize new skills or strategies, or apply what has already been learned to new tasks or activities. It is a critical step in the instructional process for multilingual learners because it allows for multiple meaningful opportunities for language learning through repeated exposure of ideas as well as practice and application of content before students are asked to work independently. Guided instruction is designed to help students under the direct purview of the teacher.

Guided instruction is generally organized to provide practical, step-by-step learning experiences for students that focus on a specific activity or task. Guidance is devised to uncover the ways to solve a problem, complete an exercise, participate in a discussion, break down information into digestible chunks, or use tools such as mentor texts or technology to complete specific tasks. Feedback is a critical component in guided instruction as it allows students to receive immediate information about their work to identify errors, correct misunderstandings, and make improvements. Based on anticipated challenges or frequently occurring errors, you can try "feed forward," which is guidance helping students with the next steps. The level of support and the tools used during guided instruction will vary depending on student progress and task complexity. For example, Holly Siggins regularly uses Canva to create scaffolded templates for her middle school students in Knoxville, Tennessee. See Figure 2.2 for an example of a Nonfiction Book Talk Guide.

FIGURE 2.2 • Scaffolded Nonfiction Book Talk Template

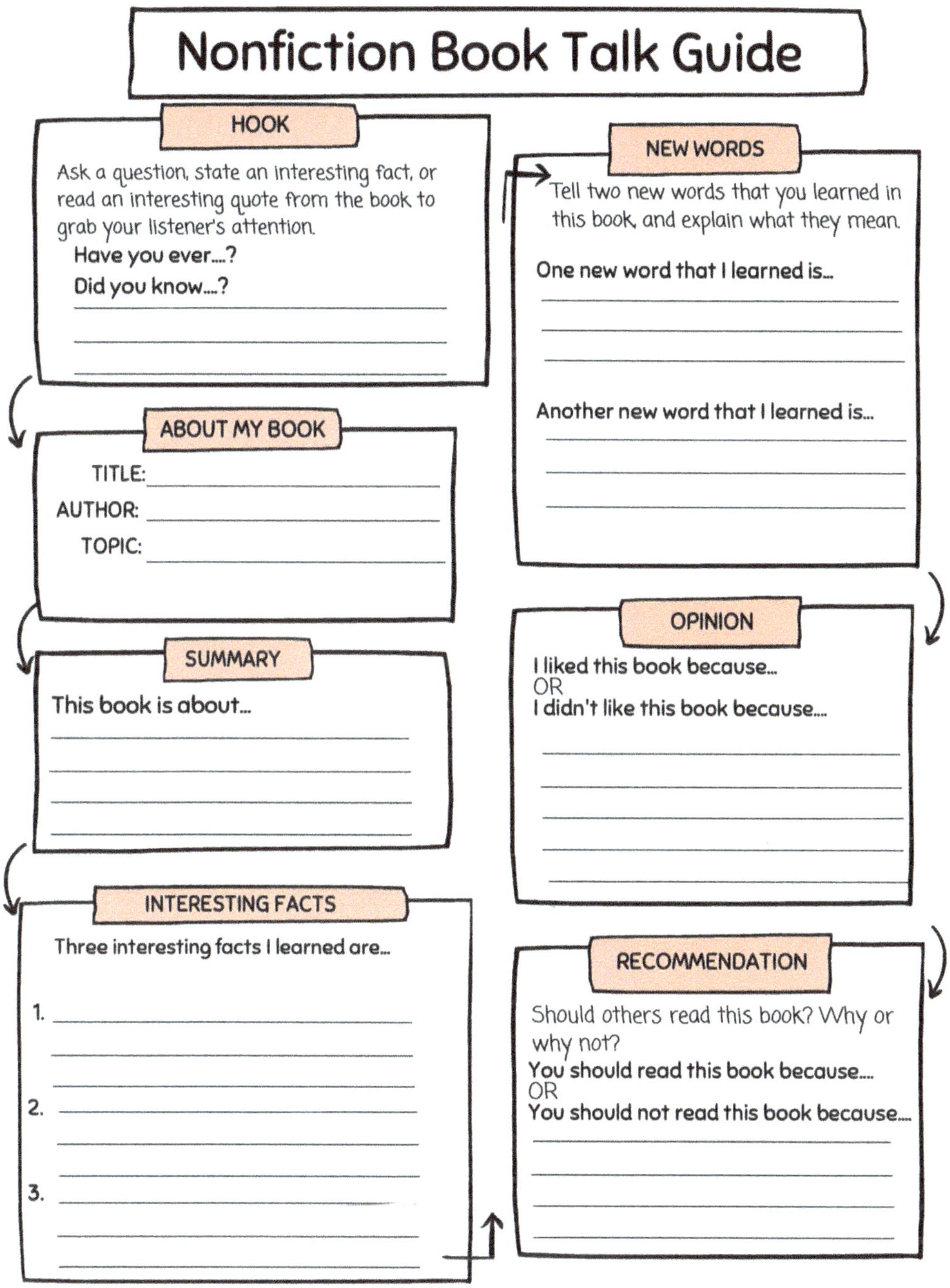

Source: Holly Siggins. Used with permission.

Not all students need the same amount or type of support, and assessing students during guided instruction is another key step. Formative assessment allows some students to move to a follow-up activity—working with peers or on their own—while other students remain with the teacher to benefit from additional guidance. In this way, teachers can tailor instruction to meet the diverse needs of students without holding back others. Grouping students for different phases of guided instruction furthers teachers' abilities to adjust the level of support, ask targeted questions, or provide additional practice to accommodate different learning needs or language proficiency levels.

ADVANTAGES OF GUIDED INSTRUCTION

Guided instruction offers multilingual learners several opportunities for language development and engagement with content. Its various structures provide supportive environments, and teachers can tailor instruction so that it is accessible for all multilingual learners. Guided instruction encourages active participation and interaction among students, increasing multilingual learners' engagement and practice across all modes of communication. It builds confidence with its step-by-step approach and supports using English for academic tasks and communication.

EXAMPLE #1: MODELING AND DEMONSTRATING

Modeling and demonstrating are strategies for guided instruction that involves showing—not just telling—students how to complete a particular task from start to finish. These practices are essential for assisting multilingual learners to better understand and internalize new concepts, skills, or processes and ultimately become independent learners. Modeling can involve teachers showing an example of a completed project and analyzing why it meets the conditions for success. However, a more effective use of this strategy involves the teacher modeling how a task is begun to how it is completed. This type of explicit instruction works best for many multilingual learners. It breaks down the process, and subsequently, the language used is directly related to each smaller step, so students can readily comprehend what the teacher is showing or describing. Modeling provides a context for learning to take place as the teacher often incorporates materials, actions, visuals, multimedia, and realia along with the steps in the process. Thus, language is attached to objects and actions while the content or task is being demonstrated. Student interactions, peer conversations, and the ability to ask questions are also incorporated during the modeling process to make learning (and scaffolding) multidimensional.

FROM RESEARCH TO PRACTICE

Abdullahi Salisu and Emmanuel Ransom (2014) describe five different types of modeling as follows:

- **Dispositions modeling** – showcasing positive character traits; modeling qualities such as integrity, empathy, courage, diligence, and so on.
- **Task and performance modeling** – demonstrating how tasks are completed from start to finish, such as conducting science experiments or solving math problems.
- **Meta-cognitive modeling** – explaining one's thinking while completing a task; expressing one's thought process when solving a problem; analyzing a theory; predicting in an experiment; inferencing during reading; and so on.
- **Modeling as a scaffolded technique** – creating multiple opportunities for repetition, discussion, and practice; pacing guided instruction according to students' needs.
- **Student-centered modeling** – providing students with the opportunity to model expected behaviors or conduct task modeling for peers when they have already mastered concepts.

Reflect on the following:

Salisu and Ransom (2014) emphasize that modeling and demonstrating are vital instructional methods for all students to develop their language and literacy skills. *What has been your experience with these five types of modeling? Are they equally manageable in your classroom? What receives more emphasis? What should be getting additional attention and why?*

____

____

____

____

Teachers may guide students through modeling and demonstrating in various ways. They read aloud to showcase fluency, expression, and pronunciation, engage students in how to decode unfamiliar words, demonstrate how to develop questions before, during, or after reading, shape how students apply reading strategies to improve comprehension, and model how to brainstorm ideas for drafting and revising written work. One of our long-time professional collaborators, K–5 itinerant English language development (ELD) teacher Dr. Katie Toppel, uses carefully constructed content and language objectives, breaks down the academic and language-based expectations for her students, and models how to complete complex tasks. See Figure 2.3 for an annotated model paragraph that shows the hook, the topic sentence, the use of descriptive words, the order in which the writer describes polar bears, as well as a conclusion. Katie does not simply project this finished product on the screen; she guides her multilingual students through the entire process of constructing a well-written paragraph.

FIGURE 2.3 ● Modelling Paragraph Writing

Appearance

Have you ever seen a polar bear? They have a lot of interesting features that help them survive in the cold Arctic habitat. First, polar bears have big fat paws, **so** they can swim in the water. Additionally, their sharp teeth are helpful because they help polar bears catch food, **so** they can't starve. Also, polar bears have thick blubber, **so** they can be warm. Finally, polar bears can use their white fur to camouflage in the snow, **so** they can hide from hunters. Now you know some ways that their features help survive.

Source: Katie Toppel. Used with permission.

One other way you can demonstrate your thinking is through a strategy known as a Think Aloud, a technique for meta-cognitive modeling. During a read aloud, you can pause at certain intervals and model your thinking about certain aspects of the text—vocabulary, author's purpose, character traits, academic content, and so on. You can pose questions or make predictions such as "I wonder why . . ." or "I think — will happen because. . ." continuing to make various text connections, inferences, visualizing, and so on, as you read. Sometimes, teachers will examine and speak to other evidence, such as diagrams, photographs, charts, and graphs, to establish other clues to the meaning of the text. To involve students in the process, engage student pairs in Turn and Talks or other activities so that they will also have practice developing their thinking about the text. For more about how to conduct a Think Aloud, please see Chapter 3.

In sum, modeling and demonstrating are synonymous, although there may be some subtle distinctions between the two practices. Demonstrating accomplishes the task of showing students what they are expected to learn; on the other hand, modeling also includes cognitive and metacognitive engagement. It is important to recognize the effectiveness of these instructional practices and how they may be effectively developed to support learning for all.

WHAT TEACHERS SAY ABOUT INSTRUCTIONAL SCAFFOLDING

Samantha Marengo, an elementary special education teacher, serves students in a co-taught classroom in Framingham Public Schools, Massachusetts. She uses affirming I-statements during small group work to articulate her own self-regulatory processes to note her observations and to model and affirm what acceptable classroom participation is like.

1. I am just ignoring any inappropriate language right now.
2. I am focused on this task for the moment.
3. I know you are doing the right thing; I can tell it from your work.

EXAMPLE #2: GUIDED PRACTICE FOR DISCIPLINARY LITERACY

Guided opportunities for meaning making are essential across all grade levels and content areas. Simply stated, disciplinary literacy refers to the subject specific (math, science, social studies, etc.) ways that members of each discipline think, talk, read, and write. More specifically, disciplinary literacy focuses on the type of comprehension and critical text analysis skills that are needed for each content area—the specialized vocabulary and sentence structures as well as the frequently used text structures and text features. For example, it is quite different to read, discuss, deconstruct, and make sense of a haiku poem compared to a math problem. Similarly, there are unique differences to account for when we teach how to write a science report versus a document-based analysis in a social studies class. Based on the vast variety of contexts you will find yourselves supporting disciplinary literacy, we have some cross-cutting strategies to offer when it comes to guided practice:

- Start with a whole-class mini lesson that incorporates modeling and explicit teaching of the target disciplinary literacy skill.
- Elicit input from students at large as you go over a whole class shared example.
- Gauge the needs of students—some might be ready to tackle tasks on their own, whereas other will benefit or require further practice.
- Support the development of disciplinary language skills and literacy practices during carefully structured, differentiated small-group instruction.
- Build students' use of essential literacy strategies under your guidance while also encouraging peer support.
- Give multilingual learners the opportunity to ask questions, make predictions, and make mistakes—both with the content and language and literacy practices.
- Provide opportunities for students to transfer newly gained disciplinary literacy skills to new tasks.
- Encourage risk-taking and tackling tasks independently while also monitoring students' progress.

See Figure 2.4 for how Elizabeth Choi, middle school ELD specialist in Knoxville, Tennessee, supports language and literacy development across the core content areas and scaffolds students' writing for mathematical problem solving.

FIGURE 2.4 ● Scaffolding for Meaning-Making and Disciplinary Writing

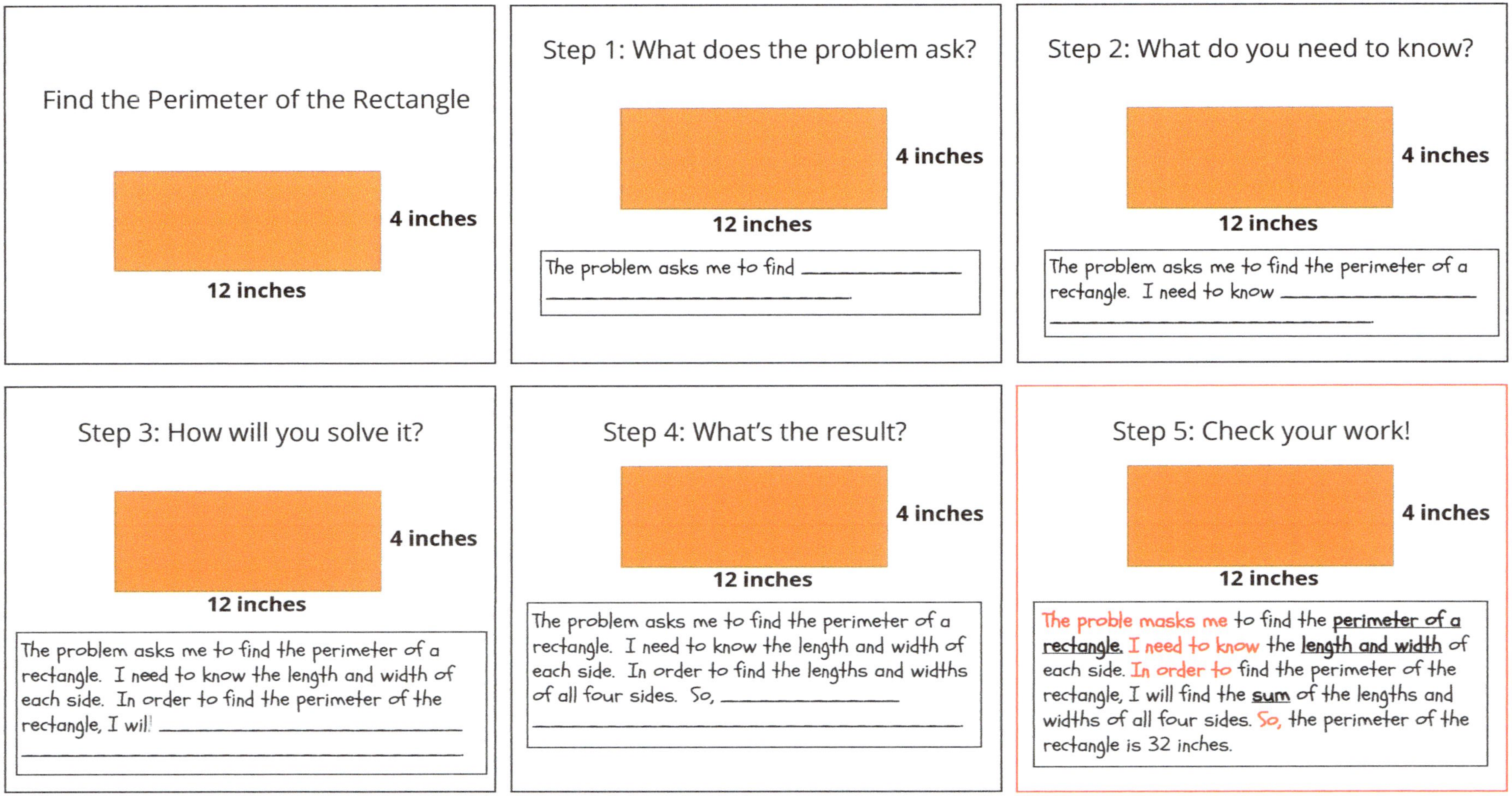

Source: Elizabeth Choi. Used with permission.

KEEP THIS IN MIND

It is critical that multilingual learners at every stage of their language and literacy development are engaged in activities that promote their reading and writing skills. Although some educators maintain that multilingual learners should obtain a certain level of fluency and facility with English before engaging in core content area instruction, we strongly believe that delaying access to disciplinary literacy is detrimental to the overall academic success of multilingual learners, particularly those students who are in secondary schools.

EXAMPLE #3: CHUNKING INFORMATION

When teachers chunk information, they break down complex content into smaller, more digestible parts, providing a reduced amount of information and language to process. While beneficial for all students, this approach is particularly significant in supporting multilingual learners because it affords them additional time to process information as well as increase their vocabulary through the repeated exposure and use of academic language. Ultimately, chunking fosters multilingual learners to have a better understanding of the subject matter by enhancing their comprehension of the material presented. An extension of this basic strategy is *Chunk-Chew-Check*:

- *Chunk* – Break down information for students using smaller quantities as previously described.
- *Chew* – Allow students the time and resources to understand new information by:
    - reflecting on how it connects to world events, other texts they have read, or their own experience,
    - partnering with other students for further discussion,
    - sketch noting the information presented (see Chapter 4),
    - completing a graphic organizer (see Chapter 5), or
    - participating in a placemat activity in which teams of students simultaneously write their understandings on a chart paper, divided like a wagon wheel, leaving space in the middle for group consensus and a summary of the topic in writing.

- *Check* – Assess student understanding through observations, questioning, or the completion of individual and group assignments.

Another example of chunking information is a *one pager*. This type of written overview of information lists the main ideas and some details of a selected topic in a bulleted fashion. In this way, students are able to read and comprehend smaller amounts of information that highlight critical concepts. One pagers can be used before reading the text or instead of reading the text, depending on students' levels of English proficiency. They can be developed with simplified text or from sentences pulled directly from the original text. You can use a one pager by reading each statement aloud, expanding on the content through discussion and definitions of vocabulary, and paraphrasing the content to verbally scaffold instruction. Take a look at the sample one-pager (Figure 2.5) written for an article entitled *I Had to Run for My Life* (Zissou, 2019).

FIGURE 2.5 • One Pager Example on A Refugee Experience

- As refugees from the Democratic Republic of the Congo (DRC), Marie Claire and her family were accustomed to being harassed in Zambia, the African country to which they had fled.
- People shouted at them in the streets, accusing her parents of stealing their jobs and draining the country's resources.
- Day after day, other kids would throw rocks at her and make fun of her for making mistakes in class and for not speaking the language.
- Eventually, Marie Claire rose to the top of her class, learning to speak English and Nyanja, a common language in Zambia.
- After more than eight years of waiting, her family's refugee application had finally been approved.
- When Marie Claire stepped off the plane in the United States, she was amazed.
- Above all else, she wants people to have compassion for refugees to understand the trauma they've been through.

Created by Maria G. Dove and ChatGPT

Other typical one pagers that chunk information for students may introduce essential vocabulary, highlight key concepts, allow for visual representation of key ideas, and may even invite students' home language to aid their understanding. See Table 2.4 for an example of how Adeline Scibelli, secondary English as a new language (ENL) teacher, introduced a lesson about the Panama Canal within a unit about imperialism in her integrated social studies content class in Baldwin, New York.

TABLE 2.4 ● Panama Cannel Vocabulary One-Pager

VOCABULARY WORD	IMAGE	DEFINITION	NATIVE LANGUAGE
Atlantic Ocean		A big body of water that **separates** Europe and Africa from North and South America.	océano Atlántico
Decrease		To become **less** or **smaller**	disminuir
Isthmus		A narrow strip of land that **connects** two larger **landmasses** and **separates** two **bodies of water**	istmo
Pacific Ocean		The world's **largest** ocean, covering more than **30%** of the planet's area.	océano Pacífico
Canal		A human-made **waterway** that allows boats and ships to **travel** from one body of water to another	canal

Source: **Adeline Scibelli. Used with permission.**

Image sources: Atlantic Ocean: istock.com/Milyausha Shaykhutdinova, Decrease: istock.com/mattjeacock, Isthmus: istock.comfrantic00, Pacific Ocean: istock.com/martinova4, Canal: istock.com/Michael Müller

Other ways to chunk information from text include highlighting the most important sentences in a text, breaking the text up by adding images, charts, tables, and so on, and placing information from the text into a completed graphic organizer. All in all, chucking information supports the unique learning needs of multilingual learners by reducing the amount of text and thereby facilitating student comprehension and language learning. See Figure 2.6 for another example from Adeline Scibelli's class, in which she chunks complex text and illustrates information to support her multilingual learners.

FIGURE 2.6 • Chunking Makes Texts More Accessible

Alliances

European powers signed treaties with one another to increase their own nations' security. These were called Alliances. **<u>Alliances</u> are agreements between nations stating that each country will assist (help) the other if they are attacked.** This meant that if one country was attacked, allied countries would help to defend them. Before World War I, the following alliances existed:

Russia and Serbia	**Germany and Austria-Hungary**
France and Russia	**Ottoman Empire & Bulgaria**
Britain and France and Belgium	
Japan and Britain	

How Alliances Led to WWI

Before the start of World War I, there were two large alliances.

1. One alliance was called the "**Allied Powers,**" and it consisted of the United Kingdom (Great Britain), France, and Russia.

2. The other was called the "**Central Powers.**" It included Germany, Austria-Hungary, and Italy.

When Austria-Hungary declared war on Serbia, Russia and France **defended** (protected) Serbia. Germany then declared war on Russia on the side of Serbia. Britain joined the war on the side of Serbia after Germany attacked France. Then, Japan entered the war. Later, Italy and the United States would enter on the Allies' side.

Source: Adeline Scibelli. Used with permission. Image source: Csh012, CC BY-SA 4.0 <https://creativecommons.org/licenses/by-sa/4.0>, via Wikimedia Commons

EXAMPLE #4: MENTOR TEXTS

Teachers select mentor texts to illustrate quality writing and use as models for students to elevate their own written work. These texts are analyzed together with students so that they better understand an author's craft, the skills and techniques used, from the use of words to the overall structure of the writing. By offering students a model of writing, they can explore how authors use language and grammatical structures effectively to create more complex text.

Mentor texts often contain rich and varied language, and multilingual learners benefit from exposure to words, phrases, and figurative language that are not ordinarily used in general conversation. After repeated exposure and practice, students will become familiar with analyzing a mentor text and applying what they have learned to their own writing. When using a mentor text, you might focus on individual words or sentences, discuss their meaning, and identify how various written elements convey ideas, thoughts, and feelings. Consider using a Think Aloud to model your thinking and analyze the text to reveal more about the author's craft for students.

Mentor texts can take various forms, including essays, passages, articles, emails, and so on. Even a single sentence might be used as a mentor text. *Sentence Dissection* (Dove & Honigsfeld, 2013) is a strategy that provides the analysis of one complex sentence selected from a text you are already using for literacy or content instruction. When using sentences as mentor text, the anticipated result is that students will use the format of the selected sentence to write their own sentences that are rich and engaging. (See Chapter 3 for more on sentence-level scaffolding.)

EXAMPLE #5: THE GRADUAL RELEASE OF RESPONSIBILITY

The Gradual Release of Responsibility (GRoR) (Pearson & Gallagher, 1983) is a routine for guided instruction that provides opportunities for students to work independently in incremental steps. Popularized and expanded by Fisher and Frey (2021), it was developed to systematically reduce direct instruction and increase student self-efficacy. The GRoR is an important method of instruction for multilingual learners because it combines multiple strategies for guided instruction. The components of the GRoR framework are as follows:

- **Focused instruction.** Teachers showcase skills, strategies, and tasks through explicit modeling involving the whole class. This approach helps students comprehend the thought processes behind tasks such as prediction, problem solving, and information interpretation.
- **Guided practice.** Some learning responsibility shifts to students as they practice skills under the teacher's step-by-step guidance. This phase

can be differentiated and applied to the entire class or small groups, proving beneficial to multilingual learners.

- **Collaborative learning.** Students collaborate in pairs or small groups to complete tasks, fostering oral and written communication. This approach, including heterogeneous grouping, is particularly advantageous for multilingual learners with varying language and content proficiency.
- **Individual learning.** Students work independently to practice and apply learned concepts. Teachers may assign independent work outside regular class time. Some multilingual learners at early stages of English proficiency may need additional instruction, guidance, or collaborative learning opportunities before they can work independently.

Planning lessons using the GRoR framework supports multilingual learners to gradually develop strategies and skills before independent application. Fisher and Frey (2021) emphasize that the framework's steps are neither linear nor prescriptive, allowing flexibility with how lessons begin and end. For example, teachers might open a lesson with an independent task (Do Now/Bell Ringer), followed by a demonstration of a skill or strategy, and conclude with students collaboratively practicing in pairs or teams.

KEEP THIS IN MIND

Guided instruction provides support for multilingual learners to learn new concepts and skills alongside learning an additional language, yet it can be challenging at times to implement. More and more, classrooms contain not only multilingual learners who have varying levels of language proficiency, but also students with interrupted or limited formal education (SIFE/SLIFE) as well as students with disabilities. For this reason, some teachers can become overwhelmed when trying to target specific student needs, select effective strategies, as well as group students for instruction. For the most part, guided instruction provides multiple entry points for content learning and many opportunities for multilingual learners to develop language and literacy. Pacing is critical to guided instruction; it allows for systemic repetition of concepts (such as multiple meaningful exposures and multimodal access to the content) and additional time for practice. Providing consistent feedback is also an essential component for guided instruction so that students correct mis-understandings and do not repeat the same mistakes.

WHAT TEACHERS SAY ABOUT INSTRUCTIONAL SCAFFOLDING

The fact that language demands are in all curriculum subjects clearly implies that teachers must be aware of using different strategies that support students in understanding content and language. For example, teachers can make the content more comprehensible through instructional scaffolding, such as illustrating meaning through demonstrations or visuals. Teachers can also have students work in small groups. Integrating speaking, listening, reading, and writing in a subject/curriculum is necessary for language acquisition.

—Migdalia Marco, bilingual educator, Patchogue Medford Schools, New York

INSTRUCTIONAL SCAFFOLDING PRACTICE #3: TEACHER CLARITY

Students need to know what is expected of them as well as how they will go about learning what they need to know and understanding what to do. For this reason, instructions, expectations, and lesson delivery need to be clear. However, for many multilingual learners, it is not always clear what is expected of them or how to approach learning with success.

Teacher clarity is associated with how teachers go about making sure that students understand what they need to learn and exactly how they will learn it. For this reason, formative assessment—frequently checking for student understanding—is a critical part of this process. Teachers also need to know when students have met with success so that they can plan accordingly.

Building on the work of Fendick (1990), Fisher et al. (2017) identified teacher clarity with the following four components:

1. **Clarity of organization** such that lesson tasks, assignments, and activities include links to the objectives and outcomes of learning
2. **Clarity of explanation** such that information is relevant, accurate, and comprehensible to students
3. **Clarity of examples** such that the lesson includes information that is illustrative and illuminating as students gradually move to independence, making progress with less support from the teacher

4. **Clarity of assessment** such that the teacher is regularly seeking out and acting upon the feedback he or she receives from students, especially through their verbal and written responses (p. 26).

Learning tasks need to be in alignment with learning targets, and planned instruction should include a logical sequence of events designed to meet identified objectives. Teachers should have a thorough command of the content being taught allowing for appropriate explanation of pertinent information at a level that all students can understand, using visuals and tools other than text, as well as pacing the lesson effectively. Guided practice, using questions, prompts, and cues to scaffold instruction, affords students opportunities that lead to deeper learning and increasing independence. Finally, formative assessment is most critical to teacher clarity. It supports teachers to adjust instruction when needed and plan future instruction accordingly.

There are five essential practices to ensure teacher clarity. How are the following integrated into your teaching already?

- Crafting learning intentions and success criteria.
- Co-constructing learning intentions and success criteria with learners.
- Creating opportunities for students to respond (i.e., formative assessment).
- Providing effective feedback on and for learning.
- Sharing learning and progress between students and teachers.

ADVANTAGES OF TEACHER CLARITY

Teacher clarity calls for clear objectives and accompanying success criteria—what students need to know and do to be successful. It incorporates explicit instruction—breaking down information into smaller parts—making learning more manageable for multilingual learners. The lesson flow and step-by-step instruction are always focused on meeting the learning targets. Language use is in line with the varying English language proficiency levels of the students. For this reason, instruction is verbally scaffolded to include a repetition of information using both simple and complex vocabulary and sentence structures. Student understanding is frequently checked through observation, questioning, and other formative assessment methods, along with providing timely feedback. In many cases, learning is connected to the real world and students' lived experiences.

EXAMPLE #1: LEARNING OBJECTIVES AND SUCCESS CRITERIA

Learning objectives are fundamental to achieving teacher clarity; they can be effectively used to guide students to meet lesson expectations. When teachers not only articulate specific learning objectives but also post and review what they mean, students are better able to know what they are expected to understand and do. Outlining a clear focus for a lesson reduces uncertainty, alleviates anxiety, and often helps to preview some of the language needed to understand lesson content. Consider the following learning objectives created for a sixth-grade science lesson:

- Students will be able to define and label the main components involved in photosynthesis, including sunlight, water, carbon dioxide, and chlorophyll.
- Students will be able to explain how plants convert sunlight, water, and carbon dioxide into glucose and oxygen.

How might you preview these learning objectives for multilingual learners? The following is an example of one possible routine for presenting them to students:

- Post the learning objectives where they are visible to all students.
- Read them aloud or have a student volunteer read them.
- Display a labeled diagram of photosynthesis.
- Check for understanding of key vocabulary, e.g., carbon dioxide, chlorophyll, glucose.
- Verbally scaffold the language used in the objectives to make it comprehensible, e.g., "Students will be able to explain how plants make food using . . ."
- Ask students to explain them using their own words, with the option of translanguaging.
- Invite students to pair up and share the meaning of the lesson objectives in their home language.

Success criteria further support student understanding by outlining the concrete steps required to achieve the learning objectives. These criteria provide students with measurable indicators of progress, helping them understand what success looks like and how to manage their own work. With clear success criteria, students can better monitor whether they are making headway in the lesson. By checking to see if they are on track, they can build their overall confidence in their learning or be better able to ask for help. Consider the following success criteria for the sixth-grade lesson on photosynthesis with the learning objectives stated previously:

- Read alone, in pairs, or with the teacher the definition of the photosynthesis process.
- Highlight important words and write definitions for unknown words in your personal glossary.
- Label the diagram provided with all the main components of the photosynthesis process: sunlight, water, carbon dioxide, and chlorophyll.
- Verbally explain to a partner each component's role in photosynthesis in English or in your home language using appropriate scientific vocabulary.
- Review the rubric for completion of the writing assignment alone, in pairs, or with the teacher.
- Complete a short, written explanation of the photosynthesis process. Use the sentence frames if needed to support your writing.

The step-by-step guidance that success criteria provide can truly enhance student understanding and performance. They minimize uncertainty and provide clear direction for students, allowing them to focus more on confidently participating in lesson activities.

EXAMPLE #2: ILLUSTRATIVE EXAMPLES AND WRITING EXEMPLARS

To foster clear intentions and enhance teacher clarity, using examples and exemplars to offer concrete models of completed work can provide powerful support for multilingual learners. By examining representations of actual assignments, students can better understand teacher expectations for the successful completion of written work. In this way, students can transfer what they have learned by analyzing these sample works to their own writing.

One type of sample work can come from actual examples of previous students' writing. By examining other students' work, students can discover various approaches to addressing the same or similar assignment, including:

- How to organize their thoughts
- The best way to structure their ideas
- What to add and exclude
- What language might be used

By analyzing the writing of their peers, students can identify strengths and areas for improvement in peer examples, helping them more clearly recognize what constitutes high-quality work. This process not only uncovers expectations for their own writing but also fosters critical thinking about their writing practices. Students might also benefit from using a checklist or guide when analyzing peer writing (see Table 2.5).

TABLE 2.5 ● Peer Writing Analysis Guide

PEER WRITING ANALYSIS GUIDE
Directions: Begin by reading the writing sample from start to finish. Next, use the following questions to guide you to analyze the work. Reread the work as needed.
☐ Does the writing address the assignment effectively?
☐ Is there a clear main idea?
☐ Are there suficient details to support the main idea?
☐ Is there a well-defined introduction, body, and conclusion (beginning, middle, and end)?
☐ Are there appropriate transitions from one idea to another?
☐ Does the vocabulary used adequately align to the topic?
☐ Are the sentence structures varied and interesting?
☐ What are the strengths in this piece of writing?
☐ What areas need improvement?
☐ What can you learn from this piece of writing to apply to your own work?
☐ What new ideas or approaches to your own writing has this piece inspired?

online resources Available for download at https://companion.corwin.com/courses/NineDimensionsofScaffoldingforMLs

Another type of sample pieces of writing are exemplars, which can demonstrate different levels of writing from developing to mastery. Exemplars can help multilingual learners truly understand the trajectory for success by examining the different stages of writing proficiency for a particular assignment. For example, when learning about argumentative writing, students might analyze a set of exemplars on a topic to determine their use of a claim, evidence, and appropriate reasoning. One piece of work might be a developing-level exemplar that identifies a claim but offers minimal evidence to support the claim. In contrast, a mastery-level exemplar might contain a hook to grab the reader's attention, background information about the topic, multiple reasons with evidence to back up the claim, and so on. By comparing these exemplars, students can be supported to identify a pathway for making their writing more proficient. These exemplar comparisons can be further enhanced by using a rubric for the assignment.

EXAMPLE #3: ASSESSMENT PRACTICES—RUBRICS, EXIT SLIPS PLUS, AND REFLECTION

The right assessment tools are crucial for multilingual learners as they can offer actionable feedback on progress toward learning goals. Assessment practices should help students to recognize their strengths and identify areas where they need to improve. Three key aspects of effective assessment for multilingual learners are:

- Ensuring that students understand the criteria for success
- Safeguarding that assessment tasks are scaffolded so students can demonstrate what they know
- Providing students with opportunities to reflect on their work—allowing them to consider what they have accomplished and how they can improve moving forward

To provide examples of these critical factors for assessment, we highlight three assessment strategies: Rubrics, Exit Slips Plus, and Reflection Journaling. Each of these practices enhances teacher clarity by providing multilingual learners with a better understanding of learning goals, support for completing assessment tasks, and opportunities to improve through self-directed learning.

RUBRICS

Rubrics provide specific measures for task completion, identifying each part of an assignment that will be evaluated as well as how students can meet with success. They are structured in a way that breaks down the components of a task into measurable criteria and describes different levels of performance for each, often using a numbered scale (e.g., 1–4) with each number representing a level of proficiency (e.g., beginning, developing. proficient, mastery). Rubrics set clear expectations for students and can support them to become self-directed learners.

Rubrics need to be accessible for multilingual learners to be of value. For this reason, consider the following guidelines when creating rubrics for an assignment:

- Use clear and simple language.
- Align rubric criteria with learning goals.
- Illustrate, model, and demonstrate what success looks like for each component identified on the rubric.
- Be specific and quantify criteria whenever possible, e.g., three pieces of evidence; no more than two spelling errors.
- Make it visual – use color-coding, icons, photographs, and so on.
- Use positive language to promote growth, e.g., use "developing" instead of "does not meet."

Teachers need to share and discuss rubrics with students beforehand, so that multilingual learners have a clear understanding of how to meet set goals. See Table 2.6 for an example of a rubric that also serves as a step-by-step scaffold for project completion from Holly Siggins's middle school classroom. Consider coupling the discussion of the rubrics for an assignment with examples or exemplars of a completed assignment.

TABLE 2.6 ● Governments Around the World Project Rubric

SLIDE #	SLIDE INFORMATION	POINTS
Slide 1	• Title of Country • Picture of flag • Your name	____/4
Slide 2	• Location of country (what continent is it in?) • Language(s) spoken • Population (how many people live there) • Image of country on a map	____/8
Slide 3	Where is the capital city? • Image of the capital city on a map • Picture of the capital city	____/4
Slide 4	What type of government does the country have? • At least three details/facts about the government (2 points each) • One image (1 point)	____/7
Slide 5	Who is the current leader or leaders of the country? • A picture of the leader (1 point) • Three facts/details about the leader (2 points each)	____/7
Slide 6	Additional information • Any other facts, details, stories, or information about the country	____/5
Slide 7	Compare and Contrast • How is the government similar to the government of the United States? (at least three similarities)	____/15
Slide 8	Compare and Contrast • How is the government different from the government of the United States? (at least three differences)	____/15
Slide 9	Sources • Include a list of websites where you found your information • All sources are cited • Information is NOT copy/pasted, but put into your own words	____/15

Presentation Skills	• Eye Contact • Loud, clear voice • Well-prepared; words pronounced correctly • Information is not read word-for-word from the slide, but explained in your own words	____/20
Total		____/100

Source: Holly Siggins. Used with permission.

EXIT SLIPS PLUS

Exit slips are quick, formative assessments in which students respond to a prompt at the end of a lesson, such as "Name three important points to remember when analyzing primary sources of information." The "Plus" refers to scaffolding these prompts so that multilingual learners can more readily respond. Consider offering sentence frames, multiple choice, or word banks to support multilingual learners to complete the assessment task. Scaffolding exit slips ensures that all students can demonstrate their understanding without being hindered by language barriers.

REFLECTION JOURNALING

Reflecting on one's learning fosters a deeper understanding by connecting prior knowledge with new insights and providing an opportunity to identify strengths and areas for improvement. Through reflection, students actively engage with the learning process and build independence. One tool to support this process is a reflection journal, a pen-and-paper, or a digital activity to foster student growth. Consider establishing a framework of questions that students can use to reflect on their learning as follows:

- What are some things I learned about today?
- What did I already know about the topic that helped me to learn?
- Which of my strengths did I use to complete today's tasks?
- What strategies did I use to help me better understand? (Consider having an accessible list of strategies that students already know and use)
- What did I find interesting about today's lesson topic?
- What might I like to learn more about?
- What did I find challenging about today's lesson?
- How do I feel about the progress that I made today?

Reflection journaling can be supported through various scaffolded writing techniques, including graphic organizers, sentence frames, and peer collaboration. Alternative means of expression, such as storyboarding or sketching, allow students to draw pictures to represent their ideas, reflect on their drawings, and use them as a reference to write their descriptions or share them orally with a teacher or peer.

KEEP THIS IN MIND

The main challenges in providing clarity for students stem from balancing the need for explicit, step-by-step instruction along with time constraints and varying student needs. In primary classrooms, there is generally ample time to provide clear introductions and use multiple scaffolds to enhance comprehension, whereas in secondary classrooms, instructional time is limited. Secondary teachers often see students for brief periods, making it challenging to establish clarity without cutting into time for completing the lesson. Another challenge is meeting the diverse learning needs of all students. More advanced students may find the scaffolds being provided unnecessary, leading to disengaging them. For this reason, grouping students who need additional support apart from other students who are ready to undertake lesson tasks might be the best way to tailor this approach.

INDEPENDENT LEARNING STRATEGIES FOR STUDENTS

To foster independent learning, teachers can empower students to internalize instructional scaffolding and apply it on their own in the following ways:

- **Self-regulation techniques.** By using self-monitoring checklists, students can learn to assess their progress, identify areas for improvement, and adjust their efforts. Various types of checklists support students in setting goals and maintaining focus, turning teacher guidance into a habit they can apply independently.
- **Provide activity choice.** Support independent learning by allowing students to engage with tasks that relate to their interests and thereby build their confidence and motivation.
- **Establish clear routines.** Give students a framework for managing their time and responsibilities, which, in turn, will help them become active, independent learners who approach learning systematically.

With these strategies and others in place, multilingual learners can develop the skills and confidence needed to navigate challenges on their own, becoming more self-directed and reflective learners.

SUMMARY

Instructional scaffolding can break down complex tasks into manageable steps, supporting students in language, literacy, and content learning. For multilingual learners, instructional scaffolding is particularly effective, as it makes lessons accessible despite their level of language proficiency. Using techniques such as leveled questioning, guided practice, modeling, and chunking information ensures all students complete lesson tasks and build their understanding to become confident, independent learners. Instructional scaffolding is beneficial for any student who needs assistance with new concepts, skills, or complex texts and can be used across general education, co-taught, and standalone ELD classes. It provides multilingual learners a structured path to academic and language learning success.

Questions

1. How can instructional scaffolding be adapted to address the varying levels of English proficiency within your classroom, ensuring that each multilingual learner engages meaningfully with both content and language objectives?
2. How might you determine which scaffold is most effective, and what indicators might signal a need for additional supports?
3. How might you effectively collaborate to design and implement scaffolding techniques that address both language and content needs in integrated classrooms?
4. What role might peer interactions and collaborative work play in instructional scaffolding for multilingual learners, and how might you structure these activities to maximize language and content development?

CHAPTER 3

Linguistic Scaffolding

"Language-learning tasks should be integrated with learning across the curriculum. Language tasks and exercises that are simply an add-on to the curriculum not only work against this, but are a frustrating experience for the teacher who then has to find time for such extra work."
Pauline Gibbons, 2015, p. 59

Linguistic scaffolding, in the broadest possible sense, means language-based and literacy-focused support for multilingual learners as they acquire new knowledge and develop their language proficiency. Through linguistic scaffolding, the full range of multilingual assets, talents, and skills students and educators possess are leveraged to ensure both *access* to the grade-level content as well as opportunities for *communication, self-expression,* and *demonstration* of new learning. In classrooms where linguistic scaffolding is embraced, teachers use multiple techniques to offer language-specific support so that multilingual learners can more fully participate and become capable learners. But there is no single, easy definition of linguistic scaffolding because of the complexities of language and literacy development. What we definitely want to avoid is a notion that multilingual learners are "in constant need of linguistic remediation" (García & Solorza, 2021, p. 512).

- When you help students recognize commonly used language features (phrases, sentence structures, signal words, etc.) within and across different content areas and when they begin to emulate features of oral and written communication that are essential for academic tasks at hand, you offer linguistic scaffolds and so much more: you also support their disciplinary language and literacy practices!
- When you focus on students' evolving levels of understanding of the intricacies of how the English language works and guide them to see those patterns, you offer linguistic scaffolds and so much more: you also support their metalinguistic awareness and skills!
- When you acknowledge and activate your students' full linguistic repertoires, including translanguaging (using multiple languages with a clear pedagogical purpose), you offer linguistic scaffolds and so much more: you also support their multilingual identities!

WHO IS IT FOR?

Linguistic scaffolds are for everyone. All students are *Academic Language Learners* (ALLs), whether English is their first and only language or their second, third, or any additional number of languages. Students need to develop language and literacy skills as these fundamental abilities serve as the cornerstone for critical thinking and overall academic success. Yet, a common (well-intentioned, yet flawed) assumption might be that linguistic scaffolding means heavily focusing on building vocabulary or expecting students to speak in complete sentences at all times or insisting on an "English-only" learning environment. We wonder what misconceptions you have encountered in your own context. In fact, would you agree that some misguided linguistic scaffolds may do more harm than good? Consider the work of Tonya Ward Singer (2025), who describes the importance of choosing, losing, and adapting scaffolding in response to students' assets. She recommends, for example, the following:

If your linguistic supports lead students to mimic without thinking, your supports are too limiting. Drop the scaffold and facilitate a low-risk opportunity for students to *engage* authentically with their own language choices and ideas - prioritizing meaningful communication over "correct" use of language. As students engage, *observe* and listen for their assets including content understandings and language choices. Use this important formative data to adapt your *supports* to help students build on their assets to thrive the task and stretch their thinking and language use in new ways. (Chapter 4, exact page number to come in March)

Linguistic scaffolds are frequently used every day in every classroom with and without multilingual learners in them, so they are more universal than you might first recognize them to be. Teachers use modeling, questioning techniques, visual supports attached to language to aid comprehension as well as offer oral and written feedback for all students to develop their language and literacy skills. Additionally, linguistic scaffolds further support multilingual learners in various ways. Here are just a few examples of how linguistic scaffolds support students at various language proficiency levels:

- They support newcomers as they process new information in their primary language and bridge that learning to English.
- They support emerging or developing multilingual learners as they recognize cognates and patterns of sentence structures that they can emulate in their own speaking and writing.

- They support advanced learners as they use their metalinguistic skills to analyze vocabulary for parts by looking for roots, prefixes, and suffixes that appear across words or compare how sentence structures are similar and different across their primary and new languages.
- They support English-proficient students in advancing their understanding of complex fiction and nonfiction texts as they identify recurring text features.

HOW IS LINGUISTIC SCAFFOLDING USED ACROSS PROGRAM MODELS?

To implement linguistic scaffolding effectively across program models, keep in mind the following:

- *In general education classes*—a large amount of complex academic language is introduced and used to deliver content, so multilingual learners will need multiple meaningful access points to comprehend and internalize what is being taught, as well as opportunities to use academic language to demonstrate their understanding.
- *In integrated, co-taught classes*—as their name suggests—both the cognitive and linguistic demands and expectations must be addressed so the students may simultaneously develop their academic knowledge, skill sets, and their linguistic competence.
- *In stand-alone—English language development (ELD) classes*, language occupies a primary purpose, so linguistic scaffolding will ensure that students stretch the boundaries of their current language use in a specially designed instructional environment.
- *In self-contained or integrated special education classes*—dually identified multilingual learners or exceptional multilingual learners will best benefit from linguistic scaffolding when their IEPs explicitly identify ways to integrate language-based supports into their academic, literacy, and social-emotional goals.

See Figure 3.1 for one frequently utilized example of linguistic scaffolding from Amy Peabody-Chieffo's third-grade classroom. Through this co-constructed anchor chart, students are reminded to try more expressive synonyms in place of commonly used words.

FIGURE 3.1 ● Synonym Chart

Source: Amy Peabody-Chieffo. Used with permission.

FROM RESEARCH TO PRACTICE

Try to visualize what Ofelia García and Cristian R. Solorza (2021) remind us of regarding the complexities of academic language:

"As language has increasingly been divided into academic and non-academic, or social, some scholars have called attention to the fact that language exists on a continuum and that it is impossible to generate a complete list of all academic features." (p. 512)

Reflect on the following:

What do you notice about how your students use language? What is your experience with, or observation of, language existing on a continuum? What academic language features (such as word choice, word formation, grammatical structures, and text markers) do you pay the most attention to in your lessons and why?

____

____

____

____

WHY IS LINGUISTIC SCAFFOLDING AN IMPORTANT APPROACH TO STUDENT LEARNING?

Academic language is an integral part of the educational lives of our students. However, George Bunch (2013) and others have cautioned about the dangers of oversimplifying "academic language" as a set of rules. We embrace the shift from merely *defining what academic language is* to exploring *how students use language at school and at home to engage in academic work.* Students can do a lot with academic language as they engage in a variety of independent or collaboratively structured academic tasks. As they do so, their language usage will vary significantly, transitioning from the initial stages of brainstorming and formulating ideas to negotiating meaning and ultimately to formally presenting their work to internal or external audiences either orally or in writing. Language is the means of communication, personal and academic socialization, in- and out-of-school learning, and much more. Within the classroom context, when you use linguistic scaffolds, you recognize that students might be ready cognitively, academically, and emotionally to work with complex concepts as well as develop new academic skills across the core content areas. Yet, the language that is necessary to communicate and to attain academic growth requires additional support.

Scaffolding as a metaphor is borrowed from construction, referring to a temporary structure that supports the builders and protects the building in its initial phases; it is also one that gets dismantled and removed. "Scaffolding as a metaphor in teaching and learning describes a system of temporary guidance offered to the learner by the teacher, jointly co-constructed, and then removed when the learner no longer needs it" (Boblett, 2012, p. 1). Here are some additional viable metaphors to consider for linguistic scaffolding:

Strike a balance—challenge the students cognitively and move their academic and linguistic development to new levels while you are offering the right amount of language process.

Build a bridge—connect what is known and familiar (linguistically and academically) with new learning and experiences.

Make language the vehicle for content attainment—plan language scaffolds strategically to get to the essence of what content is being taught. Remember what Halliday (1980/2004) emphasized about what happens in school: our students are learning language, learning *about language*, and learning *through language*.

In a recent workshop, we used a digital tool called Mentimeter to invite educators to share with us how they scaffold language in their classrooms and got a rich variety of responses (see Figure 3.2).

FIGURE 3.2 • Word Cloud Depicting Linguistic Scaffolds

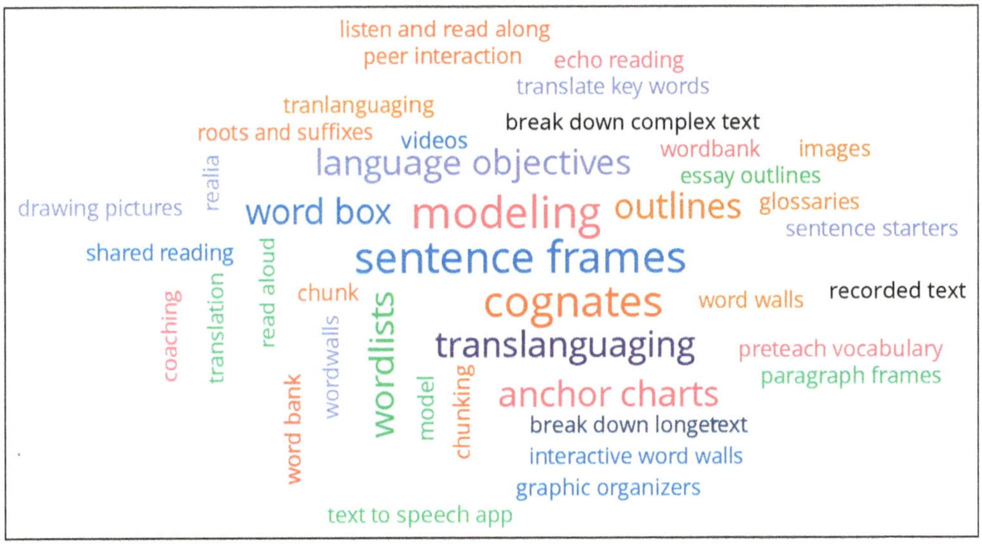

HOW DOES LINGUISTIC SCAFFOLDING SPECIFICALLY RELATE TO MULTILINGUAL LEARNERS' NEEDS?

While supporting academic language and literacy development is critical for all learners, multilingual learners especially require supports that respond to their unique linguistic needs and address the linguistic dimension of comprehension and participation. Linguistic scaffolding is essential to bolster multilingual learners' spoken and written discourse. It provides them with extended opportunities to develop functional use of linguistic forms and to learn how to use academic English across the content areas. For example, reading and discussing a poem will be quite different from engaging in mathematical conversations about a word problem. Writing a personal narrative will be uniquely distinct from a lab report when it comes to word choices, sentence structures, and text organization.

When discussing younger students, Jeff Anderson and Whitney La Rocca (2017) recognize that students are naturally curious about language; when teachers share language patterns "in bite-sized, digestible chunks," they help their students "experiment and play with these patterns with loads of talk, support, and modeling" (p. 7). Considering adolescent learners, Jeff Anderson, Travis Leech, and Melinda Clark (2021) emphasize the need for students to be invited into a process of observing and noticing how language works: "instead of drowning writers in sentences flooded in errors or lists of nevers or skills or rules, we soak them in beautiful, well-crafted sentences found in the literature already in your classrooms" (p. 9). We, too, suggest that you explore language moves (intentional ways authors use language across genres) and invite your students to try the same or similar moves in their own work. When you engage in this type of exploration, language is viewed as a tool of expression, experimentation, and innovation.

Let's embrace the duality of linguistic development to be fluid and authentic as well as a structured academic endeavor. What it means in day-to-day classroom practice is that students need ample opportunities to engage with language to express themselves (who they are and what they think or feel), to convey their understandings, and to communicate with others using all the linguistic tools available to them. Some language use will be unstructured and organic, whereas others will be well-supported and intentionally scaffolded for students.

WHAT TEACHERS SAY ABOUT LINGUISTIC SCAFFOLDING

I regularly use dialogue journals in my class. I prepare a cover page of the dialogue journal to outline personalized guidelines for each student (see Figure 3.3). For the student whose work is pictured in Figure 3.4, the dialogue journal provided an additional support to target both writing and social studies content since it was their first year in a US History class. Typically, I assign dialogue journals as open-ended tasks, but I adjusted it for this student to double-up on support. My general rule for dialogue journals is that I will match the length of writing that the student submits, which seems to motivate them to write more.

—Elizabeth Choi, middle school ELD specialist in Knoxville, Tennessee

FIGURE 3.3 ● Teacher Cover Page from a Dialogue Journal

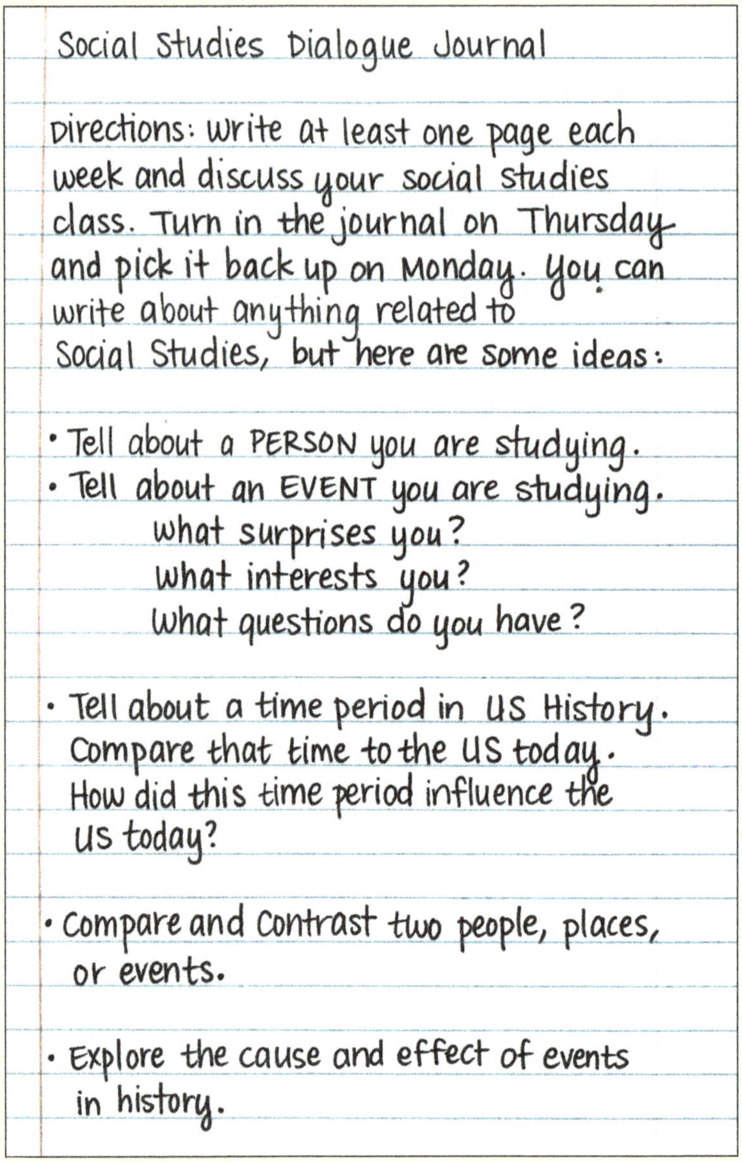
Social Studies Dialogue Journal

Directions: Write at least one page each week and discuss your social studies class. Turn in the journal on Thursday and pick it back up on Monday. You can write about anything related to Social Studies, but here are some ideas:

- Tell about a PERSON you are studying.
- Tell about an EVENT you are studying.
  - What surprises you?
  - What interests you?
  - What questions do you have?
- Tell about a time period in US History. Compare that time to the US today. How did this time period influence the US today?
- Compare and contrast two people, places, or events.
- Explore the cause and effect of events in history.

Source: Elizabeth Choi. Used with permission.

FIGURE 3.4 ● Student-Teacher Response Page From a Student's Dialogue Journal

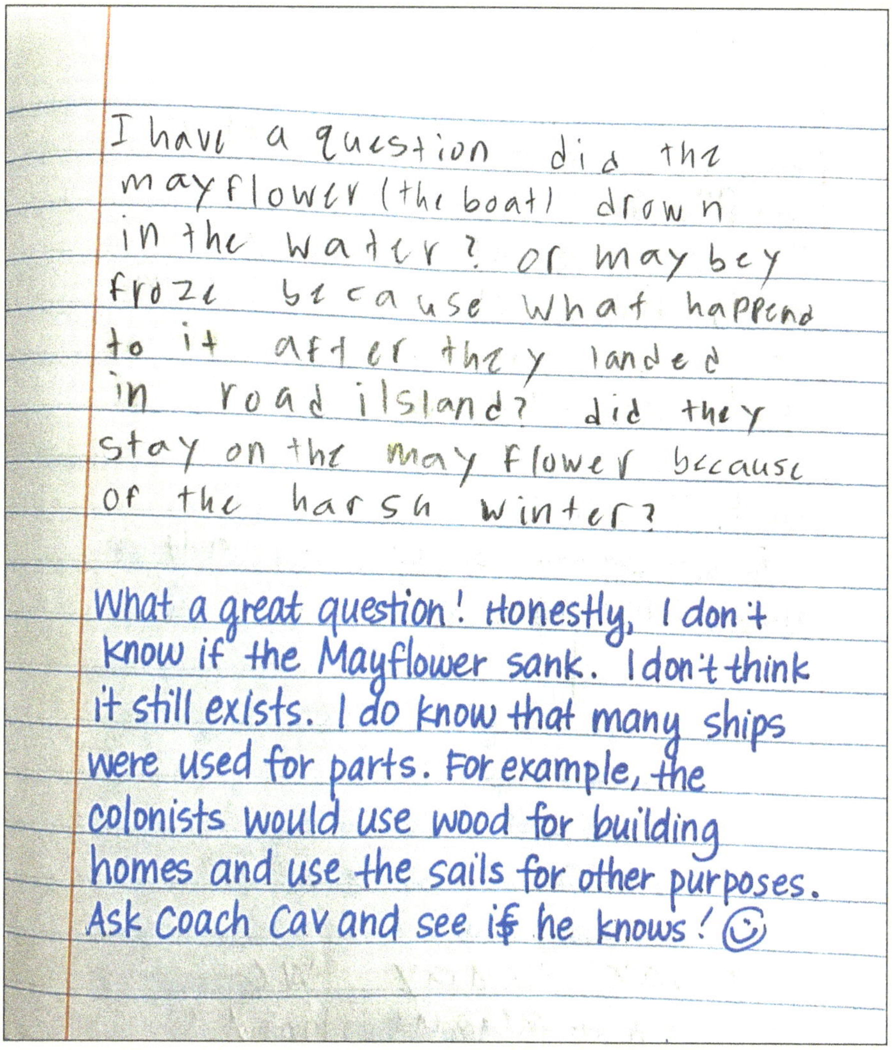
I have a question did the mayflower (the boat) drown in the water? or maybey froze because what happend to it after they landed in road island? did they stay on the mayflower because of the harsh winter?

What a great question! Honestly, I don't know if the Mayflower sank. I don't think it still exists. I do know that many ships were used for parts. For example, the colonists would use wood for building homes and use the sails for other purposes. Ask Coach Cav and see if he knows! ☺

Source: Elizabeth Choi and Student Work. Used with permission.

GETTING STARTED WITH LINGUISTIC SCAFFOLDING

Along with new concepts and complex information presented in the content areas, students must recognize, internalize, and apply the unique ways language is used in English language arts, math, science, social studies, and all other subject matters. When you plan to integrate linguistic scaffolds into the teaching-learning cycle, a board brush approach to this type of instruction may include special attention paid to one or more of the following:

- discipline-specific and generic academic vocabulary,
- phrases and idiomatic expressions associated with the target content,

- typical sentence structures and patterns of language used in the lessons,
- grammatical constructs used in academic genres,
- text-level features of standard American English, and
- interpretive and expressive language use.

But this is just the beginning; there is so much more you can do and *need* to do with linguistic scaffolding, and the next section will explore just that.

WHAT TEACHERS SAY ABOUT LINGUISTIC SCAFFOLDING

I had a Spanish-speaking newcomer start grade 4 at my school. Thanks to linguistic scaffolding, he was able to dive right into the curriculum with his classmates. Using his home language, patient rephrasing, and the appropriate context, he was quickly making connections between the treatment of Indigenous peoples in Canada and Indigenous peoples in Mexico. Language frames and vocabulary supports enabled him to attempt to interact with his classmates. From day one, he was able to fully participate in the classroom.

—Sherry Liptak, multilingual learner program specialist, Chilliwack, British Columbia, Canada

TEACHING PRACTICES OVERVIEW

There are cross-cutting scaffolding routines and approaches for linguistic support you can implement in your teaching regardless of grade levels or content areas. The following practices are expected to yield positive outcomes based on current research and evidence-based best practices. Yet a word of caution is in order. Language development is a fluid and dynamic process; while there are predictable patterns of language acquisition and keeping stages of language development in mind is important, it also varies from person to person and context to context. So, we invite you to critically reflect on how to use these language-based scaffolds in your own context. The three broad linguistic scaffolding practices we highlight here are (1) scaffolding academic language across word, sentence, and discourse dimensions, (2) building fluency and communication competence through collaborative participation, and (3) home language support and translanguaging (not just translating information). After introducing each of these scaffolding practices, we offer specific examples to aid implementation and authentic illustrations from K–12 classrooms.

LINGUISTIC SCAFFOLDING PRACTICE #1: SCAFFOLDING ACADEMIC LANGUAGE ACROSS WORD, SENTENCE, AND DISCOURSE DIMENSIONS

Academic language has been defined differently by individual researchers and practitioners. Robert Pritchard and Susan O'Hara (2016), members of the Complex Language Development Network team, originally worked with Jeff Zwiers to develop a framework for academic language and literacy development that consists of three dimensions of academic language: word, sentence, and discourse. To get started with scaffolding on these three levels, consider the following:

At the word dimension:

- Develop multimodal, multisensory support for building vocabulary (see more on this in Chapters 4 and 5).
- Create interactive word walls and word/phrase banks.
- Provide contextualized access to key terms within sentences and texts.

At the sentence dimension:

- Model academic language use.
- Generate language frames for oral interaction.
- Provide sentence starters and sentence frames for written communication.

At the discourse dimension:

- Use primary language or home dialect.
- Provide opportunities to interact with proficient English models.
- Chunk longer texts into shorter, more manageable pieces.
- Offer paragraph frames and essay outlines for written communication.

You must have noticed that these bulleted lists are rather short. This is just the beginning; there is so much more you can do with linguistic scaffolding, and the next section will explore them. Table 3.1 offers an adapted version of the three-dimensional framework, several challenges (also perceived as opportunities) that are faced by multilingual learners, and essential scaffolding practices are added based on WIDA (2020) and our own work in the field. The ultimate goal is successful academic language integration in the target core content class on the word, sentence, and discourse levels.

TABLE 3.1 ● Academic Language Dimensions, Features, Challenges, and Essential Scaffolding Practices

DIMENSION	ACADEMIC LANGUAGE FEATURES	CHALLENGES (AND OPPORTUNITIES) FOR MULTILINGUAL LEARNERS	ESSENTIAL SCAFFOLDING PRACTICES
Word level (vocabulary or phrases)	• Generic and discipline-specific academic terms • Figurative and idiomatic expressions • Words with multiple meanings • Roots and afixes	• Volume of vocabulary needed • Nuances of word meanings • Phrases and collocations • Precise use of words and phrases • Pronunciation	• Pre-teach select vocabulary • Analyze roots and word parts • Expose students to vast vocabulary through interactions with language-rich texts and experiences • Create interactive word walls • Recognize cognates • Encourage verbal exchanges • Word learning strategies
Sentence level	• Sentence structure • Sentence length • Sentence complexity • Grammatical structures • Pronouns • Context clues • Proverbs	• Complex sentences with low-frequency words • Advanced grammatical features (passive voice, participles, nominalization)	• Sentence frames, sentence starters • Sentence deconstruction and reconstruction • Sentence patterns • Mentor text at the sentence level • Repeating, recontextualizing or recasting (in more linguistically enhanced or complex ways) what students said
Text level	• Text organization and cohesion • Text craft and structure • Text density • Clarity and coherence • Text types and genres	• Reading and Lexile levels • Complexity of ideas • Background knowledge students need to comprehend • Styles and structures unique to each genre or text type	• Strategy instruction across the content areas • Genre study • Read alouds and shared reading • Guided and independent reading • Structured groupwork • Paragraph frames • Text analysis • Text annotation • Text outlines • Text deconstruction and reconstruction

Source: Adapted from Pritchard and O'Hara (2016); WIDA (2020)

online resources — Available for download at https://companion.corwin.com/courses/NineDimensionsofScaffoldingforMLs

ADVANTAGES OF THIS PRACTICE

Multilingual learners succeed when they have both authentic opportunities to use all dimensions of language across academic practices, as well as get explicit guidance in examining language as it works on each of these three levels and across the various content areas. Let's see some examples where the three dimensions of language fit together while keeping in mind that students will only develop competence with language and literacy if they have the opportunity to participate in social and academic practices in authentic contexts.

EXAMPLE #1: ANTICIPATION GUIDES

Anticipation Guides—also referred to as anticipatory guides—are designed to activate your students' prior knowledge, validate their existing understandings, and preview new material. They also help assess prior knowledge and identify misconceptions and gaps in students' knowledge as students review a list of statements related to the upcoming unit, lesson, or text. Anticipation guides not only activate background knowledge, build curiosity, and stimulate student interest in the forthcoming lesson, but they can also introduce key vocabulary. Anticipation guides are unique because they help bridge all three dimensions of academic language while also scaffolding new content and language in multiple ways:

- Students preview the entire text by reading and/or discussing a set of statements.
- Students read and evaluate a teacher-provided list of sentences one at a time about the topic.
- Students encounter key concepts and vocabulary prior to a deeper exploration of the topic.

The following examples in Table 3.2 and Figure 3.5 provide teachers with a way to identify how much information students may know about a topic or what misconceptions they may have prior to a lesson, activity, or unit overview. They may also provide teachers with data to inform their instruction.

TABLE 3.2 ● Anticipation Guide Based on Chapters One and Two in *Of Mice and Men* by John Steinbeck (1993)

Directions: Consider the following statements and indicate whether you agree or disagree, along with brief explanations for your choices, before reading the text. You can revisit your responses after reading the first two chapters to see how your understanding has evolved.

ANTICIPATION GUIDE: OF MICE AND MEN BY JOHN STEINBECK			
Dreams are essential for human survival.			
Before	Agree	Disagree	Why?
After	Agree	Disagree	Why?
Having versus not having power play a significant role in the characters' lives.			
Before	Agree	Disagree	Why?
After	Agree	Disagree	Why?
The American Dream is achievable for everyone.			
Before	Agree	Disagree	Why?
After	Agree	Disagree	Why?
Life on a ranch in the 1930s was challenging and demanding.			
Before	Agree	Disagree	Why?
After	Agree	Disagree	Why?
Friendship is an important theme in this story.			
Before	Agree	Disagree	Why?
After	Agree	Disagree	Why?

FIGURE 3.5 ● Anticipation Guide Based on a Third-Grade Unit of Study on Animal and Plant Life Cycles

Before we start learning about animal and plant life cycles, let's see what you already know and make some predictions. Write "True" or "False" for each statement below. Don't worry if you're not sure; we'll revisit these after our lesson to see how much you've learned!

1. ____ Plants and animals both go through life cycles.
2. ____ All animals have the same life cycle.
3. ____ Butterflies start their life as caterpillars.
4. ____ Plants and animals grow and change in the same way.
5. ____ A seed can grow into a mature plant.
6. ____ All animals lay eggs.
7. ____ Frogs are born as tadpoles.
8. ____ Only birds can fly.

Anticipation guides are effective scaffolding tools to support multilingual learners as they build and strengthen their content and language knowledge. They give students an opportunity to use their own experiences and funds of knowledge as they learn and develop new skills and information while creating excitement as they *anticipate* the new topic. For teachers, they give you a lens for more asset-based approaches in instruction. These tools provide you with windows of opportunity, showing you where to intentionally focus your instruction that builds on students' knowledge base and expands their skills around topics.

EXAMPLE #2: PICTURE-WORD-INDUCTIVE-MODEL (PWIM)

PWIM has recently returned to many classrooms (Ferlazzo & Sypnieski, 2022). Teachers' newfound interest may be attributed to the way PWIM supports multilingual learners on multiple levels of proficiency, through multiple modalities and on all three dimensions of academic language. You start with a picture that is of high interest to your students and is ideally connected to the core content curriculum. Place the picture in the middle of a large sheet of paper or create a margin around a digital image. First, ask your students to carefully look at the image, brainstorm, and label the picture with words that can be categorized by part of speech or grouped thematically. After you elicit, organize, or even analyze the words, direct your students to formulate sentences based on what they have noticed in the picture. After attaching words and phrases to the picture, students can discuss it and write sentences, paragraphs, or even longer texts. Remember to have your students suggest a title that best describes the picture.

Implementation choices for brainstorming and generating language include the following:

1. Whole group: through intensive teacher guidance, students respond individually.
2. Heterogenous small group: with a team leader assigned as the scribe, 4–6 students collaborate to generate possible responses to the image.
3. Intentional pairing: students with similar language proficiency level work together to co-generate vocabulary and possible sentences based on the picture.
4. Individual work: after the PWIM strategy has been introduced and practiced, students may work independently to prepare for a small group or whole group discussion based on the picture.

See Figure 3.6 for an example of how Jenna Maneri, former elementary ESL teacher, Bridgewater-Raritan Regional School District ML Coach, NJ, used the PWIM strategy with her first-grade students to support the process of generating a word list comprised of nouns, verbs, and adjectives and writing simple sentences. As a district ML coach, Jenna continues to advocate for the PWIM strategy and has designed an infographic to support her colleagues with planning and implementing PWIM (Figure 3.7).

FIGURE 3.6 ● PWIM Scaffolds for First Graders on Playgrounds

Picture Word Inductive Model (PWIM)

Name: ______________________ Date: ______________

TOPIC: ______________________________

LABEL THE NOUNS

What do you see?

I see...
There is... There are...
They have...
She has... He has...

playground playscape recess outside day

swing
tunnel
slide
ladder
seesaw
roof

plastic metal tree palm tree grass children

DESCRIBE USING ADJECTIVES

colorful
blue yellow green red orange warm
large small outdoor sunny sandy windy breezy fun empty bright

WRITE THE VERBS

play	climb	swing	run	
jump	throw	step	skip	hop
stand	can	wait	was	

WRITING CHECKLIST:

- ☑ Capital letter first
- ☑ Ending punctuation mark (. ? !)
- ☑ Spaces between words
- ☑ Writing matches picture

I see a playground. I see grass. There are trees.

There is a fun playground. There are green palm trees. The playground has a yellow slide.

The colorful, empty playground does not have any children climbing or playing.

It was a bright and sunny day on the fun playground with a warm breeze and the excited children were waiting to run and play outside during recess.

Source: Jenna Maneri. Used with permission.

online resources A blank version of this scaffold is available for download at https://companion.corwin.com/courses/NineDimensionsofScaffoldingforMLs

FIGURE 3.7 ● PWIM Planning Pyramid

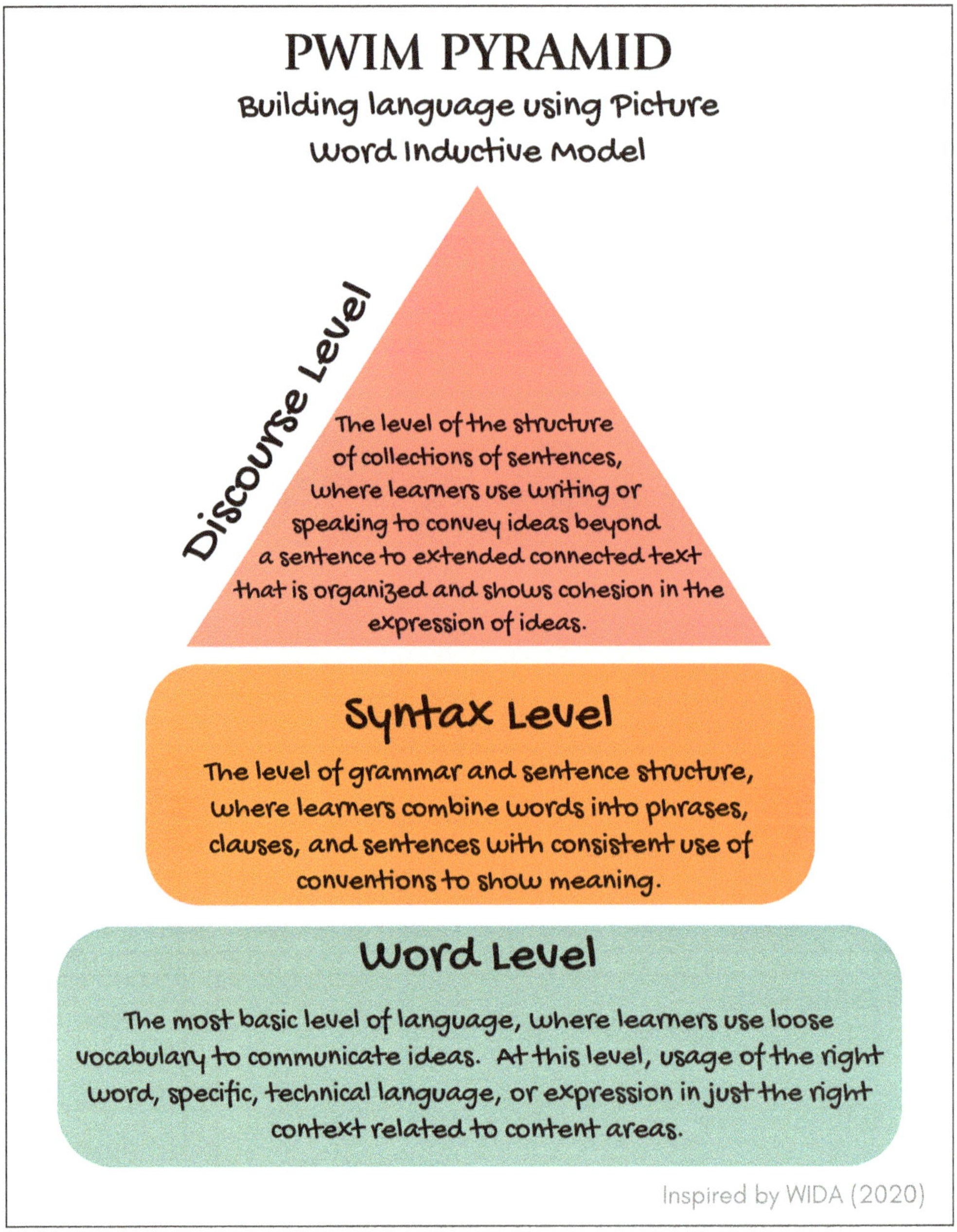

Source: Jentna Maneri. Used with permission.

EXAMPLE #3: CONTEXTUALIZING LANGUAGE: DISCOURSE—SENTENCE—WORDS

The entry point to linguistic scaffolding involving the three dimensions of academic language may be a complex, grade-level text, or a text excerpt that is shared with students through a read aloud, shared reading lesson, or multimedia experience. The initial goal is for the students to understand the gist of the text and to capture the essence of the message in the text. While they do so, they can also develop tolerance for ambiguity and use multiple strategies in combination with each other. The second step in this approach is to explore language patterns at the paragraph or sentence level as students deconstruct and reconstruct shorter chunks of the text as mentor texts. Finally, essential vocabulary is highlighted by unpacking the context in which they are embedded.

LET'S BRIDGE THE WORD, SENTENCE, AND DISCOURSE DIMENSIONS

One unique and memorable way you can integrate work with academic language across the three dimensions is the use of the power word, power sentence, and power text strategy (Dove & Honigsfeld, 2013). This lesson idea represents a cross-cutting approach to linguistic scaffolding—it can be used across content areas, grade levels, and proficiency levels!

A power word is the most important word in a sentence, paragraph, or even a text. After some modeling and lots of thinking aloud, invite students to find one (or even more than one) power word in informational text titles, in introductory sentences, and later in carefully selected short paragraphs. We have found that—with lots of practice—a *really powerful* power word gets a close to unanimous vote by any group of children! Identifying *power words* teaches students to use essential words or precise academic vocabulary in their own writing as well.

For example, in a text about the Endangered Species Act (Randall, 2023) in an online magazine called Science News Explores, the word *extinct (or extinction)* may be a power word, though the article itself suggests more than a dozen possible power words.

A power sentence is a student-friendly definition or summary account that often follows an established pattern. A power sentence can frequently be derived from the text. It may be the topic sentence or summary statement that also tends to offer a good linguistic model for analyzing and imitating the text structure. Alternately, the teacher may model sample sentences following a pattern, and students can collaboratively—and later independently—write their own power sentences about the text or topic. Here is an example from the same article about endangered species we have introduced above:

More than half of North America's 154 bat species are at risk of declining over the next 15 years. (Randall, 2023, para. 2)

First, focus on the overall meaning of the sentence, then break it down into meaningful segments. You will analyze both the meaning (what the whole sentence as well as chunks of it mean) and form (how the sentence is structured). Next, the sentence also lends itself to becoming a mentor text:

_______________ of _____________ are at risk of declining over _______years.
_______________ of _____________ are no longer at risk of declining.

As students learn more about different endangered species, the same sentence frames based on the original mentor text can provide a patterned scaffold to help make further statements.

Power texts come from high quality authentic resources that are both engaging in content and language, as well as presentation. Select an age-appropriate complete text such as an article published in *Scholastic News, Times for Kids, National Geographic*, or as we are showcasing it here, *Science News Explores*. Work collaboratively as a class or in smaller groups to generate a visual representation of the entire text by mapping out both the main ideas the author presented in the article and the structure of how those ideas were organized. First, seeing the text structure as a skeleton or frame—with the majority of the text removed—then imitating the text structure will allow students to understand the explicit organization of the text and prepare them to create similar texts in their own way. See Figure 3.8 for an example of text mapping

FIGURE 3.8 ● Text Mapping

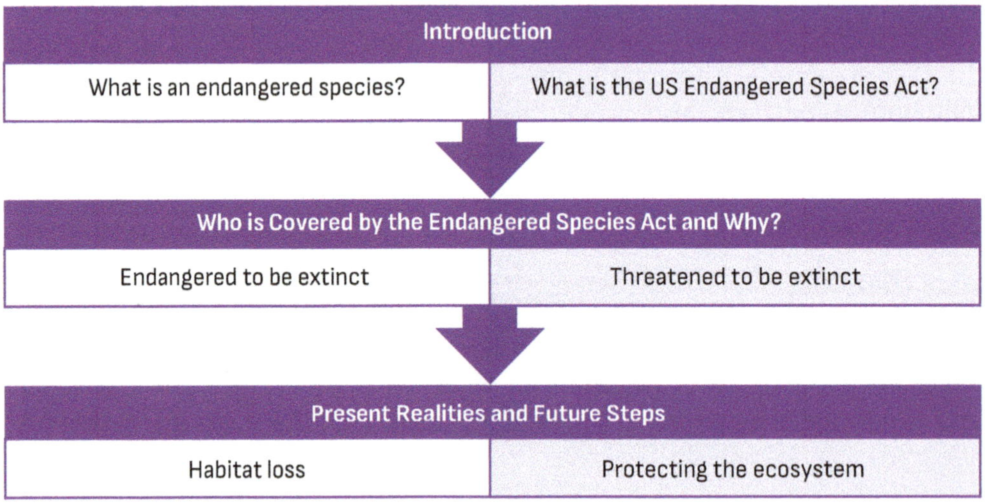

based on the entire article on endangered species we are using to showcase these scaffolding approaches of highlighting power words, power sentences, and power texts. Consider how text mapping provides access to the complex text structure of the science article as well as serves as a scaffold for students to model their own writing in the same genre.

KEEP THIS IN MIND

Academic language use is more than the building blocks it consists of. While we suggest focused attention to each dimension (words, sentences, texts), language is fluid and dynamic. Language is also functional—its very purpose is to communicate ideas, and students need to understand how it works across the disciplines in authentic ways.

FROM RESEARCH TO PRACTICE

George C. Bunch and Daisy Martin (2021) remind us to recognize students' ideas as well as support them as they develop those ideas and communicate them in various contexts:

> We need to listen to students as they use whatever linguistic resources they have at their disposal, support them in engaging in the ideas most central to the academic work at hand, and work with them to understand, and effectively craft, messages designed for different audiences and purposes. (p. 533)

Reflect on the following:

1. *There is a lot packed into this quote, so let's start by thinking of this approach as a game: We invite you and your students to become language detectives and look for typical, recurring, as well as unique ways language is used in your content area, be it math, science, social studies, and so on.*
2. *What do you notice about the way students use specific vocabulary or phrases? Are there some special ways verb tense is used or some other elements of grammar? What does a typical paragraph look like when students capture their thinking in writing? For example, in science, are you noticing how your students use language to make observations? Or the type of words and sentences they have to use to form conclusions?*

(Continued)

(Continued)

3. *The challenge (and opportunity) is clear: How do you ensure your students are successful, not just with the content mastery, but the use of these language features both for classroom discussion, day-to-day exploration, scientific meaning-making, and demonstrating their learning?*

LINGUISTIC SCAFFOLDING PRACTICE #2: BUILDING FLUENCY AND LINGUISTIC COMPETENCE THROUGH MODELING LANGUAGE MOVES AND ENGAGING STUDENTS IN STRUCTURED LANGUAGE PRACTICE

Linguistic scaffolding is also employed to prepare students to successfully participate in academic tasks linguistically. These scaffolding techniques might be labeled as instructional strategies elsewhere; we consider them pathways to successful engagement in complex academic learning while students build confidence and competence to communicate their ideas to build oracy and literacy through sustained, meaningful communicative tasks.

ADVANTAGES OF THIS PRACTICE

Language is a social endeavor. For language to grow and develop in our multilingual learners, they need ample opportunities to see how it is applied in an academic, social context, or in other words, how language serves the purpose of learning together, discussing academic content, and making meaningful connections with the thoughts and ideas of others. When students engage in regular collaborative activities, their informal discussions provide practice with spontaneous responses, which results in improved fluency. Working in tandem with others supports multilingual learners to express their thoughts and listen to others, improving their proficiency in both speaking and listening as well as their practical language skills. Building fluency and facility in English is a gradual process for multilingual learners, and regular practice with peers can significantly boost students' confidence to take risks and experiment with using and developing their language abilities.

EXAMPLE #1: THINK ALOUDS

Think Aloud is a strategy that provides students with an understanding of how to determine the meaning of unfamiliar language and the big ideas contained in a lesson or text as they listen to a demonstration of a teacher's thinking process for figuring out meaning, asking questions, making predictions, drawing conclusions, and so on, while working through a problem, task, or reading material. Its primary purpose is to clarify for learners the cognitive steps and internal dialogue that should occur to develop a wide range of critical thinking and analytical skills to make decisions, interpret data, synthesize information, recognize fallacies, and so on. A Think Aloud encourage metacognition—the awareness and monitoring of one's thought processes. It helps learners become more conscious of their thinking and problem-solving strategies. The following describes the basic steps for using a Think Aloud to make meaning for your students:

- Select a clear objective. Consider what you want the *Think Aloud* to illustrate. An objective might be how to use context clues to figure out the meaning of unknown words, the thinking behind solving a math problem, the steps to take to form a hypothesis, and so on.
- Choose a text that is relevant to the selected objective and appropriate for the grade level of your students.
- Plan how you will deliver instruction using the selected text to demonstrate your thought processes.
- Explain to students what you are going to do and why.
- Share a copy of the text, read a part of it, and model your thinking process.
- Justify your thinking process about the text. Refer to words in the same sentence and surrounding paragraph that support your thoughts, ideas, and conclusions.
- Examine titles, headings, illustrations, charts, graphs, and other visuals and discuss how they offer possible clues to the meaning.
- Encourage students to question your thinking as well as invite them to turn and talk with partners about their own ideas, analysis, or conclusions.

After modeling the activity for students, engage students in guided practice using a different, increasingly more complex text. Continue the strategy practice by having students work in small groups and *think aloud* with one another. Being explicit about the thinking process and allowing students time to practice provides a framework for students to explore and apply multiple strategies using context clues during their own reading.

WHAT TEACHERS SAY ABOUT LINGUISTIC SCAFFOLDING . . .

A recent example of linguistic scaffolding I have had this year specifically is with my new 6th grader from Ukraine. Their class is currently reading Schooled, which contains a lot of figurative language and has posed some confusion for my students. One example, the grandma's name in the story is Rain. He was really hung up on this detail since he looked up the word "rain" and translated it as precipitation, which makes total sense! I had a good conversation with him about how people sometimes have names that are words that mean other things. I shared with him how my last name is an article of clothing. He shared with me how some Ukrainian names are that way as well. He is also learning a lot of figurative language along with the rest of the class, and it is getting easier. It is something I need to check in with him frequently about as he moves along with the story.

—Jessica Vest, English as a new language (ENL) teacher, Binghamton, New York

EXAMPLE #2: TALK MOVES

Do you agree with Roskos and colleagues (2009), who over a decade ago claimed that students' "speaking and listening skills lead the way for their reading and writing skills, and together these language skills are the primary tools of the mind for all future learning" (p. vii) We have observed in many classrooms how interaction and collaboration are critical for all learning to take place. You might already use language scaffolds, also referred to as talk moves, to encourage and guide student participation and academic language use across content areas. Lauren Resnick and her team of researchers at the University of Pittsburgh Institute for Learning have developed a set of talk moves known as Accountable Talk. We appreciate how Michaels et al. (2016) clearly defines what makes talk accountable: "For classroom talk to promote learning, it must be accountable: to the learning community, to accurate and appropriate knowledge, and to rigorous thinking" (pp. 33–34). What does it mean for your classroom with multilingual learners? Use the tool in Figure 3.9 to scaffold accountable talk for your students:

FIGURE 3.9 • Accountable Talk Planning Tool

Are my students accountable to our learning community by

- ☐ listening carefully to others? If yes, how: ____________________
  If not yet, key strategies to implement: ____________________
- ☐ adding on to what others have stated? If yes, how: ____________________
  If not yet, key strategies to implement: ____________________
- ☐ asking questions and seeking proof? If yes, how: ____________________
  If not yet, key strategies to implement: ____________________
- ☐ disagreeing respectfully? If yes, how: ____________________
  If not yet, key strategies to implement: ____________________
- ☐ paraphrasing and summarizing? If yes, how: ____________________
  If not yet, key strategies to implement: ____________________

Are my students accountable for sharing accurate knowledge by

- ☐ using facts and providing evidence? If yes, how: ____________________
  If not yet, key strategies to implement: ____________________
- ☐ using precise, academic language? If yes, how: ____________________
  If not yet, key strategies to implement: ____________________
- ☐ asking others to provide evidence for their claims. If yes, how: ________
  If not yet, key strategies to implement: ____________________

Are my students accountable for rigorous thinking by

- ☐ making connections and synthesizing ideas? If yes, how: ____________
  If not yet, key strategies to implement: ____________________
- ☐ making clear statements and providing related evidence?
  If yes, how: ____
  If not yet, key strategies to implement: ____________________
- ☐ building justifications, arguments, explanations, and reasons? If yes, how:
  ____
  If not yet, key strategies to implement: ____________________
- ☐ evaluating the claims and arguments of others? If yes, how: __________
  If not yet, key strategies to implement: ____________________

Source: Adapted from Michaels et al., 2010.

online resources Available for download at https://companion.corwin.com/courses/NineDimensionsofScaffoldingforMLs

To support structured language practice, also consider the following:

- **Try conversation protocols that are modeled, explicitly taught, scaffolded, and practiced.** We are inspired by Zwiers and Crawford (2009), who emphasize the importance of teaching multilingual learners to do the following:
    - Paraphrase and summarize
    - Elaborate and clarify
    - Support one's ideas with details
    - Build on or challenge other students' ideas
    - Apply their ideas to their own lives
- **Use universal prompts as suggested by Bambrick-Santoyo and his colleagues (2013).** The more your students hear you apply prompts such as "Tell me more," "What makes you think that?" "Why do you think that is?" and "Why is this important?" to elicit more student talk, the more likely your students are going to start using and ultimately internalizing these universal prompts with their peers.
- **Provide opportunities for authentic interactions.** More recently, Jeff Zwiers (2019) has advocated for replacing pseudo-communication-heavy lesson activities with authentic communication, which has three key features:
    - Purposefully building ideas
    - Clarifying and supporting ideas
    - Filling information gaps

See Figure 3.10 for one example of how Claudia Leon, middle school ENL teacher in Bayshore, New York, scaffolds student responses for key language-based tasks, such as explaining while providing textual evidence for claims.

EXAMPLE #3. FISHBOWL

The "fishbowl" as a teaching strategy can serve as a scaffolding tool as your students take turns being contributors versus listeners in a discussion. Students in the inside (fishbowl) circle ask each other questions, share key information, and present their original ideas related to an academic topic the class is exploring. Students on the outside of the circle carefully listen to the ideas presented, take notes on how language was used to communicate the content and pay attention to the way their peers participate in the process. You can further scaffold participation in both the inside and outside circles by co-creating anchor charts and offering language models along with language choices.

FIGURE 3.10 • Anchor Chart With Sentence Starters

EXPLAIN
Textual Evidence
Sentence Starters

- This quote shows that _____
- This information states _____
- This example demonstrates _____
- The character says/does/thinks this because _____
- Based on this evidence_____
- An analysis of this _______ suggests that _________
- The author includes this information because _____
- It can be inferred that _____

Source: Claudia Leon. Used with permission.

Follow these steps to try out a fishbowl:

1. **Set up:** Place chairs in two concentric circles. A small group of students will be seated in the inner circle; a larger group will occupy the chairs in the outer circle.
2. **Preparation:** Choose a discussion topic that is meaningful, thought-provoking, and relevant to the students and the curriculum. Establish guidelines or rules for the conversation, including sentence starters and response frames.
3. **Inner Circle:** Students engage in a discussion by sharing their ideas.
4. **Outer Circle:** Students observe the discussion in the inner circle by focusing on how the key points or arguments are made, how evidence is presented, or how language is used by the inner circle participants.
5. **Conclusion:** Based on the students' age and readiness, set a reasonable timeframe and conduct a debrief with the entire class. Discuss what was observed, share key takeaways, and allow the observers to provide feedback and insights.

Here is an example we used in a middle school English language arts (ELA) class:

Learning Target: To analyze and discuss character development in a novel.

Procedure:

1. Select several short passages from a novel your students are reading with rich character development elements.
2. Select six students for the inner circle as active participants.
3. Invite the rest of the class to be observers in the outer circle.
4. Introduce one passage where character development is readily observable. Provide some guiding questions on a co-developed anchor chart to focus the discussion.
5. Students in the inner circle discuss the passage based on the scaffolded chart.
6. Students in the outer circle actively listen, take notes, and prepare for the debriefing.
7. After the discussion, bring the whole class back together for a debriefing session.
8. Invite the outer circle students to share their observations and thoughts about the discussion. Facilitate a whole class discussion about the character development in the novel based on the first passage.
9. Repeat the protocol with a new passage and a new group of six students in the inner circle.

The structured opportunity this strategy provides for students to be both on the speaking and listening side of the conversation can help you ensure that students develop both metacognitive and metalinguistic awareness. After roles are reversed and the inside circle switches places with the outside circle, bring the students back together to debrief. Consider the following set of questions to discuss after the fishbowl activity is completed:

- What has the inside circle accomplished?
- How has the conversation evolved?
- What were some "talk moves" used?
- How did the speakers get their listeners' attention?
- How did participants show active listening?

To guide students in the outside circle in their observation, a note-catcher template such as the one in Table 3.3 can be offered.

TABLE 3.3 ● Note-Catcher for Fishbowl Observations

NAMES OF STUDENT INSIDE THE FISHBOWL	DID THEY USE ANY KEY WORDS? IF YES, WHAT?	DID THEY ASK ANY QUESTIONS? IF YES, ABOUT WHAT?	DID THEY BUILD ON OTHER MEMBER'S IDEAS? IF YES, HOW?
Student 1			
Student 2			
Student 3			
Student 4			

KEEP THIS IN MIND

Using oral academic language publicly may present a special challenge for some students. Creating multiple meaningful, highly engaging opportunities for students to develop academic oracy is essential, but it may evoke anxiety in some students. Let's also acknowledge that there may be some overlap between these recommendations and the ones you will also see in the chapters discussing multimodal and collaborative scaffolding. When it comes to planning for linguistic scaffolds, collaboration between and among ELD specialists, general education teachers (K–5 classroom teachers and secondary content area educators), and other special area teachers and paraprofessionals enhance linguistic access for all students, but teachers need time, resources, and opportunities to co-plan.

LINGUISTIC SCAFFOLDING PRACTICE #3: MULTILINGUAL ACCESS AND FORMS OF EXPRESSION

Tapping into the students' home languages mean recognizing students' complex identities and acknowledging the rich linguistic heritages and unique literacy lives of their family, community, and country of origin. The home language or primary language also turns out to be a powerful tool that allows access to complex academic content and opportunity to express themselves and participate in academic and social situations.

So, we can also think about using the lens of multilingualism and multiliteracy as a scaffolding pathway.

In a safe and supportive classroom environment, multiple languages are used regularly and purposefully to build background knowledge, comprehend complex text, develop new skills, or transfer existing ones into a new context to demonstrate learning. This intentional use of students' home languages fosters linguistic confidence, encourages deeper engagement, and affirms students' cultural selves as valuable assets in the learning process.

ADVANTAGES OF THIS APPROACH

Students' home language can be considered a foundation for learning and must be honored as one way to access and build new understanding and skills. "Rather than framing students' uses of [their home languages] as markers of deficiency, teachers can recognize, praise, and investigate student language use to inform classroom meaning-making" (Pacheco et al., 2019, p. 77). It is becoming more widely accepted that we can provide richer learning opportunities when students use their full linguistic competencies as they speak, write, read, and listen in any language available to them and engage in multilingual and multimodal endeavors in and out of class. They can create videos, engage in discussions or debates, keep reading logs, add entries into their notebooks, participate in inquiry-based projects, and so on, across multiple languages and literacies.

EXAMPLE #1: HOME LANGUAGE SUPPORT

To support the use of several languages in the classroom, consider the following approaches to be meaningfully incorporated in the classroom:

- **Anchor charts:** More than one language can be used to capture students' ideas and to include all students' voices and experiences. Students can help co-construct these charts, including cognate charts, and contribute their ideas in multiple languages.
- **Multilingual signs, charts, and graphs:** Classroom spaces such as posters on the walls or student work samples on bulletin boards tell a complex story of who occupies that environment, who belongs, and whose languages and identities are valued. Include both teacher-created signs and student-generated work that includes multiple languages.
- **Electronic devices such as dictionaries or translators:** Teaching students how to use digital tools as linguistic scaffolds creates an opportunity for enhanced independence.
- **Peer bridges:** Classmates who speak the same primary language may work together to offer each other context, follow-up discussions, or clarifications that support the generation of new knowledge.

- **Parallel texts:** Make the same text available to students in English as well as in their home languages (being mindful if the students have the necessary literacy skills).

More specifically, see some examples from classrooms where students' home languages are not only honored but utilized as scaffolds. Figure 3.11 depicts Claudia Leon, a middle school ENL teacher's Cognate Word Wall, and Figure 3.12 is an excerpt from Tan Huynh, a secondary English as an additional language (EAL) teacher's biology exam.

FIGURE 3.11 • Academic Word Wall With Spanish Cognates

Academic Vocabulary	Spanish cognates
explain	explicar
identify	identificar
illustrate	ilustrar
discuss	discutir
predict	predecir

Source: Claudia Leon. Used with permission.

FIGURE 3.12 • A Scaffolded Exam Question

Look at the **chemical equation** for aerobic cellular respiration below. The real formulae (រូបមន្ត 数式) have been replaced by letters:

$$6A + B \rightarrow 6C + 6D$$

a. Substance (សារធាតុ 物質 sustancia) *A* is a gas (ឧស្ម័ន).

What is it?____________

b. Substance *B* is a nutrient (សារធាតុចិញ្ចឹម: 栄養素 nutritiva)

What is it? ____________

c. Substance *D* is also a gas: What is it? ____________

d. **Outline** a factor (a reason) other than A and B that can affect (ប៉ះពាល់ change) the rate (ល្បឿន speed) of **cellular respiration**.

____

____

Source: Tan Huynh. Used with permission.

EXAMPLE #2: TRANSLANGUAGING AS A SCAFFOLD

Earlier in this chapter, we shared several metaphors for linguistic scaffolding. Here is a powerful one to capture the essence of translanguaging—when we stop forcefully and artificially separating languages and language practices, we understand the *corriente*, river current, of multilingual language use and embrace how languages flow freely into each other (Maldonado Rodríguez & Krause, 2020). Translanguaging is defined by Ofelia García and Li Wei (2014) as a process in which, "bilingual speakers select meaning-making features [from multiple languages] and freely combine them to potentialize meaning-making, cognitive engagement, creativity, and criticality" (p. 42). The use of the students' full linguistic repertoires optimizes learning and making sense of what is being explored in the classroom. Or as Nelson Flores (2020) reminds us, multilingual learners build their lives on their *full language architecture*, so our responsibility is to honor that and capitalize on that gift. Translanguaging has also been recognized as part of a systemic approach to cultural inclusionary practices (Xu & Valdez, 2023).

To utilize translanguaging pedagogy as an approach to linguistic scaffolding, consider the following strategies for your classroom:

- Students preview the new lesson in their primary language—participate in the target lesson in English and review the concepts or skills in their primary language again (Freeman & Freeman, 2007).
- Students use bilingual dictionaries and discuss concepts with same-language partners in the language of their choice.
- Students research a topic online and using print-based resources in the language of their choice.
- Students access concepts and skills in their primary language first (watch a video, read a short text, interview their family or community members).
- Students use both languages in their speech and writing
- Students draft in one language and produce the final response in the other.

WHAT TEACHERS SAY ABOUT TRANSLANGUAGING

One example of culture and translanguaging in my classroom happened when I was teaching summarizing, and students used cultural words to explain the content to others. One misunderstanding of "summary" was when one student said, "Summary is chisme" [gossip]. Students started debating the meaning of the word "chisme." The same word had multiple variations depending on students' home countries, and my students discussed whether their own ways of saying "chisme," "chismoso," "chismado," "cotilleo" [gossip], "bulo" [gossip, fake news] were the right ways to say that word. Every student believed deeply their variation of that word was the only correct way. We 'Googled' the word together and saw that there was no correct word because all the words meant the same: gossip but were used with different variations. After clarifying that gossip was not summary, we went on to "Google" synonyms for summary in Spanish and found words such as "sumario"[summary], "epitome" [brief summary], "extracto" [summary], and "resumen" [summary]. The lesson about summary was enriched by the discussion with students and the use of cultural and word variations, as translanguaging was used here to clarify content and to find synonyms for words making the classroom discussion richer. See Figure 3.13 for another example for translanguaging from a student's essay.

—Sinelia Espindola Peixoto, EdD, middle school EL/ELA teacher

FIGURE 3.13 ● Student Writing Sample With Translanguaging

Dear Miss. Peixoto. Hello, today I`m gonna tell you about why students should wear uniforms to school.

Many times we have asked ourselves what would happen if we would wear a uniform to school. The truth is that I would feel very comfortable. Not only would it simplify many things like choosing a home every day, not only that, it also has many benefits. So I think students should wear uniforms to school como una farda.

Many people think that wearing a uniform is bad because it prevents freedom of expression, but I think the opposite. Clothes may represent something for many, even for me, but after all, it is school, we cannot go to school with any clothes that we have. Some clothes can have a phrase that offends many people or with improper clothing. Some evidence that supports my opinion is from "garrampa.es" that says "The use of uniforms prevents students from wearing inappropriate clothing, such as t-shirts with offensive phrases". As evidence, if students must wear uniforms, we could prevent them from wearing inappropriate clothes to school and avoid many kinds of problems. In my old school, I wore a uniform in my school in Peru and the truth was that I felt very comfortable. I think that in schools that approved of students wearing uniforms, he almost did not open bullying because somos iguales. When all the students wore the same clothes, nobody would bother no one for the clothes you wear.

Source: Student work. Used with permission.

KEEP THIS IN MIND

A common misconception is that the home language or translanguaging should be used only with newcomers or entering/emerging level students—or not at all. Holding onto—or rather, fully embracing and continuing to grow in—one's language or languages beyond the initial stages of English language development is critical. Students often need to navigate and process their understandings while bridging their language development from early acquisition development through proficiency. In many cases, multilinguals do this throughout their lifetime, developing a healthy identity and growing into bi-/multi-lingual and bi/multi-literate future leaders in society.

INDEPENDENT LEARNING STRATEGIES FOR STUDENTS

When students internalize linguistic scaffolding, they use their metalinguistic consciousness to support their own language development intuitively. What is metalinguistic awareness? Similar to metacognition, defined as thinking about thinking, metalinguistic processes are best conceptualized as thinking about how languages work and how a person uses language. The bilingual or multilingual brain is highly apt to conduct many comparative analyses between and among languages all the time. In a recent conference presentation, Brianna Adachi and Hyonsuk Cho (2024) recognized the importance of demonstrating how different languages express the same grammatical structures to raise metalinguistic awareness. See Table 3.4 for an example of how comparatives are structured differently in Spanish and Japanese.

TABLE 3.4 ● Helping Develop Metacognitive Awareness

ENGLISH	SPANISH	JAPANESE
Hotter temperatures	Temperaturas más altas **[temperatures more highs]** Temperatura: temperature Más: more Altas: high (plural)	より暑い気温 (yori atsui kion) **[more hot temperature]** Yori: than/compared to Atsui: hot Kion: temperature

Students might also apply linguistic scaffolds they learned from their teachers, from peers, or using digital tools. When they observe their teachers thinking aloud and comprehending aloud (Zwiers, 2014), and when they are encouraged to try the same practices with peers and on their own, these scaffolding tools may continue to serve as independent, self-directed learning tools. For example, students might transfer vocabulary learning strategies or comprehension strategies from the classroom to their own learning contexts related to academic content and beyond. As they develop their interpretive and expressive competencies, we need to be mindful of designing contingent scaffolds that are closely aligned to students' incrementally expanding capacity with language and challenge them to experiment and use language on their own. You will notice that your students have internalized linguistic scaffolds when they start using them without prompting, when they remind their peers of these scaffolds, when they reflect on their own learning, when they name the scaffolds, and so on.

WHAT TEACHERS SAY ABOUT LINGUISTIC SCAFFOLDING

Dr. Nadia Khan-Roopnarine, professor of teacher education and former New York City ELA educator, shared with us a powerful anecdote that captures a student's agency and intuitive brilliance to scaffold learning for himself:

During our lesson today, students were working in small groups. One group worked with my co-teacher to close-read sections of our class novel. The independent group read and completed tasks that did not require additional teacher support beyond the embedded scaffolds. And, a group of students worked with the ESOL co-teacher on acquiring new vocabulary in short sections of the novel. Juan [pseudonym] was working in my heterogeneous group on comprehension. Our novel is written primarily in English but has a smattering of Spanish. Juan used our class calendar to look ahead to what we were reading today. He pulled out all of the phrases in Spanish in advance and used them as anchors to guide his comprehension of the chapter. During the group's read aloud, Juan demonstrated an incredible confidence that I had not seen him exhibit previously. Though he only correctly answered about half of the questions he attempted, his participation in the small group discussion was indicative of a fully engaged mind. When class was over, I asked Juan privately what inspired him in our discussion today. He explained that being able to understand some of the text made him more interested in finding out more about the story. He found that the phrases throughout the chapter helped guide him, the same way context clues can guide readers to comprehend a sentence.

Juan's work today was a moment of true learning for me. I only helped students understand the meaning of one sentence at a time and never applied a comprehension strategy to the structure of an entire chapter. Moving forward, I plan on taking Juan up on his strategy and having him teach it to others to further increase collaboration and engagement in our class.

SUMMARY

Linguistic scaffolding is an essential practice to advance and accelerate multilingual learners' language and literacy development. These scaffolds provide multilingual learners with access to grade-level content while offering them opportunities to engage in both structured and authentic ways to use language as they demonstrate new learning and build on their funds of knowledge.

Questions

1. What are the top three strategies presented in this chapter that are readily applicable to your own context?
2. Which scaffolding practices presented here might present challenges in your context? Why and how might you overcome those challenges?
3. Which ideas outlined here have you had previous experience with, and how might you further refine your practice based on this chapter?
4. Observe your students' use of linguistic scaffolding on their own: What choices are they making? How can you further support their independence with scaffolding?

CHAPTER 4

Multimodal Scaffolding

> *"Multimodality allows all students to use multiple means to engage, interpret, represent, act, and express their ideas in the classroom. For example, as students read, they also might refer to illustrations or diagrams, and as students write, they might also represent their ideas numerically or graphically."*
> *WIDA, 2020, p. 19*

Multimodal scaffolding refers to providing access to information and opportunities for self-expression through multiple modes of communication, such as spoken, written, and visual language. Student learning is supported by getting information, acquiring new skills, expressing ideas, and producing new content in text and non-text formats through multimodalities. Other methods for acquiring information include examining photographs and responding to video clips using text, images (including emojis and memes), audio and video recordings.

You might be thinking, well, isn't it just good teaching? Yes, it is! Yet multilingual learners consistently need good teaching as well as multiple opportunities to be exposed to language and literacy in English, whereas their English-proficient peers may be able to tackle complex tasks with less intentional attention to multimodality. Just about everything students encounter out of school in the "real world" involves gathering information through multimodalities, therefore, all students will benefit from intentional planning through these different mediums:

- Writing essential questions, learning objectives, and success criteria on the board, adding visuals to some of the keywords, and simply pointing to the written text as it is presented offers multimodal scaffolds and so much more. These instructional techniques show students that there is a strong interrelationship among verbal, written, visual, and gestural cuing, and they can rely on a combination of those systems to learn.

- Making a range of resources available to students on a specific topic (such as print-based, web-based, textual or visual, video, and audio-supported materials) offers multimodal scaffolds, giving students the choice to access, explore, and evaluate a wider selection of instructional materials.
- When students are invited to first visualize what they are reading about and then use multimodality in their responses to new learning, they are offered multimodal scaffolds and so much more. Students are motivated and empowered to connect their learning to a range of modalities that they wish to use while their creativity is nurtured.
- When students combine linguistic and nonlinguistic (language-based and nonlanguage-based) modes of expression while they are acquiring English as an additional language, they are offered multimodal scaffolds. Students' multimodal communicative competence is enhanced, ensuring earlier and richer participation in academic and social learning activities.

You might be wondering how it is possible to accomplish all this. See Figure 4.1 for an example of a multimodal representation of a key concept from Sasha Engelsman's co-taught high school science class. All key science terms for the upcoming unit were illustrated in a similar manner for the interactive word wall she co-designed with her colleagues. The four languages other than English included Spanish, Vietnamese, Hindi, and Arabic, making it not only multimodal but multilingual as well.

FIGURE 4.1 • Multimodal, Multilingual Presentation of a Key Concept on a Science Word Wall

Entropy:

The amount of disorder in a system

La cantidad de desorden en un sistema.

Số lượng rối loạn trong một hệ thing

ປະລິມານຄວາມຜິດປົກກະຕິໃນລະບົບ

سـستمی کـی در ینظم یب زانیم

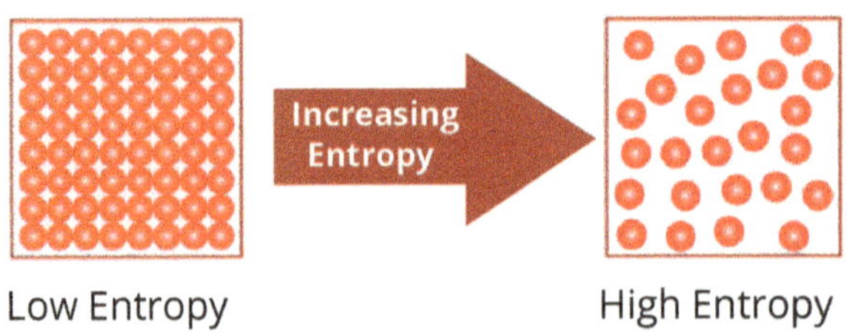

Source: Sasha Engelsman. Used with permission.

WHAT TEACHERS SAY ABOUT MULTIMODAL SCAFFOLDING

Last year, during my first year of co-teaching with a fellow chemistry teacher, I created a word wall in the front of our classroom highlighting the most important terms from our unit of study. In our classroom, we had multiple multilingual students and a great variety of languages represented. To acknowledge and celebrate the many languages that our students speak, the chemistry word wall incorporated the languages of our class. By the end of the semester, the word walls became only English word walls as our newcomers were bridging over to higher English proficiency, but an electronic version of our word wall (nothing special, just a Google Slide deck) was always made available for students to translate the definitions of terms on their own if they felt that they needed it or wanted it. The focus of the word wall was to create an image-rich resource for students to associate a term with. Chemistry is filled with such abstract concepts like entropy. These images were incorporated into assignments and sometimes also assessments.

—Sasha Engelsman, English language (EL) science specialist
at West Ottawa High School, Minnesota

WHO IS IT FOR?

Multimodal scaffolds may be implemented in any classroom where students are invited to fluidly and meaningfully move across modes of expression or even break down modality boundaries. That sounds very poetic, and indeed it can be! When learning experiences are not limited to one mode of communication, students see more opportunities for creative self-expression and risk-taking as they experiment more with using their emerging or expanding language skills alongside visual, auditory, digital, and other emerging modes of expression. Here are just a few examples of how multimodal scaffolds work across the language proficiency levels you might have in your classroom:

- They support newcomers as they draw images that match key vocabulary words written in English and also in their home languages.
- They support emerging or developing multilingual learners as they storyboard a sequence of events.
- They support developing students as they capture their ideas with pictorial notes, also referred to as sketchnotes.

- They support advanced learners as they create infographics in lieu of, or in addition to, more traditional, written research reports.
- They support English proficient students as they engage in contemporary multiliteracies (such as digital multimodal projects) while discussing data presented in visual formats and collaboratively discuss and prepare a multimedia presentation based on their analysis and interpretation of such data (see more on this in Chapter 7).

Providing intentional opportunities for students to use multimodal scaffolds throughout a lesson opens the door to learning and provides a pathway toward success for all!

HOW IS MULTIMODAL SCAFFOLDING USED ACROSS PROGRAM MODELS?

Multimodality has generated a lot of interest in the field of education, both among researchers and practitioners. For example, Scott Grapin (2019) distinguishes between a weak (illustrative) and strong (communicative and disciplinary) version of multimodality. He cautions against using a narrow definition and placing multimodal tools merely in service of language-based learning. Instead, he reminds us that multimodal tools are "legitimate meaning-making resources in their own right" (p. 34) and advocates for a strong version of multimodality because "it turns a deficit view of ELs [English learners] as lacking the linguistic resources needed to participate meaningfully in the content areas into an asset view that capitalizes on the diverse meaning-making resources they bring to the classroom" (p. 35).

While we fully embrace an asset-based philosophy towards working with multilingual learners, here we take an *integrated* view of multimodality. Based on our extensive field-based experience and research-informed practices, we consider it both a specific pathway to meaning-making within and across the core content areas *and* a powerful scaffolding tool for language and literacy development (also within and across all academic disciplines). Students need to know that there is more than one way to access challenging content or express their complex ideas. You can use multimodal scaffolding effectively across program models when you keep in mind the following:

In *general education classes,* using the principles of Universal Design for Learning (UDL) (CAST, 2024) will result in multiple means of:

1. Engagement—students are motivated and engaged in the lesson in multiple ways when educators:
    a. Welcome students' interests and embrace their multidimensional identities

   b. Foster students' efforts and nurture their persistence
   c. Recognize and enhance students' emotional capacity and readiness for learning

2. Representation—the content of the lesson is presented in multiple formats, thus ensuring that all students can access it and transfer it to new knowledge through:
   a. Multiple perceptual modalities (auditory, visual, tactile, kinesthetic) infused in the lesson
   b. Language-based, visual, or symbolic presentation of content
   c. A variety of opportunities for meaning-making

3. Action and Expression—during the lesson, students have options for expressing and demonstrating what they have learned and can do through:
   a. Interacting with tools and accessible materials (including technologies)
   b. Choice opportunities for responding to the content of the lesson (including creative use of tools and multimedia)
   c. Purposeful use of strategies and resources

In *integrated, co-taught classes*, in addition to using UDL-based practices, each teacher can take on specific roles to *show*, not just *tell*, the students what the new learning is about. While one teacher is reading aloud, the other teacher models note-taking on the smartboard or creates an anchor chart. While one teacher is modeling an experiment, the other teacher is explaining the steps that need to be followed and captures and projects brief notes digitally about each step with some pictorial reminders. As one teacher explains the various roles needed to complete an interactive group assignment, the other teacher shares a role and responsibility chart which identifies each group, individual roles and expectations for each student in the group, and the overall assignment.

In *stand-alone, English language development (ELD) classes*, especially when implemented with entering and beginning (Level 1 and 2) students, seeing and hearing the language and content simultaneously is critical. For example, using a document camera, a read aloud can more easily be followed by all students since the book pages are enlarged on the screen. Teachers can also combine physical movements or gestures with language-based prompts for the students to commit commonly used commands or content-concepts to memory with ease. Such "mapping of language" to action helps students on all proficiency levels each time new directions or new concepts are introduced.

In *self-contained or integrated special education classes*, dually identified multilingual learners or multilingual learners with exceptionalities (Honigsfeld & Cohan, 2024) frequently have complex *access needs* identified by their individual education plans (IEPs) or 504 plans to ensure that they, too, can meet their educational, linguistic, and social-emotional development goals. Multiple access points, multiple modes of processing information, multiple language-based, visual, or symbolic teacher presentations of content or student representation of their learning may be explicitly and implicitly included in lessons with multilingual learners. For example, students use illustrated, color-coded puzzle pieces that show the steps of the scientific process.

For language to develop, your students need the opportunity to go beyond offering brief responses. Multimodal expression honors multilingual learners across all grade levels, all proficiency levels, and all content areas and ensures more student-generated classroom communication and authentic sharing.

FROM RESEARCH TO PRACTICE

Based on Kress's (2010) pioneering research into multimodality, Sophia Diamantopoulou and Sigrid Ørevik (2022) have applied multimodality to the field of English as an Additional Language (EAL) and noted that

> English is learned and taught through a multiplicity of modes that reach beyond speech and writing. These modes, embodied (e.g., gaze, facial expression, and movement) and disembodied (e.g., image, moving image, layout, space, sound, and music), are *orchestrated* to produce a range of texts through which pedagogies are realized and learning happens (p. 6).

Reflect on the following:

The authors introduce two less commonly used categories (embodied and disembodied modes of communication), which prove to be helpful for us to further refine our understanding of the origins or types of multimodalities to include in our teaching. Have you heard of these two terms? Think of how body language, gestures, eye contact, proximity, or even a simple movement of leaning into a conversation may add more layers to communication in your classroom. Also, consider how nonlanguage-based tools, such as visuals or auditory experiences, establishing a system of signals, or playing soft instrumental music in the background during silent reading time can impact (enhance or interfere) with meaning making.

What are your experiences with these modes of communication? How do you plan for them, or how they show up incidentally during a learning experience? What might be the implications of this research for your day-to-day practice in the classroom to harness the power of multimodality as a scaffolding approach?

____

____

____

____

WHY IS MULTIMODAL SCAFFOLDING AN IMPORTANT APPROACH TO STUDENT LEARNING?

Through multimodal scaffolding, students have access to the same information through several channels or modalities. Multimodality is also inherent to and essential for how students make meaning, access new information, and respond to or engage in disciplinary practices. All students are able to both interpret and express ideas with greater flexibility when using multimodal resources, as well as multiple languages (revisit Chapter 3 for more on translanguaging). Think of your own classroom (or a classroom you visit frequently as a coach, colleague, or administrator) and consider the following:

- ***What types of resources are available for students? And can they access them with support or independently?***
    - A kindergarten class usually bustles with so many visual resources, right? How can teachers ensure that as students move up in the grade levels, there continue to be grade- and age-appropriate multimodal tools at their fingertips?
- ***What modes of communication are privileged and supported?***
    - If teacher talk dominates the classroom, students are asked to listen a lot and navigate one main channel of communication. When visuals, interactive processing, and meaning-making time are essential parts of instruction, students can develop a stronger ownership of their own learning.
- ***What discipline-specific multimodal meaning-making is taught and practiced explicitly?***
    - Consider how students learn to make sense of graphs, diagrams, and pictograms as well as practice the language that is needed for such meaning-making. Providing an array of tools in multiple modalities helps students become more independent as they navigate their own learning.
- ***How are students afforded multiple access points to the lesson through multimodal tools and learning opportunities? How are they afforded multimodal interpretations of complex target texts unique to each discipline?***
    - Without simplifying or reducing the cognitive complexity, multimodal representations of the same complex text or lesson open access points for students while also teaching disciplinary practices.
- ***How might students be given a choice to express themselves in multiple ways?***
    - When it comes to note-taking, ensure students capture their thinking in multiple ways that include visual representations,

including sketchnotes, diagrams, pictorial representations, and nonvisual representations through stop and jots and margin notes.

These tools provide multiple entry points for students to access grade-level academic curriculum while ensuring autonomy through a variety of response techniques to evidence their learning.

WHAT TEACHERS SAY ABOUT MULTIMODAL SCAFFOLDING

A highly effective strategy I created is to use a set of Stretch Texts that allow MLLs access to grade-level instruction and incrementally increases in rigor and literacy demands. All new topics should be introduced with "Big Picture Videos," preferably in the native language of students, that provide an overview of the topic and any background information that is needed to orient and prepare students for instruction. Stretch Texts begin with creating straightforward, concrete content instruction anchored by resources with simplified and chunked dual language texts, lots of visuals, essential vocabulary, and constant quick formative assessments embedded within. The next level of resources created are chunked and provide dual language text but have a higher literacy demand, less visuals, and embed higher order thinking questions as formative assessments. At this point, students are prepared to engage in grade level texts scaffolded with minimal modifications such as native language support or reduction of text length. Through the use of Stretch Texts, students gain access to rigorous content while developing their English language proficiency and are prepared to succeed on grade level summative assessments as well.

—Amanda Haleiko, English as a new language (ENL) teacher, North Shore Central School District

HOW DOES MULTIMODAL SCAFFOLDING SPECIFICALLY RELATE TO MULTILINGUAL LEARNERS' NEEDS?

When multiple modalities are available simultaneously to support multilingual learners' language and literacy development, students can SWIRL—speak, write, interact, read, or listen (see more about SWIRL later in this chapter), as well as view or create image- or video-based resources.

They also can demonstrate their understanding through textual and visual representations, having the opportunity to develop both foundational skills and more advanced, complex meaning-making across content areas, language domains, and literacies.

Multimodal scaffolding helps double the support for processing complex information or ideas—also referred to as *dual coding* (the interconnected mental process of verbal and visual processing): students access information through multiple channels. As researchers Qi Si and colleagues (2022) observe, "The pictorial and textual contents in picture books are useful resources for students to generate discussions with their critical thinking, logical reasoning, creating interpretations, and judging skills" (p. 287). So, there is a lot more to adding pictures to text than making it look prettier or more enticing. Multimodal scaffolding is well aligned to students' needs for *message abundancy* or information received in multiple meaningful ways and multiple accessible modalities (Hammond et al., 2018). Similarly, inviting students to respond through multiple modalities enhances their opportunity to demonstrate their learning. See some examples from Nicole Sibiski's integrated high school ELA/ENL classroom, where she uses art-based and multimodal student participation. She establishes clear and consistent content and language objectives based on the literary exploration of Julia Alvarez's (2010) novel *In the Time of the Butterflies*. (Notice how the language objectives written as *I can* statements also serve as linguistic scaffolds and self-assessment guideposts for the students):

Content Objective:

We will investigate how the Mirabal Sisters exhibited six different types of courage.

Language Objectives:

- *I can choose one of the four Mirabal Sisters to deepen my understanding of how she demonstrated courageous actions while opposing the dictatorship of Rafael Trujillo.*
- *I can cite evidence from the text,* In the Time of the Butterflies, *to show how the character demonstrated each type of courage.*
- *I can write at least three different examples for each courageous category.*
- *I can brainstorm possible symbolic representations for each type of courage and how it relates to my character.*
- *I can explain in writing how my character responds.*

- *I can explain, in writing, why I think each event shows each type of courage.*
- *I can write complete sentences in English.*
- *I can properly cite my evidence using MLA formatting.*
- *I can envision how I will be presenting my end product to the class.*

To accomplish these ambitious goals, see in Figure 4.2 how Nicole uses a carefully constructed, color-coded scaffold that guides students' analysis of the literature through the lens of the six types of courage represented in the novel (physical, social, intellectual, spiritual, moral, and emotional).

FIGURE 4.2 ● Scaffolded Literary Analysis Template

Chapter ________________	Page #s:____________
Description of event #1: **Description of event #2:** **Description of event #3:**	**Quote #1 to support description (cited in MLA):** **Quote #2 to support description (cited in MLA):** **Quote #3 to support description (cited in MLA):**
How the character responds:	**Why do you think this event shows __________ courage? Explain using complete sentences.**
***(#1): _(Character's name)_ responds by...** ***(#2):** ***(#3):**	***(#1) This event shows ____ courage because...** ***(#2)** ***(#3)**

Source: Nicole Sibiski. Used with permission.

Students complete the template one event at a time in a digital notebook. In addition, Nicole invites her students to sketch out scenes from the readings and to work on more fully developed artistic renditions of the types of courage represented by their chosen character(s) in the novel. See Figure 4.3 for one of her high school students' written works discussing an example of social courage, Figure 4.4 for the student's sketch, and 4.5 for the student's final painting about Patria (one of the Mirabel sisters) demonstrating all six types of courage.

FIGURE 4.3 • Student Written Response Using the Scaffolded Prompts From Figure 4.2

Description of Event & Chapter: 4

Patria went to her baby's grave to check if the baby's dead body was still there.after she was suspecting that her husband could remove her dead baby's body from his grave.

Quote to support description & Page # (cited in MLA):

This quote supports social courage "So I went to the graveyard and enlisted a couple of campesinos with the excuse that i have forgotten the baby's virgencita medallion." (Page 54)

How the character responds:

Patria responds doing the actions that she thinks that are okay, as sending the campesinos to dig her baby's dead body grave.

Why do you think this event shows __________ courage?

This event shows socal courage because she is risking of being rejected because of what she is doing, people don't see it right. So she is risking, consequences or reaction from the campesinos cold be bad.

Source: Student work. Used with permission.

FIGURE 4.4 • Student Sketch Accompanying His Written Response

Source: Student work. Used with permission.

FIGURE 4.5 ● Student Painting Depicting Six Types of Courage

Source: Student work. Used with permission.

GETTING STARTED WITH MULTIMODAL SCAFFOLDING

When planning multimodal scaffolds, you may incorporate the following *teaching* strategies as well as create opportunities for students to try them as *learning* strategies:

- Using gestures, facial expressions, and vocality such as intonation, stress, and pitch to accompany teacher talk and enhance comprehension.
- Attaching language to actions (also referred to as mapping actions) as you demonstrate something for students.
- Choosing multimodal texts such as picture books, graphic novels, and richly illustrated print-based readings to benefit from dual coding. Quick tip: Explore the recommended list of graphic novels by the American Library Association (2022) or Scholastic (2023)—see link in the reference list.
- Exploring the types of multimodal representations that are unique to each academic content area to engage in authentic disciplinary practices (students will graph in math and science, use timelines in

history, examine maps in geography, analyze optical illusions in art, interpret blueprints in technical subjects, describe archival photographs in ELA, and so on).

- Accessing multimodal digital resources such as digital audio recordings, films, video clips, and interactive webpages (see more in Chapter 7 on digital scaffolding) to offer varied access points.
- Presenting mini-lessons through multiple modalities including oral, written, and visual modes simultaneously to reinforce the message being presented.
- Creatively combining graphics that represent complex concepts with language-based scaffolds such as labels, captions, short descriptions, and spoken or prerecorded explanations to enhance comprehension.
- Inviting student choice in selecting and analyzing resources that will support their learning as well as in demonstrating new learning (oral and written text, visual representations, graphic organizers, videos, animation, etc.).
- Engaging in project-based learning that allows for students to "comprehend and compose meaning across diverse, rich, and potentially complex forms of multimodal text, and to do so using a range of different meaning modes" (Victoria State Government, 2018, para. 6).

FROM RESEARCH TO PRACTICE

When Carrie Symons and Yue Bian (2022) researched ways refugee-background youths attempt to make meaning of complex texts, they reported the following:

> A linguistic orientation to meaning-making includes the practices of encouraging and employing the full range of literacy modalities (reading, writing, listening, speaking, viewing, and representing) to communicate and negotiate meaning; building connections among students' contributions to one another and the content through discussion; leveraging students' contributions to learn about who they are (e.g., their languages, identities, backgrounds, and cultures) and how they think; analyzing and explicitly addressing potential language demands in planned and spontaneous classroom discourse; recognizing and afirming students' meaning-making efforts to sustain their engagement; and using aspirational mirror texts, as well as less familiar texts, to provide scaffolded opportunities for applying comprehension strategies. (p. 12)

Reflect on the following:

While this quote could very well support linguistic scaffolding discussed in Chapter 3, we chose to highlight it here in Chapter 4 since the researchers emphasize (a) the importance of applying a full range of literacy modalities by going beyond listening, speaking, reading, and writing to include viewing and visually representing, and (b) students' identities and agency to be nurtured as well. What further connections can you make between research and practice in your own classroom regarding multimodal and linguistic scaffolding?

(Continued)

(Continued)

____

____

____

____

TEACHING PRACTICES

There are several powerful multimodal scaffolding practices to choose from. We are introducing a new and improved version of SWIRL we call SWIRL + (plus), since it includes some additional dimensions to the previously well-established approach to integrating modalities. We are going to present several practical strategies for connecting visualization or visual input to oracy and literacy. Finally, we are making a strong case for—and supporting it with several examples of—student-created visuals.

MULTIMODAL SCAFFOLDING PRACTICE #1: SWIRL +

The idea of a SWRL-ing or SWIRL-ing classroom has become more and more widespread. The common notion is the importance of integrating the four language domains and reordering the traditional sequence—listening, speaking, reading, and writing to—to a new sequence—speaking, writing, reading, and listening, and as such, prioritizing the expressive or productive language domains. Burkins and Yaris (2013) and Cooper (2012) blogged about it, emphasizing the need for active engagement with language and literacy tasks. Anderson (2015) suggests that "language components are interrelated following a format of SWIRL (speaking and writing integrated with reading and listening) that give opportunity for social and academic language development in a holistic and meaningful way" (p. 73). Here, we interpret the *I* in SWIRL as *interaction* to emphasize how students interact with each other and complex materials. Additionally, we add a plus (+) to represent visual literacy. While "SWIRL +" may be applicable to just about any learning experience, here is an example for project-based learning (PBL). As your students participate in PBL, they will:

Speak to each other to discuss the available resources and plan the project.

Write, sketch, or draw to identify the steps necessary for completing the activity.

Interact with each other as they negotiate the product design and completion.

Read and use print and digital resources that inform their steps in completing the project.

Listen to each other as well as to digitally available video or audio recordings that are relevant to the project.

Plus (+) visually interpret diagrams and *visually represent* their projects through sketchnotes.

WHAT TEACHERS SAY ABOUT MULTIMODAL SCAFFOLDING

By their nature, multimodal scaffolds offer more than one avenue for students to access the content and meet the objectives of a lesson. This fact immediately puts students at ease because they can see more than one path for success and increases the likelihood they will engage deeply with a lesson. The more students engage, the more confident they become in using their strengths to persevere and succeed. When students are challenged by some aspects of a multimodal activity, as they surely will be, they can rely on their strengths in one area to gain skill and confidence in others. Through multimodal instruction, students enter a continual cycle of applying their strengths while building skills and gaining confidence. This cycle leads to classroom success in the immediate sense but, when internalized, promotes lifelong learning.

—Alycia Owen, ELD coach

See Figure 4.6 for two students engaged in a SWIRL+ learning opportunity in Alycia Owen's secondary classroom, where she regularly sets up "annotation stations." Students read a visually enhanced text, they talk and listen to each other as they discuss their interpretations of the assignment and critical reflection on the text, as well as add their annotations on the large pink paper.

FIGURE 4.6 ● Students Work in Pairs to Make Sense of Dual-Coded Text (having both print and pictorial input)

Source: Alycia Owen. Used with permission.

Another example of turning text annotation into a SWIRL + activity was shared with us by Elizabeth Choi, featured earlier in Chapter 3. Elizabeth scaffolds her students' interaction with complex texts by using a slightly modified, illustrated set of text annotation symbols (see Figure 4.7). However, she takes this frequently used approach to the next level by turning the text-mark ups into sentence frames so students interact with each other as well, based on the readings (see Figure 4.8).

FIGURE 4.7 • Text Annotation Codes

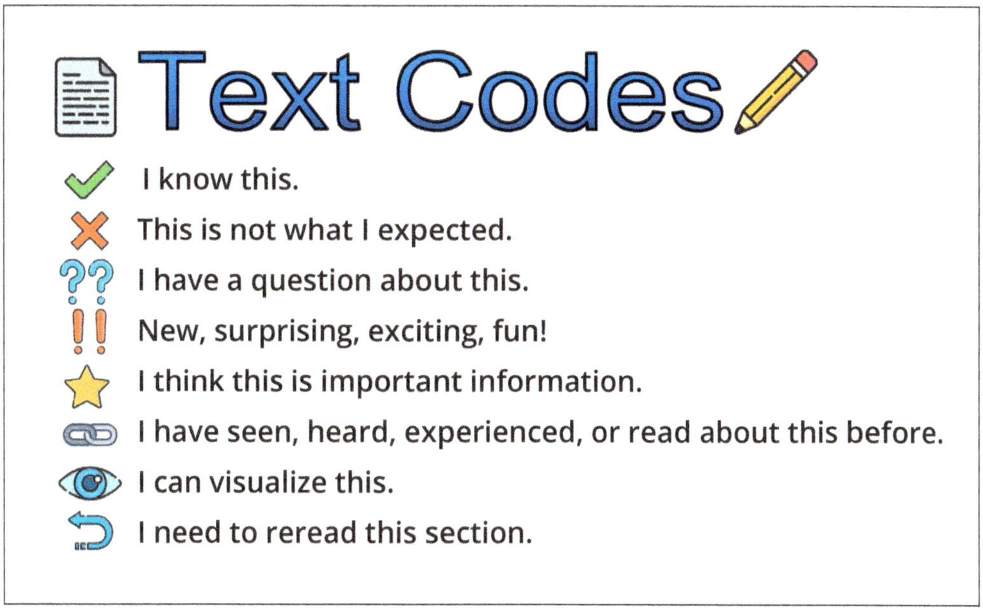

Source: Elizabeth Choi. Used with permission.

FIGURE 4.8 • Text Annotation Codes Turned Into Text Talk Prompts

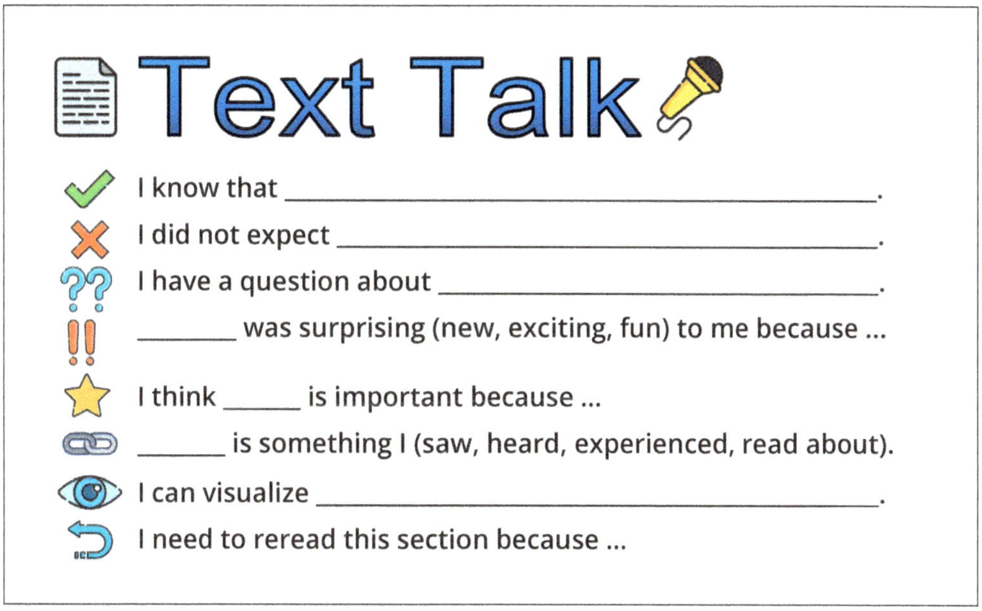

Source: Elizabeth Choi. Used with permission.

ADVANTAGES OF THIS PRACTICE

At the core of language development is student voice—active participation, and critical engagement with the content, academic language and literacy practices—and the authentic identities of students and their peers. Oracy is critical for literacy, including visual literacy, to develop. Students need ample opportunities to talk and write—in any language of their choice. They should talk to English-speaking peers, same-language partners and to their teachers and other adults in the classroom and school environment. Within content classes, students also need to actively participate in academic conversations and authentic writing opportunities with peer and teacher guidance and support to make sense of what is being taught. Here are some examples of how to engage students across the content areas:

- In math, engage students in math talk and draw special attention to (a) the way students explain their thinking and (b) the precision of language needed to fully engage in disciplinary conversations.
- In social studies, have students pose their own questions, establish their own line of inquiry, and participate in respectful debates and critical conversations around issues they sincerely care about, read about, and write about.
- In science, engage students in task-based discussions that build on hands-on explorations and multiple representations such as diagrams, outlines, sketches, and video-recorded responses, as well as in inquiry that provides additional opportunities for oracy and disciplinary literacy.
- In language arts, select nonfiction and fiction pieces to discuss those that are relevant to students' lives and invite students to share their own examples; use "pairing" strategies which simultaneously introduce the informational/nonfiction and fiction versions of a topic; embrace multiliteracies or "text multiplication" as you explore multimedia resources, video clips, and films in addition to print-based materials about the same topic.
- In music, invite students to share personal and cultural experiences with musical traditions and songs related to the lesson.
- In visual arts, have students share their plans for their work, the processes they engage in, and their final products.

Why is this so important? "By providing multiple opportunities for students to negotiate meaning in disciplinary conversation together, we can engage multilingual learners in the interactions that, over time and with appropriate modeling, enable them to become increasingly effective in expressing and exploring ideas" (Nordmeyer et al., 2021, p. 65). Sustained, authentic, and well-supported academic conversations coupled with similarly sustained, authentic, and well-supported writing, reading, listening, and visual meaning-making opportunities pave the way to meaningful, equitable classroom experiences for multilingual learners.

KEEP THIS IN MIND

While the "SWIRL +" acronym seems to suggest a set order of the language domains to be integrated, you do not need to follow this sequence—speak, write, interact, read, listen, and visually engage—when planning multimodal learning activities. Instead, focus on making sure you give students "the tools to have extensive, productive discourse [that] will enable them to substantiate their claims with evidence whether it is science-centered, political in nature, or pleading their case with their parents as they get older" (Craddock, 2021, p. 53). Intentional planning for "SWIRL +" is essential for a balanced, well-organized opportunity for students to engage in all modalities that build on each other within one learning experience.

EXAMPLE #1: TALK MOVES (ENHANCED WITH ANCHOR CHARTS AND MOVEMENTS)

Students' participation in academic conversations can be scaffolded in multiple ways. One strategy is to co-construct norms for classroom conversations. Figure 4.9 illustrates an anchor chart that exemplifies what the shared expectations are and what they actually mean in the classroom context. Co-constructing expectations for conversations is important for several reasons. It helps create a positive and effective learning environment, avoids misunderstandings, empowers students to be a part of the decision-making process, and supports the development of a positive classroom culture. As you co-develop similar anchor charts with your students, keep in mind to co-define what these experiences look like, sound like, and feel like in the classroom and add illustrations to better support multilingual learners.

Additional strategies include creating simple charts or table tents with sentence stems and common questions for academic conversations that generally support students when they converse in pairs or teams as follows:

Clarifying Questions

- Could you explain what you mean?
- Can you provide an example?
- What evidence do you have to support your claim?

- How is this relevant to your point?
- Have you thought about __________?

Sentence Stems for Responses

- I noticed that ______________
- I like how you said that_______
- I would like to add __________
- I agree with _________because_________
- I disagree with _______because________
- I still wonder about____________
- Thank you for noticing that _______

FIGURE 4.9 ● Class Discussion Rules and What They Look or Sound Like

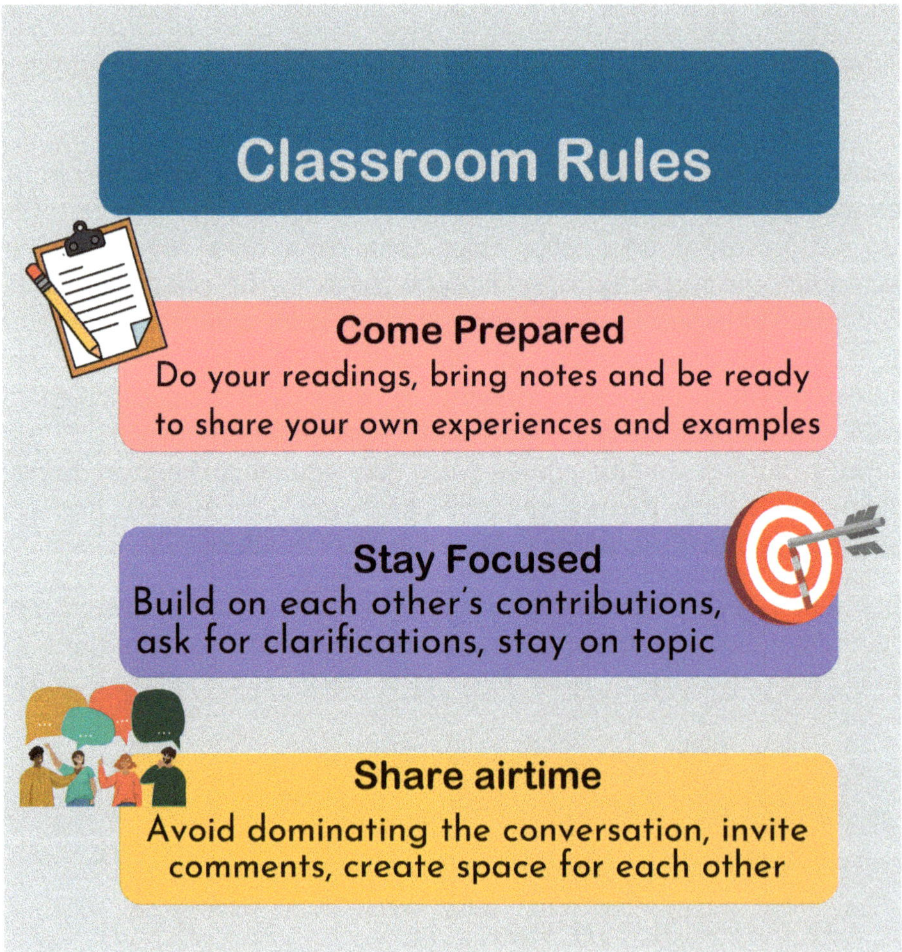

Another important scaffolding approach is to co-create illustrated sentence frames for students to see how language may be used in specific contexts or for specific purposes. By doing so, we ensure that our students "feel safe to go public with their ideas" (Michaels & O'Connor, 2015, p. 335). Keep in mind that sentence frames, just like all scaffolding tools, must gradually fade and make way for student independence. They can be regularly revisited and replaced with more advanced, enhanced, or updated choices. Table 4.1 is an example of a digital anchor chart that can also be used as a personalized handout to support students when they have conversations about cause and effect.

TABLE 4.1 • Cause–Effect Sentence Frames

QUESTIONS:
What happened? What caused it to happen?
What is the effect? What are the important factors that cause this effect?
KEY VOCABULARY AND PHRASES:
Because
This led to
As a result
So
If ___, then ___
For this reason,
Another reason why
Consequently
ONE-SENTENCE CAUSE–EFFECT FRAMES:
If _______, then _______________.
If ______, it will lead to _______.

(Continued)

(Continued)
________ results in _______.
The effect of _______ is _______.
CAUSE–EFFECT PARAGRAPH FRAMES:
One reason ______happens(ed) is that ______.
Another reason is ________.
These factors can lead to _______.

EXAMPLE #2: QUICK WRITE, QUICK DRAW COMBINED WITH TURN AND TALK

Quick writes or quick draws are similar to the think-jot-pair-share strategy. Students get productive wait time and an opportunity to choose whether they wish to gather their thoughts by writing down a few ideas or creating a sketch or a (not-too-elaborate) drawing. The essence of a quick write or quick draw is that it is fast—so remind your students not to second guess themselves, not to go into too many details. Instead, they should fully immerse themselves in capturing their thoughts verbally or visually without lifting their pen or pencil.

EXAMPLE #3: HEAR IT—READ IT—PICTURE IT!

In this activity, students listen to a story read aloud to them but are not shown any of the illustrations in the book, including its cover. During the reading, pause periodically and invite students to draw their own illustrations to match the section of the book that was just read. Students may create a quick sketch of the story idea on paper, an erasable whiteboard, or a tablet. To prevent students from creating elaborate drawings during the reading and hinder the progression of the book, request students divide their paper or whiteboard into four equal boxes to reduce the area for students to sketch their illustrations. In a variation of this activity, students stop to create marginal notes in the form of illustrations of text they read or you read to them. As an extension to this activity, students can create their own book jackets for the story in question. With all book illustrations, students can participate in a *gallery walk* in which all their drawings are displayed, and students have an opportunity to walk by and examine each student's drawing and compare the artistic elements that were apparent in the collection.

MULTIMODAL SCAFFOLDING PRACTICE #2: CONNECT VISUALIZATION OR VISUAL INPUT TO ORACY AND LITERACY

Interpreting visual representations or creating mental images are two distinct but interrelated processes. The multilingual brain has an advantage of being skilled in accessing multiple systems, so visual input/visualization connected to oracy and literacy will naturally enhance language processing and language development.

- Before presenting visuals to students, reflect on what students might observe:
  - *How will they make sense of this image?*
  - *How will they describe the overarching message of the image?*
  - *What will they zoom in on to identify specific details?*
  - *What inferences can they make based on the image?*
- When teachers guide students to create mental images, they learn to pause, make connections, and use their prior knowledge as well as their imagination. To support students in their process of visualization, consider asking them the following:
  - *What would you see if you were watching a movie about ________?*
  - *When we are reading this book, how do you imagine the main character to look?*
  - *If you closed your eyes, what images would pop into your mind?*

When students view existing images or ones created in front of their minds' eyes and at the same time talk, read, or write about those images, they rely on multiple ways to express themselves.

ADVANTAGES OF THIS PRACTICE

The initial access to this selection of scaffolding activities is image-based. The reduced linguistic load will result in reduced fear or anxiety around language use. Let's agree that multilingual learners have a robust knowledge base, are inquisitive, and have curious minds. They want to learn and engage with complex learning opportunities. A visual entry point will help provide the impetus for student engagement and much more—students will also have a more nuanced opportunity for observing details, processing information available through visual input, or imagining what the story/information is about as they connect new learning with their prior knowledge.

EXAMPLE #1: SEE IT-SAY IT.

Using only drawings, photographs, or other still images that tell a story, wordless books can promote rich conversations, discussions, and the use of the students' full linguistic repertoires. Focusing on illustrations gives students the opportunity to gather information from visual representations of a story, a strategy that can bolster reading comprehension.

- Begin by previewing the wordless book page by page.
- Refrain from telling the story; instead, name items in the illustrations and invite students to do so as well.
- Pose questions and probe students to begin describing what they see and formulate more complete thoughts by adding some explanations or predictions about what they are looking at.
- Subsequently, ask students to tell the whole story from the wordless book, either the whole class with students taking turns telling part of the story using one illustration at a time or in small groups that are teacher-led or student-led, depending on grade level and student ability.

Additionally, use books with text for this activity by covering the words, having students tell the story from the illustrations, and then by reading the story. Wordless books promote student use of varied vocabulary and oral language as well as presenting ideas for story writing. It is important to note, wordless books are not just for early childhood or elementary students. In fact, there are quite a few wordless books or picture books that explore serious topics that are better suited for Grades 5 and up. See Table 4.2 for a short selection of our favorites.

TABLE 4.2 • Recommended Wordless (or Almost Wordless) Picture Books

ELEMENTARY SCHOOL
Chalk by Bill Thomson
Flotsam by David Wiesner
Journey Trilogy by Aaron Becker
Zoom and Re-Zoom by Istvan Banyai
The Red Book by Barbara Lehman
Flashlight by Lizi Boyd
Small Things by Mel Tregonning

A Ball for Daisy by Chris Raschka
Wave by Suzy Lee
Mirror by Jeannie Baker
The Paper Boat: A Refugee Story by Thao Lam
Hike by Pete Oswald
Boat of Dreams by Rogério Coelho
MIDDLE SCHOOL
Arrival by Shaun Tan
Unspeakable: The Tulsa Race Massacre by Carole Boston Weatherford & Floyd Cooper
The Undefeated by Kwame Alexander and Kadir Nelson
Dreamers by Yuyi Morales
Nicky and Vera: A Quiet Hero of the Holocaust and the Children He Rescued by Peter Sis
The Wall by Eve Bunting and Ronald Himler

EXAMPLE #2: VISUAL THINKING STRATEGIES (VTS)

VTS originated in museum education programs to guide students, of all ages, in interpreting artwork (https://vtshome.org/). Using VTS can support an open-ended, shared inquiry guided by three core questions (with no right or wrong answers) on any grade level or content area:

1. *What is going on in this picture?*
2. *What makes you say that?*
3. *What else can you find?*

After modeling how to use the three guiding questions on a sample image, use various grouping configurations to invite more risk-taking, student-to-student interactions, and critical thinking. Students jot down their initial thoughts and turn and talk to one partner to begin the shared meaning-making. Next, open up the conversation to a larger group of four students by combining two, two-member partnerships. Due to the open-ended nature of the activity, students begin to offer their contributions in response to images that can include reproductions of art, contemporary or historical photographs, drawings, and so on. And they will do so with more confidence since there is no need to seek affirmation from the teacher.

Marva Cappello and Nancy Walker (2016) suggest that there are many similarities between close reading and VTS protocols: both require students to analyze the text or the image, to ask text- or image-dependent questions, to engage with the text or image multiple times whether through reading or viewing, and to identify evidence for claims they make in the text or image.

For students in upper grades, try the New York Times Learning Network (n.d.) "What's Going on in This Picture?" series. Every week, the New York Times publishes and moderates a live online discussion about an intriguing photograph published without a caption. It is recommended for ages 13+. You can join in this global lesson with your secondary students by using your own photographs (see Andrea's picture from an Alaskan trip in Figure 4.10), or invite your students to share some of their pictures for similar shared explorations.

FIGURE 4.10 ● Authentic Photographs Spark Lively Discussion Using VTS

Bubble-Net Feeding Humpback Whales off the Coast of Alaska—not to be shared until the students have completed the VTS activity

EXAMPLE #3: DATA TALK

Data talk is a form of accountable talk that involves interpreting visually represented information. Common visual data displays include pie charts, bar graphs, color-coded maps, pictograms, illustrated timelines, and so on. These visuals can be digitally created or simply drawn, generated by or with students, or obtained from published sources. Students need productive wait-time to closely examine a graph, diagram, or other type of data display. They take verbal or pictorial notes of their interpretations and prepare for a small group data talk to answer two key questions:

1. What trends or patterns are present in the data display? (Claim)
2. What makes you say that? (Evidence and reasoning)

The goal is for students to engage in shared meaning-making, and they can accomplish this goal by describing what they see in the data display and restating the data verbally. As they analyze the information, they can share insights about the data trends, generate claims and counterclaims, and probe and challenge each other. Through their discussions, they can link their own ideas to others' reasoning, negotiate meaning, ask for clarification, and co-develop defendable arguments.

KEEP THIS IN MIND

Remember to invite students who are in the earlier stages of language development to use their full linguistic repertoire, including their home or primary languages, or rely on bilingual peer bridges to make sense of visual input. In addition, visualization might have to be connected to concrete objects and taught explicitly first. For example, you cannot ask your students to visualize an orange tree if they have never seen, touched, smelled, or tasted an orange or have no idea if oranges grow on small or very tall trees. Start with tangible items and easy to follow steps:

1. Hold up a small, everyday object, such as a fork, from the school cafeteria.
2. Have students closely look at it for a few moments.
3. Ask them to close their eyes and think of the same object.
4. Have them keep seeing it in their minds' eyes without opening their eyes for as long as possible.
5. Have them check to see how closely the image in their mind matches the actual object when they open their eyes.

Repeat the same exercise with other, more complex objects and model the use of descriptive language while the students are examining the objects. Try the same when their eyes are closed to make sure they can continue to describe what they are looking at. Continue to expand the visualization journey with photographs or pieces of art before you ask your students to recreate a memory (such as something very familiar, such as their room, their home, etc.). Finally, move on to encouraging the use of their imagination during the visualization process—for example, have students see themselves climb a mountain, try a new sport, or swim in a lake or pool for the first time. Transferring visualization to the literacy or core content class will also be highly beneficial, but we can't assume the students have done it before or know how to, so take the time to ensure this approach to multimodal teaching is successful.

WHAT TEACHERS SAY ABOUT MULTIMODAL SCAFFOLDING

Multimodal scaffolding is a bit of a no-brainer to me—the more varied ways that information is presented or expressed, the higher the likelihood of success, right? I want to know what a student knows or can do (not just what they know or can do in English) so I know what they are bringing to the lesson and what I can add and connect to. This is most helpful to me with kinders. We had an enthusiastic and outgoing newcomer in our class, but we couldn't rely on the translation apps. With gestures, images, realia, cognates, etc., we were all able to engage with lessons in the classroom.

—Sherry Liptak, multilingual learner program specialist, Chilliwack, British Columbia, Canada

MULTIMODAL SCAFFOLDING PRACTICE #3: STUDENT-PRODUCED VISUALS

When students are engaged in not just processing or interpreting but producing information via visual tools, they are developing visual literacy in new ways—they are not just consumers of visual input but creators as well. Even in the earliest stages of language development (some refer to it as the silent period), the multilingual mind is never silent; students are thinking and can express their ideas and emotions, as well as represent their new learning in many different ways, including visually. When students produce images (by ways of simply drawing or sketching), taking visual notes rather than writing words, annotating texts with symbols, or more artistically expressing themselves by illustrating, painting, or collaging, they communicate in a new modality while also constructing their own knowledge and understanding, engaging in active learning, and developing ownership of their learning.

ADVANTAGES OF THIS PRACTICE

When students visually express themselves, they can employ a range of higher order thinking skills. They select, evaluate, and organize information that will be visually captured, which also ensures student choice and learner agency! Engaging their imagination and visual expression is also a form of liberation in a text-heavy academic context. When drawing or sketching is integrated into learning in a nonjudgmental, nonevaluative way (no one is grading the visuals students produce), visual forms of expression may also prove to be therapeutic by way of reducing stress, anxiety, or the impacts of trauma. Students don't have to consider themselves artistically talented to give themselves permission to produce work that shows what they know or to experiment with different forms of expression (just simply switching from pencils to pens, markers, crayons, and so on) to breathe life into their learning.

FROM RESEARCH TO PRACTICE

If we have not persuaded you yet about the power of student-created visuals, see what Myra Fernandes et al. (2018) found in their research about the influence drawing has on memory.

> Drawing improves memory by encouraging a seamless integration of elaborative, motoric, and pictorial components of a memory trace. That is, to transfer a word into a drawn visual representation, one must elaborate on its meaning and semantic features, engage in the actual hand movements needed for drawing (motor action), and visually inspect one's created picture (pictorial processing) . . . The mechanism driving the drawing effect is one that promotes the seamless integration of these codes, or modes of representation, into one cohesive memory trace, and it is this that facilitates later retrieval of the studied words. (p. 304)

Reflect on the following:

Some students love to doodle, others can fully immerse themselves into elaborate artistic creations, yet others claim "they can't draw." Knowing the diversity of talents and interests that exist in any classroom, how can you make sure drawing adds to the learning process and enhances the processing and retention of new and difficult information? In what ways can all students benefit from it?

____

____

____

____

EXAMPLE #1: CONCEPT MAPPING

According to an academic definition of a concept map, it is a "node-link diagram in which each node represents a concept, and each link identifies the relationship between the two concepts it connects" (Schroeder et al., 2018, p. 431). More simply put, it is a graphic organizer that helps teachers and students categorize key concepts from a unit of study (or a text) visually while also showing meaningful connections between the main idea, supporting details, and other relevant pieces of information. To introduce this strategy, start with a whole-class activity and build a concept map with your students on a readily available topic such as the weather. Once students understand the process, move on to more complex concepts and shift to small group or individual concept mapping tasks. It is really critical to model for students how to make connections between the central concept and the first tier of supporting ideas and how to revise the map if your conceptual understanding changes. Starting with a blank concept map or adding visuals (drawings, photographs, cut-out pictures) will help all students benefit from this strategy (Reading Rockets, 2023). See Figures 4.11 and 4.12 for how Sasha Engelsman co-creates differentiated concept maps with her secondary science students. She also offers a word bank that her students can tap into as they work in small groups or individually to complete the concept maps.

FIGURE 4.11 • Matter Concept Map—Version 1

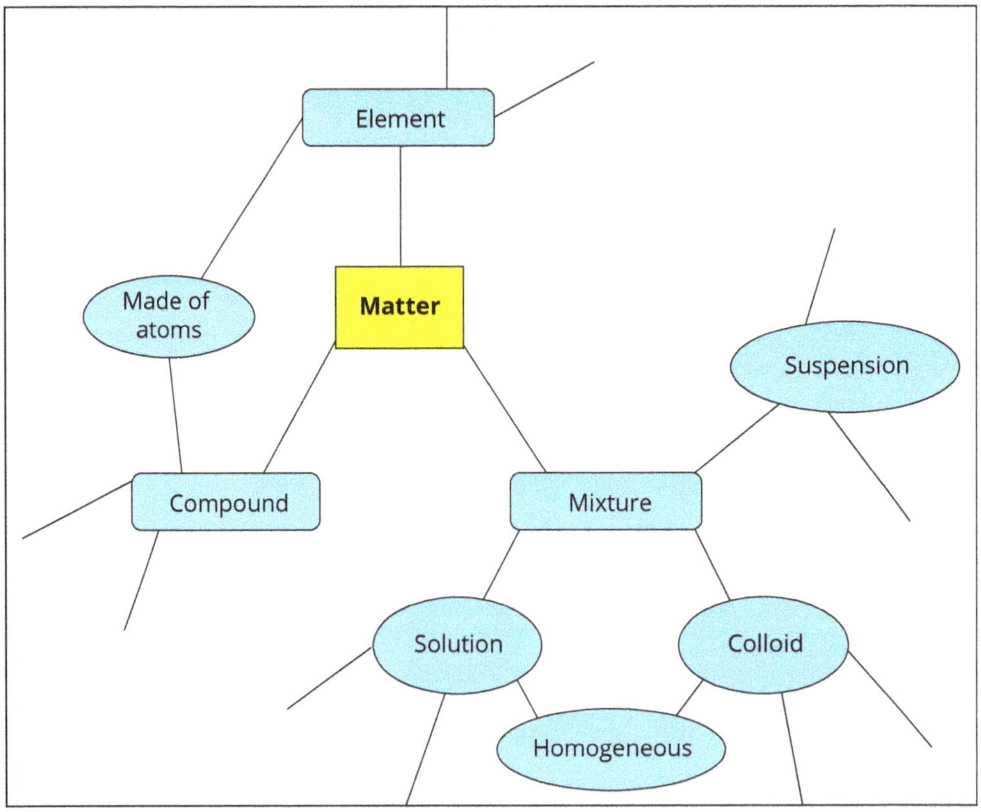

Source: Sasha Engelsman. Used with permission.

FIGURE 4.12 ● Matter Concept Map—Version 2

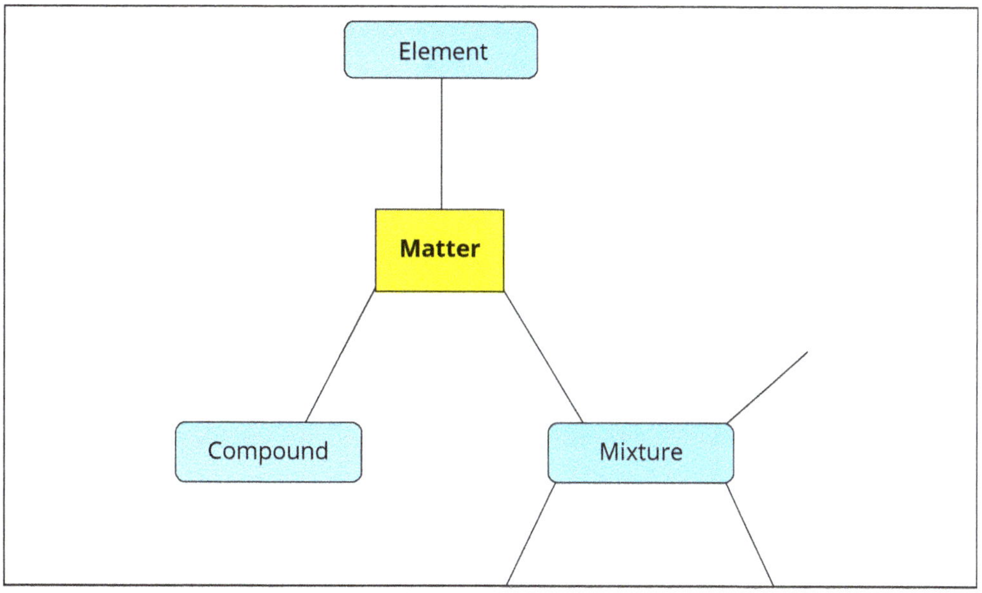

Source: Sasha Engelsman. Used with permission.

EXAMPLE #2: DRAW-TO-LEARN

It is hard to imagine a classroom in which a teacher would not grab a piece of chalk, a marker, or a stylus pen to quickly draw something to better illustrate or clarify a point. Be it a vocabulary word to illustrate, a couple of stick figures to refer to opposing historical figures, a rough outline of a map to show the journey of the protagonist, a math problem to solve, a predicted outcome of a science experiment, and so on! These quick visuals enhance understanding and engagement. See Figure 4.13 for a student-created

FIGURE 4.13 ● Student-Created Multimodal Poster

Source: Student work. Used with permission.

poster with guidance from Pushpanjali Sengupta, multilingual facilitator and heritage language coach at Bellevue Public Schools in Washington.

Whenever possible, we embrace the process of our students' *drawing to learn*. Let's look at the flip side of it, too. As Kim Quillen and Stephen Thomas (2015) suggest, drawing to learn is a strategy that uses student drawings to support conceptual development, model building for scientific processes, or simply for understanding new information. These drawings can range from being representational (looking realistic) to abstract, from including some, a lot, or no words, and from depicting objects to capturing relationships or complex processes. When working with multilingual learners, you don't need to be an artist to (sooner or later) fully embrace the notion of *drawing to teach*. A great place to start is with illustrated vocabulary cards, such as in Figure 4.14, based on the **K. I. M.** strategy—**K**ey idea, **I**nformation, and **M**emory clue (Ford & Ford, 2014). With your students, you can co-develop a three-column chart, write a vocabulary word or key idea under *K*, its definition (or essential information) under *I*, and a picture or drawing under *M* to commit the word to memory.

Similarly, you can take any graphic organizer (see more on graphic scaffolding in Chapter 6) and add a visual to make them multimodal. Better yet, have your students work on these multimodal versions:

- A Venn diagram with photo cutouts, drawings, or a combination of words and images
- A timeline with illustrations to represent key dates in a person's life or historical period
- A T-chart with images on one side and verbal notes on the other
- A flow chart showing a sequence of events through visuals and text-based information

FIGURE 4.14 ● K.I.M.

K (KEY IDEA)	I (INFORMATION)	M (MEMORY CLUE)
Plate tectonics'	• The Earth's outer layer is broken into big pieces called tectonic plates. • These plates fit together like a puzzle. • The tectonic plates are not fixed in place.	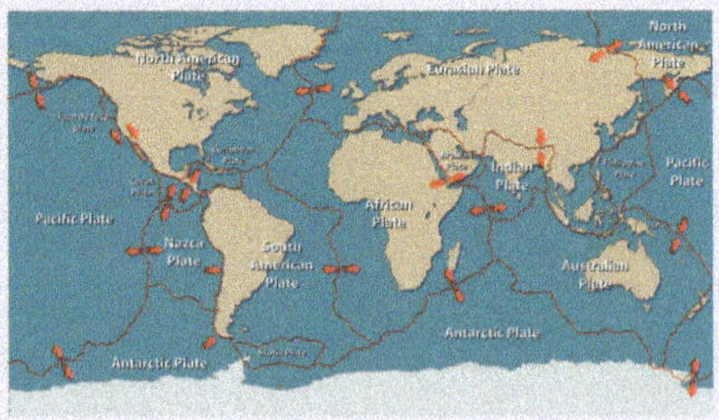

Source: istock.com/blueringmedia

EXAMPLE #3: STORYBOARDING

Storyboarding, as a tool, originated in the movie industry, and it has been used as a visual representation of how movie scenes are sequenced using a series of panels. Each panel shows one action from one camera angle, so when the panels are put together, the entire series reveals the movie maker's vision of how the film would unfold.

Building on the visualization strategy we introduced earlier, storyboarding can be used as a pre-writing scaffold, during which students are guided step-by-step to visualize and illustrate the beginning, middle, and end of stories. The panels could be more nuanced, allowing for additional details, but we suggest starting with a limited number first. Storyboarding encourages students to grow their ideas and clarify story details in a multimodal fashion. In this way, students explore writing a more complex narrative that is organized using three or more panels, each designated for part of the story. In addition, it may also pave the way for students to turn their storyboards into skits or even short videos they can produce.

See Table 4.3 for a simple template and Figure 4.15 for a student example from Elizabeth Choi's middle school classroom using the digital tool for storyboarding. Elizabeth asked one group of students to use the StoryboardThat app (https://www.storyboardthat.com/) to illustrate and retell a classic story from Greek mythology (check out Chapter 7 for more explanation of digital storytelling).

TABLE 4.3 ● Storyboard Template

PARTS OF THE STORY	BEGINNING	MIDDLE	END
Illustrations			
Brief summaries			

Source: Elizabeth Choi. Used with permission.

online resources Available for download at https://companion.corwin.com/courses/NineDimensionsofScaffoldingforMLs

FIGURE 4.15 ● A Student Example of a Completed Storyboard Using StoryboardThat

Source: Student work. Used with permission.

The images incorporated in these strategies may be partially or fully student created. Rather than giving students a blank piece of paper, you can model the use of visual tools to get them started. You may choose to provide a partially completed image for students to complete, but always offer them a choice—students can stay with your model or think outside the box and create their own visuals. Similarly, students should have a choice to work alone, in pairs, or in collaborative groups to complete any one of these activities. In fact, when students have the opportunity to collaborate on creating visuals, they naturally add language to their work by describing it, soliciting input, and building on each other's ideas. On the other hand, when students are dually identified as multilingual learners with a disability that limits verbal communication, teachers may be able to provide the necessary linguistic details first. Students can then demonstrate their understanding of complex concepts through visual representations of their thinking, as observed in a co-taught class with Dr. Elena Dokshansky, ENL teacher, and Melissa Dinelli, special education teacher at Buffalo Public Schools, New York (see Figure 4.16). During a class presentation, a student with selective mutism whispered responses into one of the teachers' ears who repeated and co-presented with the student in this fashion.

FIGURE 4.16 ● Student Artwork With Teacher-Created Storyboard Text

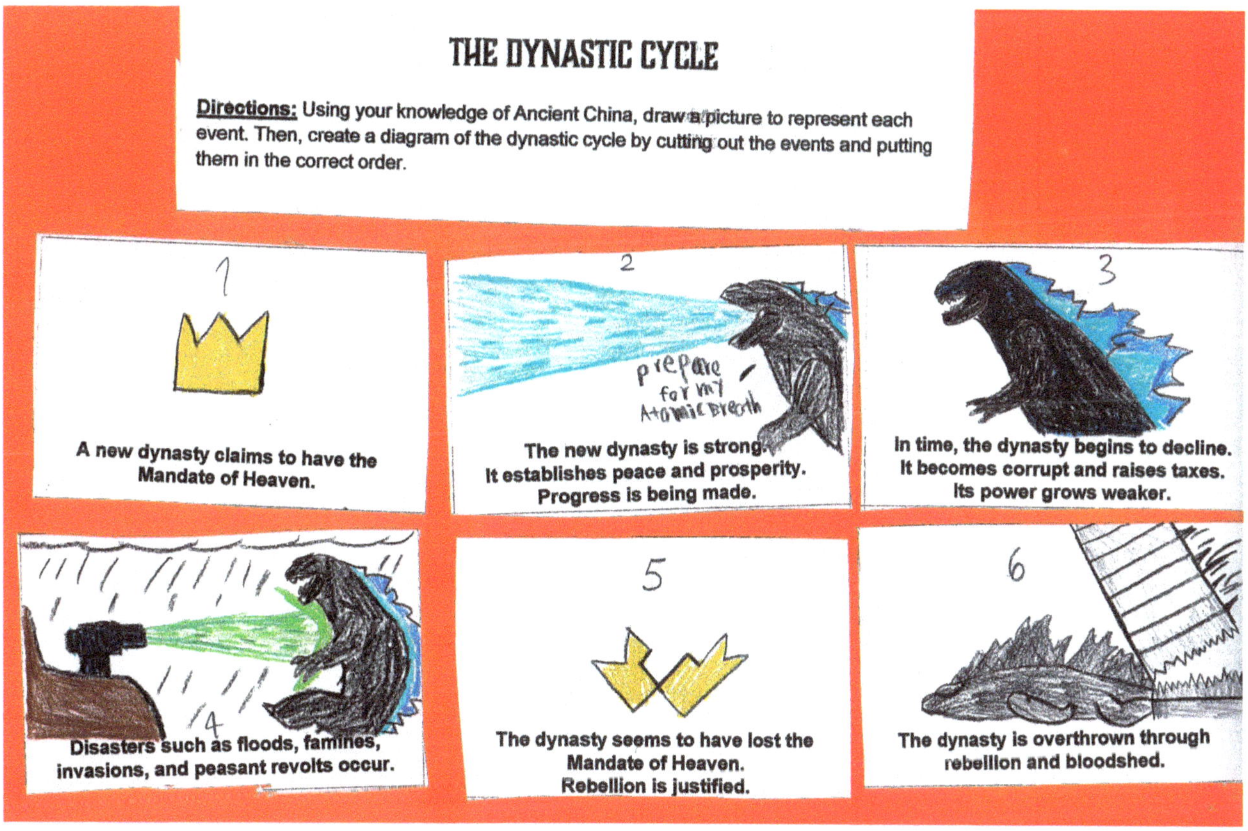

Source: Student work. Used with permission.

INDEPENDENT LEARNING STRATEGIES FOR STUDENTS

Students engage in multimodal disciplinary practices when they interpret a graph in math, create a pie chart in a science class, analyze an illustration or historic photographs in ELA, and examine and respond to political cartoons in social studies. These multimodal learning opportunities naturally lend themselves to teacher modeling and the necessary "fading," so students can fully benefit from this type of learning on their own. Multimodality seems to be an everyday occurrence across core content areas, and they are even more common in special subject matters such as music, art, health and well-being, computer science, library, and so on. While teacher modeling and shared classroom experiences with multiple modes of representation and expression are critical, students must learn and internalize how to locate, interpret, and use multimodality strategically with their peers and on their own to increase their understanding of difficult topics and to successfully complete complex tasks. (For more on how teachers model instruction, see Chapter 2.)

Luckily, multimodal learning tends to be highly motivating and actively engaging. It offers lots of embedded choices for students. To further encourage students' transitioning to independence with self-directed multimodal learning, use the following self-assessment tool, adapt it to be better aligned to your students' age level, or create one like in Table 4.4 with your students.

TABLE 4.4 ● Self-Assessment of Multimodal Learning Choices

MY MULTIMODAL LEARNING CHOICES	ALWAYS	SOMETIMES	NOT YET
• I like to draw pictures or diagrams of what I read.			
• I like to watch videos that explain key concepts.			
• I like to have the freedom to express myself verbally or visually.			
• I like to make connections to real-life experiences.			
• I like to discuss what I am learning.			
Overall, I...			
I need to work on...			

online resources Available for download at https://companion.corwin.com/courses/NineDimensionsofScaffoldingforMLs

SUMMARY

Multimodal scaffolding is uniquely positioned to support multiple access points for students simultaneously. By virtue of combining two or more modalities within a single lesson or single task, educators are more intentional about presenting information in multiple ways so that a range of students (multilingual learners included) will have access and develop understanding. Planning and delivering instruction and assessment through multiple resources and modalities will give students numerous ways to engage with the content and language to demonstrate their new learning.

Questions

1. What are the dimensions of multimodal teaching and learning practices?
2. How does multimodal scaffolding support multilingual learners?
3. What other scaffolding dimensions overlap with multimodality, and how would you capitalize on them concurrently or sequentially?

CHAPTER 5

Multisensory Scaffolding

> *"For multilingual learners, the selection and sequencing of tasks within and between lessons, and their access to message abundancy, is critical. It assures that students have opportunities to visit and revisit key concepts; that their learning can progress in small steps, and that they have the time to learn relevant aspects of language and literacy as they engage with these concepts."*
> *Jennifer Hammond, 2023, p. 16*

We learn best when we are fully present, and our senses are fully engaged. When we awaken our senses, we can foster deeper cognitive and emotional connections between our prior and ongoing learning. Sensory experiences leave lasting impressions that not only trigger our memories but also aid in recalling learned information. By obtaining information through a combination of visual, auditory, and tactile sources as well as kinesthetic movement, we can increase our retention of knowledge and skills and convert abstract concepts into practical applications.

Designing enhanced instruction through sensory experiences is crucial for fostering deeper engagement for multilingual learners. When students' senses are fully activated, they are more likely to internalize language learning, improve their retention of content, and increase their ability to apply what they have learned in new contexts. To create lessons that are accessible to multilingual learners, incorporating rich sensory input can foster meaningful connections to the language and content they need to learn.

In our exploration of comprehensive instructional supports in this volume, we now turn our attention to the power of multisensory scaffolding for multilingual learners. In this chapter, we explore how multisensory approaches to learning can provide access points for students to grade-level curriculum while they are still developing fluency in English. By tapping into students' senses, we expand our repertoire of scaffolding strategies, making learning experiences more engaging, memorable, and accessible.

It is widely acknowledged that connecting to multiple senses can deepen cognitive processing, strengthen memory, and support engagement in learning (Dubois et al., 2021; Wolfe, 2001; Zull, 2002). In a classroom context, this means incorporating materials, activities, and learning supports that encourage students to interact with content by engaging the senses. To promote active engagement, multisensory scaffolding can encompass a range of tools and techniques designed to provide multilingual learners with multiple pathways into the learning process.

WHO IS IT FOR?

A multisensory approach to scaffolding instruction is for multilingual learners as well as all students who would benefit from additional support for making content and language understandable. Providing resources and activities that capitalize on visual, auditory, tactile, and kinesthetic encounters can incorporate students' learning preferences as well as cultural backgrounds, as different cultures emphasize varied ways of interacting with the world. Multisensory scaffolding can further enhance student engagement and comprehension by providing multiple pathways for processing and retaining information and making abstract concepts more concrete. When thoughtfully implemented as well as used in combination with one another, these scaffolding approaches create dynamic and inclusive classrooms that support all learners as they deepen their language, literacy, and content learning.

HOW IS MULTISENSORY SCAFFOLDING USED ACROSS PROGRAM MODELS?

In classroom settings, multisensory scaffolding approaches support the instruction of multilingual learners in general education, co-taught, and integrated English language development (ELD) classes by increasing engagement, improving retention, and reducing cognitive overload as follows:

- In *general education classes*, visual aids in the form of organized text (e.g., steps in a process), success criteria, informational charts or diagrams, photographs with accompanying vocabulary, and the like, make learning content more accessible and meaningful for multilingual learners. Other multisensory materials that accommodate diverse learners' needs might include hands-on materials such as using math manipulatives, a recorded reading of printed text, and learning activities such as gallery walks in which students move around the classroom to complete various tasks. See Figure 5.1 for how Lani Perez-Santana, who teaches multilingual learners at John Overton High School in Nashville, Tennessee, creates a visually appealing anchor chart to support all her students in mastering math concepts and the language of mathematics while also playfully putting students at ease at the same time.

FIGURE 5.1 • A Visually Engaging Anchor Chart That Teaches Content and Language

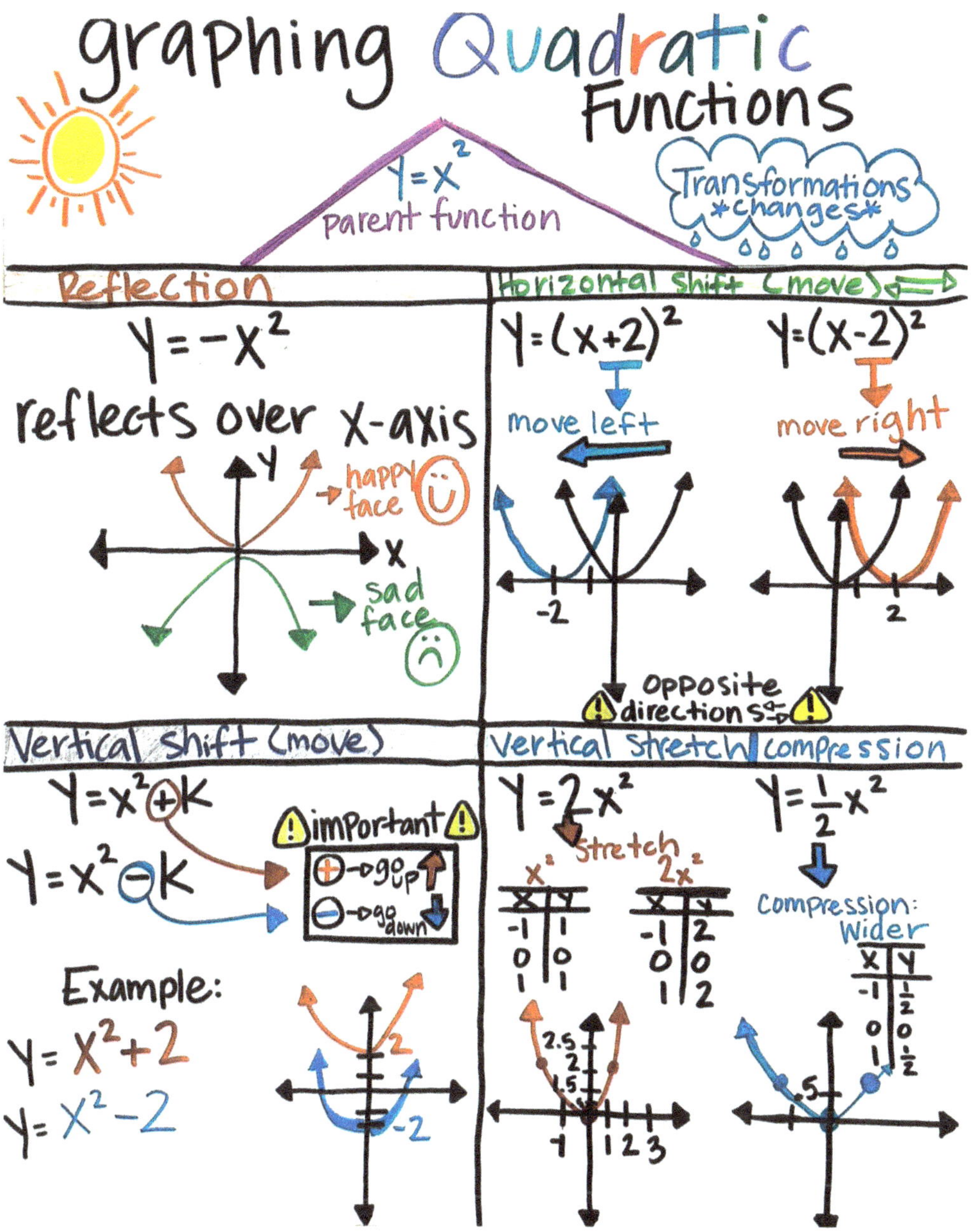

Source: Lani Perez-Santana. Used with permission.

- In *co-taught classes*, multisensory scaffolding approaches foster inclusivity for multilingual learners by leveraging the strengths of both teachers to deliver instruction. Co-teachers can deliver instruction collaboratively, with one teacher verbally explaining information while the other teacher provides visual support through diagrams, noting critical vocabulary, producing photographs, or using realia and manipulatives. Instruction can be further tailored through flexible grouping or individualized multisensory supports.

- In *standalone ELD classes*, creating a multisensory, language-rich classroom can engage multilingual learners' senses to reinforce learning. Visual supports such as word walls, labels, and images; auditory representations such as songs, chants, and read-alouds; tactile tools like word tiles or manipulatives; and kinesthetic activities using dance and movement make words and concepts more understandable.
- In *self-contained or integrated special education classes with dually identified multilingual learners*, multisensory scaffolding addresses students' linguistic and cognitive challenges through targeted support. This approach offers diverse ways for students to access and engage with the content, reducing cognitive or linguistic overload and building on personal strengths to promote meaningful learning.

Across all educational settings, multisensory scaffolding approaches create inclusive, supportive environments where multilingual learners are better able to actively participate in learning. These approaches can provide for diverse learning needs and various proficiency levels. However, implementing multisensory scaffolding effectively requires thoughtful consideration of classroom space, preparation time, and available resources.

Classroom space and class size play critical roles in multisensory approaches to learning, as these methods often involve hands-on activities, movement, and collaborative work. Teachers need both flexible and ample spaces that can accommodate activities like setting up learning centers or lab stations as well as the space to store the necessary equipment and materials. Smaller classroom sizes or using a shared classroom space might limit opportunities to use certain approaches.

The time to prepare multisensory activities is equally important, and designing lessons that integrate multisensory elements requires creativity and additional effort. The gathering of materials, creating visual aids, or preparing technology for interactive lessons all take more time. In particular, co-teachers need time to collaborate, coordinate, and align their instructional strategies to meet the needs of multilingual learners effectively.

Despite these challenges, the investment in multisensory scaffolding approaches is worthwhile. Using these techniques can foster academic and linguistic growth and provide equitable learning opportunities for multilingual learners. Prioritizing space, time, and resources for these strategies ensures that learners are supported in ways that leverage their diverse strengths and needs. By integrating visual, tactile, auditory, and kinesthetic experiences into instruction, teachers can reduce barriers to learning.

WHAT TEACHERS SAY ABOUT MULTISENSORY SCAFFOLDING

A multisensory scaffolding approach is one of my favorite methods for supporting my English learners. This scaffolding approach is very important because students learn best when information is presented in multiple ways. Using manipulatives during a math lesson has been so helpful for my students. Physical objects help students develop a better understanding of number sense. You can also create multiple opportunities for students to practice and work with different quantities when using math manipulatives. As I work with my English learners, illustrations and pictures help build the bridge to comprehension and kickstart conversations. When reading a text where students might be unfamiliar with vocabulary words, the illustrations help them build meaning and understanding. While retelling a story, rather than re-reading the entire text, I will use a picture walk for my English learners to highlight the most important parts of the story. Additionally, the use of audio and video representations for my English learners has been very helpful in building awareness of context. Videos can increase motivation for different learners and the visual aspect supports students' ability to remember compared with simply listening to a text. I love to show BrainPOP Jr. videos to my students because they love Annie and Moby, and the visuals really help my English learners build comprehension.

—Nancy Weng, first grade bilingual teacher, Brooklyn, New York

WHY IS MULTISENSORY SCAFFOLDING AN IMPORTANT APPROACH TO STUDENT LEARNING?

Multisensory scaffolding is a key approach to student learning because it engages multiple senses, and thereby enhances comprehension, retention, and overall academic success. Moreover, this approach promotes active engagement, which is central to effective instruction and critical for sustained learning. When students interact with content using multiple sensory experiences—visual, auditory, tactile, and kinesthetic—they are more likely to stay focused and motivated, resulting in meaningful learning.

One of the key benefits of multisensory scaffolding is its alignment with how the brain processes information. Decades of neuroscience research have suggested that activating multiple neural pathways reinforces learning by creating stronger connections in the brain (Clark & Paivio, 1991; Dubinsky & Hamid, 2024). For example, pairing spoken language with visual cues, such as diagrams or videos, allows students to associate abstract concepts with concrete representations, making learning more accessible and meaningful. Similarly, incorporating hands-on activities or movement enables learners to physically engage with content, which is especially beneficial for kinesthetic preferences for learning.

Providing information that engages the senses in multiple ways is a fundamental aspect of this method. Macro-level multisensory methods, such as incorporating large muscle movements (e.g., using gestures or physical activities), allow students to actively participate and physically connect with learning tasks. Conversely, micro-level methods, which focus on small muscle movements (e.g., writing, manipulating objects, or tracing letters), help students internalize concepts on a detailed level. Combining these approaches with visual and auditory modalities ensures that all learners are supported effectively.

Gamified multisensory scaffolding activities offer another dimension to this strategy, making learning even more interactive and enjoyable. For instance, incorporating games that involve sound, visuals, and touch not only fosters engagement but also improves learning effectiveness and motivation. Learners in sensory-rich environments tend to develop stronger language and communication skills. Such environments promote retention and understanding through active involvement and enjoyment.

Multisensory scaffolding can transform learning for all students. It fosters an engaging, supportive educational environment and enhances cognitive processing. By incorporating multisensory methods for learning, teachers can be better equipped to build lessons that break down complex concepts into manageable and relatable parts, making abstract ideas more concrete and understandable. See Figure 5.2 for an example of how Courtney Gilpin, biology teacher, and Selvi Oyola, English language development teacher (now director of multilingual learners and equity), collaborate to attend to their students' content and language development while integrating sensory experiences.

FIGURE 5.2 • High School Biology Example of Using Small Manipulatives and Visuals

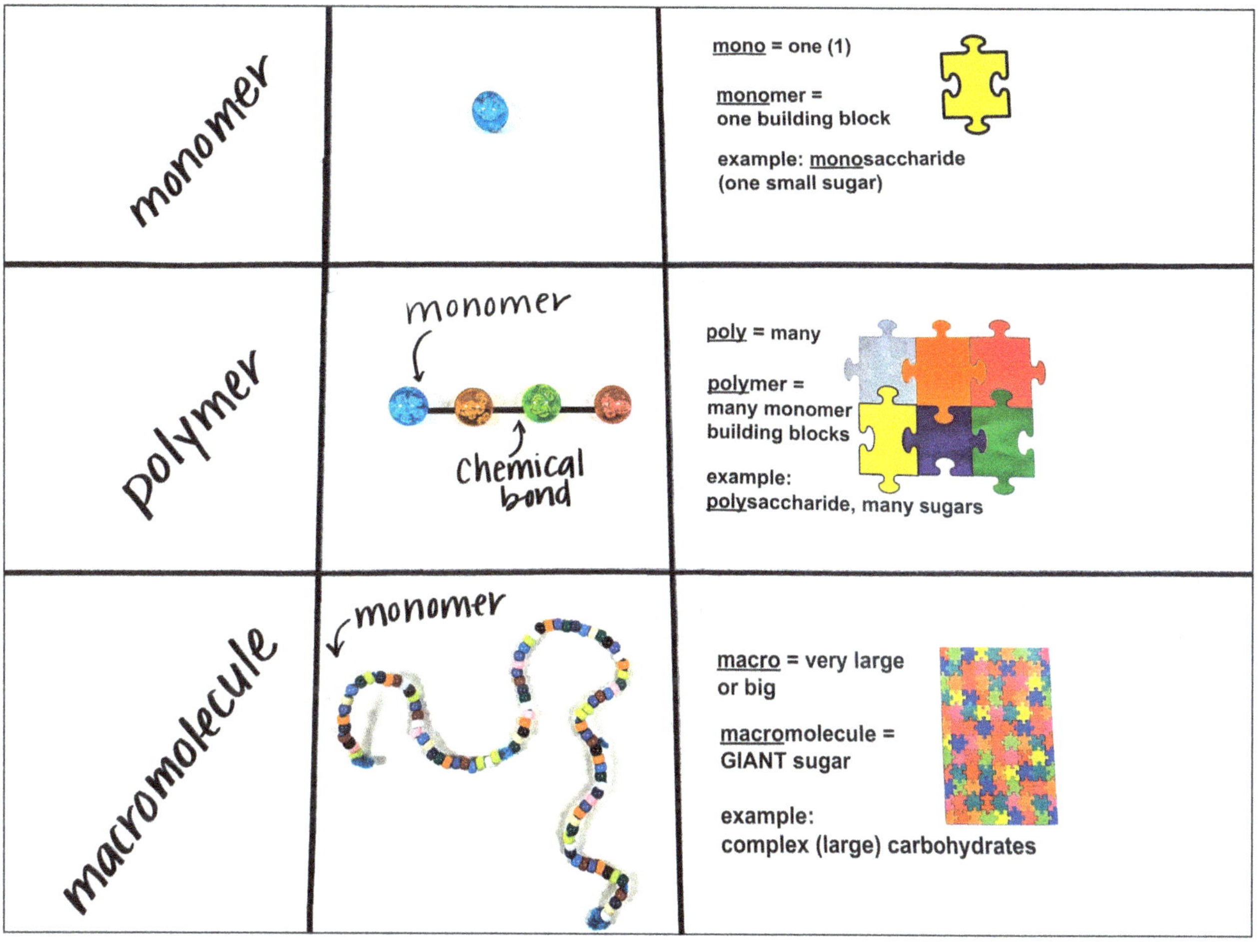

Source: Courtney Gilpin and Selvi Oyola. Used with permission.

HOW DOES MULTISENSORY SCAFFOLDING SPECIFICALLY RELATE TO MULTILINGUAL LEARNERS' NEEDS?

To address the unique challenges multilingual learners encounter developing their content knowledge alongside a new language, multisensory scaffolding provides engaging and accessible pathways for learning. By tapping into multiple senses through visual, auditory, tactile, and kinesthetic activities, this approach supports multilingual learners in making language and content more comprehensible, creating opportunities for meaningful learning experiences. Consider how learning new vocabulary—from foundational to academic—becomes clearer and more meaningful when words are paired with visual representations such as drawings, photographs, or videos. Think about how difficult it might be for a language learner to remember the pronunciation of new and uncommon words yet hearing them repeated and practicing them using audio recordings can enhance their pronunciation and confidence in using the language in real-world contexts. Moreover, tactile and kinesthetic activities, such as using math manipulatives, skywriting (using fingers in the air to write words), role-playing, or moving about the room to complete different tasks, allow multilingual to practice language and content interactively. These strategies provide immediate, concrete experiences that link language to meaning. All in all, engaging multiple senses can deepen understanding, reinforce retention, and encourage active participation, making the learning process both memorable and fun! See Table 5.1 for examples and benefits of multisensory scaffolding.

TABLE 5.1 ● Examples of Multisensory Scaffolding for Multilingual Learners

MULTISENSORY EXPERIENCES	STRATEGY EXAMPLES	BENEFITS FOR MULTILINGUAL LEARNERS
Visual	Images, anchor charts, graphic organizers, and videos	Builds language in meaningful context; supports content learning
Auditory	Songs, rhymes, chants, and recorded text	Enhances listening skills, pronunciation, fluency, and understanding of language patterns
Tactile	Base-ten blocks, 3D models, science experiments, and time capsule creation	Provides discovery learning to promote critical thinking, curiosity, creativity, and innovation
Kinesthetic	Historic event reenactment, mock trials, gallery walks, Total Physical Response (TPR), and scavenger hunts	Strengthens engagement and authentic language use promoting communication and collaboration in real-world contexts.

Multisensory scaffolding supports students at various stages of language proficiency. While students who have yet to acquire much fluency in English benefit from the inclusion of visual and hands-on tasks, more advanced-level students might be involved in discussion-based activities. It also supports students in developing their language skills alongside their content learning when they are engaged in real-world, sensory experiences. For the most part, the various nature of multisensory strategies addresses the many needs of multilingual learners by making learning accessible, interactive, meaningful, and memorable. It creates pathways for both language and content learning, ensuring that multilingual learners are supported to reach their full potential. See Figure 5.3 for a chant that Pushpanjali Sengupta, multilingual facilitator and heritage language coach at Bellevue Public Schools, Washington, codeveloped with her 4th-grade students, who were studying the impact of weathering on the environment.

FIGURE 5.3 ● Weathering Chant Poster

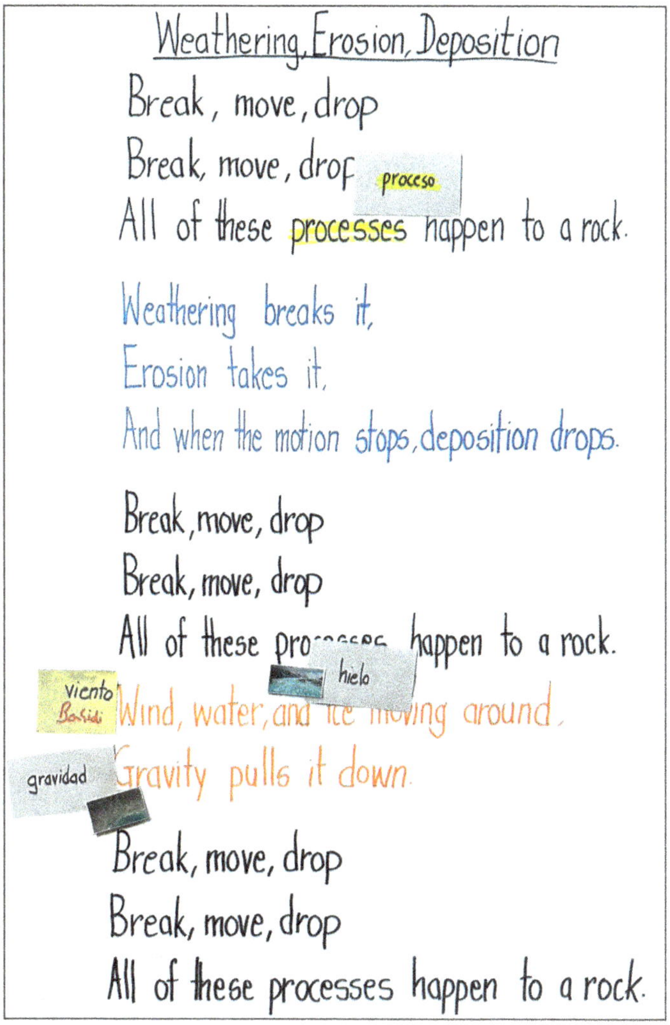

Source: Pushpanjali Sengupta. Used with permission.

FROM RESEARCH TO PRACTICE

There are various seminal research studies that support the use of multisensory scaffolding. Clark and Paivio (1991) were among the first to describe Dual Coding Theory (DCT) as a psychological theory that explains how the brain processes information through two separate systems: one for visual images and one for language. DCT indicates that these two systems work together to support various cognitive functions, including emotion, motor skills, and other areas of psychology. It also suggests that combining verbal and visual information enhances memory and understanding.

Mayer's (2005) and Sweller's (2010) research studies explore how different sensory experiences impact learning. Their findings indicate that presenting information through multiple sensory channels can enhance retention and problem-solving abilities, supporting the broader concept of multisensory learning.

(Continued)

(Continued)

One longitudinal study using control and experimental groups determined the effects of multisensory learning on academic performance (Prasannakumar, 2018). In this study, students were divided into control and experimental groups. The experimental group was taught using a multisensory integration approach, while the control group followed traditional methods. Results from the post-tests showed significant improvements in the experimental group's memory recall, memory recognition, visual retention, and imagery compared with the control group, suggesting that multisensory learning methods had a positive impact on memory and overall academic performance.

Reflect on the following:

How can visual and verbal information be effectively combined to support both language acquisition and content understanding for multilingual learners?

How can teachers design lessons that present information in manageable sensory formats to avoid overwhelming students while maximizing retention?

What methods can be implemented to measure the impact of multisensory learning?

____

____

____

____

GETTING STARTED WITH MULTISENSORY SCAFFOLDING

When considering the different aspects of multisensory scaffolding, a first step might be to create a print-rich classroom environment. Both elementary and secondary classrooms need to be filled with purposeful and accessible charts, graphs, timelines, images with labels, word walls, and so on, to support the comprehension and language development of multilingual learners.

Visual scaffolds are a cornerstone for teaching multilingual learners; they provide distinct reference points and offer context without lengthy verbal explanations. When students can visualize a concept, they can remember it more readily.

Simple ideas for using auditory scaffolding include reading aloud (along with echo reading and shared reading) and incorporating songs and chants to enhance access to complex language and to increase student language use.

Consider using meaningful oral repetition when teaching new vocabulary and ideas. Encourage students to chorally produce responses when appropriate to reinforce their understanding and use of language patterns.

Tactile learning often requires more preparation to either acquire or design and produce materials. Some activities, such as using everyday objects or simple materials, may involve minimal planning. However, it is often worth the extra effort it takes to incorporate these scaffolding strategies because they allow students to physically engage with abstract concepts in meaningful ways.

There are some quick and easy ways to start using kinesthetic activities that will get students out of their seats and moving. One general strategy requires students to stand up depending on their responses to a series of statements. For example, if students believed a statement were true, they would stand up, or if they thought it were false, they would remain seated. Students might be asked to answer yes/no questions in a similar way. Other ideas that have little preparation include acting out new vocabulary words, using body movements to remember new concepts, or playing games that require one person to ask a question and then toss an object (e.g., ball, bean bag) to a classmate who will have to answer it.

By integrating multisensory strategies into your teaching, you can make content more accessible, promote active learning, and support language development for multilingual learners.

Here are some general ideas to ensure these strategies are most effective:

- Consider how you might combine two or more techniques to complement one another and increase student engagement, such as combining visual, auditory, tactile, and/or kinesthetic ideas for learning in the same activity.
- Allow students to practice using the same or similar sensory techniques multiple times to build their autonomy, for example, creating word maps on large chart paper with colorful markers or arranging vocabulary words with magnetic tiles on a board.
- As with all scaffolding practices, adapt strategies to meet individual students' needs (remember that sometimes a strategy is a scaffold, and sometimes a strategy has to be scaffolded).
- Provide students opportunities to reflect on and share their learning; for instance, have them build a strategy chart in which they identify techniques that have been most helpful to them and add their reflections on the effectiveness of the strategy, thus building metacognitive awareness and autonomy (see Table 5.2 for a sample strategy chart).

TABLE 5.2 ● Multisensory Strategy Reflection Chart

STRATEGY	WAS THIS STRATEGY HELPFUL?	WHY WAS IT HELPFUL OR NOT? ADD YOUR REFLECTION ON THE STRATEGIES YOU USED IN THIS COLUMN.
Comic strip story summary	Yes/No	Visualizing to summarize the story: ____________________
Listening to a book while reading	Yes/No	Hearing the text to enhance your comprehension: ____________________
Using word tiles to create sentences	Yes/No	Manipulating word tile to help you write: ____________________
Using graphic organizer	Yes/No	Using a graphic organizer to connect ideas: ____________________
Creating a song or rap to remember terms	Yes/No	Using rhythm and rhyme to aid memory: ____________________
Watching a video clip	Yes/No	Visual/audio techniques for comprehension: ____________________
Acting out scenes from a story	Yes/No	Moving your body to comprehend better: ____________________

online resources — Available for download at https://companion.corwin.com/courses/NineDimensionsofScaffoldingforMLs

This chart should be adapted to include the strategies students are currently using. It can also be altered to incorporate more visuals or icons (such as smiley faces) for younger or less English proficient students. As with all other tools in this book, we invite you to adjust the complexity and grade-level appropriateness of the reflection prompts.

TEACHING PRACTICES

Multisensory scaffolding engages all learners because it leverages various sensory pathways to enhance engagement, understanding, retention, and application of what students have learned. In this section of the chapter, we will uncover three general multisensory practices. The first scaffolding practice combines visual and audio techniques, as both are essential in language acquisition, such as pairing written text with verbal explanations or audio recordings to reinforce comprehension and overall retention. Tactile techniques follow, incorporating hands-on learning tools such as manipulatives or realia, allowing learners to physically interact with physical objects to acquire vocabulary, content, and abstract concepts. Finally, we explore kinesthetic learning strategies, which involve movement and physical activity, connecting students to learning through action.

MULTISENSORY SCAFFOLDING PRACTICE #1: VISUAL AND AUDIO TECHNIQUES

Visual and auditory approaches to learning are essential for multilingual learners because they provide multiple pathways to access information. Visual aids, such as charts, images, and diagrams, help clarify complex concepts, while auditory elements, like narrated lessons or read-alouds, support language development. Together, these approaches bridge language gaps, allowing multilingual learners to engage with grade-level content through active participation in meaningful activities. Integrating these strategies can create a supportive environment where multilingual learners can thrive academically and build their confidence.

Multilingual learners often understand subject matter at a deeper level than their English proficiency might suggest. However, many of these students remain silent, particularly in general education classes, due to fear of not being able to express their ideas. Teachers often struggle with how to present rigorous, grade-level content to students who are still developing their language skills. To avoid student frustration—and sometimes their own—they may resort to segregating these learners, assigning them busy work, or relying heavily on language learning programs through interactive devices like tablets or Chromebooks. While these approaches may seem practical, they isolate students and limit their access to meaningful grade-level content.

Incorporating visual and auditory approaches to instruction can transform the classroom experience for multilingual learners, not only making content more accessible but also building their self-assurance and participation. Consider how:

- Videos with closed captioning expose learners to language in context, combining auditory input with written words to introduce new vocabulary and sentence structures
- Interactive whiteboards combine visuals, diagrams, and teacher narration to engage multiple senses and make complex concepts easier to grasp
- Text-based tools, such as voice typing, provide valuable support for multilingual learners, enabling them to express their ideas
- Online read-aloud books combine visual and auditory elements, allowing students to hear fluent reading while following along with text and pictures, strengthening their listening and reading skills

Just as important, visual and auditory supports benefit all students in the classroom, not just multilingual learners. They can enhance comprehension, reinforce learning, and create a more inclusive environment where every student feels able to contribute.

ADVANTAGES OF THIS APPROACH

The main advantages of using visual and auditory approaches, especially for multilingual learners, include increased comprehension, engagement, and language learning along with fostering students' sense of belonging due to their ability to participate alongside their peers. The abundance of images, videos, and songs available on the internet provides varied and dynamic ways to present information to students, making abstract concepts more tangible. Visual and audio platforms offer contextual clues that support students to uncover meaning without relying solely on spoken information from the teacher or text devoid of context. These resources not only make learning more accessible and interactive but also foster a deeper connection to the material, helping students feel more capable in their ability to engage in learning.

EXAMPLE #1: SKETCHNOTES

A sketchnote is a visual notetaking task which combines drawings, symbols, and color with written words to design a portrait of information. This approach takes notetaking to the next level, tapping into student creativity and fostering personalization by combining visual, auditory, and even tactile sensory domains to provide a cognitively engaging activity that enhances understanding and retention.

Sketch noting can help learners organize complex information. By representing ideas through images and words, students can make connections between concepts more explicit. Think about how students might be listening to a description of the water cycle and create a visual representation of the sun heating a body of water, causing evaporation and water vapor rising to form clouds. Consider how you might create a sketchnote along with students, using chart paper or a document camera, to further support entering and emerging multilingual learners to make abstract concepts more concrete and accessible.

Sketchnotes encourage active listening and engagement. As learners listen to content instruction, watch a video, or participate in discussions with their peers, they can summarize information either individually or in pairs via sketch noting. Through this process, students can uncover meaning and deepen their comprehension. It truly involves multilingual learners to actively learn alongside their English-fluent peers.

This approach to notetaking requires all students to think about the information being presented during a lesson and to focus on key ideas to complete the task in contrast to passively transcribing or copying notes. It is adaptable to various content areas for learning, such as:

- In social studies, creating timelines with words and drawings
- In English language arts, mapping out storylines, characters, themes, and relationships
- In math, sketching out a word problem
- In science, drawing steps in a process such as the life cycle of a plant

You can encourage the use of sketchnotes in various ways, such as modeling the technique during lessons, providing templates, or incorporating it into projects. Whether used individually or collaboratively, sketchnotes transform notetaking into an impactful learning experience that helps students process, remember, and apply information more effectively.

WHAT TEACHERS SAY ABOUT MULTISENSORY SCAFFOLDING

Mary Sue Ragsdale, a K-6 ELD teacher, models sketch noting and scaffolds this mode of expression for her students. See Figure 5.4 for what Mary describes as follows:

These sketchnotes were used in a 6th grade class during a Myths unit. Not only was the class made up of several language learners, but students who were visual learners and needed additional process time. This strategy became a foundation for building comprehension and giving students anchors for sharing and developing their analytical thinking, whether in fiction or non-fiction texts. Normally, when I am previewing a text, I assess the vocabulary, phrases, and sentence structures that may be the trickiest, along with what the most important events are—and I plan our sketchnotes around those first. Then, as we are sketching together, we decide on the most meaningful icons of pictures to represent our ideas. Sometimes, the kids have similar ideas to what I sketched when I prepared for the lesson, and sometimes, they have even better ideas, so we change the sketch! My goal with this strategy is to give them visual places to store pockets of thought that we can develop and return to. And . . . I've seen many positive outcomes from an approach like this to help kids tackle a tough text! It is naturally engaging and a great avenue for everyone to participate and build small wins.

FIGURE 5.4 ● Sketchnote Examples

Source: Mary Sue Ragsdale. Used with permission.

FROM RESEARCH TO PRACTICE

Sketchnotes as legitimate forms of meaning making are getting both researchers' and practitioners' attention. They have been scientifically defined as "a combination of language, image, graphs, mathematical symbolic notation, and other visual resources" (Fernández-Fontecha et al., 2020, p. 11), and have also been featured in online postings by several practitioners as powerful tools for active student engagement, self-expression, and joyful learning.

In a 2019 article, Terada tackles the question of why drawing is such a powerful memory tool as follows: "Unlike listening to a lecture or viewing an image—activities in which students passively absorb information—drawing is active. It forces students to grapple with what they're learning and reconstruct it in a way that makes sense to them" (para. 7). Similarly, in a blog entry, Valentina Gonzalez (2020), multilingual learner literacy expert, connects sketch noting to pre-writing, reading, listening, or vocabulary development. Among its many benefits, Ms. Gonzalez identifies how sketchnotes provide recall and memory enhancement, stress relief, and opportunities for creativity.

Reflect on the following:

How can visual tools like sketchnotes be used to promote active learning and deeper understanding? What roles do creativity and self-expression play in helping multilingual learners engage with and retain new information?

EXAMPLE #2: VIDEO VIEWING

Using videos can be an effective way to scaffold instruction for multilingual learners, offering unique opportunities to enhance learning through visual and audio perceptual modes. This approach involves introducing new concepts, language, and skills through a medium that offers support for students to engage cognitively and build comprehension of grade-level curriculum as well as be used as a springboard to practice verbal and written language. Presenting information via videos can bridge gaps in knowledge, cater to diverse learning needs, and offer students those "ah-ha" moments when spoken language may not be as meaningful as visual representations. Here are some effective strategies for using videos to scaffold learning for multilingual learners:

- *Preview and Pose Questions*: Before showing the video, activate students' prior knowledge by previewing key vocabulary and concepts. Pose guiding questions to focus their attention and encourage them to look for specific information as they watch.
- *Chunk Information Into Segments*: Break videos into shorter, manageable segments. To reinforce understanding, pause to ask questions, facilitate discussions, and turn and talks. Students might also use a template to jot down ideas before, during, and after the video (see sample template in Table 5.3).
- *Connect Audio With Written Words*: Use videos with captions to improve comprehension and support literacy learning.
- *Encourage Recreation*: Have students actively engage with the content by recreating what they watched. They can make their own videos, summarize the content in their own words orally, or express their understanding through written work.
- *Turn the Sound Off*: Challenge your students to watch a short, carefully selected video excerpt with the sound off. Depending on the content of the video, invite them to make educated guesses of what is being said, recreate a dialogue, or make predictions or other details about the context or content of the video.

These strategies make video-based learning interactive and meaningful, helping multilingual learners process and internalize new information effectively.

TABLE 5.3 ● Video Viewing Template

WATCH & WONDER: VIDEO VIEWING ACTIVITY
Name of video/topic:
What I know about this topic (before viewing):
Ideas from the video:
Visual notes and drawings (what I saw):
Words I need to know:
Questions I have:
The most important thing I learned:

online resources Available for download at https://companion.corwin.com/courses/NineDimensionsofScaffoldingforMLs

EXAMPLE #3: RECORDED TEXT

Digitally recorded text can support multilingual learners by providing them with accessible, repeated exposure to spoken language, allowing them to listen to standard pronunciation, intonation, and natural speech patterns while simultaneously reading the text, further aiding comprehension, language development, and student engagement. It is a versatile scaffolding tool that can provide access to more complex texts for multilingual learners. By providing students with access to both spoken and written language, recorded text accommodates diverse learning needs and strengthens students' ability to make connections between oral and written language.

In primary schools, the recorded text supports early literacy and foundational language skills. Teachers might record themselves reading a picture book aloud while displaying the corresponding text and illustrations on a screen or interactive whiteboard, allowing young learners to connect spoken words with print and visual images. Students can listen to these recordings repeatedly, practicing pronunciation and fluency either individually or in groups. There also is a plethora of picture book readings readily available via YouTube. Beyond the use of picture books, consider recording a set of step-by-step instructions for students to follow paired with visual aids such as labeled diagrams to be used at a learning center or station to help multilingual learners complete tasks independently.

In secondary schools, the recorded text supports more complex content and academic language. Teachers might provide a recording of a primary source document being read aloud, with key vocabulary highlighted on-screen and definitions provided. This dual-mode delivery helps multilingual learners to be less intimidated by complex language and text. Consider how students might listen to a chapter of a novel while following along with the printed text, bridging gaps in decoding skills or unfamiliar language. Recorded information, paired with slides that include visual summaries or graphic representations of information, can also enable multilingual learners to focus on key ideas without the stress of keeping up with notetaking.

Recorded text empowers multilingual learners by offering them access to content repeatedly, autonomy to pace their own learning, and opportunities to build their language and literacy skills. (Revisit Chapter 4 for more on multimodal scaffolding.)

KEEP THIS IN MIND

When using visual and audio techniques with multilingual learners, ensure that materials used are culturally relevant, age-appropriate, and aligned with grade-level curriculum. Visual aids should be clear and explicitly connected to the content being presented, and audio recordings should be paced appropriately according to students' facility with spoken English. A key factor in using these scaffolding tools is to provide opportunities for students to interact with the language and content being presented.

MULTISENSORY SCAFFOLDING PRACTICE #2: TACTILE TECHNIQUES

Tactile learning techniques offer an inclusive and engaging approach to learning that removes common barriers for students so that they may more fully participate. For students who have yet to gain fluency in English or are still developing confidence in their overall language skills, traditional pencil-and-paper class activities can be intimidating. They can heighten stress and discourage students from taking risks, especially for those who are reluctant to write despite being confident speakers. In contrast, tactile strategies are alternative ways of learning that emphasize critical and creative thinking as well as social interaction. Many of these approaches involve manipulating preprinted materials or working with real objects (also referred to as realia), allowing students to focus on building content knowledge and vocabulary with minimal, if any, written output. For multilingual learners, this type of learning is more accessible and supports their full participation in general education classes.

Tactile learning engages students cognitively by encouraging them to process and organize information in active, meaningful ways. By manipulating materials, students analyze, categorize, and connect ideas, fostering deeper comprehension. This approach shifts the focus from passively receiving information to actively engaging with it to figure things out, further enhancing their problem-solving skills.

Teamwork and social interaction are often essential components of tactile learning. Collaborative tasks such as constructing models, categorizing items, and interactive sentence building encourage students to discuss their thinking and share ideas, promoting oral language practice in a low-stakes environment. In this way, tactile learning makes abstract ideas more concrete and ensures more equitable learning experiences for multilingual learners.

ADVANTAGES OF THIS APPROACH

Tactile learning activates multisensory engagement, which supports cognitive processing by making abstract concepts more concrete. Handling and manipulating materials provide physical interaction with content that helps students explore and internalize key concepts in new ways. For multilingual learners, this hands-on approach reduces the linguistic load while enabling them to access content knowledge and engage fully. These activities often scaffold the cognitive demands of tasks, making them accessible while still intellectually challenging. By integrating tactile strategies, educators create inclusive environments that support cognitive engagement and help students construct meaning through active, purposeful experiences. See Figure 5.5 for a collection of rocks that help students closely examine and distinguish among the three main types of rocks based on how they were formed (igneous rocks—formed when lava cools and solidifies; sedimentary rocks—formed from preexisting rocks and organized materials; and metamorphic rocks—formed under conditions of high heat or pressure).

FIGURE 5.5 ● Rock Collection for Student Classification

EXAMPLE #1: MAKING WORDS

This activity requires students to manipulate letter cards as directed to spell new words. It is highly engaging and supports students to develop a better sense of spelling patterns while demystifying the process. Unlike traditional methods that focus on copying word lists for spelling practice, this strategy actively engages students in analyzing and applying word family patterns, fostering long-term success with accurate spelling.

Using a specific set of small letter cards for the lesson, students create words in a step-by-step fashion as directed. The teacher uses a corresponding set of large letter cards displayed on a card chart at the front of the class or manipulates a virtual set of cards on an interactive whiteboard. The lesson generally begins with students forming two- and three-letter words and progresses to longer words. Students are given time to spell each word independently or in pairs while the teacher circulates to assess their progress. Afterward, one student is invited to display the word for the class using the teacher's set of cards.

The activity concludes with students attempting to form a "secret word" by using all the provided letters. To further scaffold this task for multilingual learners, offer clues, such as the number of letters in the word, and emphasize the number of letters to change or which letters to remove or add to transform one word into another. Consider preparing and displaying cards that contain completed words or add words to a list as they are created. An example of a lesson on making words can be found in Figure 5.6.

FIGURE 5.6 ● Making Words Lesson

Distribute the following letters to each student: *a, a, e, c, k, n, p, s.* Ask students to follow these directions.

1. Take two letters and make the word *an.*
2. Add one letter and make the word *can.*
3. Don't change any letters, and don't take any away. Just add one letter and make the word *cans.*
4. Change one letter and turn cans into *caps.*
5. Change one letter and turn *caps* into *naps.*
6. Don't change any letters, and don't take any away. Add one letter and make the word *snaps.*
7. Now, take away all the letters, and let's start again.
8. Take three letters and make the word *can.*
9. Add one more letter to *can* and make the word *cane.*
10. Add one more letter to *cane* and make the word *canes.*
11. Take away the middle letter in *canes* and add one letter to make the word *cakes.*
12. Now, use all the letters to make the secret word (*pancakes*).

(Adapted from Dove & Honigsfeld, 2013).

EXAMPLE #2 LIST-GROUP-LABEL

The List-Group-Label strategy combines brainstorming with semantic mapping to engage students' prior knowledge, expand their vocabulary, and help them understand relationships between groups of words. In this activity, students brainstorm a list of words related to a topic within a teacher-set time frame. They then use critical thinking skills to organize the words into categories they identify and create labels or titles for each group. Typically, this strategy is conducted in pairs, trios, or small groups and can be applied before, during, or after reading a text. Alternatively, lists can be generated as a whole class, with students collaborating to complete the categorization and labeling process.

To differentiate instruction, teachers can modify the strategy in these ways:

- *Word Sorts*: Teachers provide printed lists of words alongside titled categories. Students, working with a partner, cut out the words and sort them into the predefined categories (see Figure 5.7 for an example).

FIGURE 5.7 • American Revolution Word Sort

- *Photo Sorts*: Instead of words, students are given a small collection of photos (sourced, for example, from Google Images) to group and categorize. Labels for the categories can be either teacher-provided or student-created.

EXAMPLE #3: FOLDABLES

Foldables, introduced by Dinah Zike in 1992, are versatile graphic organizers designed to help students identify and organize information in an engaging, hands-on manner. These two- or three-dimensional notes are created by folding standard 8 × 10 sheets of plain paper into various configurations, making them an excellent resource for visually representing story elements or other types of content. Their tactile and creative format often motivates even the most reluctant learners to participate actively, offering a fun and approachable way to engage with writing and organizing ideas.

This approach to writing can be used across disciplines and tailored to suit a wide range of learning objectives and student needs. Foldables can be used to create flip books, layered booklets, accordion-style organizers, or even pyramid-shaped commentaries (see Figure 5.8 for an example). Each configuration supports different types of information organization, from sequencing events in a story, comparing and contrasting concepts, or summarizing key points from a story, lesson, or unit of study.

KEEP THIS IN MIND

When considering tactile approaches for learning, remember that students often spend a significant amount of time on tablets, Chromebooks, and such, and they may need practice with working in pairs or teams to complete certain tasks. Tactile activities provide a hands-on alternative to digital tools that can stimulate the senses in unique ways. Purposeful tactile tasks should connect to learning objectives and incorporate collaboration and problem solving while reducing the passive nature of screen-based learning. These activities cater to diverse needs, ensuring inclusivity and accessibility. Meaningful tactile tasks can foster dynamic, screen-free engagement, helping students process and apply knowledge in enriching and even playful ways.

FIGURE 5.8 ● Story Elements Foldable

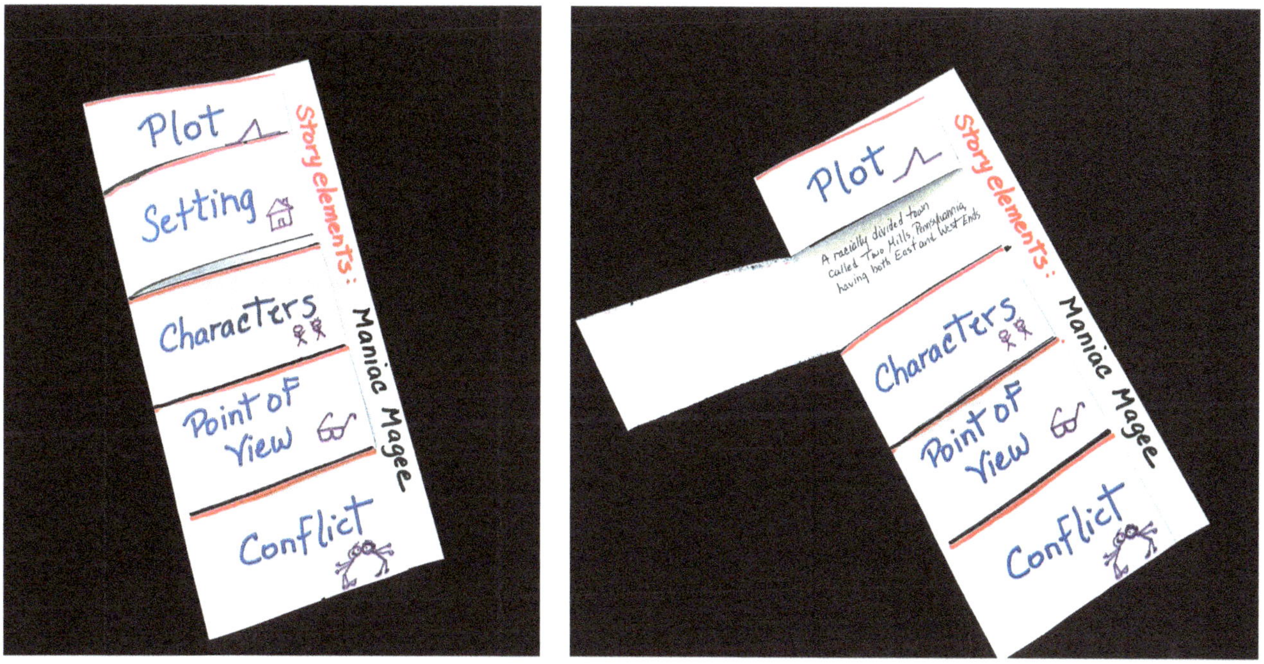

MULTISENSORY SCAFFOLDING PRACTICE #3: KINESTHETIC TECHNIQUES

Movement is a powerful tool for learning, as it not only improves physical engagement but also strengthens cognitive connections. For multilingual learners, kinesthetic techniques make language learning more interactive and accessible. As students physically embody concepts, their understandings are reinforced, and they are better able to retain new information through movement.

The development of muscle memory is a significant advantage of kinesthetic learning. Tracing letters, using hand gestures to associate words with meanings, or role-playing scenarios are all tasks that can help students anchor new knowledge in the brain. These approaches enable students to internalize language structures and vocabulary through repetition and action, improving comprehension and recall. When students physically engage with content, such as acting out verbs or participating in movement-based language games, they are more likely to remember and apply what they have learned.

Kinesthetic activities also increase attention and focus, especially for students who may find traditional classroom tasks less engaging.

Activities like performing skits, movement games, and gallery walks in which students move about the room to examine different images, objects, and materials require active participation, drawing students into the learning process. These approaches reduce reliance on passive learning in which students sit and listen to a great deal of teacher talk. Instead, they encourage students to collaborate, examine, decipher, explain, and so on, fostering skills essential for language learning and academic success.

Incorporating movement into instruction provides students with a dynamic way to engage with content while fostering deeper learning and retention. Physical activities stimulate the brain by requiring students to engage actively with their environment. For multilingual learners, movement is particularly beneficial because it reduces the reliance on written or spoken language alone, making language acquisition more tangible and accessible. Movement also plays a vital role in increasing student attention and maintaining focus. Activities that require physical engagement help learners reset their energy and remain attentive during lessons. See Figure 5.9 for how Jennifer Edwards uses movement in her high school ELD class to review math concepts.

FIGURE 5.9 ● Movements Enhance Muscle Memory

Source: Jennifer Edwards. Used with permission.

ADVANTAGES OF THIS APPROACH

Much like visual, auditory, and tactile techniques, kinesthetic approaches to learning provide multisensory reinforcement, enabling learners to process information in ways that support deeper comprehension and retention. These techniques promote inclusivity, which is critical to the success of multilingual learners because they allow all students to fully participate in learning activities in general education classes as well as demonstrate their understanding without relying solely on language. These techniques provide opportunities for personal expression, allowing multilingual learners to connect with content meaningfully.

WHAT TEACHERS SAY ABOUT MULTISENSORY SCAFFOLDING

We make up hand motions for our vocabulary! It is so much fun; the kids love it (and so do I). For example, we recently read a book on friendship, Leon and Bob (James, 1997). The four vocabulary words we focused on were rushed, army, halfway, and waved. For rushed, we pretended to run in place; for army, we did a salute gesture; for halfway, we gestured small with our thumb and index finger; and for waved, we waved. As I read the text, the students were provided with visual vocabulary cards for each vocabulary word, and whenever they heard one of the four words, they would do a signal with their middle and index fingers showing a "V," and they say, "SUPER VOCABULARY!" and gesture for the vocabulary word they heard while saying the name. For example, if they heard rushed, they would hold up their finger "V" and say, "super vocabulary," followed by saying "rushed" with the gesture of running in place.

—Kristina Jackson, ENL & special education dual certified teacher, Stony Point Elementary School, North Rockland Central School District, New York

EXAMPLE #1 ROLE PLAYING

Role-plays are versatile instructional tools that can be tailored to suit a variety of learning objectives. One engaging approach to role-playing is called *Act It Out*, which combines physical movement with language exploration to help students better understand nuanced vocabulary and concepts. To help multilingual learners grasp subtle differences in meaning, it's important to make these nuances tangible and visible. Using kinesthetic activities such as acting out word meanings, playing charades, or engaging in pantomime can make shades of meaning more explicit and memorable. These interactive methods not only reinforce vocabulary but also enhance comprehension in a fun and engaging way.

To implement a pantomime activity, prepare a set of cards with words that vary in shades of meaning (e.g., synonyms for verbs like "run" such as "dash," "jog," and "sprint"). Divide the class into teams. One team selects a card, discusses the word's meaning, and chooses a team member to act it out. The other teams take turns guessing the word being pantomimed.

Another way to plan a role-playing activity is through Reader's Theater, a scaffolding strategy that transforms storytelling into an interactive learning experience. Reader's Theater engages reluctant readers and multilingual learners by providing them with story scripts to read and perform in small groups, enhancing their reading fluency in a low-anxiety activity. Unlike traditional plays, students do not memorize their lines; instead, they read directly from their scripts, using minimal props and costumes to enhance their performances.

To introduce Reader's Theater, follow these steps:

- Choose an age- and grade-appropriate script or create your own using one of your students' favorite storybooks.
- Either duplicate the script and distribute copies or provide the script for students on electronic tablets.
- Read the script aloud to the class and then have students read along with you chorally.
- Divide the class in half, assigning each group alternating character parts to read aloud.
- Further divide students into small groups, assigning individual roles for practice and rehearsal.
- Once prepared, invite students to perform for the class. For a broader audience, teachers might invite other classes or parents to watch a polished performance.

Reader's Theater builds fluency, pronunciation, intonation, and expressiveness. As students become comfortable with the format, assign different scripts to each small group and encourage frequent practice. Scripts can also be adapted to accommodate varying reading levels, ensuring all students can participate meaningfully. For advanced activities, students may even write their own scripts. Online resources provide numerous Reader's Theater scripts, and recorded performances on platforms like YouTube can serve as examples or inspiration. This approach not only strengthens reading skills but also boosts confidence and fosters creativity in an engaging, inclusive setting. For more on Reader's Theater, see Chapter 9.

EXAMPLE #2 GALLERY WALKS AND CAROUSEL

A Gallery Walk combines kinesthetic learning with peer collaboration, creating a suitable way for multilingual learners to explore and reflect on a topic. To implement this strategy, prepare five or six exhibits related to a topic under study and place them around the classroom on walls or tables. These exhibits can include a mix of texts and visuals, such as short poems, song lyrics, proverbs, quotes, images with or without text, photographs, cartoons, charts, and graphs. Students, initially working in pairs or small teams, and later individually, move around the room, examining at least three exhibits of their choice.

As students engage with each exhibit, they complete a scaffolded gallery-response sheet designed to guide their reflections and encourage connections to personal experiences or prior knowledge (see an example of a Gallery Response Sheet in Figure 5.10). This reflective process promotes critical thinking and helps students synthesize the material. Gallery Walks are particularly effective for multilingual learners, as the combination of visuals and varied text types supports comprehension and makes abstract concepts more concrete.

FIGURE 5.10 • Gallery Walk Response Sheet

Name______________________________ **Date**________________________   Directions: Visit each station in the gallery walk. Read, observe, or examine the material presented. Respond to the questions in the spaces provided below.
Station 1____________________________   *What did you learn at this station? What stood out to you? Why?*

(Continued)

(Continued)

Station 2__________________________ *What did you learn at this station? How does it connect with something you already know?*
Station 3__________________________ *What did you learn at this station? What questions does this station make you think about?*
Station 4__________________________ *What did you learn at this station? How might this information be useful or important?*
Reflection *What is one thing you found most interesting during the gallery walk? Why?*

online resources Available for download at https://companion.corwin.com/courses/NineDimensionsofScaffoldingforMLs

Building on the interactive nature of the Gallery Walk, the Carousel strategy emphasizes team collaboration and brainstorming. In this approach, large sheets of paper are placed around the room, each labeled with a question or topic related to the lesson. Divide the class into small groups, assigning each group to a starting station. Students discuss the prompt at their station and write their ideas, answers, or reflections on the paper. After a set time, groups rotate to the next station, where they add to or respond to the previous group's contributions. This continues until all groups have visited each station. The Carousel encourages active participation, reinforces prior knowledge, and fosters collective learning. Figure 5.11 illustrates a Carousel activity where teams of students analyze and discuss former students' writing posted around the classroom to evaluate the accuracy of their claims and the strength of their supporting evidence. Both Gallery Walks and Carousels are adaptable across subjects, making them versatile tools for engaging students in meaningful exploration and dialogue.

FIGURE 5.11 • Carousel Activity

EXAMPLE #3: "ON YOUR FEET" DISCUSSIONS

When students are asked to move about the classroom to engage in discussions rather than remaining seated at their desks, their level of participation tends to increase. Kinesthetic activities are essential for elementary-age children, as passive experiences tend to lead to disengagement as well as having little lasting impact on learning. They are equally critical for secondary school learners, as physical engagement can reenergize students and promote deeper cognitive connections to the material. The strategies that follow are research-based and pioneered by Kagan and Kagan (2015), who designed them to promote cooperative learning and active student engagement. They are simple yet powerful examples of "on your feet" discussions that enhance participation and can influence learning outcomes. For multilingual learners, incorporating these strategies into learning fosters peer collaboration, deeper comprehension, and ideal opportunities to practice language skills, making learning meaningful, memorable, and enjoyable.

Four Corners. This strategy assigns a specific category or label to each corner of the classroom, tailored to grade level, curriculum, and learning objectives. For younger students, the corners might represent the four seasons, supporting an activity where students select a season based on guided questions or prompts, whereas older students might encounter character names from a story or opinion-based options like Agree, Strongly Agree, Disagree, or Strongly Disagree.

To prepare for this interactive activity, students first complete an individual task that prompts them to reflect or analyze. Examples include:

- For Early Elementary Grades: Students are given cards showing different types of food items, such as ice cream, soup, watermelon, and hot chocolate. They decide which season the food is most associated with and move to the corner labeled for that season.
- For Story Discussions (All Grades): Students are given a scenario or a specific event from a story, such as "helped a friend in need" or "solved a problem creatively." They determine which character from the story matches the description and move to the corner labeled with the corresponding character's name.
- For Opinion-Based Topics (Upper Grades): Corners are labeled with Strongly Agree, Agree, Disagree, or Strongly Disagree. The teacher presents a statement such as *"Homework should be optional for students,"* and students move to the corner that reflects their opinion on the topic.

Once students are in their chosen corners, they engage in group discussions about their choices. Using sentence frames, guiding prompts, or modeled responses, they share their reasoning and discuss their choices with peers.

Inside Outside Circle. To begin, each student creates a set of cards with a question related to the topic on one side and key points or answers on the other. For students who require additional support, partially completed cards or guided notes should be provided. The class is then split into two equal groups. One group forms an inner circle, standing with their backs to the center, while the other group forms an outer circle, facing inward toward a partner in the inner circle. Each pair (one inner-circle and one outer-circle student) works together using the cards to guide their discussions. The inner-circle students begin first by posing a question from their cards to their paired outer-circle partners who are expected to respond. They then switch roles to ensure mutual participation.

After a set time, the teacher signals the outer-circle students to shift one position to the right, creating new pairs. The process continues, with each round providing fresh opportunities for interaction and engagement. This strategy can be scaffolded further by having students in the outer circle work in teams to answer inner-circle partner questions. In this way, multilingual learners might be supported by other students who have more fluency in English as well as speak their partner's home language.

Line Up and Fold. This strategy is similar to *Inside-Outside Circle,* but the activity is conducted in a straight line instead of a circle. To begin, have students organize themselves into a single line according to a specific order, such as by the month and day of their birthday, the alphabetical order of their names, or using cards with content-related information to arrange themselves in a logical sequence. Once the line is complete, ask the student at one end to walk to the opposite end, followed by the others, so the line "folds" into two, creating pairs with students facing one another.

To guide their interaction, students can use cards with questions or prompts or other material according to the directions of the teacher to prompt their discussions. The students on one side of the folded line start by asking a question or sharing information, while their partners listen and/or respond. Afterward, roles are reversed so both students actively contribute to the exchange.

After a set time, one side of the line is signaled to shift by a few positions while the other side remains stationary, forming new pairs. This process repeats, allowing students to engage with multiple peers while discussing the assigned topic.

Stand Up, Hand Up, Pair Up. Start this activity by asking students to complete a task related to a literacy or content-based topic. Next, direct students to follow these steps:

1. Stand up, holding a card or notes with your prepared material.
2. Raise your hand and look around the room for a partner.
3. Choose a partner from a different table or group, someone you do not regularly talk with.

Once students have paired up, they discuss the prepared topic using their notes or cards. After finishing their discussion with one partner, students raise their hands again to signal they are ready to find a new partner. They then pair up with a different classmate and repeat the process. This continues for several rounds, allowing students to engage in discussions with multiple peers.

KEEP THIS IN MIND

When using "on your feet" discussions, consider if there is enough room for students to move around safely and comfortably. Rearrange desks or other furniture as needed to create open spaces for the activity. Ensure there is sufficient time for each round of discussions to keep the activity engaging and focused. Remember to offer sentence starters, word banks, or guiding questions to help multilingual learners participate confidently as well as demonstrate each new strategy to reduce confusion.

WHAT TEACHERS SAY ABOUT MULTISENSORY SCAFFOLDING

To illustrate how I use multisensory scaffolding in teaching English learners, I will highlight specific strategies to teach the reading skill of cause and effect. I also use the Read-Write-Talk Cycle, which integrates reading, writing, and discussion to increase comprehension and support language learning to develop the four modalities of listening, speaking, reading, and writing.

I engage English learners through multisensory scaffolding techniques incorporating many visuals, charts, songs, and videos. I start by introducing the Cause-and-Effect song set to the tune of the Addams Family theme and available on YouTube. Students follow along with the printed lyrics displayed in the video and clap at designated intervals, creating a fun and interactive learning experience. Next, I frontload vocabulary and share words that signal cause and effect, e.g., since, due to, on account of = cause; therefore, consequently, as a result = effect. I demonstrate cause and effect using bubble gum—blowing a bubble (cause) and the bubble bursting (effect). As I offer additional examples displayed on a slide deck, students engage by giving a thumbs up or down in response to the questions I ask. They then explain their answers, identifying whether each example represents a cause-and-effect scenario.

I demonstrate how to use the T-Chart graphic organizer to note cause and effect occurrences (see Figure 5.12).
They are also given opportunities to match cause and effect sentences during guided practice. Next, I use the Read-Write-Talk-Cycle. My English learners read a short selection on what plants need to grow. They then jot down some cause-and-effect ideas from the reading on a T-Chart and then turn and talk to a partner to share some of their ideas. Finally, students are invited to make green slime and answer questions following the activity in writing, such as What causes the slime to be green? and What is the effect of adding water to the cornstarch? Using multisensory strategies is very important for our English learners!

—Rosemary Zavaglia Rutigliano, ENL teacher, Brooklyn, New York

FIGURE 5.12 • Cause and Effect T-Chart Slide

Some causes have only one effect, but some have more than one effect. In our example below the rain caused three effects.

CAUSE	EFFECT
It rains very hard all day.	There are puddles on the ground.
It rains, and I go out.	I get all wet.
It is raining.	People stay inside.

INDEPENDENT LEARNING STRATEGIES

Students easily incorporate and adapt multisensory scaffolding strategies for independent learning. Color-coding and highlighting key ideas or themes in notes or readings can help students categorize and prioritize information effectively. Using texts and materials that are read aloud can support content and language learning and reinforces comprehension. Tactile strategies, such as using flashcards, are easily created with minimal materials, provide hands-on exploration, and are particularly effective for remembering vocabulary or new information. Students can also be taught how to break down content into smaller chunks of information and review each segment while incorporating some type of movement or sound. Sketching and drawing to represent ideas or summarize information are also strategies that can carry over from the classroom to use independently. These strategies can empower students to personalize their learning, remain actively engaged, and take ownership of their study process.

SUMMARY

This chapter emphasizes the importance of engaging multiple senses in learning, particularly for multilingual learners. Sensory-rich instruction—including visual, auditory, tactile, and kinesthetic techniques—supports students to deepen cognitive connections, improve memory, and make abstract concepts tangible. Multisensory scaffolding creates access points to grade-level curriculum and academic language. It fosters inclusivity and active engagement, which are critical for multilingual learners. Strategies that scaffold learning like visual aids, manipulatives, auditory supports, and movement-based activities, provide multilingual learners with a wide range of pathways to understand and retain content. These approaches can accommodate individual learning needs and reduce students' feelings of being overwhelmed. By implementing multisensory scaffolding thoughtfully, all teachers can create dynamic, inclusive classrooms that support language, literacy, and content learning.

Questions

1. How do multisensory scaffolding approaches benefit multilingual learners in accessing grade-level curriculum and academic language?
2. How can teachers use visual aids (e.g., diagrams, charts) alongside verbal instructions to reinforce new language concepts and content knowledge?
3. What strategies can be used to incorporate multiple sensory modalities?
4. How can educators track the effects of multisensory learning in their own classrooms?

CHAPTER 6

Graphic Scaffolding

> *"Graphic organizers scaffold learning on the back-end when students must construct linkages about the relationships between the concepts they have just learned or encountered in the learning experience or task."*
> *–Fisher, Frey, & Almarode, 2023, para. 8*

Graphic scaffolding transforms traditional instruction into a visually engaging and structured learning approach that makes complex academic content accessible to all students, particularly multilingual learners. Unlike traditional teaching methods that rely heavily on verbal instruction, graphic scaffolding creates multiple pathways for students to understand new content through carefully designed visual tools that make abstract concepts more accessible and help students organize their thinking in new ways. This chapter explores how graphic scaffolding enhances classroom instruction by providing strategic support for all learners, with particular attention to how these tools address the unique needs of multilingual students working to access academic content and develop language and literacy skills.

Graphic scaffolds are powerful strategies that help students to organize and retain information, link concepts together, and think critically and creatively about their learning in all content areas (Francis, 2022). Implementing them for learning goes beyond simple visual aids by creating systematic frameworks or organizers that guide students through the process of understanding, connecting, and applying new concepts. For example, when studying a literary text, students might progress from using a character trait web with prewritten vocabulary to creating their own analysis diagrams that demonstrate a deeper understanding of character development. Next, they may capture key events on a plot diagram, and then they may summarize their understanding of the text using a story elements graphic organizer. These visual tools serve as both learning supports and bridges to more complex thinking, allowing students to build on their existing knowledge while developing new academic skills.

Providing graphic scaffolds at every stage of a lesson, gives students the structures they need to organize, retain, and process information:

- When you begin a lesson with graphic scaffolds, you can activate students' prior knowledge, establish clear learning objectives, create a framework for organizing new information, and help students anticipate the lesson's key concepts and their relationships.
- When you incorporate graphic scaffolds within a lesson, you can support active engagement with new content, guide students in organizing incoming information, help them make connections between concepts, and provide structured opportunities for processing and understanding key ideas.
- When you include graphic scaffolds while you are teaching, you can make abstract concepts concrete and visual, helping students see relationships between ideas and transform complex information into manageable, structured representations.
- When you add graphic organizers to the end of a lesson, you can help students synthesize key learning points, review essential concepts, consolidate their understanding, create a visual summary that can serve as a study tool for future reference, and even assess their learning.

Providing graphic scaffolds across all language domains supports students with strategic access points to improve overall comprehension and communication skills:

- In reading, graphic scaffolds help students analyze text structure and organization, identify main ideas and supporting details, and track narrative development and genre features.
- In writing, graphic scaffolds support students to develop clear plans and outlines, organize their ideas logically and sequentially, visualize the structure of their composition, and transform brainstormed concepts into coherent written arguments or narratives.
- In speaking, graphic scaffolds guide students to map out key talking points, sequence ideas logically, maintain fluency through visual cues, and construct well-organized oral presentations with clear transitions between main ideas.
- In listening, graphic scaffolds provide students with ways to focus on key information, capture important details systematically, recognize organizational patterns in spoken content, and visualize relationships between concepts as they process auditory information.

By virtue of graphic scaffolds being visual in nature, they support students both in accessing information and representing their own understanding and ideas visually.

The effectiveness of graphic scaffolds stems from their ability to support multilingual learners at different stages of language development and content mastery, acting as flexible scaffolds that can be adapted to meet varying student needs. By offering a variety of graphic organizers, you can accommodate different learning preferences, give students options to process information in ways that work best for them, and develop their flexibility in organizing and representing knowledge across various formats. An intentional approach to using graphic organizers helps students develop both cognitive flexibility and deeper content understanding as well as multimodal ways of self-expression. (Look back at Chapter 4 for more on multimodal scaffolding.)

WHAT TEACHERS SAY ABOUT GRAPHIC SCAFFOLDING

I use graphic scaffolds frequently. They help my students better understand abstract concepts by providing concrete examples and breaking down topics into smaller parts they understand.

—James Ridgely, English for speakers of other languages (ESOL) teacher, Mattituck, New York

WHO IS IT FOR?

Graphic scaffolding is a versatile instructional approach that benefits learners across all grade levels and abilities. While particularly effective for multilingual learners and students with learning differences, these visual tools support all students in organizing their thoughts, processing new information, and demonstrating their understanding. From elementary students beginning to grasp basic concepts to secondary students who tackle more complex academic tasks, graphic scaffolding provides a flexible framework that can be adapted to meet diverse learning needs and objectives.

You might find graphic scaffolding especially valuable when planning and implementing tiered, differentiated instruction, as these tools can be modified in complexity and support level to more closely respond to individual student needs. For multilingual learners at earlier stages of their language development, highly structured organizers with clear prompts and partial completion can build greater confidence and success. As students develop their language proficiency, you can gradually reduce the level of support, encouraging more independent thinking and organization of content. Graphic scaffolds easily lend themselves to becoming part of lifelong, self-directed study skills and learning tools.

HOW IS GRAPHIC SCAFFOLDING USED ACROSS PROGRAM MODELS?

Graphic scaffolding actively engages students throughout the learning process in a variety of classroom and virtual settings, including general education, integrated co-taught, stand-alone English language development (ELD), and self-contained special education classes as follows:

In *general education classes*, graphic scaffolds serve as comprehensive support tools that address multiple elements of learning. They can be adjusted through strategically designed templates with integrated language support that help multilingual learners develop critical thinking skills through structured activities such as comparative analyses and sequential thinking tasks. Consider how you might introduce concepts using partially completed organizers for note-taking or structured comparison matrices, giving multilingual learners the framework needed to organize their thoughts and demonstrate understanding. Through careful observation and assessment, teachers can identify when to increase support or fade scaffolding by strategically adjusting elements within graphic organizers to support students developing language proficiency and content knowledge. This flexible approach allows for differentiation by providing multiple versions with varying levels of support, allowing students to select tools that best enable their efforts while working toward shared academic goals.

In *integrated, co-taught classes*, graphic scaffolds leverage the distinct expertise of content teachers and ELD specialists to support diverse learners. Adjusting the level of graphic support can become particularly dynamic as teachers collaborate to create differentiated versions of organizers while maintaining rigorous content expectations. Content teachers identify key academic concepts while ELD specialists ensure appropriate language supports are embedded within descriptive, sequential, comparative, and causal thinking tasks. In co-taught settings, two (or more) teachers actively monitor and adjust the implementation of scaffolds. Through careful co-planning, collaborating teachers create targeted scaffolds for different purposes—from planning templates with integrated language supports to assessment tools that allow students to demonstrate understanding in multiple ways. This collaborative approach enables real-time support and adaptation, with one teacher leading instruction while the other monitors student engagement with the scaffolds, gathering data about effectiveness and providing targeted assistance. The presence of two (or more) teachers facilitates a dynamic use of resources, ensuring that graphic scaffolds remain responsive to both content and language development needs across all learners.

In *stand-alone ELD* classes, graphic scaffolds are strategically implemented across multiple elements to support intensive language development alongside academic growth. ELD teachers carefully calibrate scaffolds to align with students' English proficiency levels while maintaining high academic expectations. Attention is paid to how graphic support can enhance learning foundational language skills and key language functions for academic tasks while embedding specific vocabulary and grammatical structures into language-based learning activities. Teachers design graphic scaffolds that serve multiple purposes—from planning templates that guide academic discourse to assessment tools that help students demonstrate understanding while developing English proficiency. This focused approach ensures that students not only master essential language skills but also develop transferable strategies for success across content areas. Through careful attention to these elements, teachers can gradually release support as students gain confidence and independence, helping them build both the linguistic and academic skills needed for success.

In *self-contained special education classes*, graphic scaffolds are implemented to address both language development and specific learning needs outlined in students' individual education plans (IEPs). The instructional purpose takes on particular significance in special education settings, as scaffolds must simultaneously support IEP goals and language development. This comprehensive approach ensures that students receive appropriate support while working toward both language and IEP objectives. Through careful monitoring and collaboration with support staff, teachers can adjust graphic scaffolds as needed, creating a learning environment that promotes both academic success and increased independence. Graphic scaffolds are selected to provide consistent, predictable structures that help students develop both organizational skills and content understanding, whether through modified Frayer models with tactile elements (Model Teaching, 2022)—breaking down a concept through its definition, characteristics, examples, and non-examples, or simplified concept maps with integrated visual cues. See Figure 6.1 for an example of how Jenna Maneri, a district multilingual learner coach in Bridgewater-Raritan Regional School District, New Jersey, has modified the well-known Frayer Model by adding color-coded multilingual prompts and ensuring that—whenever possible—cognates are recognized.

FIGURE 6.1 ● Modified Frayer Model

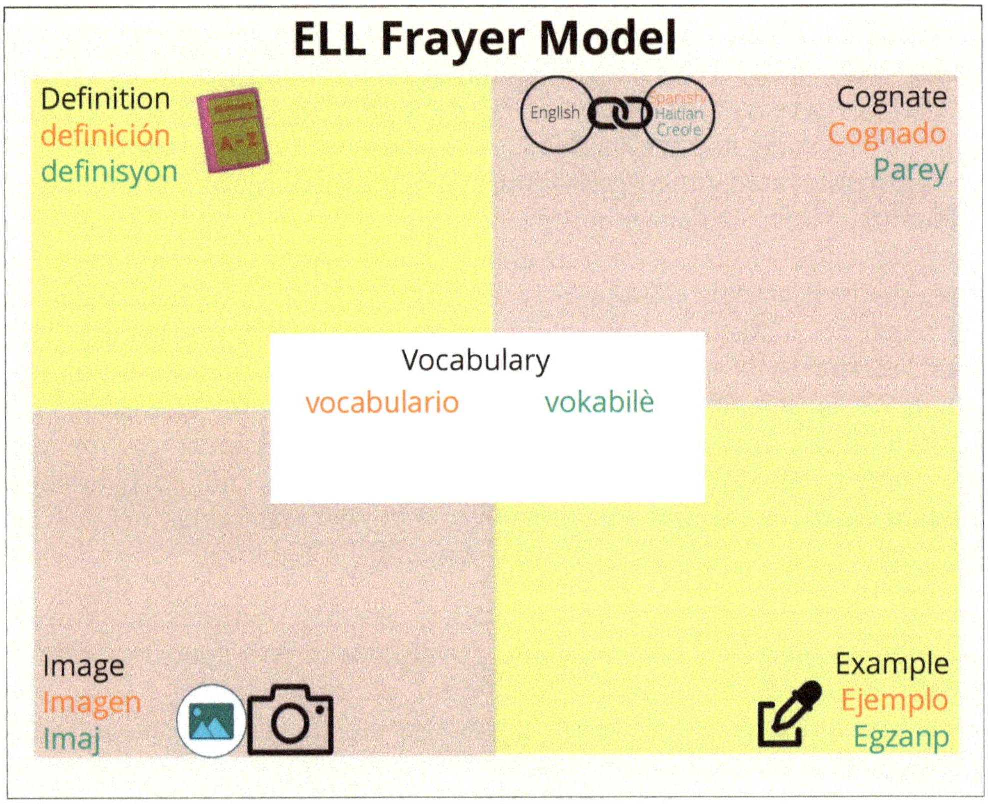

Source: Jenna Maneri. Used with permission.

WHY IS GRAPHIC SCAFFOLDING AN IMPORTANT APPROACH TO STUDENT LEARNING?

Graphic scaffolding represents a fundamental shift in how we support student learning, particularly for multilingual learners and students who benefit from visual and structured approaches to accessing core content and developing language and literacy simultaneously. Rather than simply presenting information, graphic scaffolding actively engages learners in the process of connecting, analyzing, and constructing knowledge while developing critical academic language skills. As classrooms become increasingly diverse in terms of students' language backgrounds, learning preferences, and educational needs, graphic scaffolding enables teachers to differentiate instruction effectively while maintaining high academic expectations for all students. Adeline Scibelli, secondary social studies/ English as a new language (ENL) teacher in Baldwin, New York, likes to create scaffolded note-catchers for her students. One recurring graphic scaffold in each social studies unit is a political cartoon analysis grid that invites students to engage in a structured, step-by-step process as they make sense of the image. See Figure 6.2 for the template and notice that additional scaffolding strategies, such as the use of students' home language, are also used.

FIGURE 6.2 ● Graphic Support for Analyzing Political Cartoons

POLITICAL CARTOON ANALYSIS (POST)	
People: List the people you see	**Objects:** List any objects you see
Symbols: Are any of the objects meant to symbolize something? What does each symbol mean? **(¿Hay símbolos en la imagen? ¿Qué son?)**	**Text:** List any words or phrases you see in the text that are really important.
Describe what is happening in the cartoon:	
What is the message of the cartoon? (¿Cuál es el mensaje de la imagen?):	

Source: Adeline Scibelli. Used with permission. Image source: istock.com/ andrewgenn

FROM RESEARCH TO PRACTICE

Jennifer D. Green and Beth Dillard (2021) discuss why and how, at times educators must "scaffold the scaffold" and create unique graphic organizers that are closely aligned to both their students' needs and the learning context:

Scaffolding is a critical part of teaching. It is important to include bridges that take students from what they can do on their own to what they are still learning to do . . . [helping them] *analyze language at a deep enough level to [create] meaningful language.* (p. 70)

Reflect on the following:

How do the unique needs of your students, including their language proficiency levels, influence your approach to scaffolding and the design of graphic organizers? How do you decide when a graphic organizer or other scaffold needs to be adapted or layered with additional support to help students access deeper levels of language and

(Continued)

(Continued)

content understanding? What strategies do you use to assess the effectiveness of a scaffold in real-time, and how do you adjust or add layers to it ("scaffold the scaffold") during instruction?

___

___

___

___

HOW DOES GRAPHIC SCAFFOLDING SPECIFICALLY RELATE TO MULTILINGUAL LEARNERS' NEEDS?

Graphic scaffolding serves as a critical bridge between language acquisition and academic content mastery for multilingual learners, providing structured support that addresses both linguistic and cognitive needs. Through its multidimensional approach, graphic scaffolding creates accessible pathways for multilingual learners to engage with complex academic content while developing their English language proficiency. This visual and structured approach helps students organize their thoughts, develop academic language, and demonstrate their understanding regardless of their current English language level.

Graphic scaffolds support both academic achievement and language development goals:

- Planning scaffolds help students organize their thoughts before speaking or writing in English.
- Comprehension scaffolds support their understanding of complex texts.
- Assessment scaffolds allow students to demonstrate their knowledge even as they develop English proficiency.
- Metacognitive scaffolds help students reflect on both their content learning and language development.

Such a purposeful implementation creates a supportive learning environment where multilingual learners can thrive.

For emerging level multilingual learners, graphic scaffolds might include home language support, bilingual word banks, and complete sentence frames. As students develop greater language proficiency, supports can be gradually reduced while still maintaining access to key academic vocabulary and language structures, ensuring students can engage meaningfully with content while building their English skills.

Graphic scaffolds prove particularly useful for multilingual learners as they provide nonlinguistic representations that support comprehension and expression. They help students connect the dots between their conceptual understanding and their emerging English skills, allowing them to grasp complex relationships and ideas even as they develop proficiency in academic English. For example, Sundar (2022) shares that "concept mapping is expected to facilitate meaningful learning—learners *purposefully* **connect** new information with their PRIOR knowledge" (p. 41). Concept maps and all other graphic scaffolds, in general, provide an interactive, hands-on approach for students to develop new content concepts effectively, to systematically internalize complex thoughts, and to engage with academic language aligned to content goals. Whether using hierarchical formats to show vocabulary relationships or cyclical formats to demonstrate processes, visual organizers help students understand and communicate academic concepts regardless of their current language level.

By serving multiple instructional purposes, calibrating support levels, providing visual representations, and making thinking processes visible, graphic scaffolds create accessible pathways for students to engage with grade-level content while developing English proficiency so that multilingual learners can build conceptual understanding and language simultaneously as well as demonstrate their learning visually.

WHAT TEACHERS SAY ABOUT GRAPHIC SCAFFOLDING

Graphics help make learning more exciting and engaging. I see it improving student engagement and motivation. I also use graphic scaffolding to provide students with an alternative assessment form. This type of assessment is meaningful and engaging.

—Erin Holtkamp, ESOL teacher, West Hempstead, New York

GETTING STARTED

Getting started with graphic scaffolds requires thoughtful planning and a clear understanding of learning objectives and student needs. It is tempting to be creative and try to introduce a lot of fancy designs, interesting graphics, or digital templates. We suggest you begin by selecting one or two familiar graphic organizers that align with specific content goals and student language levels rather than introducing multiple formats simultaneously. Start with highly structured yet simple graphic scaffolds that include clear examples. You can further support the use of graphic scaffolds with word banks and sentence frames to build student confidence and understanding of how to use these tools effectively. As students become comfortable with basic formats, gradually introduce new organizational structures and reduce the level of support while maintaining consistent visual formats across lessons.

When incorporating graphic scaffolds into instruction, consider how to ensure that multilingual learners are making connections and thinking actively about how they are using the tools you provide them, not just plugging in information. Considering the big picture while keeping the end in mind is essential. For multilingual learners, let's think about how we can use our ABCs for graphic scaffolds to:

- Activate prior knowledge.
  - *How will this practice be built in before, during, and at the end of the lesson? How will multilingual learners connect to what they already know and have learned? How will they seek information if they do not know or understand something? Will this be included in the graphic scaffold, or is this something we are figuring out beforehand?*
- Build on funds of knowledge.
  - *What in- and out-of-school knowledge do my multilingual learners have about the topic? What do they know about other things to help them understand the topic? How will they explore new ideas and concepts that help them grow their understanding? How will they connect new learning to their original thoughts and ideas?*
- Construct meaning from learning and express it in writing, reading, listening, speaking, and interaction through visual representation.
  - *How do multilingual learners take what they know or are learning and apply their knowledge? What skills do they need? How do they evidence their learning? What will they create? Which components do students need, and how will the graphic scaffolds support them? What do the supports look like? How will language and content be structured and connected to help multilingual learners make meaning? How will students co-construct learning?*
- Develop their understanding of responsibilities and how they will be successful.
  - *How will multilingual learners know what they need to do? How will they know they have completed a task/goal/activity? How will the graphic scaffold support them? How will they be held accountable? What will success mean?*
- Enhance their autonomy and independence.
  - *How will multilingual learners be motivated to be independent? What does success mean for them? How will they use their skills to grow their knowledge? What will they produce independently? How will we gradually remove the scaffolds to help multilingual learners have more autonomy?*

Consider how, when, and why graphic tools are used to support multilingual learners' learning. According to Wang et al. (2018), students better understood the materials they learned, and overall performance increased after using graphic scaffolds. Graphic scaffolds are versatile as they are designed to help students reach grade-level academic expectations while simultaneously supporting academic language and literacy development.

TEACHING PRACTICES

As you begin designing and using graphic scaffolds (or enhance your current practice regarding this type of scaffolding), determine how you can best address multilingual learners' complex language needs as they learn and develop new knowledge and skills in mathematics, the sciences, social studies, language arts, the creative arts (music, art, drama, etc.), and other special subject areas. We invite you to consider five key decisions to make about graphic scaffolding practices when designing and implementing them:

- Instructional purpose (to ensure content goals and objectives are aligned to graphic scaffolds)
- Key language uses (to prioritize ways language is used across the core content areas)
- 3M levels of support (to distinguish among maximum, moderate, and minimum amounts of support offered to students)
- Cognitive processes (to reveal the kinds of thinking skills required)
- Visual format (to ensure accessibility and ease of use/implementation)

See Table 6.1 for a more detailed explanation of each component. Together, they provide a comprehensive framework of practices that guide the process of selecting and adapting graphic scaffolds to enhance student learning.

TABLE 6.1 • Components of Graphic Scaffolds

COMPONENTS OF GRAPHIC SCAFFOLDS	OVERVIEW
Instructional Purpose	Focuses on specific learning objectives and educational goals the lesson is designed to achieve. Centers on the learning targets of a lesson, such as supporting planning, enhancing comprehension, fostering metacognitive development, or guiding assessment.
Key Language Uses (WIDA, 2020)	Focuses on the predominant way(s) language is used in a particular lesson or lesson sequence: • **Narrate:** Telling a story or recounting events in chronological order.

(Continued)

(Continued)

COMPONENTS OF GRAPHIC SCAFFOLDS	OVERVIEW
	• **Inform:** Presenting facts and details about a topic. • **Explain:** Providing reasons, causes, and analysis to clarify a concept. • **Argue:** Presenting a perspective and supporting it with evidence to persuade an audience.
3M Levels of Support	Focuses on the degree of guidance and structure provided—maximum, moderate, and minimum—allowing for the gradual release of responsibility as students develop proficiency and/or independence. Ranges from highly structured scaffolds (maximum), which provide substantial guidance, to minimal scaffolds that encourage greater independence.
Cognitive Processes	Focuses on specific thinking skills and mental operations that the scaffold aims to develop or facilitate (such as description, comparison, and analysis). Addresses different ways of spatially organizing and representing information graphically aligned to the cognitive processes.
Visual Format	Determines how and by whom the graphic scaffolds are created. Encompasses traditional, word-processed, and digital designs.

When creating graphic scaffolds, first and foremost, keep learning targets in mind to ensure multilingual learners are actively engaged in the learning process and not simply copying or regurgitating information. Multilingual learners should be explicitly taught how to use these tools with time to practice them. Demonstrate how to use these tools, share your metacognitive strategies as you work, and invite students to gain insights into their own thinking processes by asking questions about how they might use these graphic tools.

Once you have a general overview of the direction for the lesson or unit, begin planning how to intentionally support multilingual learners throughout the process. Providing multilingual learners with clear instructions and expectations is crucial to their success. Yeung et al. (2017) note that the clarity of scaffolds provided with associated visuals improves student engagement, motivation, and understanding of course content. As you plan for and develop graphic scaffolds, decide ahead of time what exactly students need to do. Many students work more efficiently when:

- expectations are clear and specific,
- concepts are broken down into small, manageable parts,
- the focus is on what students need to know and do,
- there is a visual flow showing students what to do, and
- students understand the outcomes.

If students get stuck, encourage them to incorporate other dimensions of scaffolding on their own, which often leads to deeper understanding, more meaning-making, and greater retention.

When combining a discussion of thinking activities with graphic tools, you honor your students' agency in the learning process. These scaffolds evolve with students' language development, offering progressively more sophisticated opportunities for academic language use while maintaining content accessibility. Multilingual learners, at the earliest stages of their language development, most often start with heavily supported graphic organizers that include substantial home language connections, visual cues, and basic English vocabulary along with cognates. Adjust the level of support provided through graphic scaffolds based on students' progress, gradually reducing support as they become more independent. Simultaneously, consider increasing the complexity of these scaffolds to respond to students' changing needs. Build in time to provide feedback to students on how they are accessing and applying the tools to their own learning and allow them to collaborate with peers and co-assess their work.

GRAPHIC SCAFFOLDING PRACTICE #1: OVERALL SUPPORT FOR INSTRUCTIONAL PURPOSE

Instructional purpose focuses on the specific learning objectives and educational goals the scaffold is designed to achieve. This practice includes supporting various aspects of the learning process, from initial planning and organization to comprehension, assessment, and metacognitive reflection. Each purpose-driven graphic scaffold is tailored to facilitate particular aspects of the learning journey, helping students achieve specific educational outcomes while developing their independent learning capabilities.

Implementing graphic scaffolding for instruction requires the strategic alignment of graphic supports with specific learning objectives and pedagogical goals. Begin by clearly identifying the instructional purpose, whether it's activating prior knowledge, introducing new concepts, supporting comprehension, or facilitating assessment, and then selecting or designing appropriate graphic tools or organizers that directly support these aims. For example, when the purpose is to activate prior knowledge, you might use a KWL chart, which tracks what students know, want to learn, and have learned about a topic, or a concept map, a visual organizer that illustrates relationships between ideas using connecting lines and labels. These tools can help students connect new information to existing understanding. The implementation of these scaffolds should include explicit modeling of how to use them effectively, with clear connections made between their purposes and the intended learning outcomes.

ADVANTAGES OF THIS APPROACH

The advantages of focusing on the instructional purpose when devising graphic scaffolds are significant and multifaceted. Teachers can better maintain clear alignment between visual supports and learning objectives, ensuring that graphic organizers serve as purposeful tools rather than mere accessories to instruction. By aligning specific types of graphic organizers to different instructional purposes, various cognitive processes and learning preferences are better supported while clear pathways are provided for student progression. Additionally, a targeted approach to implementation helps students develop metacognitive awareness of how different organizational tools support various learning tasks, enabling them to become more strategic and independent learners who can select appropriate scaffolds for academic purposes and language acquisition.

EXAMPLE #1: GRAPHIC SCAFFOLDS FOR PROJECT PLANNING

Project planning scaffolds serve as essential organizational tools that help students navigate complex, multi-step assignments while developing crucial time management and self-regulation skills. By breaking down larger projects into manageable chunks with clear timelines and checkpoints, these scaffolds make the process less overwhelming and more accessible for learners who are just beginning to develop their project management abilities. These visual organizers not only support immediate task completion but also help students internalize effective planning strategies that they can apply to future academic challenges.

An example of a project planning scaffold can be found in the implementation of a human rights project that requires careful guidance for multilingual learners through a complex set of social issues while developing research and advocacy skills. Students select a specific human rights issue they feel passionate about, comprehensively research the topic, analyze information to write summaries, and finally develop potential solutions, which culminate in a community showcase where they share their findings and proposed solutions. Over a six-week period, scaffolding is provided for each phase of the project as follows:

- Step 1: Select an issue: Students identify a human rights issue (Interest web—central circle with branches for brainstorming ideas)

- Step 2: Research: Record background, statistics, and existing solutions (Research matrix with columns to collect data)
- Step 3: Analysis: Summarize impacts and identify stakeholders (Stakeholder map to visualize the connections between stakeholders and impacts)
- Step 4: Action Planning: Design solutions and advocacy materials (Problem-solution chart to connect identified challenges with possible solutions)
- Step 5: Showcase: Plan the presentation of findings and proposals (Presentation planner to structure and refine the showcase)

(See blank copies of each of the highlighted graphic tools on the book's companion website.)

EXAMPLE #2: GRAPHIC SCAFFOLDS FOR COMPREHENSION

Comprehension scaffolds serve as critical tools that guide students through the complex process of understanding and analyzing text (both fiction and nonfiction pieces) across various content areas. These scaffolds can be strategically implemented to support different aspects of learning from initial understanding to deep analysis and synthesis of content. By providing structured frameworks for processing information, making connections, and organizing thoughts, these scaffolds help students develop both their comprehension skills and their metacognitive awareness of how they understand new information.

One type of graphic scaffold for comprehension is plot mapping, a powerful visual tool that helps students break down and understand the essential elements of narrative texts while developing their reading comprehension and analytical skills. By providing a structured framework for identifying and organizing key story components such as characters, setting, plot events, and themes. These scaffolds help young readers visualize how different parts of a story work together to create meaning.

To model using a plot map, begin by reading a selected story together as a class, then systematically fill in the map section by section, using different colors to distinguish various elements while incorporating drawings and symbols to enhance understanding. Throughout this process, creating strategic discussion points at each branch of the map helps multilingual learners develop a deeper comprehension of the narrative elements.

In *The Lightning Thief*, Riordan (2005), builds upon the rich mythology and modern adventure elements that make this novel engaging and highly appealing to young adult readers. See Figure 6.3 for a student-created plot map as part of an independent reading project in Christine Lopez's middle school English Language Arts class. A map like this can be developed gradually as students read, with strategic opportunities to make predictions and connections between modern and mythological elements. Students can also update the map with character developments, locations, and key events as they read and analyze the text. Graphic scaffolds could also focus on helping students understand how ancient myths are woven into contemporary settings while tracking Percy's hero's journey.

FIGURE 6.3 ● Student-Generated Plot Map as Graphic Scaffold

Source: Student work. Used with permission.

EXAMPLE #3: GRAPHIC SCAFFOLDS FOR METACOGNITION

Many researchers and practitioners alike recognize that metacognition plays an important role in students' learning. It is frequently defined as consisting of at least two dimensions such as metacognitive knowledge (thinking about thinking or understanding how one develops new knowledge) and metacognitive skills (planning, monitoring, and evaluating one's own thinking). Thus, graphic scaffolds may prove to be useful in supporting students by (a) understanding their thinking and learning process and (b) making strategic plans for thinking and learning and reflecting on their success in doing so. A graphic tool such as the template in Table 6.2 invites students to keep track of their own thinking and develop metacognitive awareness.

TABLE 6.2 ● "Lift a Line" Metacognitive Tool

WHAT I READ:	WHAT I THINK IT MEANS:	HOW I FIGURED IT OUT:

online resources Available for download at https://companion.corwin.com/courses/NineDimensionsofScaffoldingforMLs

You may also create other simple graphic templates to support students' reflection on their learning by keeping a record of their thinking in double-entry journals, reflection logs, or learning logs that provide age- and grade-appropriate headings and prompts. Better yet, ask your students to decide what types of templates or graphic formats would work best for them.

EXAMPLE #4: ASSESSMENT SCAFFOLDS

Graphic scaffolds can be easily leveraged not merely as instructional strategies but as assessment tools as well. When the goal is to guide and support students in demonstrating their understanding and showing (not just telling or writing about) what new learning they have developed, graphic representations can come in handy. When graphic scaffolds are used for assessment purposes, there are several options to consider:

1. Self-Assessment and Goal Setting Templates (see Table 6.3 for a frequently used vocabulary self-assessment tool).
2. Teacher-created graphic scaffolds are partially completed graphic organizers provided to students to complete an assessment task, such as the example in Figure 6.4.
3. Student-created graphic scaffolds are independently developed graphic outlines that multilingual learners may create as representations of their understanding. They can be accepted as final submissions, as partial submissions, or as drafts (see Figure 6.5 for a 9th-grade student's example of a historical analysis paragraph).

TABLE 6.3 ● Vocabulary Self-Assessment Tool

VOCABULARY	MY KNOWLEDGE OF KEY WORDS			
	I HAVE NEVER HEARD OF IT	I HAVE HEARD OF IT, I THINK I KNOW WHAT IT MEANS	I KNOW IT VERY WELL	I CAN TELL OR WRITE A SENTENCE WITH IT

Source: Adapted from Beck et al. (2002)

FIGURE 6.4 ● Text Comparison Chart

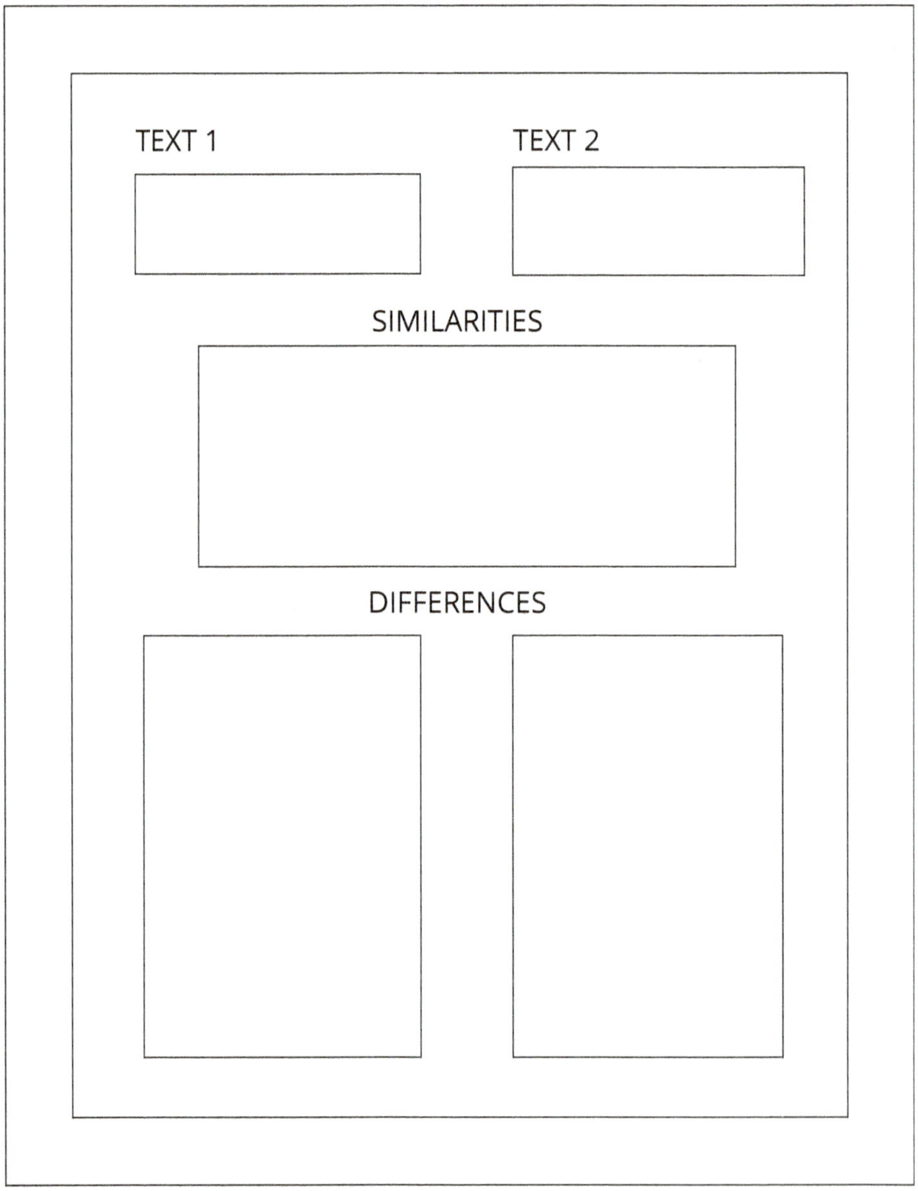

FIGURE 6.5 ● Historical Paragraph Graphic Organizer

TOPIC SENTENCE/MINI-THESIS
Gandhi's nonviolent approach worked because he made many moves where it financially hurt the British.
THE FIRST PIECE OF EVIDENCE
one great example of this is the Great Salt March. Gandhi and many of his followers rejected use of British salt, and marched for 25 days to the ocean and made their own salt. This and many other acts of civil disobedience are the reasons that Mahatma Gandhi was so successful in his journey and to liberate India from British rule.
RELEVANCE
This evidence is extremely relevant because the salt march was one of his most important act of civil disobedience and one that got recognized the most by the world.
THE SECOND PIECE OF EVIDENCE
Gandhi states "every one of us was firm in the resolution of passing his term in jail in perfect happiness and peace." This was written while Gandhi and many of his followers were in prison for acts of civil disobedience.
RELEVANCE
this evidence shows that even though Gandhi's followers and him were imprisoned for their "crimes", they never gave up hope and gratefully took their sentence, staying true to their beliefs of nonviolence. This once again proves that they are very determined in their pacifist choices, even when given terrible circumstances such as this.
THE CONCLUSION
With all of this evidence it is clear that Gandhi and all of the people who believed in him were true to their cause and they proved it in many ways.

Source: Student work. Used with permission.

GRAPHIC SCAFFOLDING PRACTICE #2: KEY LANGUAGE USES

When designing graphic scaffolds, it's important to keep language functions in mind. According to (WIDA, 2020), the four key language uses—narrate, explain, argue, and inform—capture how language is typically used when students attempt academic tasks across subjects:

- To *narrate*—or to recount of events in a story, typically in a sequential manner
- To *explain*—or to clarify ideas, concepts, or stages in a process by breaking them down into understandable steps or components
- To *argue*—or to present evidence and reasoning to support a claim, often used to persuade others or justify a viewpoint
- To *inform*—or to convey facts or descriptions to provide details about a subject

Incorporating WIDA's key language uses into graphic scaffolds makes certain that instruction is aligned with lesson expectations while providing multilingual learners with meaningful, accessible, and differentiated support, fostering academic language development across the curriculum.

Explicit guidance on language functions is essential for multilingual learners, and graphic scaffolds play a key role in helping them organize their thoughts and use language effectively.

While focusing on key language uses, teachers must also consider effective differentiation by addressing the unique language-learning needs of each student. For example, newcomers may be provided with graphic organizers along with word banks or sentence frames to structure their responses, while more advanced multilingual learners can use the same tools that are adapted for students to respond with more detailed and complex answers. This adaptability safeguards that all students benefit from graphic scaffolds.

ADVANTAGES OF THIS APPROACH

Focusing on language functions provides multilingual learners with targeted support for both academic and linguistic growth. By highlighting how language is used to narrate, explain, argue, and inform, teachers can design purposeful graphic scaffolds that align with real-world communication and academic expectations. This approach helps multilingual learners effectively engage in learning tasks while developing practical skills and transferable strategies that support success across various contexts. It also enables students to grasp not only the necessary vocabulary and grammar but also the underlying structure and purpose of their communication. As a result, they gain confidence in expressing ideas, analyzing information, and participating in discussions.

EXAMPLE #1: GRAPHIC SCAFFOLDS FOR NARRATING

Graphic scaffolds for narrating provide multilingual learners with structured support to organize and express their ideas when telling a story or recounting events. Tools like story maps lead students to identify key narrative elements such as characters, setting, problem, events, and resolution, guiding their storytelling to be cohesive and clear. These scaffolds help learners sequence events logically and include necessary details, making the narrative easier to follow. An example of a graphic scaffold for narrating to help students organize their knowledge and ideas about the subject of recycling can be found in Figure 6.6. It is an abbreviated story map that provides basic questions that guide multilingual learners to "map out" a narrative text about recycling in their community. The map contains examples of possible answers. Like all graphic scaffolds, this story map can be adjusted to meet students' individual needs (see Practice #3 in this chapter for modifying graphic scaffolds for multilingual learners).

FIGURE 6.6 ● Story Mapping: Narrating About Recycling

Title: Recycling: Creating Cleaner Living Spaces

Who is involved?
- students
- families
- community

Where does it happen?
- home
- school
- parks
- playgrounds

What needs to be solved?
- no recycling bins
- people's understanding of recycling

What are possible solutions?
- launch a recycling campaign
- students teach their families about recycling

EXAMPLE #2: GRAPHIC SCAFFOLDS FOR EXPLAINING

Graphic scaffolds for explaining help multilingual learners clarify processes, concepts, or systems. Organizers such as flowcharts, spider maps, Venn diagrams, and T-Charts help students to visually structure and present information logically and sequentially by showing relationships between main ideas and supporting details. These scaffolds encourage learners to break down complex ideas into manageable steps, making their explanations clear and accessible. These tools build both comprehension and communication skills. Figure 6.7 is an example of a spider

FIGURE 6.7 ● Spider Map: Explaining About Recycling

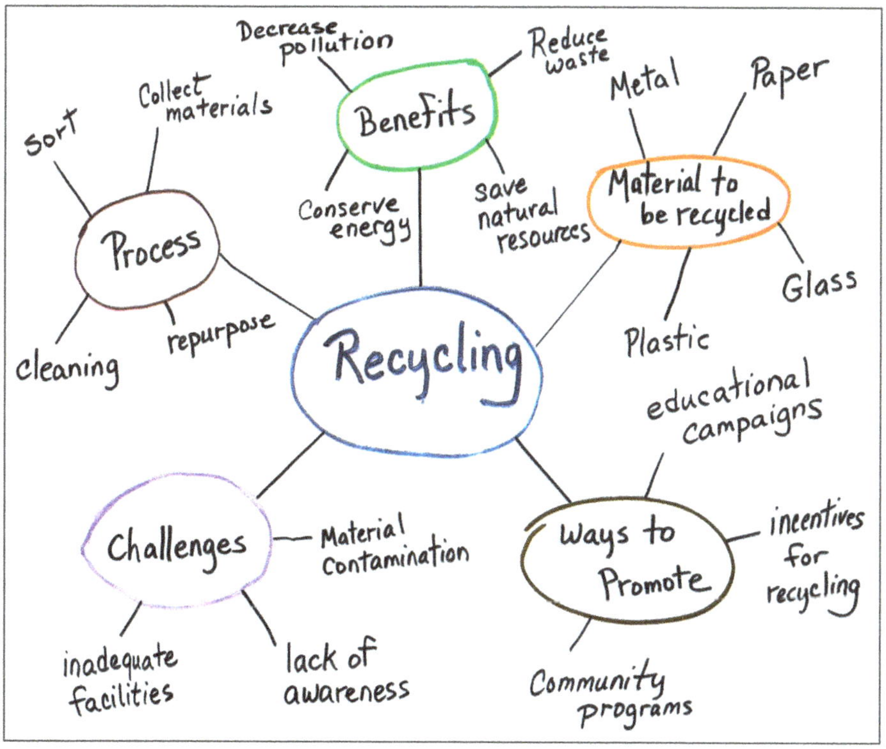

map that can be completed as a whole class to explain the different aspects of recycling.

EXAMPLE#3: GRAPHIC SCAFFOLDS FOR ARGUING

Graphic scaffolds for arguing viewpoints provide a framework for students to organize their claims, identify their supporting evidence, and draw conclusions in a clear and persuasive manner. Organizers such as persuasion matrices, T-Charts, mind maps, and concept maps can all be used to support multilingual learners to visually separate their main argument from supporting points, counterarguments, and conclusions. These scaffolds help learners focus on building logical connections between their claims and evidence, ensuring their argument is well-supported and coherent. They also can encourage critical thinking by prompting students to anticipate and address opposing views. With clear prompts for each component of an argument, these scaffolds empower students to construct persuasive and structured responses, enhancing their ability to engage in academic discourse. Figure 6.8 is an example of a partially completed persuasion matrix that identifies a claim about recycling and supporting evidence to justify the claim.

FIGURE 6.8 • Persuasion Matrix: Developing an Argument About Recycling

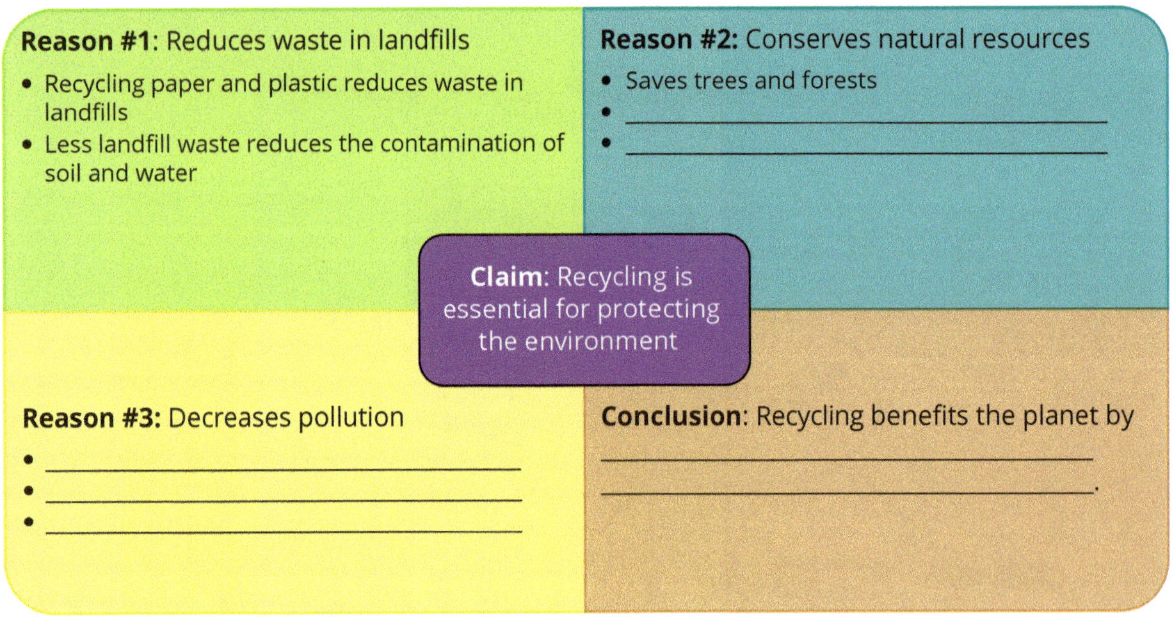

EXAMPLE #4 GRAPHIC SCAFFOLDS FOR INFORMING

Graphic scaffolds for informing help multilingual learners organize and present facts in a way that is clear to their audience. Tools like fact charts, information webs, and category grids allow learners to break down complex topics into key ideas and supporting details. These scaffolds guide students to focus on accuracy and relevance, ensuring their information is concise and well-organized. By using these scaffolds, students can effectively convey important information, improving both their comprehension and their ability to communicate ideas. Table 6.4 is an example of a partially completed chart to scaffold information gathering with key facts about recycling on one page. Notice how the first two rows are completed as models, and subsequent rows in the chart invite students to provide the missing information.

TABLE 6.4 • Fact Chart: Informing About Recycling

FACT CHART: RECYCLING		
CATEGORY	**DETAILS**	**EXAMPLES**
Materials	Paper, plastic, glass, metal, electronics	Newspaper, soda cans, plastic bottles, old cell phones
Benefits	Reduces landfill waste, conserves resources, decreases pollution, saves energy	Saves 17 trees per ton of recycled paper, cuts energy use in aluminum production by 95%
Process	Collecting, sorting, cleaning, repurposing materials into new products	
Challenges		Dirty containers in bins make materials nonrecyclable
Actions		

Source: Created by Maria Dove and ChatGPT

GRAPHIC SCAFFOLDING PRACTICE #3: DIFFERENTIATING 3M LEVELS OF SUPPORT

Multilingual learners undoubtedly require varying levels of support based on their language proficiency, general literacy skills in both their home language and English, prior knowledge, and familiarity with academic content and vocabulary. This naturally leads to the critical question: What types of support do they need, and how can I effectively provide it? One possible answer is the use of graphic scaffolding, tailored to students' needs, as an effective way to support multilingual learners. By differentiating the level—maximum, moderate, or minimum—and the type of graphic scaffolding, you can ensure that all learners engage meaningfully with the content while supporting their language learning.

For newcomer, entering, or emerging multilingual learners, scaffolds should be highly detailed and offer substantial guidance. Maximum support might include bilingual labels, visuals such as drawings or photographs, and partially prefilled graphic organizers. These scaffolds help make learning easier by letting students focus on key ideas without being overwhelmed by the challenges of language.

Multilingual learners who are developing or expanding their English proficiency might receive more opportunities for independence than newcomers while still accessing key resources. Moderate support can provide targeted assistance, such as key vocabulary provided with some translations or simplified definitions for clarity and partially completed graphic organizers using sentence stems to further guide students toward independent thinking.

Advanced multilingual learners may benefit from minimum support, where the scaffolds focus primarily on enhancing academic vocabulary and promoting critical thinking. New academic vocabulary might be highlighted and defined but not translated. Blank graphic organizers can be paired with guiding questions to encourage multilingual learners to focus on, analyze, and synthesize information.

In short, graphic scaffolding can be a game-changer for multilingual learners to succeed, no matter their language level. By adjusting the support, you can meet students where they are and provide them with the tools they need to access content and grow their language skills. See Table 6.5 for a summary chart suggesting some further distinctions among the three levels.

TABLE 6.5 • Differentiating Graphic Scaffolds Based on the 3Ms

3M LEVELS OF SUPPORT	POSSIBLE APPROACHES TO DIFFERENTIATING GRAPHIC SCAFFOLDS
Maximum	• Model an entire example with an anchor chart, provide sentence frames within the chart, and provide a word/ phrase bank. • Provide a completed model showing the flow or sequence of events • Offer images and sentence starters for them to complete the chart. • Include pictures on some parts of the web and words on others. Have students complete what is missing.
Moderate	• Model one part or one component of the diagram as an example. • Provide the beginning, middle, or end of the chart and give students a model of what the other sections may include. • Complete one part of the web or map to provide a model and have students complete it. • Offer a model within one-two parts (tree branch, map bubbles) of the diagram or map completed.

Minimum	• Continue providing a partially completed model and a blank map or web. • Encourage students to create their own chart and complete it based on prior learning. • Include an anchor chart for reference and give students a blank tool. • Invite students to complete the activity on their own or with one peer.

online resources Available for download at https://companion.corwin.com/courses/NineDimensionsofScaffoldingforMLs

ADVANTAGES OF THIS APPROACH

As with many scaffolding strategies, leveling graphic scaffolds ensures that multilingual learners receive the right amount of support when needed. Tailored graphic scaffolds organize information in meaningful ways, making new or complex content and language more accessible. For beginning learners of English, highly supported graphic scaffolds reduce frustration, clarify meaning, and foster task completion. Similarly, intermediate learners benefit from the added guidance to complete work independently while reinforcing key language usage. Similarly, advanced learners can tackle more challenging tasks with minimal support, focusing on building their independence as learners. By differentiating the design of graphic scaffolds, multilingual learners are better able to engage meaningfully with the material alongside their peers, ensuring equity while addressing the unique needs of each learner.

EXAMPLE #1: T-CHART WITH MAXIMUM SUPPORT

A T-Chart is a simple tool that helps students compare two ideas, organize information, or show how two things are related. It has two columns separated by a line, making it look like the letter "T." The left column is used for one idea or category, and the right column is used for the other idea or category. An example of a graphic scaffold with maximum support to help students analyze the internal and external conflicts in the novel *Maniac Magee* can be found in Table 6.6. It is a partially completed T-Chart that provides the structure and guidance multilingual learners need to engage with the lesson objective (internal and external conflicts) using the novel's contents. The chart includes a few examples of internal and external conflicts partially filled in, such as Maniac's feelings of isolation and his struggle with understanding how others feel on one side as well as his experiences with racism or conflict on the other. Bilingual prompts are included for further clarity and cognates (encounters—encuentra) are used for support. Consider using pictures of the characters or drawings of items that represent key ideas to enhance the T-Chart as well as strategically pair students to work on the task together.

TABLE 6.6 ● T-Chart With Maximum Support

INTERNAL CONFLICTS (CONFLICTOS INTERNOS)	EXTERNAL CONFLICTS (CONFLICTOS EXTERNO)
Maniac feels he doesn't belong because (siente que no encaja porque) ____________ ____________.	Maniac encounters racism when (encuentra racismo quando)____________ ____________.
Maniac doesn't understand why people are (no entiende por qué las personas son) ____________.	Maniac has a conflict with the boy, Mars Bar, when____________ ____________.
Maniac ____________ ____________.	Maniac ____________ ____________.
Word bank lonely (solitario) isolated (aislado) prejudice (prejuicio) pressure (presión)	**Word bank** bullied/intimidated (intimidado) bites a candy bar (muerde una barra de chocolate) fights (peleas) threatens (amenaza)

EXAMPLE #2: T-CHART WITH MODERATE SUPPORT

Let's adapt the same T-Chart (Table 6.6) to provide scaffolding for multilingual learners who demonstrate more advanced language skills and greater fluency in English compared with students at the entering and emerging levels of proficiency. In this version (Table 6.7), there is less reliance on translation, but shorter sentence starters are still included to provide support when needed. Consider providing a one-page reference sheet summarizing the key events in the novel, highlighting internal and external conflicts.

TABLE 6.7 ● T-Chart With Moderate Support

INTERNAL CONFLICTS	EXTERNAL CONFLICTS
Maniac feels ____________ because ____________ ____________.	Maniac encounters ____________when ____________ ____________.
Maniac doesn't understand ____________ ____________.	Maniac has a conflict with ____________, when____________ ____________.
Maniac ____________ ____________.	Maniac ____________ ____________.
Word bank lonely (solitario) isolated (aislado) prejudice (prejuicio) pressure (presión)	**Word bank** bullied/intimidated (intimidado) bites (muerde) fights (peleas) threatens (amenaza)

The difference between the T-Chart designed for maximum support and the one designed for moderate support might seem subtle, but it is intentional because each chart reflects the gradual release of responsibility to the learner. With maximum support, the T-Chart is designed to get students to engage with the concepts of internal and external conflict while gaining comfort and confidence in using English. In contrast, the moderate support T-Chart provides fewer cues, encouraging more independence.

EXAMPLE #3: T-CHART WITH MINIMUM SUPPORT

Let's further adapt the T-Chart for multilingual learners who are approaching full proficiency in English and require minimal scaffolding. In this version (Table 6.8), sentence starters and translations are removed entirely, encouraging students to generate their own responses independently. To support their critical thinking and deeper analysis, guiding questions are included within each section of the T-Chart, prompting students to explore the internal and external conflicts in the novel. Additionally, students can reference the text directly to identify key events and provide evidence.

TABLE 6.8 • T-Chart With Minimum Support

INTERNAL CONFLICTS	EXTERNAL CONFLICTS
How does Maniac feel about belonging? What pressures does Maniac face in Two Mills? What are some things Maniac does not understand about other people?	How do other characters treat Maniac unfairly? What happens when Maniac crosses racial lines?

KEEP THIS IN MIND

Graphic scaffolding serves as a powerful instructional tool that enhances student learning, comprehension, and retention by making information more accessible and memorable through visual representation. By providing multilingual learners with diverse approaches to engage with content through graphic scaffolds, educators create a welcoming and safe learning environment where students feel confident taking risks and gradually develop greater autonomy in their learning process. This scaffolded approach not only builds students' capacity and self-confidence but also increases the likelihood of meeting learning objectives as students take ownership of their learning journey, while the opportunity to create and revise their visual representations of concepts and relationships provides concrete evidence of their growth and understanding over time.

PRACTICE #4: SUPPORTING COGNITIVE PROCESSES ALIGNED WITH GRAPHIC DESIGNS

The cognitive process component addresses the specific thinking skills that the scaffold aims to develop or facilitate. These scaffolds are designed to support various mental operations, from basic descriptive thinking to more complex analytical processes like comparing, sequencing, and establishing causal relationships. Each type of cognitive scaffold provides a structured approach to organizing and processing information in ways that align with specific thought patterns and reasoning skills. Ritchhart (2015) reminds us that "the chief goal of instruction, right alongside the development of content understanding, is the advancement of thinking" (p. 33).

To demonstrate the use of each of these graphic scaffolds, we will use a third-grade science unit on the water cycle to illustrate how a hierarchical scaffold can explore its processes, a cyclical scaffold can show its continuous nature, a linear scaffold can examine its role in weather patterns, and a spatial/categorical scaffold can compare its effects across different environments. Most educators guide their students' thinking about the water cycle by graphically representing the process as pictured in Figure 6.9.

However, when you wish to explore the thinking process associated with learning about the water cycle, other types of graphic scaffolds are available:

1. Descriptive scaffolds help students describe, classify, and organize information and develop conceptual understanding. These graphic scaffolds typically take the form of webs, concept maps, tree maps, and brainstorming diagrams. See Figure 6.10 for a concept map that captures students' existing knowledge about water.
2. Comparative scaffolds aid in analyzing similarities and differences between two distinct entities such as places, people, concepts and so on. The graphic scaffolds frequently used to compare and contrast two items are Venn diagrams, T-Charts, or double bubble maps. When more than two items are compared and contrasted, the Venn diagram can be augmented with additional overlapping circles, or further columns can be added to a T-Chart. See Figure 6.11 for a graphic scaffold comparing and contrasting how the water cycle takes place in deserts versus rainforests.
3. Sequential scaffolds support the understanding of processes and/or chronological relationships of events. Typical graphic representations associated with sequencing are timelines, flow charts, or flow maps. Continuing with our theme of the Water Cycle, see Figure 6.12 for an example of how the process of evaporation, condensation, precipitation, and collection is captured along with factors that affect each step in the process.

FIGURE 6.9 ● Water Cycle—Graphic Representation to Scaffold Understanding

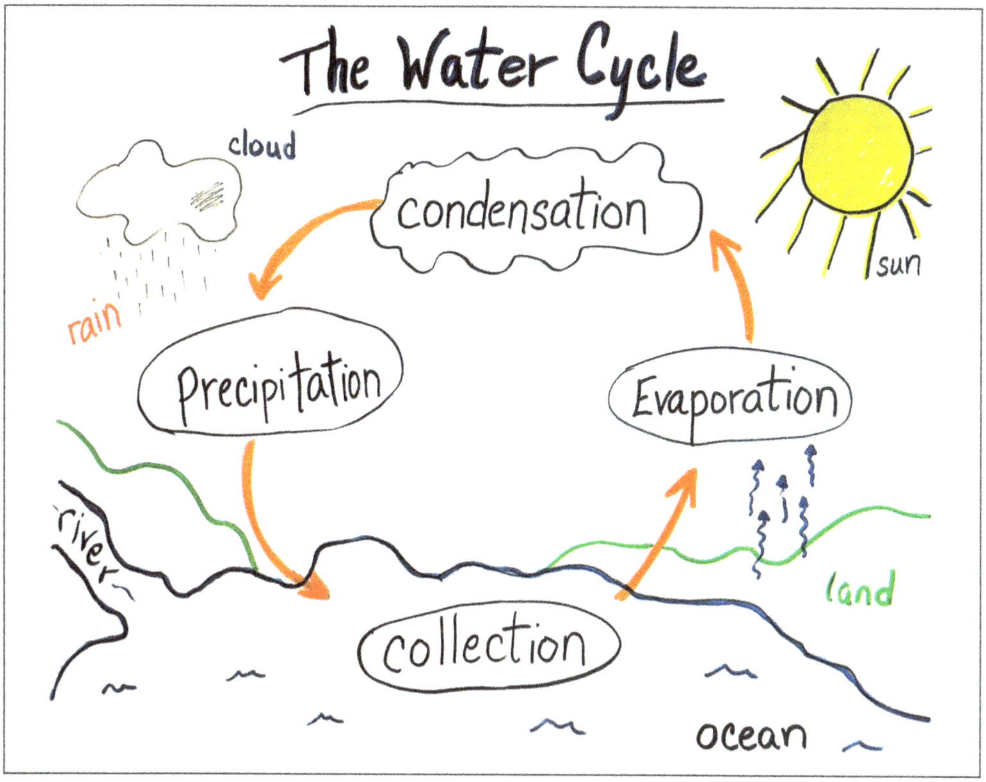

FIGURE 6.10 ● Concept Map: What Do We Know About Water?

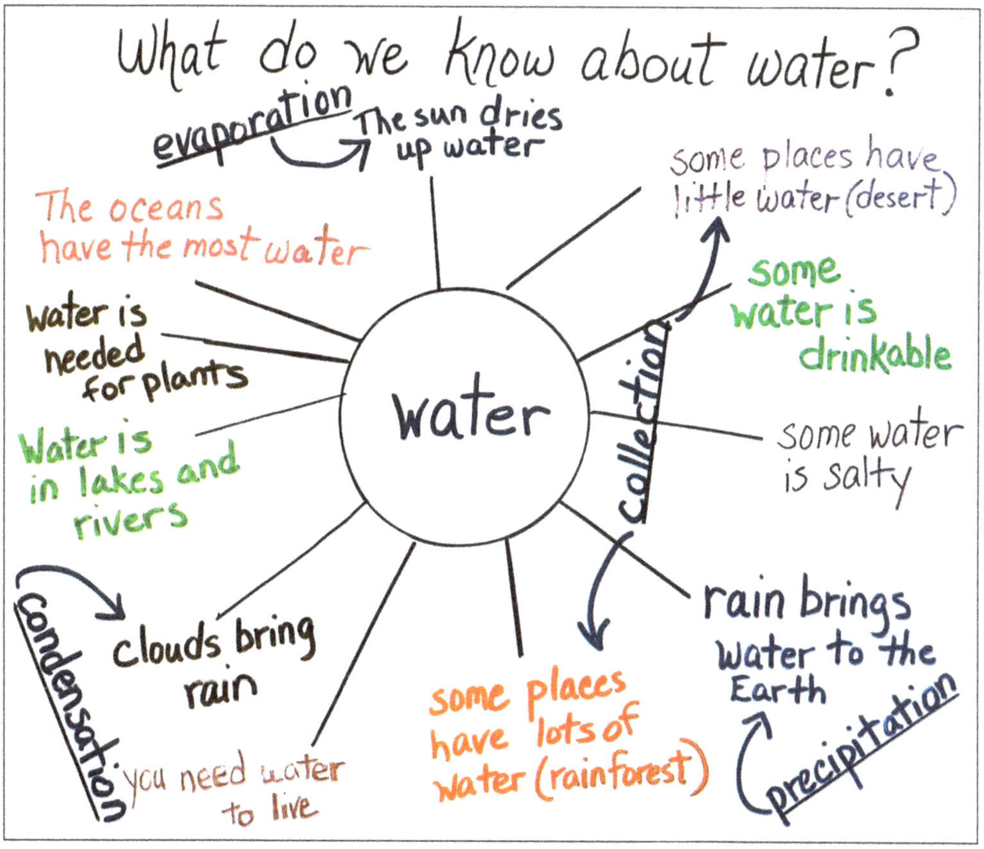

FIGURE 6.11 ● Venn Diagram About the Water Cycle in Two Different Climates

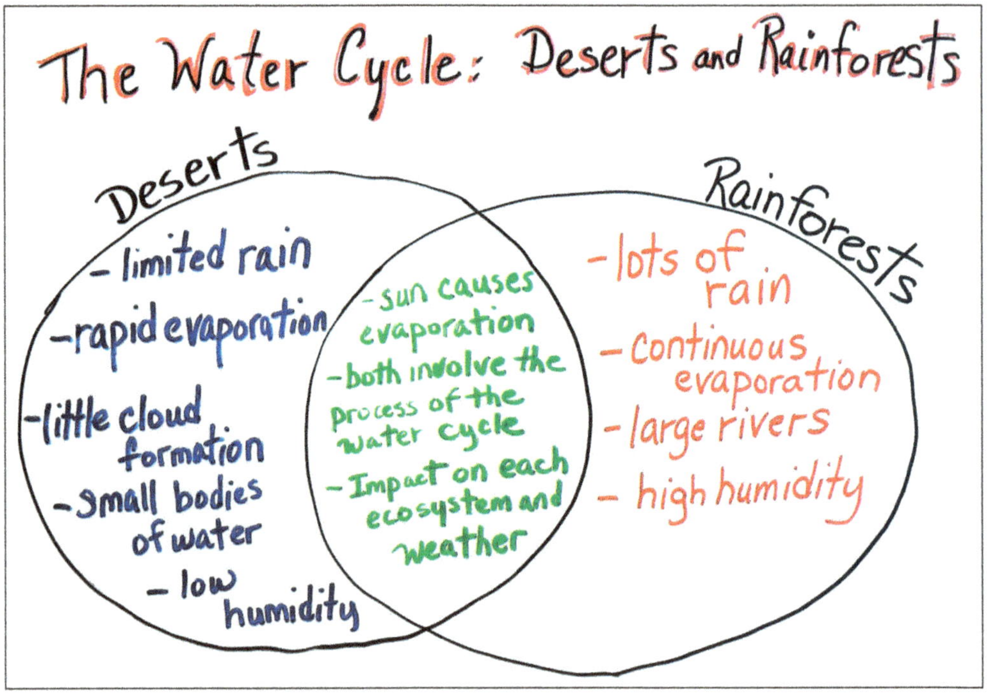

FIGURE 6.12 ● Flow Map to Show the Factures Impacting Each Phase of the Water Cycle

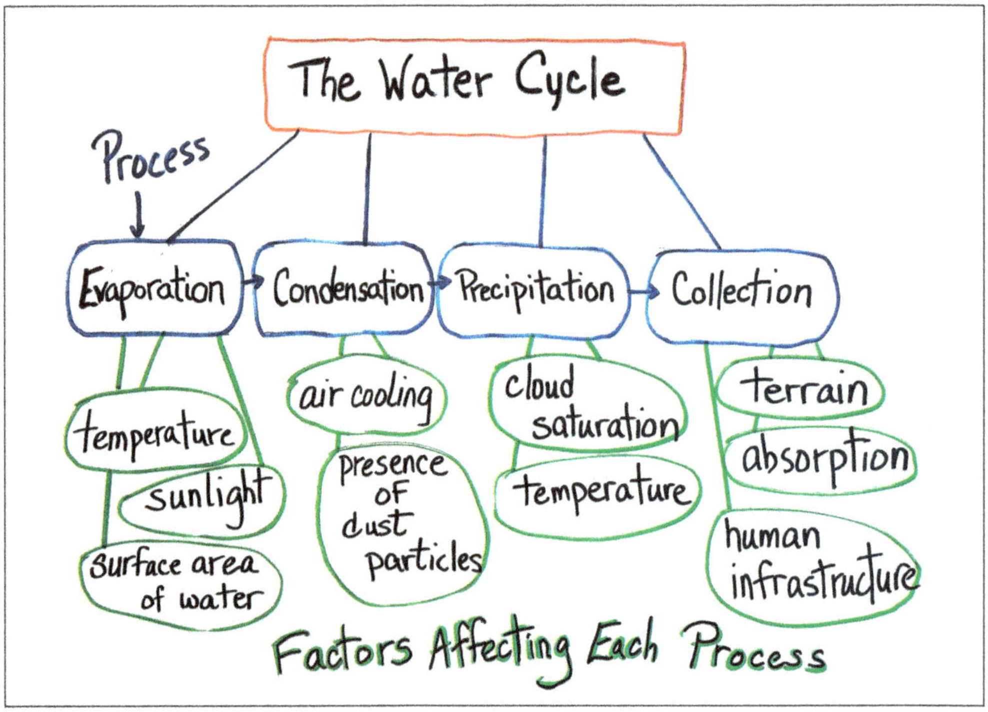

4. Causal scaffolds assist with understanding cause-effect relationships, and they are frequently represented with a flowchart or a fishbone diagram. At times, students may struggle with understanding that the cause is why something happens, and the effect is what actually happens as a result of the cause. Clue words or signal words may be helpful for multilingual learners to associate the casual relationship with certain language features, yet graphic or visual scaffolds can further enhance students' thinking processes. See Figure 6.13 for a flow-chart version of the water cycle to emphasize the causal relationships.

FIGURE 6.13 ● Graphic Scaffold to Support the Casual Relationship in the Water Cycle

GRAPHIC SCAFFOLDING PRACTICE #5: DETERMINING VISUAL FORMAT OR DESIGN

In addition to all the previous suggestions regarding graphic scaffolding, effective use and implementation also require intentional planning of the format or the design of the graphic scaffold. The following questions will help.

Who creates them?

→ Teacher- or student-created or co-created graphics

What medium is going to be used?

→ Traditional paper and pencil templates; chart paper with markers; digital tools such as SmartArt in Microsoft Word, templates available on Canva or other graphic design apps, AI-enhanced designs

What are some unique design features?

→ Intentional use of lines and shapes, color-coded elements, photographs, or drawings

How will the graphic scaffold be completed?

→ Modeled by the teacher, co-created with the students; student groups working collaboratively, completed by students interdependently

Our recommendation is that you start by modeling the use of visual organizers, demonstrating how to break down complex information into manageable components while thinking aloud about organizational choices. This process might involve beginning with basic concept maps or Venn diagrams before progressing to more complex visual arrangements. Provide clear templates or frameworks initially, gradually reducing this support as students develop greater competence in organizing their own visual representations.

There should be regular opportunities for students to practice creating and modifying their own graphic scaffolds through guided practice sessions where students work collaboratively to organize information visually and receive immediate feedback and suggestions for improvement. Incorporate specific instruction on visual literacy skills, such as identifying key relationships, establishing hierarchies of information, and using appropriate visual elements to represent different types of connections. It is essential to maintain a balance between providing structure and allowing for creative expression, ensuring that students understand the fundamental principles while developing their own effective approaches to visual organization.

ADVANTAGES OF THIS APPROACH

The advantages of intentionally focusing on the design features and choices encompass both cognitive and pedagogical benefits, particularly for diverse learners and multilingual students. This approach supports various learning and cognitive preferences, making complex information more accessible to students who may struggle with traditional text-based learning while enhancing memory retention through multiple pathways for recall that utilize visual, spatial, and verbal processing systems.

EXAMPLE # 1: A PARTIALLY COMPLETED CONCEPT WEB ON CHART PAPER

Concept webs prove especially valuable as they leverage spatial reasoning and visual processing to enhance comprehension and retention. The radial structure naturally draws attention to the core concept while supporting unlimited expansion through branches and sub-branches, making it particularly well-suited for exploring complex topics with multiple interconnected elements. The flexibility of concept webs allows learners to continuously add new information, revise existing connections, and develop increasingly sophisticated understanding as they engage with the content. Additionally, the process of creating and modifying concept webs actively engages learners in metacognitive practices, helping them reflect on their own understanding and identify gaps in their knowledge that need further exploration. There are typically four features of a concept web: the central node with the main idea, topic, or theme; branches, which are the lines connecting the central idea to related subtopics or details; subtopics with key points or ideas connected to the main concept; and connections with visual links showing how ideas are related to each other, often annotated with words or phrases.

A weather systems unit starts with students sharing daily weather observations, connecting science to personal experience. The concept map develops gradually with five main branches: temperature, precipitation, air pressure, wind, and clouds (see Figure 6.14).

FIGURE 6.14 • Weather Systems Concept Map

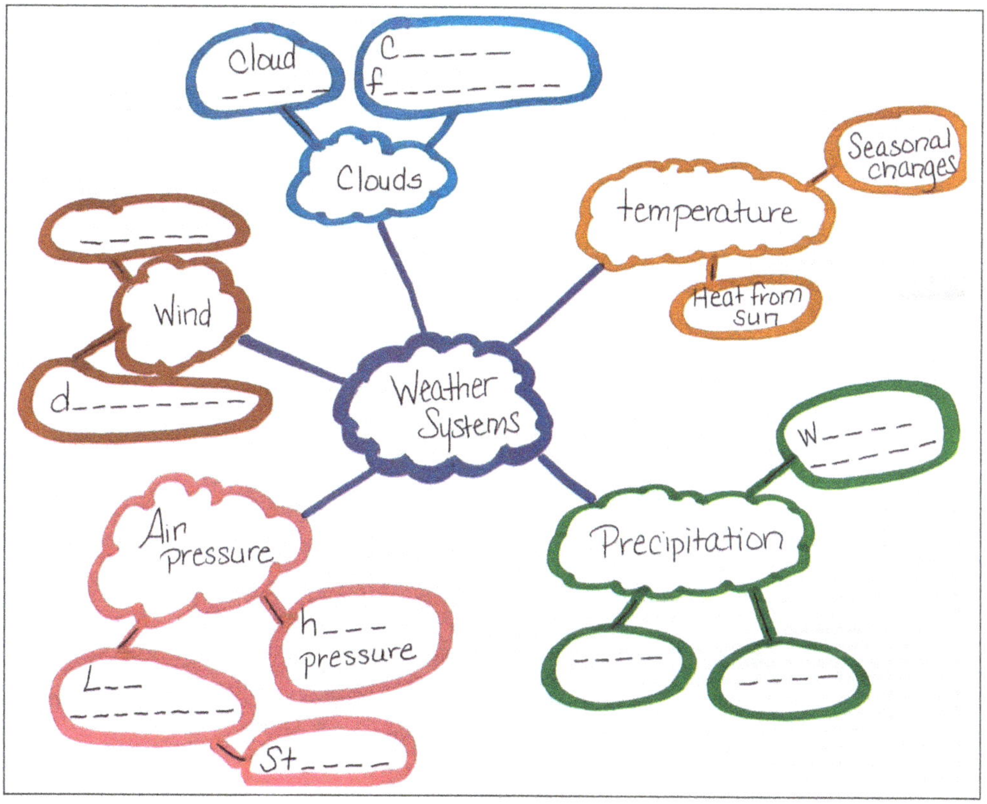

EXAMPLE #2: A SMARTART TREE DIAGRAM

Tree diagrams organize information hierarchically, starting with a central idea or decision (root) and branching out into categories, options, or outcomes. They can be used to problem-solve, classify, and even map out potential outcomes. The tree diagram in Figure 6.15 demonstrates how to analyze themes in Shakespeare's "Romeo and Juliet," by breaking down complex literary analysis into organized, hierarchical relationships in a systematic, scene-by-scene exploration of the play. It helps introduce key themes like love, conflict, and fate through Act 1 passages, guiding students to collect textual evidence and expand thematic branches collaboratively. You can add color-coding or symbols to track connections (e.g., red for fate, blue for conflict), while discussions and debates may refine the diagram. As a co-constructed, evolving tool, it supports class discussions, essay planning, and thesis development, fostering deep literary analysis and interpretation.

FIGURE 6.15 ● Romeo and Juliet Tree-Diagram

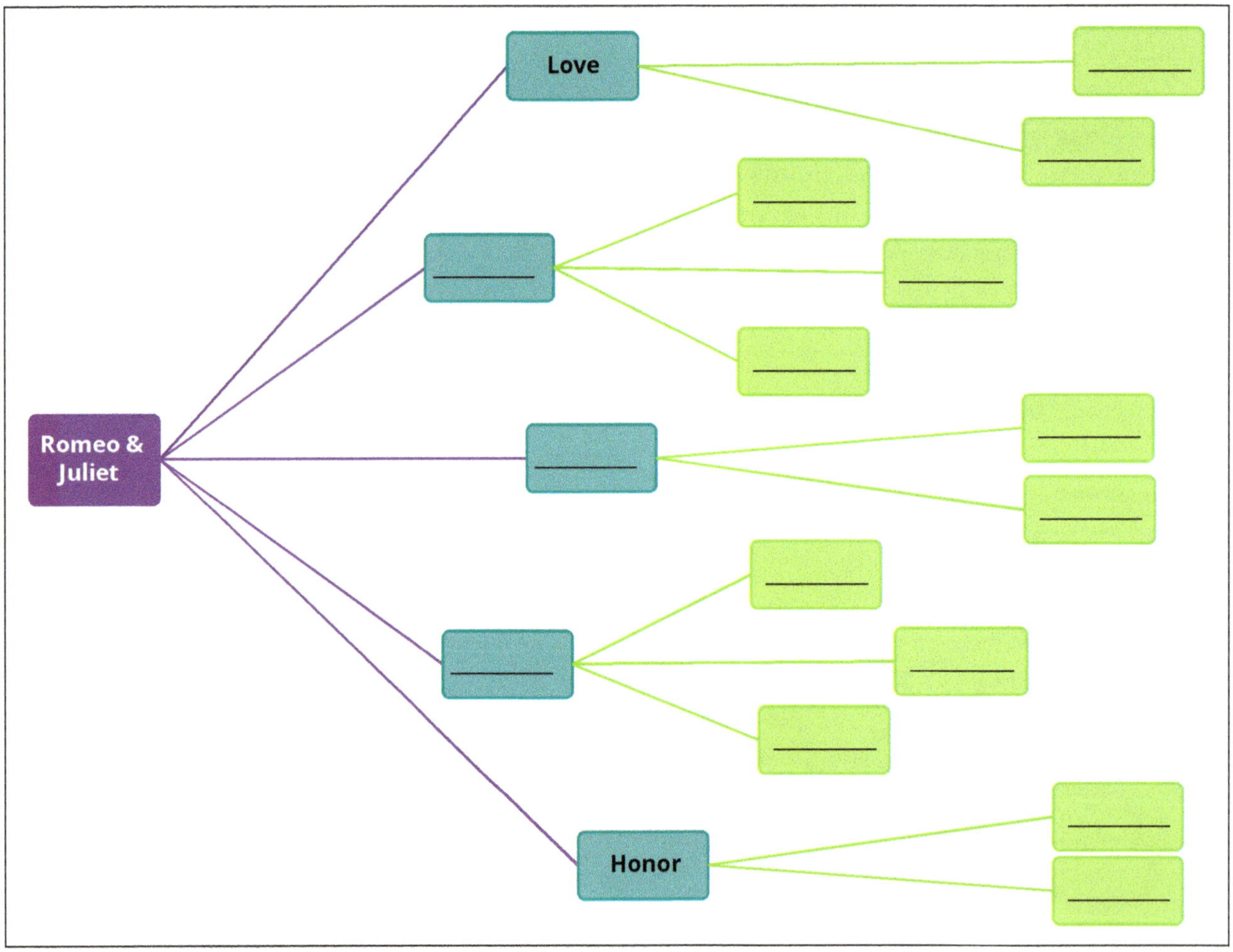

EXAMPLE #3: A WORD-PROCESSED FISHBONE DIAGRAM

Fishbone diagrams are ideal to showcase cause-and-effect relationships and can identify and organize potential effects of a problem or outcome. It looks like a fish skeleton, with its "head" indicating the problem and the "bones" representing categories of causes, such as issues with people, practices, technology, and so forth. The use of fishbone diagrams in studies provides multilingual learners with a powerful visual tool to analyze complex historical events and their multiple causes.

The following fishbone diagram (see Figure 6.16) helps learners break down the various factors that led to a pivotal moment in history, the American Revolution, making abstract concepts more concrete and understandable. By examining the interrelated causes of the growing tensions through categories such as taxation, British Control, and propaganda, students can better comprehend how these various elements worked together to spark revolutionary change. Consider how this graphic scaffold may support learning over several days exploring the central question: "What caused the American Revolution?" Day 1 introduces the concept, connecting to students' understanding of fairness. Day 2 establishes major categories related to the growing tensions: Taxes, British Control, and Colonial Rights. Day 3 adds specific events with primary sources and visual symbols, while Day 4 focuses on connecting events and creating timelines. This structure helps students analyze the Revolution's complex causes.

FIGURE 6.16 ● Fishbone Diagram Identifying the Causes on the American Revolution

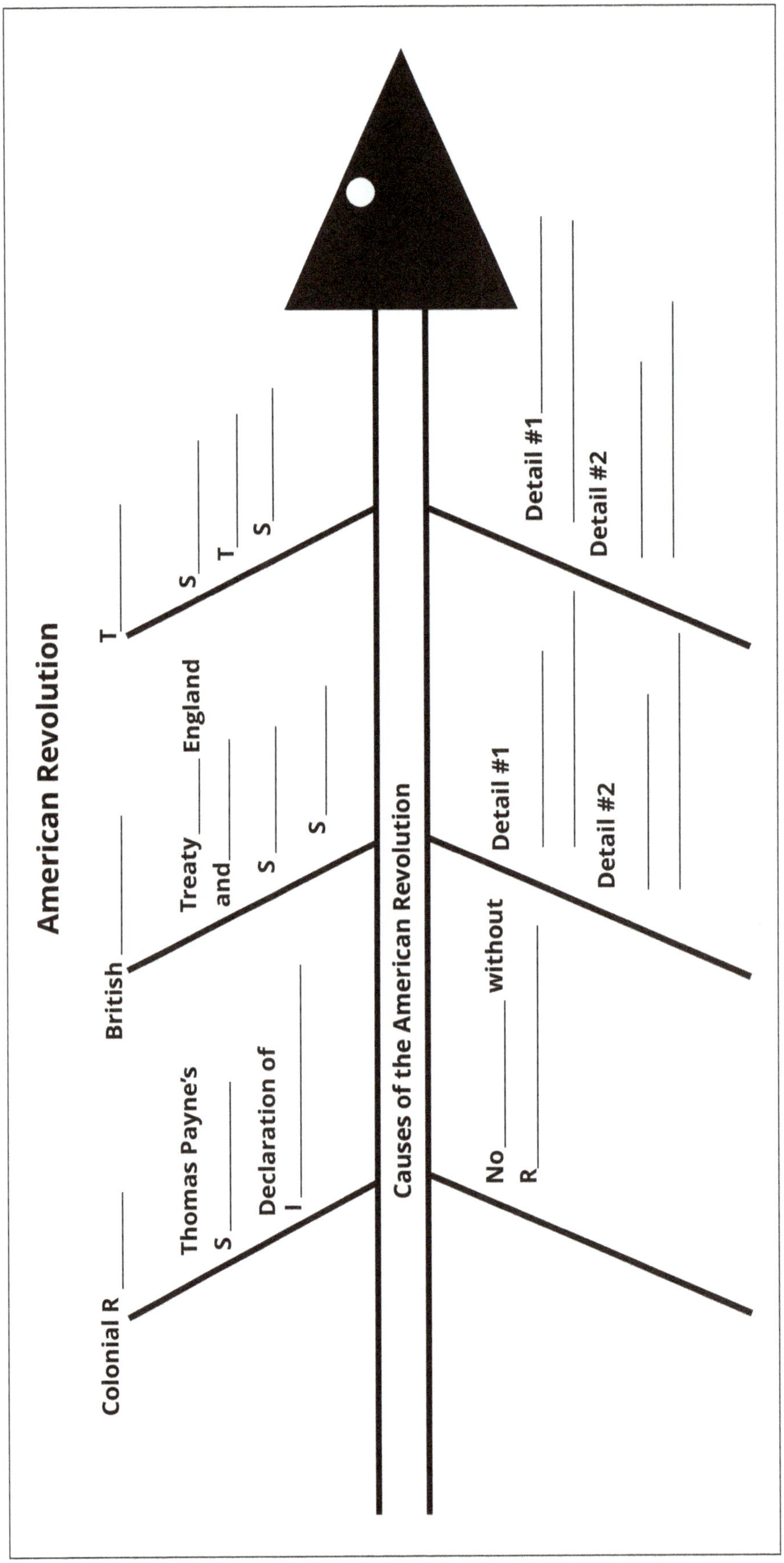

KEEP THIS IN MIND

As you begin using graphic scaffolds or continue enhancing their implementation in your classroom, consider how you address multilingual learners' various language needs as they learn new skills and develop content knowledge in mathematics, the sciences, social studies, language arts, the arts, and other special and core subject areas. Consider the following reflection questions:

- What must multilingual learners achieve from a language and content perspective? (Expectations)
- What language skills do multilingual learners need to know to achieve the intended expectations? (Expertise)
- What will learning look like for multilingual learners, and how will they use graphic scaffolds to demonstrate their learning? (Evidence)
- What checkpoints will we intentionally build into instruction to identify where multilingual learners are in the learning process? (Milestones)
- How will we know our multilingual learners have met the learning targets? (Mastery)
- How will multilingual learners know they are successful? (Self-Assessment)

INDEPENDENT LEARNING STRATEGIES FOR STUDENTS

Independent learning strategies with graphic scaffolds empower students to take ownership of their learning process while maintaining structured support. Students begin by selecting appropriate graphic organizers that match their task, whether it's a simple T-Chart for compare/contrast activities, a story map for narrative comprehension, or a concept web for exploring complex ideas. They learn to break down assignments into manageable steps, using sequential flow charts or checklist templates to track their progress and maintain focus.

Students develop self-monitoring skills by using structured reflection tools, such as any variation of the well-known KWL charts (Know, Want to know, and Learned) or learning logs with visual prompts. These scaffolds help them identify areas where they need additional support while celebrating their achievements. As students become more proficient, they can customize their graphic organizers, combining different elements to create personalized learning tools that address their specific needs and learning preferences.

The practice of implementing graphic scaffolds serves as a springboard to independence for multilingual learners, providing them with greater control of their learning while maintaining necessary support structures. This flexible approach can incorporate various tools such as flow charts, sequencing illustrations, tables, diagrams, and graphic organizers, all of which can be enhanced with strategic annotations to support comprehension. Through this scaffolded approach, multilingual learners discover new information, construct meaning through deep learning, and retain information more effectively as they take supported risks in their learning journey, gradually developing the confidence and skills needed for independent academic success.

SUMMARY

Graphic scaffolding combines five essential elements: instructional purpose, key language uses, three support levels, cognitive processes, and visual formats. Instructional purpose ensures content goals and objectives align with the selected graphic scaffolds. Key language uses help prioritize how language functions across core content areas. The 3M support framework distinguishes between maximum, moderate, and minimum levels of assistance offered to students. Cognitive processes reveal the thinking skills required for comprehension and application. Finally, visual format considerations ensure accessibility and ease of use. These elements work together through tools like concept maps and sequencing charts to help students organize information and develop thinking skills. The approach particularly benefits multilingual learners by making abstract concepts concrete, building independence, and supporting academic language development through multiple entry points to complex content.

Questions

1. What are the most effective ways to provide access to complex information for multilingual learners using graphic scaffolds?
2. How are visuals tailored to specific learning tasks, different student learning preferences, and linguistic abilities?
3. How can we provide practice opportunities and activities for students so they develop independence with the scaffolding tools and even create their own?
4. How can you make sure that graphic scaffolds are clear, easy to understand and implement, and transferrable across grade levels and content areas?

CHAPTER 7

Digital Scaffolding

"We need to find sustainable ways to be limber, nimble, energized, and practical in our tech-rich future in education."
Heather Pacheco-Guffrey, 2021, p. 12

The use of digital scaffolding in the classroom has revolutionized the learning process for multilingual learners, transforming traditional teaching methods, and offering creative, dynamic, and interactive types of instruction that were previously unimaginable. By incorporating various media, digital scaffolding supports the development of language and literacy and makes learning complex concepts more comprehensible and engaging. This scaffolding approach improves students' overall access to general education curricula, supporting multilingual learners in a more inclusive learning environment.

When you think of digital scaffolding, what are some examples that immediately pop into your mind? Do you think of the dynamic cues provided by tools like Microsoft Word and Google Docs, such as auto-completion algorithms that help turn ideas into complete thoughts? You must have seen this in action last time you were composing an email or text message and . . . boom! Words, phrases, or even complete sentences were suggested. You might have readily accepted those suggestions or simply shook your head and wrote your own conclusions. Do you think of that experience as an example of digital scaffolding?

How about taking advantage of spellcheck, readily available across so many digital tools! There seems to be a diminishing need to look up words in a traditional dictionary to check for spelling. Document editors and search engines like Google, can not only verify word meanings, but also model standard pronunciation, illustrate word usage within a sentence, and more.

In the classroom context, there are ever-evolving multilingual digital dictionaries and translation apps that are getting increasingly sophisticated as they offer access to complex language. The digital world is expanding by the minute, so we need to acknowledge that many more new tools and ideas will be around by the time you read this book. To stay current and relevant, we use the term digital scaffolding in a much broader sense than merely listing digital tools or apps. In this chapter, we define it as an all-encompassing construct for a range of digital resources that strategically support students' academic, linguistic, and social-emotional learning, as well as nurture 21st-century digital literacy skills.

- When you introduce basic technology tools to your students, you offer digital scaffolds and so much more: you also assist multilingual learners to acquire language, literacy, and academics, especially when intentionally integrating tools for entering and emerging English learners and students in early elementary grades as well.
- When you regularly integrate digital tools into your teaching, you offer digital scaffolds and so much more: you also support your students' evolving digital identities—which refers to the students' relationship with their own digital skills and online presence!
- When you challenge yourself and your students to learn about and try out new digital tools, you offer digital scaffolds and so much more: you also support their curiosity, risk-taking, and authentic engagement with technology—and the ever-changing world, which now includes Generative Artificial Intelligence (AI)—as they grow up!
- When you help students evaluate and carefully select digital tools that enhance and enrich their learning, you offer digital scaffolds and so much more: you also support their adaptability or agility to be critical consumers and digital content creators! See Figure 7.1 for an example of how Holly Sawyer, NCBT, lead EL teacher at Oscar Smith High School in Chesapeake Public Schools, Virginia, models creating an infographic and Table 7.1 for making the digital content creation a reflective and interactive task with scaffolded support.
- When you guide your students to use digital tools responsively, in an ethical manner, you offer digital scaffolds and so much more: you also teach them to protect their privacy online, to respect intellectual property and copyright laws, to learn to interact, communicate and collaborate with others safely online . . . or, in other words, to develop digital citizenship!

FIGURE 7.1 • Teacher-Created Infographic (Using Canva)

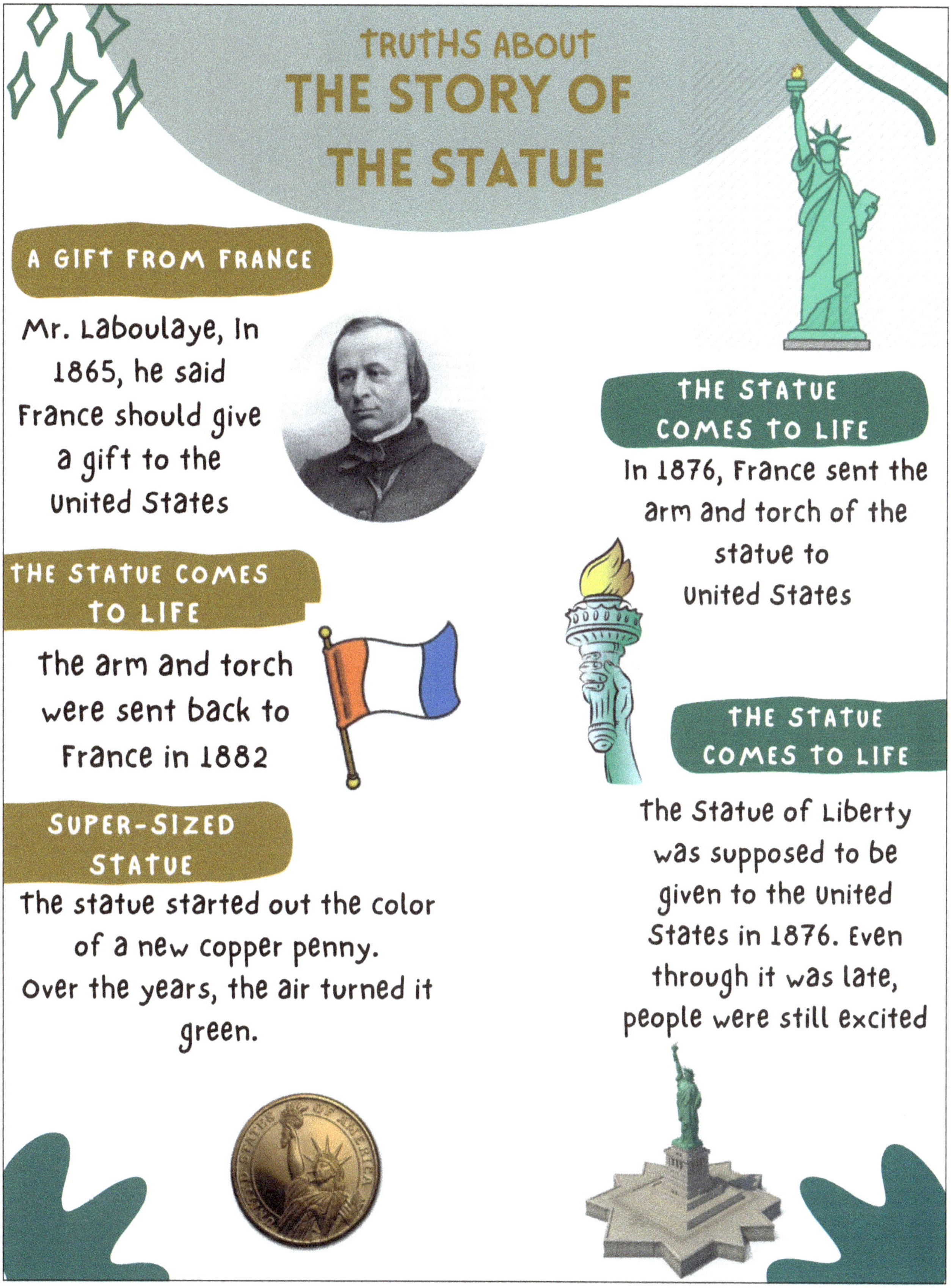

Source: Holly Sawyer. Used with permission.

TABLE 7.1 ● Scaffolded Partner Talk to Discuss Infographics

ASK	ANSWER
Hi! What's your name?	My name is ______________.
What kind of design is this? Where did you create it?	This design is an infographic. I created it in Canva.
Can you define infographic?	An infographic is ______________.
Why did you select this template?	I selected this template because ______________.
Where did you get your research? The book, the virtual field trip, or Google?	I got my research in ______________.
What is the title?	The title is ______________.
What is your most interesting fact?	My most interesting fact is ______________.
What is your least interesting fact?	My least interesting fact is ______________.
How did you feel during the creation of the project? And why?	I felt ______________ because ______________. **+ emotions**: successful, excited, creative, accomplished **– emotions**: unsure, uncertain, nervous
Can you justify some capitalization choices?	Sure! I capitalized __________ because __________. I capitalized __________ because __________. I capitalized __________ because __________.
How do you feel about this project?	I feel like I ______________. ↑ -I could teach another how to create an infographic in Canva. -I could do this again with confidence. -I could use more practice.

Source: Holly Sawyer. Used with permission.

WHO IS IT FOR?

Digital scaffolds can be used successfully with multilingual learners at all levels of English proficiency. The following examples demonstrate the versatility of digital tools in supporting multilingual learners. Just keep in mind, no one digital scaffold should be restricted to use with specific subgroups of students.

- They support newcomers by providing visual and interactive support to convey meaning, develop new vocabulary, and grasp concepts without relying on text. They allow for greater repetition and reinforcement of developing skills.
- They support newcomers and their families as they become familiar with and begin to navigate a new school system, get essential documents translated, or learn important information being presented in visual and multimodal formats.
- They support emerging or developing multilingual learners as they expand their vocabulary, build their background knowledge across a range of core content area topics, as well as get real-time feedback on their language and literacy development.
- They support more advanced learners to stay motivated and engaged with challenging content, language, and literacy learning opportunities and refine their language use. They allow students the autonomy to seek information when language and concepts are unclear.
- They support English-proficient students to learn to use technology responsively and productively. They learn to navigate and evaluate information and discern credible sources as well as offer opportunities for students to communicate and collaborate with one another more effectively.

WHAT TEACHERS SAY ABOUT DIGITAL SCAFFOLDING

Jason Raymond, digital media arts teacher at the Burlington Technical Center in Vermont, shares his philosophy of nurturing student agency and day-to-day practice of guiding English language learners (ELLs):

Rather than functioning in my role as a media arts teacher in working with ELL students, I often imagine myself in the role of their producer. From this vantage point, I am less focused on the deficits of my students and more on maximizing their assets through the tools of media arts. For ELL students, many of whom often speak several languages, have talents in several art forms (i.e., music, dance, drawing, or painting), have strong interpersonal skills, and a pronounced resilience finding these strengths is not difficult. Rather than defining the tasks to be created, I also orient myself to where my students gravitate their attention. Many of my ELL students from Congo, having spent time in refugee camps in Tanzania, are fans of Tanzanian hip hop and R&B styles, avid viewers of Bollywood films from India, watch Korean dramas, and Japanese anime and are obsessed with the English Premier and the Champion's League soccer. Understanding their global perspectives, I work to build a sense of shared interest, a feeling of trust, and a connection as consumers of these media forms, and use these shared points of reference to unpack the media arts curriculum (including composition, basic effects for filmmaking, and other components of audio, photography, and film production). This is often the preliminary condition for building the motivation for co-creating their own media artworks.

Unlike students from the small New England state we share, my ELL students have a broad, global audience of potential fans to communicate with. Once we have developed a body of work, through the immense power of social media, these students are able to build an audience comprised of viewers and listeners both locally, regionally (in Canada and New England), nationally (across the United States where other communities have settled), and globally (often reaching back to the countries where they were encamped because the styles are similar to those of that region and to the countries where they originated because of their unique blend of tribal and other languages). Suddenly, students who were introduced to me at the beginning of the year as a level 1 or 2 in their language abilities are coordinating music videos with a reach of 10 to 20,000 followers, building press kits for their album's releases, and negotiating music video shoots with producers back in Africa and local producers here in Vermont.

HOW IS DIGITAL SCAFFOLDING USED ACROSS PROGRAM MODELS?

You can implement digital scaffolding effectively across all program models with some strategic and intentional focus on high-impact choices:

In *general education classes*, online learning management systems (LMS) with a range of digital tools and scaffolds ensure that teachers can communicate clear expectations, provide access to learning materials, and establish routines and structures on a previously less familiar platform. For example, Canvas, Seesaw, and Google Classroom are being utilized for managing students independently in and out-of-class work and displaying or sharing students' learning with others such as peers, teachers, and families. In addition, digital scaffolding can be used directly with multilingual learners who need support with academics and language learning by adding early access to the content (such as using the flipped learning approach and inviting students to preview content via a video clip before it is introduced in class).

In *integrated, co-taught classes*, digital scaffolds can make complex content available and meaningful to all students through easily accessible resources and tools. For example, when students learn about the Holocaust by reading Anne Frank's diary, they can take a virtual tour of the Anne Frank House in Amsterdam and experience multimodal learning that expands their understanding of the hardships depicted in the book (https://www.annefrank.org/en/museum/web-and-digital/).

In *stand-alone English language development (ELD) classes*, technology tools can be used to tailor instruction to individual needs to provide access to basic language features and to accelerate language and literacy learning through meaningful practice. For example, some students might be using a digital scaffold on a tablet to develop or practice vocabulary and reading comprehension, while other students might be using a particular app to write a response to what they have already read.

In *self-contained or integrated special education classes*, assistive technology tools are regularly implemented as determined by students' Individualized Educational Programs (IEPs). There are dozens, if not hundreds, of assistive technology tools that support student learning. For example, text-to-speech applications allow students to listen to printed material and follow along with the text while making connections between what text looks like and sounds like.

WHAT TEACHERS SAY ABOUT DIGITAL SCAFFOLDING

There is no question that teachers have been facing a rapidly changing educational landscape for quite some time. Language teaching and learning have evolved dramatically in recent years with the integration of digital learning platforms and one-to-one mobile devices. Fast-forward to 2025, and there is yet another new frontier for educators to explore—the use of Artificial Intelligence (AI) in the classroom. Have you tried it out in your classroom yet? If you are currently using AI, you have already discovered that it is a dynamic tool that is helping teachers personalize instruction and save time. However, it isn't a replacement for teaching. AI can help teachers create scaffolded lesson plans and complete administrative tasks. It can help teachers to quickly differentiate learning tasks and tier assessments according to English proficiency levels. It can also curate appropriate and culturally relevant content while adapting materials to fit students' interests. If you feel unsure about using AI for education, I invite you to begin by exploring AI for yourself. Ask your colleagues which tools they have been using. Research some of the most popular tools and start experimenting on your own. Try out an AI chatbot like Bing Copilot or ChatGPT. You'll quickly discover that writing a clear and effective prompt or question is the secret to success! Test out different AI education platforms like MagicSchool, Brisk, and Diffit and find one that meets your needs. After you've had some time to experiment, teach one lesson that has incorporated AI in some way. Notice what works and what needs to be modified and then teach another lesson using AI. Although trying something new may feel overwhelming at times, remember, we teachers are experts at adjusting. We do it every day in the classroom. So how do we embrace all these rapid technological changes? We focus on our students. We remember that we are life-long learners, and we lead by learning.

—Heather Rubin, Long Island regional bilingual education resource network coordinator

We certainly share Heather's passion for technology, yet we are aware of some deep-rooted concerns as well. Perhaps you are like many educators and parents who find it troubling that most school-age youths spend hours of screen time every day dedicated to nonacademic activities, such as content browsing, social media usage, online peer interactions, gaming, and so on. Digital devices are not going away, and screen time may continue to increase, so as adults, we must be mindful of how much additional screen time and what kind of meaningful possibilities are added to students' *daily digital allowance* (Ray, 2023). The challenge is to deeply reflect on and determine how we can be international and strategic about students' in and out-of-school digital tool usage and make sure they are beneficial for students' academic, language, and literacy learning. Consider the following suggestions to be more strategic with technology and digital scaffolding:

1. Connect school learning with out-of-school cultural experiences, including digital practices:
   - *For example, have students research their cultural heritage online and design a website to clarify myths and misconceptions about their cultures.*
2. Create authentic connections between (a) what students do in digital spaces and what they already know about digital tools and (b) what may advance their academic and linguistic development in school:
   - *For example, invite students to select online resources and digital tools that best align with particular tasks.*
3. Build on students' natural curiosity to learn something that is brand new:
   - *For example, challenge your students (and yourself) to try out a new tool that promises to provide better access to language and literacy development or to learning in general and analyze its impact on student outcomes.*

4. Add criticality to your teaching and invite students to make it their second nature:
    - *For example, invite students to ask ChatGPT or another generative AI tool to answer a question and then guide students through the process of evaluating the response for accuracy or bias.*
5. Involve students in making decisions about choosing digital tools while supporting their digital agency:
    - *For example, introduce students to two or more digital tools that promise to accomplish essentially the same (or something similar), have students analyze the tools, and compare them for effectiveness and ease of use. Further, students may discuss or write about each tool or even engage in a debate about them.*

WHAT TEACHERS SAY ABOUT DIGITAL SCAFFOLDING

Kandice Adams and Louise Herington from Apple Valley Unified School District in California use Pear Deck to scaffold reasoning when they teach CER (claim, evidence, reasoning) structure. As secondary co-teachers, they have found that their students typically make strong claims but don't always follow through with the reasoning. This is how they use Pear Deck, to scaffold the reasoning portion of the task:

We have done a four-corner activity kinesthetically, with students physically moving to the four corners of the room and vocalizing their reasoning. That activity is engaging and effective for our extroverted students but is not inclusive for all students, including some of our English language learners and special education students. To solve this issue, we have structured the activity digitally using Pear Deck, which increased student engagement to nearly 100%.

The Pear Deck slides in Figure 7.2 were used as an anticipatory guide for the theme of the book, as well as a scaffold for reasoning. After introducing the task, we reviewed the rules presented on Slide 1. Slide 2 invited students to drag their icon (a Pear Deck feature) to the corner that best fits their opinion. We gave a few moments for this, then revealed the screen displaying the class response on the projector. Slide 3 offered students a chance to provide reasoning. We gave students some time to respond, then revealed all of their responses on the projector. We scrolled through their responses slowly and read a few out loud, being mindful to choose a variety of opposing viewpoints. At this point, we also gave students an opportunity to voice their viewpoints. Finally, after students had a chance to see other's perspectives, they could change their initial viewpoint using Slide 4. We do this as a way to build students' expectations of opposing views, eventually leading to learning counterclaims.

FIGURE 7.2 ● A Digital Version of the Four Corners Activity

Four Corners Activity

How to participate:

-For each claim provided, decide whether you:

Strongly agree-No one can change your mind!

Agree-With enough evidence, someone may be able to change your mind.

Strongly disagree-No one can change your mind!

Disagree With enough evidence, someone may be able to change your mind.

ONCE YOU DECIDE, DRAG YOUR ICON TO THE CORNER THAT REPRESENTS YOUR OPINION.

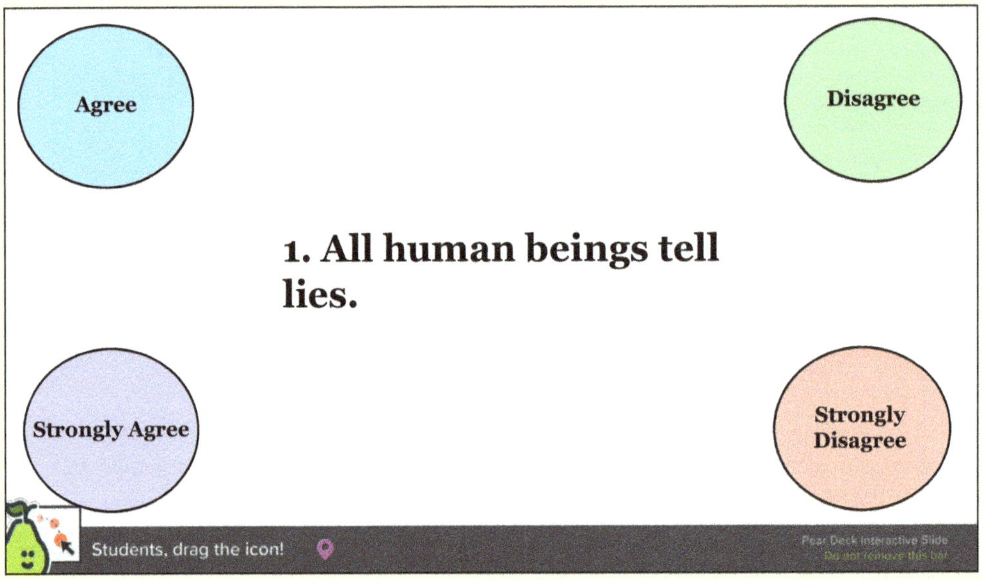

Reasoning:

Now that you have decided whether you strongly agree, agree, strongly disagree, or disagree, you need to explain why you believe that. Use the sentence starter, and in a few sentences explain your opinion. Remember, we will share responses on the projector, but they are anonymous! No one will know which response is yours, except me.

Sentence starter:

"I (strongly agree, agree, strongly disagree, or disagree) that all human beings tell lies because ____________________________________.

Students, write your response!

Pear Deck Interactive Slide
Do not remove this bar

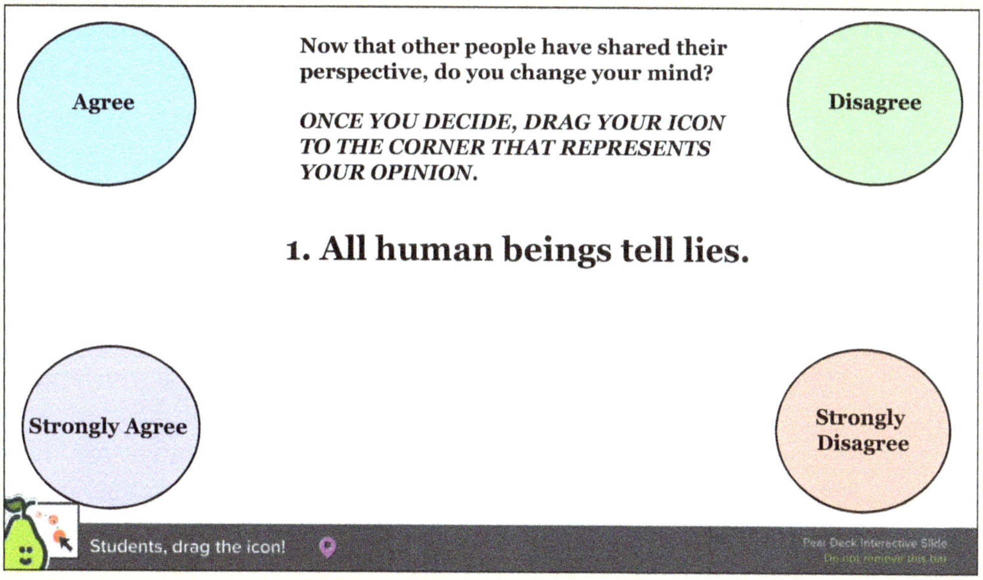

Source: Kandice Adams and Louise Herington. Used with permission.

FROM RESEARCH TO PRACTICE

Digital tools, including AI, are here to stay. Sheri Vasinda and Jodi Pilgrim (2022) challenge the notion of treating digital scaffolds in a traditional sense as temporary, removable constructs. Instead, they suggest that digital tools can be used in more sustainable and flexible ways without expecting them to fade; in fact, they claim that digital scaffolds offer new opportunities to engage with literature and build users' more contemporary, multiliterate identities.

> We argue that everyday digital tools with inclusive features are new literacies options, that are readily available given equitable access to the Internet, devices, and software. They provide opportunities for learners to demonstrate their multiliterate agency and experience school success. (p. 44)

Reflect on the following:

What has your experience been with digital tools that remain an integral part of students' learning? Are digital, multiliterate identities an important consideration in your work with multilingual learners? How would you balance the approach presented in Sheri Vasinda and Jodi Pilgrim's research with a seemingly opposing point of view of limiting screen time?

____

____

____

____

WHY IS DIGITAL SCAFFOLDING AN IMPORTANT APPROACH TO STUDENT LEARNING?

Access to digital technology is quickly expanding both in schools and in students' homes. Digital tools have the power to provide multimodal, multilingual, and multisensory experiences for students as they watch and listen to videos, simulations, or animations. Digital scaffolds can help build foundational knowledge and understanding or may offer enrichment opportunities as students take virtual tours of national parks, monuments, and museums. Digital scaffolds may also support student interaction as they use educational apps such as EdPuzzle, Seesaw, Nearpod, and so on to practice skills. Why might current and emerging technology tools and scaffolds provide new, enhanced, and exciting opportunities for multilingual learners to learn? In our emerging assessment of well-established and newly emerging trends, digital scaffolds have the potential to:

- Encourage collaboration between the teacher and students.
  - ***How?*** *Productivity suites such as Seesaw, Google Workspace, Canvas, and Office 365 can support student-teacher interaction while also helping students with notetaking and a range of organizational skills.*
- Develop language skills through listening, speaking, reading, writing, viewing, and visually representing their understanding.
  - ***Why?*** *Multilingual learners build their comprehension and expand higher-order thinking skills when accessing digital content.*
- Demonstrate new knowledge and understanding (such as screencast tutorials or interactive multimedia presentations).
  - ***How?*** *Students create multimedia presentations by using text, audio, images, and video to tell digital stories that show mastery of content.*
- Adapt content to adjust lexical or syntactic complexity based on students' language and literacy levels.
  - ***What?*** *Multilingual learners are provided read-aloud options and are engaged with interactive and bilingual content.*

However, our strongest, most compelling argument for integrating digital scaffolds is that through digital access points and resources, students develop proficiency both with the target content and language, as well as develop 21st-century technology skills. We must also recognize that most students no longer merely receive and interpret information, or develop new skills or, enhance them via digital supports. They can take a more active role and create, not just consume, digital content.

A QUICK SELF-CHECK

How prepared are you to use digital scaffolds? Let's find out! Try the Technology Readiness Survey in Figure 7.3, adapted from Rubin et al. (2022), to help identify the types of technology you are currently using, your comfort level with using technology, and how technology is employed. We recommend that you jot down detailed answers to each prompt and share your responses with colleagues.

FIGURE 7.3 • Technology Readiness Survey

1. What is your overall reaction to technology use for teaching and learning?

___

___

2. Which digital tools do you use for teaching and learning? Why?

___

___

3. What challenges do you face in integrating technology in your teaching?

___

___

4. What supports do you need to effectively integrate digital learning resources into your teaching?

___

___

5. How does your technology use support all students'—specifically multilingual learners'— access to new and dificult learning?

___

___

(Continued)

(Continued)

6. How does your technology use support students'—specifically multilingual learners'— expressive skills and interactive group work?

____

____

7. How confident are you when using technology in your classroom learning environments?

____

____

8. What are the key technology skills your students need to develop to be future-ready?

____

____

Source: Adapted from Rubin et al. (2022).

online resources Available for download at https://companion.corwin.com/courses/NineDimensionsofScaffoldingforMLs

HOW DOES DIGITAL SCAFFOLDING SPECIFICALLY RELATE TO MULTILINGUAL LEARNERS' NEEDS?

Strategic use of digital scaffolds offers much-needed opportunities for multilingual learners to meaningfully engage in rigorous learning. These scaffolds are designed and implemented to provide students with access to new learning by (a) frontloading (pre-teaching or previewing) upcoming lessons such as in flipped learning; (b) being available in the moment to provide access to both content and language and literacy learning such as using electronic dictionaries, thesauruses, or using a range of possible apps; (c) serving as tools for reviewing or revisiting teacher-recorded or curated materials; and (d) offering enrichment and extended learning opportunities through educational games such as Kahoot!, BrainPOP ESL, and many more.

GETTING STARTED WITH DIGITAL SCAFFOLDING

When you plan to offer digital scaffolds, your instruction may include the following and many more tools or approaches:

- Digital recordings to provide access to new learning (Screencastify, Loom)
- Multimedia presentations created by the teacher and the students to develop fluency and facility with English and express ideas (Padlet, Nearpod)

- Digital storytelling to enhance multimodality (Book Creator, Adobe Express, VoiceThread, Stop Motion Studio, Make Beliefs Comix)
- E-books, blogs, and web-based reading materials to offer multiple entry points (Epic!, Newsela, News in Levels, Starfall)
- Digital whiteboards to ensure interaction and expression (Witeboard)
- Instructional apps or extensions to digital platforms (Flip, EdPuzzle, Pear Deck)
- Web-based learning games to lower students' affective filter (Kahoot!, Gimkit)
- Student and parent messaging tools to stay connected and help organize student learning (TalkingPoints, Remind, WhatsApp)
- Adaptive software to practice content skills (DoodleMath, Zearn, Prodigy, Mathspace)

A BIT MORE ABOUT AI

AI is ever evolving—at the publication of this book, it is hard to predict precisely where it is heading and where it is going to land in a year or two within the educational context to better support multilingual learners. If you are among early adopters, you might consider some of the most promising aspects of AI-supported tools and scaffolds in your classroom and how they are best used to support multilingual learners. If you are approaching AI with some concerns, rank the following statements:

Which of the following limitations are you most concerned about, why, and how are you planning to address these challenges?

___ Teachers and students may become overly dependent on AI tools.

___ AI tools might hinder multilingual learners from becoming proficient in English.

___ AI tools may diminish or hinder critical thinking.

___ AI may provide inaccurate, misleading, superficial, or biased information.

___ AI may present a threat to student data privacy.

___ Others: ____

HARNESSING AI AS A SCAFFOLDING TOOL

Wherever you stand with AI, the proliferation of AI-enhanced educational and productivity tools is evident everywhere. Take a look at our "A-to-Z with AI" in Figure 7.4 and cross-check which of these tools might hold promise as a digital scaffold, which of them you are familiar with, which you might be intrigued by, and what others not listed here you might be using already.

FIGURE 7.4 ● A-to-Z With AI

A is for Animated Drawing: to bring students' drawings to life

B is for Brainly: to help students get answers to challenging homework questions; B is also for Bing Image Creator: to turn verbal directions into images

C is for ChatGPT: to get answers to any questions; C is also for Carnegie Learning: to help create personalized learning plans; C is also for Craiyon: to create art with this image generator app

D is for Diffit: to create leveled differentiated resources on any content/topic

E is for ELSA Speak: to practice pronunciation

F is for Formative AI: to design digital assignments and offer real-time feedback

G is for Grammarly: to help with spelling and grammatical structures; G is also for Google tools such as Google Translate; Google Earth Studio, or Google Gemini

H is for Hello History: to allow students to have life-like conversations with historical figures

I is for Immersive Fox: to transform text into multilingual videos; I is also for Image Creator: to generate images from text

J is for Jumpspeak: to engage in AI-partnered dialogues; J is also for Julius AI: to visualize and animate math problems

K is for Khan Academy's Khanmigo: to provide students feedback and respond to student inquiries; K is also for Knowji: to teach vocabulary by combining audio and visual inputs, cartoons, etc.

L is for LanguaTalk: to practice conversations with personalized interactions

M is for MagicSchool AI: to provide over 60 AI tools both for students and teachers

N is for Note Genie: to help take notes with AI-powered transcription

O is for Owlift: to offer complex concept simplification, discussion question generator

P is for Perplexity AI: to answer questions and provide citations as links

Q is for Quizlet: to practice with AI-driven flashcards, tests, and games; Q is also for QuillBot: to help with paraphrasing and to check text for grammar and plagiarism

R is for Recall: to serve as a summarization tool

S is for Socratic: to serve as a personal tutor and to offer personalized learning; S is also for Speechify: to turn text into audio

T is for Textbuddy: to provide AI-powered editing and multilingual translations

U is for Unreal Speech: to convert text to speech with humanlike voices

V is for Vimeo AI: to create videos with AI support

W is for We Made A Story: to create age-specific children's stories; W is also for Wisdolia to transform study materials into multilingual interactive flashcards

X is for X Detector: to detect AI-generated content in multiple languages

Y is for Yippity: to convert any piece of information into question-and-answer prompts and flashcards

Z is for zSpace: to help students use augmented and virtual reality (AR/VR) in science and technology

WHAT TEACHERS SAY ABOUT DIGITAL SCAFFOLDING WITH AI

Kelly Cray, cultural and language support educator at Burr and Burton Academy, Manchester Center in Vermont, has found several meaningful opportunities for AI integration in her classes:

I advocated for mixed-level classes a while back as they add so much enrichment, creating space for children to learn from each other and create a sense of kinship and camaraderie. But being a grade teacher in a mixed-level class is challenging on so many counts; AI has made me the teacher I always dreamed of being. Suddenly, I can do a million things at once. For example, for a warm-up, I ask ChatGPT to create leveled warm-up speaking prompts for my English language development class and give 2 words of the day for them to use. Theme:

Famous Art Language foci: supporting details, past progressive. Students are A2-C1 (International Baccalaureate levels approximately corresponding to Levels 2-5).

AI's Response:

"Words of the Day:

1. Masterpiece *(noun)*: a work of outstanding artistry, skill, or workmanship.
   Example: The Mona Lisa is considered a masterpiece of the Renaissance.
2. Portray *(verb)*: to depict or represent in a work of art or literature.
   Example: The painting portrays a woman sitting by a window.

Leveled Speaking Prompts

A2 Level:

1. What were you doing the last time you saw a painting or a picture?
   (Example: I was walking in a museum when I saw a beautiful masterpiece.)
2. Look at a famous painting. Describe it. What do you think is happening in the picture? Use "was/were + -ing."
   (Example: The artist was painting a woman who was smiling softly.)

B1 Level:

1. Think about a famous painting you know. What was the artist likely doing or thinking while they were creating it?
   (Example: While Van Gogh was painting Starry Night, he might have been feeling emotional.)
2. Imagine you are looking at a painting. What details in the picture support the idea that it is a masterpiece?
   (Example: The details of the light and shadows in the picture make it a masterpiece.)

B2 Level:

1. Describe a famous artwork. What do you think the people in the painting were doing when the artist portrayed them?
   (Example: In The Last Supper, the people were talking and eating together when Da Vinci portrayed them.)
2. How do you think an artist prepares to create a masterpiece? Give specific details to support your answer.
   (Example: Before creating a masterpiece, the artist might have been sketching many ideas and studying other works of art.)

C1 Level:

1. Choose a famous piece of art. How does the artist portray emotions or actions in the scene? What supporting details in the artwork make it a masterpiece? *(Example: The details in The Persistence of Memory portray a surreal world where time seems to be melting away.)*
2. If you were interviewing a famous artist from the past, what questions would you ask about their process while they were working on their masterpiece? *(Example: What were you thinking while you were painting this scene? What details were most challenging to portray?)"*

ChatGPT. (2024, December 8). Leveled speaking prompts for English language development. OpenAI.

The AI gets to know what you often ask for; here, it gave two choices per level because that is something I usually ask for; I like students to have choices. From here, I can edit and tweak the prompts as needed. I can also ask AI to include sentence stems or word banks if the students need them. In my class, I work with my students to learn to choose the most challenging prompt that they can be successful with. It takes some time and practice for students to hit their stride. At the beginning of the year, my students generally try to pick the highest-level prompts and not fully answer the question. I spend time sharing sample responses and going over expectations with my students. I think the most important part of scaffolding is helping the student feel empowered and inspired. This can be hard. There is a lot of stigma against asking for "help." Or getting another version of something. That is why I like to include all levels in everything I do, from speaking and writing prompts to even reading passages. When students choose, it reduces the stigma. I also try not to judge. If I see some higher-proficiency students choose a lower-level prompt. They might have a lot going on; maybe they slept poorly or worked late; perhaps that prompt is the best for them today. If I have a student constantly working below their potential, a one-on-one conversation usually solves the problem.

TEACHING PRACTICES

We are using the six modes of communication (listening, speaking, reading, writing, viewing, and visually representing) introduced by WIDA (2020) as an organizational principle for this section of the chapter. First, we explore how digital scaffolds can provide students with access to new learning and engage them in interpretive processes of language use previously called receptive skills, including listening, reading, and viewing. Next, we move on to the expressive domains of language previously dubbed as productive language skills, including speaking, writing, and visually representing, and highlighting successful tools and strategies for those modes of communication. We are only highlighting well-established, reliable, and teacher-tested apps, websites, and resources in this section, with the understanding that there are many more options available and even more will emerge in the coming months and years.

DIGITAL SCAFFOLDING PRACTICE #1: MULTIMODAL DIGITAL SUPPORT TO ACCESS NEW LEARNING

Multilingual learners need access to grade- and age-appropriate core content to be successful academically. It is easier to achieve this goal when they become and stay motivated and engaged in the learning tasks their teachers design for them. When it comes to the complex nature of language and literacy development, students develop comprehension skills across the modalities to develop new knowledge and understanding. Strategic use of digital tools as scaffolds across the three interpretive modes of communication ensures multiple entry points and various meaningful exposure to complex ideas and authentic yet accessible language input.

WHAT TEACHERS SAY ABOUT MULTIMODAL DIGITAL SCAFFOLDING

Source: istock.com/mladn61

When we think about creating immersive language experiences for our students, Canva can be a great tool to bring vocabulary and text to life. Presentation slides that include multimodal options, such as sound files and video loops, pull learners into the learning. For example, for a read-aloud of Come On, Rain! by Karen Hesse, there is a reference to a "gramophone," a long since used music player that eventually was replaced with the term "phonograph." This sound is referred to and sets the scene for the hot day of old where the main character roams her town and experiences different sounds and feelings as she does so. Inserting a picture and a sound loop that is playing the sound of a gramophone into the slides, this can be shown and played in the background while this page is read, helping the story come to life in the imagination of our readers, and giving context to a rather obscure word.

Sarah Forbes, kindergarten multilingual learner support teacher and co-teacher at John F. Kennedy Elementary School, Winooski, Vermont

EXAMPLE #1: DIGITAL TOOLS TO SUPPORT AND SCAFFOLD LISTENING

Listening and processing information without any other types of input or communication channels is a tall order for many students, not just language learners. Imagine how challenging it might be for students to listen to the many announcements blasted over the school loudspeaker day in and day out! (By the way, this rather antiquated use of technology is successfully augmented in major airports with digital message boards that allow travelers to see and hear announcements, and it is available in multiple languages nonetheless!)

When multilingual learners hear their teachers or their peers talk, there may be limited opportunities for them to make sense of such auditory input. Students can certainly ask the speaker to repeat what they have just said, and they may even request that they slow down a bit or explain what was presented again. In addition to well-established, more traditional ways to enhance understanding, a range of digital media tools are available to boost comprehension and exposure to novel ideas. They give multilingual learners the opportunity to listen to authentic language, and while doing so, they can adjust the rate of speech, pause and rewind a recording, or repeat a listening task as many times as needed. Thus, real-life verbal input can be augmented with digital sources so students may listen to commercially available or teacher-created read-alouds, kid- or teen-friendly educational podcasts, news reports, interviews, and a wide variety of recordings. Some of the most reputable and long-standing resources include Audible (audiobooks and podcasts by age group), National Public Radio (NPR) with several kid-friendly podcasts (e.g., *But Why: Podcast for Curious Kids*).

Our advice is to not limit yourselves to merely sharing digital content. If you wish to create your own recordings with professional sound quality—or better yet—set your students up to start recording, interviewing, and listening to each other's work, there are easy-to-use apps such as Podbean or GarageBand available.

EXAMPLE #2: DIGITAL TOOLS TO SUPPORT AND SCAFFOLD READING

Multilingual learners can access fiction and nonfiction texts electronically through websites and apps, including e-books. Some online digital platforms such as Newsela, Time for Kids, and News in Levels provide accessible news reports tailored to a wide range of ages and reading levels. Similarly, TumbleBooks and CommonLit provide the same literary text on multiple Lexile or reading levels. Teachers may select the most appropriate version of the text for students, and multilingual learners may determine which level is most accessible to them. Some reading websites also offer a range of extension activities, including vocabulary-building exercises, videos, and games such as DOGO News, ReadWorks, Epic!, Reading A-Z, and Tween Tribune.

Assistive technology—more frequently utilized with students with special needs—makes reading digital content accessible for all who need it through text-to-audio features, which benefits all multilingual learners by allowing students to read the text or follow along while they listen simultaneously. These tools can be customized to match individual reading speeds and comprehension levels, enabling students to pause, replay, and adjust the pace, as needed, for optimal understanding. Additionally, many assistive technology platforms now include built-in translation features, vocabulary support, and visual aids that help bridge language gaps and reinforce meaning. The integration of these multimedia elements not only supports diverse learning preferences but also promotes greater independence and confidence among students as they develop their reading and language skills. Some examples of this assistive technology include text-to-speech tools such as NaturalReader, Read&-Write, Voice Dream Reader, and Speechify; translation tools such as Snap&Read, DeepL, and iTranslate; and visual support tools such as line readers, dyslexia-friendly fonts, and high contrast modes.

Yet another new kind of digital tool that enhances reading and creates scaffold access points by making it interactive is commonly referred as a social reading tool, in which students can highlight text, add comments and discuss their understanding of digital text with their peers and teachers either online or in person. In her research, Elif Burhan-Horasanlı (2022) emphasizes how "DSRs [digital social readings] transform reading into an interactive practice, through which students can follow, like, and respond to each other's annotations and thus build shared attention and more focused conversations around text(s)" (p. 3). Some annotation tools can be used with middle and high school students as well via private rooms that teachers can set up (such as within the platform *Hypothes.is*). Others, such as *Perusal* or *NowComment*, require teachers to upload a text selection for students to use as an anchor text for annotation and class discussion. Based on the linguistic and content-based focus of these selections, they can also serve as mentor text for writing assignments.

Samantha Sova (2024), a secondary ELA teacher, creatively reignites the love and joy of reading in her students with book tasting: periodically, she offers her students to browse or sample multiple books across genres, reading levels, themes, and so forth. We recommend a technology-enhanced version of it by creating a "digital playlist" for a class, a group, or even an individual student and inviting students to get a taste of as many texts as possible without imposing a particular text or even genre and incorporating a variety of formats including articles, e-books, blogs, podcasts, and interactive stories that can be easily accessed across different devices and platforms to accommodate diverse learning preferences and schedules.

EXAMPLE #3: DIGITAL TOOLS TO SUPPORT AND SCAFFOLD VIEWING AND VISUALLY PROCESSING

Viewing and visually accessing or interpreting information requires practice and skills like reading comprehension. Viewing and visual processing may include any kind of image, from photographs or drawings to diagrams or graphs, as well as watching and making sense of movie clips, video presentations, TED talks, and so on. Instructional videos and other visual resources can be found across platforms such as YouTube, Khan Academy, Discovery Education, TedED, and more.

Another well-regarded platform is The New York Times Learning Network, which publishes an extensive section of up-to-date, high-quality news items online, along with ready-to-use instructional materials. In addition to reading, this open-access platform invites students to closely examine images in two categories—photographs and graphs—and ponder the following open-ended questions:

- What's going on in this picture?
- What's going on in this graph?

Many teachers we work with further scaffold visual literacy tasks by using VTS (Visual Thinking Strategies) scaffolding strategies (look back to Chapter 4 for examples).

In addition to looking at and analyzing digital images, video-viewing—both for previewing or reviewing lessons—has been widely used for instructional purposes. We suggest that videos may serve as powerful digital tools and scaffolds as well. If you have ever browsed YouTube for instructional materials, you must have found a huge selection of children's books that are read aloud by actors, voice artists, or teachers like you; some even have animated versions available. Once students watch a video version of a book, they can move on to analyze it by using the print version of the text. If there are film adaptations of reading materials, students can compare and contrast the two versions of the same story. In addition to YouTube, some well-established video platforms include:

- FluentU: uses clips from TV shows, movie scenes, and even music videos for learners to watch with or without subtitles
- Discovery Channel: broadcasts high-quality nature shows
- National Geographic: broadcasts high-quality nature shows
- AsapSCIENCE: has grown into one of the largest educational channels on YouTube, sharing videos related to science and technology
- History Channel: broadcasts high-quality shows related to history and current events

- PBS Kids: produces educational shows and games for all ages
- Khan Academy: helps students practice at their own pace

Whichever platform, app, or digital tool you are using, consider a scaffolding template, such as the one in Figure 7.5, when the goal is to ensure students interact with the digital content in a structured fashion.

FIGURE 7.5 ● Basic Scaffolding Template

Pre-viewing: Ask predictions
  Introduce one or two key essential vocabulary words or phrases
  Have students complete anticipatory guides
Viewing: Show the video twice
  First viewing: Ask big-idea questions and aim to get to the gist
  Second Viewing: Have students look for some specific details
  Encourage text-based or visual notetaking
Post-viewing: Have students discuss what they saw
  Compare their new understanding with their predictions
  Have them revisit their anticipatory guides

online resources Available for download at https://companion.corwin.com/courses/NineDimensionsofScaffoldingforMLs

There is an abundance of visual resources that may be strategically integrated into lessons for multilingual learners. A unique visual tool that could scaffold and support learning is Virtual Reality (VR). Students wear a headset that blocks out the physical environment and displays artificial content (virtual reality) that allows them to be present and interact in a computer-generated, immersive environment that simulates a 3D interactive experience. This simulation technology has made its way into many classrooms because it brings the world to life and allows students access to a variety of experiences. Simpler, more accessible learning opportunities that build background knowledge and provide unique visual experiences without VR equipment include:

- "Flying" anywhere in the world with Google Earth. You can walk the streets of any major city, hike mountains, explore river estuaries and ocean beaches.
- Taking a virtual trip to major museums and galleries in the United States and beyond. The 360-degree view of exhibit halls or the close-up examination of artifacts or paintings on display support students' interaction with otherwise inaccessible or hard-to-reach places and objects of importance.
- Watching live camera feeds from interesting spots, such as famous intersections in metropolises (e.g., 42nd street of New York City), zoos and wildlife sanctuaries from around the world (e.g., Zoolife with 24/7 streaming from numerous locations or the U.S. National Park Service

via www.nps.gov), historical sites and other points of interest from around the globe (e.g., EarthCam https://www.earthcam.com).

In Figure 7.6, Victoria Seelinger previews what her students will be experiencing by using VR during a favorite learning activity. In order to celebrate students' cultural identities and backgrounds, she encourages her students to visit their countries of origin or ancestral homes virtually. She also models the appropriate use of the device.

FIGURE 7.6 • Previewing How VR Can Support Student Exploration

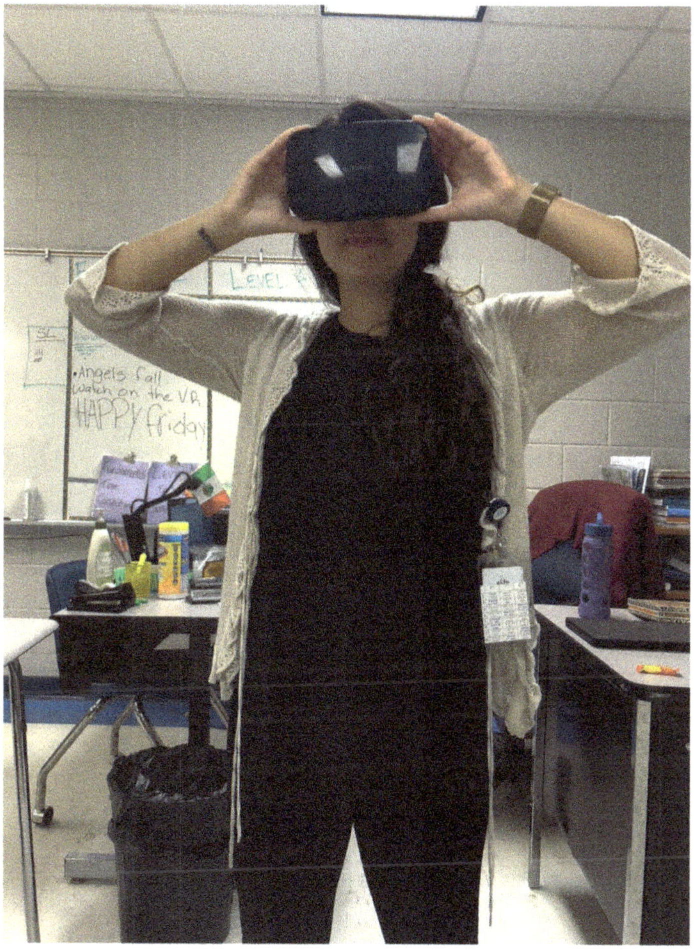

Source: Victoria Seelinger. Used with permission.

ADVANTAGES OF THIS PRACTICE

With the expansion of technology tools, multimodal digital supports are also expanding in their importance and impact on student learning. They provide much-needed and varied access to new learning or to practice and application of language and literacy skills. Some scaffolds may serve the purpose of offering immediate access to language and literacy learning, such as speech-to-text technology or spellcheck, whereas some may be used in tandem with other scaffolds, such as digital recordings students can watch or listen to while also accessing print-based materials.

The use of technology may be highly motivating for many students. It lets them engage in learning in ways that parallel many of their outside school activities. Students are generally well versed in communicating on digital platforms such as text messaging and video chats, as well as enjoy various video games that foster creativity, critical thinking, and problem solving. One of the most important motivating factors for using digital tools is how they can provide personalized learning for students, which is particularly important for multilingual learners. They allow students to work at their own pace, thereby affording them greater autonomy. Additionally, these tools offer students timely feedback, which can further spark motivation and encourage engagement.

KEEP THIS IN MIND

All external digital content and tools, including apps, must be carefully vetted for quality and appropriateness. Ensure that any material you plan to have students listen to, read, or view is carefully reviewed for (a) content, (b) language, (c) overall technical quality and ease of use, and (d) need for any prior contextualization and background building. Even if you feel pressured for time, do not show or use anything you have not previewed fully. Be mindful of any websites that might be blocked by your district or are free only with excessive embedded advertisements.

DIGITAL SCAFFOLDING PRACTICE #2: MULTIMODAL DIGITAL SUPPORTS AND SCAFFOLDS TO DEMONSTRATE LEARNING

For language and literacy to grow and expand across subject matters, instructional and noninstructional contexts, modes of expression, and so forth, multilingual learners need multiple meaningful opportunities to express themselves—to talk, write, and visually represent their thinking and understanding. Student engagement and active participation across language domains ensure varied opportunities to formulate their ideas in a new language and new learning contexts. Jenna Maneri, former elementary English as a second language (ESL) teacher and School District ML Coach at Bridgewater-Raritan Regional in New Jersey, uses various digital tools with students to engage in independent research. Based on students' reading level and language proficiency, she curates a range of digital resources so students can read books, listen to read-aloud books, and watch videos before completing a graphic organizer about the subject of their research. Additional scaffolds include sentence frames and paragraph outlines. Jenna integrates Vocaroo (an online voice recording app) so students could practice reading their sentences and re-record themselves, if necessary, before submitting the speaking part of their assignment (see Figure 7.7). This also serves as practice for the oral presentation they would be giving at the end of the unit.

FIGURE 7.7 ● Scaffolding With Voice Recording and Sentence Frames

1. Introduction
Let me tell you about ________________

2. Childhood
______was born _____ *(date and location) at*_____.

3. Famous For
___________ is famous for _______________.

4. Major Accomplishments
One of ______ accomplishments is ______________.
Another accomplishment is _______________.

5. Key Life Events
One key event in _________'s life was ______.
Another key event in her life was ___________.

6. Famous Quote
___________ is famous for saying "_____________"

Source: Jenna Maneri. Used with permission.

FROM RESEARCH TO PRACTICE

Before we explore these three modes of communication, let's tap into what research says. Loren Jones et al. (2022) investigated how teachers took on the role of digital composers and modeled the use of digital scaffolds for their multilingual students. They referred to a combination of tools as digital jumpstarts that helped students develop autonomy and increased their motivation while engaging in digital storytelling. The researchers concluded:

(Continued)

(Continued)

"Analysis of digital jumpstart projects that the teachers created, their lesson plans, and their written reflections revealed that digital jumpstarts can effectively provide students with planned scaffolds that support language and content development through the incorporation of multiple modes, key terms and definitions, translations, and connections to students' lived experiences." (p. 1)

Reflect on the following:

Have you tried digital storytelling? If so, what worked? If not yet, how would you consider incorporating digital jumpstarts? How might they impact student learning?

____

____

____

____

EXAMPLE #1: DIGITAL TOOLS TO SUPPORT ORAL EXPRESSIONS OR SCAFFOLD SPEAKING

When multilingual learners participate in typical classroom interactions, they may be talking with classmates, contributing to a small group or whole class discussion, sharing their ideas directly with the teacher, or presenting their work in front of the whole class. It may require significant courage on behalf of the student and strong encouragement on behalf of the teacher for multilingual learners to contribute to classroom discourse. For these reasons, using various forms of digital media gives students the opportunity to:

- record their thoughts and offer an explanation (by adding a voice recording to a Google slide),
- engage in an asynchronous video or audio discussion (by using digital discussion platforms such as WeVideo),
- narrate a digital story that they created (such as by using Book Creator),
- create their own podcast (such as Soundtrap for Education), and
- provide audio feedback on their classmates' work (such as in Canvas).

When students are invited to record their ideas, they may or may not plan what they are going to share. They might create an outline, write out some key phrases or sentences, seek peer or teacher feedback before recording, or even rehearse what they are going to say. Alternatively, students may use digital tools to capture their ideas more spontaneously. An added benefit is that students can re-record as many times as needed until they are satisfied with the result. They may also receive feedback on an earlier recording and make a new attempt at their work.

EXAMPLE #2: DIGITAL TOOLS TO SUPPORT AND SCAFFOLD WRITING

Multilingual learners, just like all students in K-12 classrooms, frequently use traditional tools such as paper, pencils, pens, crayons, and markers for writing to capture their thoughts, take notes, or communicate their ideas in more formal ways. With the rise of school-based technology integration and the prevalence of one-on-one devices such as tablets, iPads, Chromebooks, and laptops, digital learning resources are becoming an integral part of everyday writing tasks. Therefore, it is important to recognize the power of technology as students develop new literacy identities and become authors of digital content for either their immediate or larger audiences. E-books, blog posts, class websites, and as well as other digital tools can create authentic opportunities for writing. Platforms such as Storybird, Edublogs, and WriteReader not only facilitate writing but also create a collaborative, low-anxiety environment for students. See Figure 7.8 for an example of how Mariel Gómez de la Torre–Cerfontaine, K-8 ESL teacher at Summit Virtual Academy, Rowan Salisbury Schools in North Carolina, models a writing task in two ways. She deconstructs the task and shares her own completed paragraph to add clarity to her expectations and to offer instructional support for her students.

Digital text creation is one emerging trend among educators who recognize the possibility and impact of multimodality in writing instruction and student self-expression. We adapted the CLICK model from Robin Jocius (2020), suggesting a protocol for teachers to provide scaffolds for students as they compose multimodal text:

- C: Collaborate with peers, which makes digital, multimodal content creation interactive and social.
- L: Loop, which refers to the process of teachers providing supporting materials and guidance on how to use appropriate digital tools.
- I: Increase the complexity of the assignment, which gives students time and opportunity to adjust to incrementally more challenging assignments and to become more comfortable with multimodal composing.
- C: Critique each other's work, which allows for peer feedback and further edits.
- K: Know the process of multimodal composing, which helps develop metacognitive and metalinguistic awareness.

FIGURE 7.8 ● Task Modeling and Product Modeling With WriteReader

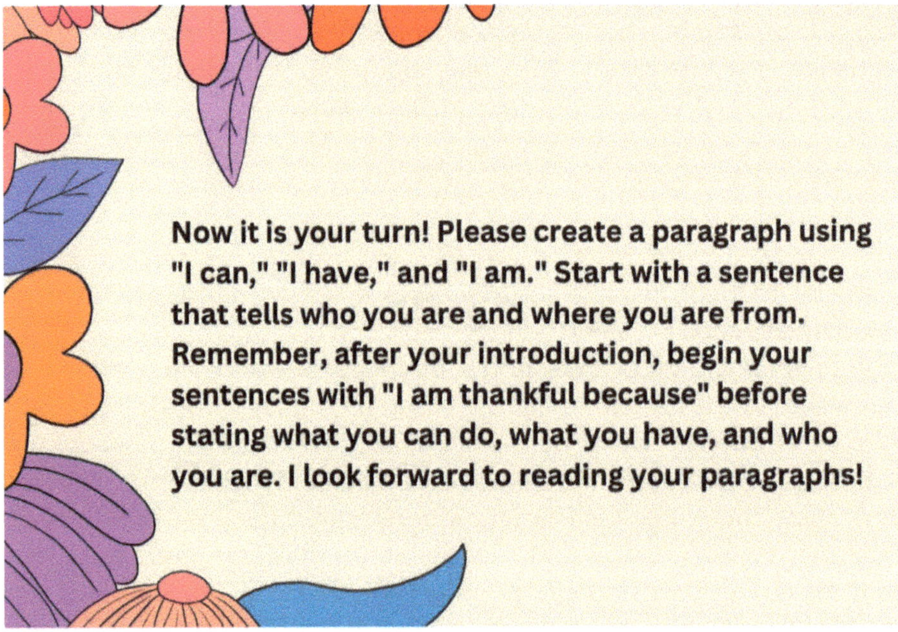

You can use my example: My name is Mariel Gómez de la Torre, and I am from Lima, Peru. I am thankful that I have a family. I have a house, friends, and students. I am brave because I moved to another country. I am adaptable, having lived on three different continents.

Source: Mariel Gómez de la Torre-Cerfontaine. Used with permission.

EXAMPLE #3: DIGITAL TOOLS TO SUPPORT AND SCAFFOLD VISUAL REPRESENTATION

Drawing, sketching out ideas, taking notes visually, and trying other engagements in visual self-expression or demonstration of learning can be highly motivating when digital tools are used. When multilingual learners create a visual product, they must collect and organize information from multiple text-based and visual sources and determine how to best convey meaning visually. Simple devices, such as stylus pens for touch screens or more intricate tools and programs, such as Educreations or PowToon, can facilitate student self-expression and communication through visual imagery. See Figure 7.9 as an example of how Michelle Gill, an ELL teacher at the Abbotsford School District in Canada, uses Book Maker to scaffold a game called "This or That." Next, take a look at Figure 7.10 for a template she gives her students so they could create their own "This or That" prompts. Her digital scaffolds are combined with linguistic and interactive scaffolds.

FIGURE 7.9 ● Teacher Example of "This or That" Task

Source: Michelle Gill. Used with permission.

FIGURE 7.10 ● Scaffolded Template for the "This or That" Task

OPEN ENDED QUESTION	
Write your answer below. Then, when instructed, discuss your answers with your partner or group. Use the second box to take notes on what their answers were in the space provided. 1. Create your own "This or That" prompt.	
Your answer:	**What did your partner or group say?**

Source: Michelle Gill. Used with permission.

EXAMPLE #4: DIGITAL TOOLS TO SUPPORT AND SCAFFOLD PARTICIPATION IN LEARNING THROUGH GAMES

When multilingual learners feel anxious or nervous about using their new language, they might shy away from participating in learning experiences or contributing their ideas to class discussions. Zaretta Hammond (2015) powerfully positions gamifying learning as a culturally responsive pedagogical choice when she claims that "Games are the power strategy for culturally-grounded learning because they get the brain's attention and require active processing. Attention is the first step in learning. We cannot learn, remember, or understand what we don't first pay attention to" (para 10). We believe that gamifying learning and creating a learning environment where students actively use language with their affective filter lowered (Krashen, 1988) are also pathways to linguistically responsive pedagogy that may be well supported by digital scaffolds.

When students play a game, mistakes are less awkward or not embarrassing at all. Making mistakes and taking risks are part of any game. For this reason, there are several digital tools that can scaffold learning by turning it into a game-like activity. Two favorites among many teachers are Kahoot! (this platform has an extensive selection of quizzes and games that invite both collaboration and competition among students) and Gimkit (this tool acts as a game show and requires students to demonstrate their understanding of a topic by using strategic thinking and collaboration).

ADVANTAGES OF THIS SCAFFOLDING APPROACH

Digital scaffolds not only support students' academic attainment and language and literacy development, but they also serve as impactful tools of motivation and self-expression. These tools provide ways for students to engage with material that is accessible and personalized, and they can break down complex tasks as well as offer immediate feedback. Additionally, they can offer students various ways to express their ideas and communicate what they know and have learned. The combination of the support and the freedom for students to express their ideas using multiple platforms makes the use of digital scaffolds a powerful instructional practice.

KEEP THIS IN MIND

Digital tools are not the panacea. There are numerous translation tools available (e.g., Google Translate) that can be used to support multilingual learners. However, we deliberately stayed away from advocating for them in this chapter to avoid over-reliance on translation apps as the go-to strategy for one-stop solutions to support students.

WHAT TEACHERS SAY ABOUT DIGITAL SCAFFOLDING

My collaboration and mutual coaching with our school's media specialist, Grace Campbell-Sheran, includes bots she's built and trained to connect state content standards with WIDA ELD standards and the school's lesson planning format. We're playing around with asking for specific help in creating lesson plans and lesson activities. For example, I told one bot that it should always suggest QSSSA—Question, Signal, Stem, Share, Assess (Seidlitz et al., 2024) instead of turn and talk and also provide sentence stem suggestions. I've asked it to help me write exemplar essays and grade-level texts to explain a science image about energy transfer. In this way, properly trained AI is helping to scaffold the way I can build lesson materials both for ESL classes and for content area classes.

—Tamara Coburn, multilingual learner instructional coach, Konnoak Middle School, Winston-Salem/Forsyth County Schools, North Carolina

INDEPENDENT LEARNING STRATEGIES FOR STUDENTS

Today's K-12 students are technologically savvy—they often know and do more with digital tools than some of their teachers. As educators, our role is to recognize the full potential technology holds when integrated with sound pedagogy and utilized for sustained, authentic, and equitable content, language, and literacy development. When digital scaffolds are coupled with equity-focused strategies, teachers recognize the urgency of the learning context and attend to students' immediate, unique needs by attending to the following:

1. Ensure access to devices both in school and at home. But simply handing students a shiny new Chromebook or laptop will not do the trick! Make sure students develop competence using these tools independently.
2. Evaluate accessibility tools that were tested, used, or are needed. All students, not only multilingual learners, should benefit from tools that

better help them access the curriculum. Closed captioning, PowerPoint presentations with voiceovers, electronic highlighters, screen readers, calculators, low-tech math supports, magnification, and text-to-speech options are choices students must be aware of and integrate into their own learning as needed.

3. Leverage students' emerging expertise and talents when it comes to not merely using technology and accessing material digitally but also developing new content.
4. Establish routines that encourage independence and critical, responsible use of technology, including digital tools or apps such as Duolingo, Imagine Learning, and Starfall.

SUMMARY

Digital scaffolding is an essential practice to advance and accelerate multilingual learners' content, language, and literacy development by harnessing contemporary technology tools and pedagogies. This rapidly expanding field brings some new challenges and opportunities to educators to enhance their support for multilingual learners in previously unimaginable ways. While we highlighted some well-established digital tools in this chapter, we are fully aware that by the time you read this book, many new tools will be available to students and educators alike. Our main goal was to emphasize the pedagogical decisions you would need to make to intentionally integrate technology to enhance student motivation, access to learning, and self-expression.

Questions

1. Which strategies and recommendations in this chapter affirm your practice, and which ones challenge you to try something new?
2. How do you integrate digital scaffolding with other forms of scaffolding?
3. What role does AI play in your current teaching? What potential applications do you see for the future?

CHAPTER 8

Scaffolding Social-Emotional Learning

"Teachers who respect and invite students' cultures into the classroom have opportunities to expand the understanding and perspectives of everyone."
Gloria Ladson-Billings, 2021, p. 76

Social-emotional scaffolds help establish and implement nurturing learning environments geared to support students' overall health and well-being through intentional strategies that meet students where they are socially and emotionally. They are crucial skills that are taught to multilingual learners because they offer support to develop their capacity to navigate their often complex personal and social lives, contributing to their overall success. Without these skills, multilingual learners sometimes face a range of challenges including communication difficulties, behavioral issues, anxiety, and problems adapting to new learning spaces as well as navigating challenging academic content.

Through social-emotional learning (SEL) strategies, teachers focus on more than academics as they build relationships with students and support their social-emotional development in the classroom through a multi-layered approach. Building solid relationships and connections with multilingual learners strengthens the classroom community and, in turn, enhances positive learning environments that support the health and well-being of all students (Honigsfeld et al., 2021).

Teachers act as role models as they demonstrate healthy examples of empathy, self-control, effective communication, and other social-emotional skills students need to develop. By scaffolding these skills, teachers help to meet students where they are as individuals, encouraging them to express themselves and share their thoughts, beliefs, and insights while validating their identities (Ironside, 2024) within and outside the classroom.

What questions do you ask yourself or reflect on daily to ensure students' social-emotional growth along with academic and language development? Which of these everyday social-emotional learning strategies are already part of your daily practice?

- ***Establishing a supportive and inclusive environment:***
    - Are they remaining engaged in class activities and discussions?
    - Are students acting differently on a particular day?
    - Are they showing signs of stress and anxiety?
    - Are they interacting differently with their peers?
    - Is there a trigger that sets them off on a day that seems routine?

    Why is a safe, supportive, and inclusive environment essential? Establishing an environment that encourages students to feel safe helps them share their thoughts and express their feelings. It also promotes open communication and discussion.

- ***Providing safe spaces:***
    - Are there clear procedures and expectations in place that promote respect and safety?
    - Are there regular check-ins with students to gauge their emotional well-being?
    - Do students check in with peers when they recognize a change?
    - Do some students have moments when they seem to shut down?
    - Do students quickly get angry or frustrated in routine situations?
    - Are there signs that something has changed or is troubling them outside school?

    Why is providing safe spaces essential? Providing students with a space in your classroom or the school building where they feel safe, unjudged, and at ease enables them to take a minute to breathe, step away from a situation, or have a quiet moment. Safe spaces foster personal control and support for their social and emotional needs on their terms. In addition, safe spaces help students become more aware of themselves and their own feelings and recognize the feelings of others. This sense of security and emotional support creates a community of learners who care about one another.

- ***Implementing classroom meetings:***
    - What structure or format might be used to conduct class meetings?
    - How can meetings be inclusive, where all voices are heard and valued?

- What if some students disagree about something but will not discuss it?
- What if some students are easily distracted or focus on things that may not be important?
- How can one ensure that class meetings are relevant and productive?

Why is implementing class meetings essential? Providing opportunities for students to meet as a group, share their thoughts, voice their concerns, and simply be heard allows them to build and be a part of a classroom community as well as supports their self-worth, a sense of belonging, and their personal growth.

- ***Incorporating mindfulness practices:***
  - Do students get anxious before lunch or prior to a specific subject?
  - Are some students worried when they come to school or before they leave for the day to return home?
  - How might mindfulness practices benefit students' overall well-being?
  - What specific mindfulness techniques would be most effective with students?
  - How can mindfulness practices be incorporated into daily routines or learning academic content?

  Why is incorporating mindfulness practices essential? Identify times students appear to be the most anxious and incorporate activities to change their mental direction or put them into a state of relaxation to help them cope with whatever they may be facing.

WHO IS IT FOR?

Teaching social-emotional skills and scaffolding these techniques equip all students with the essential tools to navigate their personal, social, and academic lives. Specifically for multilingual learners, it includes fostering their cultural identity, which contributes to their overall well-being and success. By incorporating and scaffolding these skills within the curriculum, students can achieve academically and become well-rounded individuals who integrate into the wider community, positively contributing to society and being better prepared to face the complexities of life.

In addition, social-emotional scaffolding benefits multilingual learners' overall well-being and accomplishments. It enables them to navigate the challenges of content and language learning and cultural adjustment while developing the skills necessary for success in school and beyond.

We use the CASEL (n.d.) framework, a comprehensive, evidence-based approach that covers multiple aspects of student development, to show the connection between social-emotional skills and academic achievement. The framework has five core competencies: self-awareness, self-management, social awareness, relationship skills, and responsible decision-making (CASEL, n.d.). Each element significantly supports the whole child in meeting academic standards by coupling it with their nonacademic needs. In Table 8.1, we identify each competency and give an overview of how each element supports social-emotional development.

TABLE 8.1 ● The Components of Social-Emotional Learning

ELEMENTS OF SOCIAL-EMOTIONAL LEARNING	OVERVIEW
Self-Awareness	Understanding and recognizing one's own emotions, strengths, weaknesses, and values. Self-awareness includes developing emotional literacy and self-reflection skills.
Self-Management	Learning to regulate and manage one's emotions, impulses, and behavior. Self-management involves stress management, self-control, and coping with challenges.
Social Awareness	Developing empathy and the ability to understand and appreciate the feelings and perspectives of others. The social awareness component includes recognizing and valuing diversity and cultural competency.
Relationship Skills	Developing the ability to build and maintain positive and healthy relationships with peers, teachers, and others is a crucial aspect of social-emotional learning. Relationship skills involve communication, active listening, cooperation, and conflict resolution.
Responsible Decision-Making	Making ethical and responsible choices based on ethical and social norms. Responsible decision-making includes understanding the consequences of one's actions and problem-solving.

Source: Adapted from CASEL (n.d.)

WHAT TEACHERS SAY ABOUT SCAFFOLDING SOCIAL-EMOTIONAL LEARNING

In my curriculum, the final unit of the year is a personal narrative unit. In this unit, students read examples of memoirs in different genres—graphic novels, children's books, and short excerpts from autobiographies. Then, students complete a variety of activities to generate ideas for their own stories that they could turn into a "comic book" based on their experiences. Students create timeline maps of key events, relationships, and/or places in their lives. This timeline map is one activity completed as part of our brainstorming. The timeline maps not only support their understanding of plot sequencing but also invite students to deeply reflect on their past and more recent experiences, their friendships, and other relationships, and the ups and downs in their lives (See Figure 8.1 for one student example).

—Jennifer Edwards, English as a second language teacher, Hamilton High School, Ohio

FIGURE 8.1 ● Student Personal Timeline With Explanations

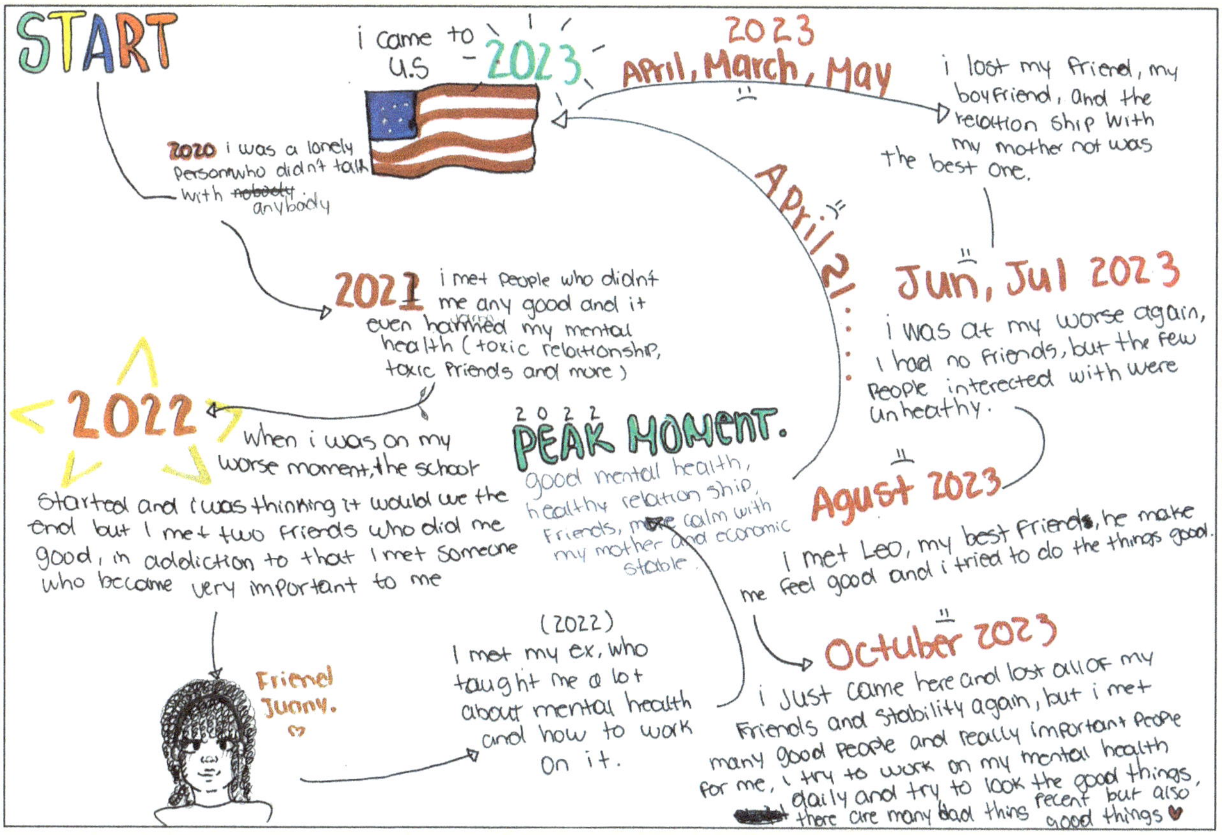

Source: Student work. Used with permission.

HOW IS SCAFFOLDING SOCIAL-EMOTIONAL LEARNING USED ACROSS PROGRAM MODELS?

From an emotional perspective, meeting students where they are is paramount to supporting them academically. Academic learning can only occur effectively when students' nonacademic needs and circumstances are thoughtfully addressed. For this reason, social-emotional learning has become part of the fabric of many schools and classrooms.

Numerous school districts have implemented the CASEL framework as part of their social-emotional programs, providing a structured approach to support all students while allowing for targeted interventions when needed. Popular programs include Second Step, designed for PK-8 students and focuses on learning, empathy, emotion management, and problem solving, to help students gain confidence, set goals, and make better decisions (Shi et al., 2022). Promoting Alternative Thinking Strategies (PATHS) aims to reduce aggression and behavior issues by developing social and emotional skills (National Center for Education Evaluation at IES, 2021). RULER, developed by the Yale Center for Emotional Intelligence (n.d.), teaches five key emotional intelligence skills—recognizing emotions in oneself and others, understanding the causes and consequences of emotions, labeling emotions with a nuanced vocabulary, expressing emotions in accordance with cultural norms and social context, and regulating emotions with helpful strategies. This method fosters a healthier, more equitable, and compassionate society. Some other programs that are used in schools use a more holistic approach to learning and may include:

- Character education: aims to instill positive values, including respect, responsibility, and honesty;
- Anti-bullying: fosters a positive school climate;
- Conflict resolution: focuses on communication, problem-solving, and negotiations; and
- Mindfulness practices: reduce the effects of and help manage anxiety and stress.

As you read through these ideas, reflect on whether you have any of these initiatives in your school community. Are there other related district- or school-wide programs?

Many SEL programs impact the entire school community and help create a welcoming and affirming climate for all students. Generally, school-wide programs set the direction for teachers' approaches in their classrooms. When schools do not have a structured program, teachers often implement social-emotional learning routines and strategies they have devised to support students from a nonacademic perspective.

- In *general education classes*, teachers may create social-emotional learning routines to support students throughout the day or within an instructional period. They may start the day by meeting students in the hallway or greeting them at the door. This routine might be followed up with a morning meeting and various daily check-ins. Students may also have a cozy Zen Zone or Quiet Corner in the room with comfortable seating to independently self-monitor their feelings.
- In *integrated co-taught classes,* which include students with general education identification as well as students with specific needs, including special education and multilingual learners and the teachers that service them, each teacher implements social-emotional learning techniques during the lesson. For example, while one teacher conducts the morning meeting, the other may encourage students to share their ideas. For multilingual learners who feel uncomfortable speaking English in a whole group setting, the teacher may scaffold the discussion by providing sentence starters or sharing their own thoughts to get the students to join the conversation. Another example of scaffolding social-emotional learning techniques might be when one teacher verbally guides students through a calming breathing exercise ("inhale for four counts, hold for two, exhale for six") while the other teacher physically demonstrates the technique, showing students exactly how to position their bodies, control their breath, and maintain proper posture throughout the exercise.
- In *stand-alone classes* for English language development (ELD), teachers incorporate daily routines for multilingual learners that embed social-emotional learning into lessons, simultaneously supporting ELD to help students navigate a new culture and language. Teachers further scaffold these lessons using anchor charts that feature vocabulary with corresponding emojis that correlate with different feelings or display cognates that give students a clearer understanding of how their home language and English relate.
- In *self-contained classes*, which provide intensive, specialized instruction to students with specific needs in smaller class-size environments, teachers may help students build self-confidence and self-regulate their emotions by engaging them in discussions about their feelings using a mood meter. To implement this strategy, break students into pairs or small groups and provide them with specific talking points to discuss how they are feeling using the mood meter. The teacher may also guide students to reflect on their learning experiences knowledge about a particular topic, and to evaluate their progress, and set goals for their learning.

Social-emotional learning is incorporated throughout all ELD program models and embedded in the context of lessons to support students at all levels of learning. We understand that students may not be receptive to learning if their affective filters are up (Krashen, 1982). To support students at every stage of their academic and language development, we must ensure they feel safe and valued holistically, not just from an instructional vantage point. See Figure 8.2 for an example of how a safe environment is co-constructed in Kristin Chouinard's second-grade co-taught classroom in Framingham Public Schools, Massachusetts.

FIGURE 8.2 ● Co-Constructed Anchor Chart Showing Appreciation for the School Community

Source: Kristen Chouinard. Used with permission.

WHY IS SCAFFOLDING FOR SOCIAL-EMOTIONAL LEARNING AN IMPORTANT APPROACH TO STUDENT LEARNING?

Since the COVID-19 crisis, social-emotional learning has become a central focus in education. Schools have identified its critical role in helping students cope with stress, build resilience, and redevelop communication skills. Recognizing the importance of students' social-emotional development has led to a critical shift in the curriculum to move beyond academics and support the whole student.

To develop a rationale for scaffolding social-emotional learning, we revisit the five components of CASEL introduced earlier in this chapter: self-awareness, self-management, social awareness, relationship skills, and responsible decision-making—to address some key pointers about how to go about scaffolding social-emotional learning instruction. In Table 8.2, we offer our guidance about what to keep in mind when implementing each of the components and the overall impact it may have on students, including multilingual learners.

TABLE 8.2 ● Implementing Scaffolds for Social-Emotional Learning

SOCIAL-EMOTIONAL LEARNING COMPONENTS	WHAT DOES IT MEAN AND INCLUDE?	HOW DO YOU SCAFFOLD IT?	WHAT SHOULD YOU KEEP IN MIND?	WHAT STUDENT IMPACT SHOULD YOU EXPECT?
Self-Awareness	This involves understanding one's own emotions, thoughts, and values, and recognizing one's strengths and limitations.	Self-awareness can be scaffolded in a classroom through activities that encourage self-reflection, such as journaling, mindfulness exercises, or discussions about personal experiences and feelings.	Teachers should create a safe and supportive environment where students feel comfortable exploring and expressing their thoughts, feelings, and experiences without fear of judgment.	Students with strong self-awareness tend to have higher self-confidence, better decision-making skills, and better emotional and behavioral management.
Self-Management	This refers to the ability to regulate one's emotions, thoughts, and behaviors in different situations.	Self-management can be scaffolded in a classroom through teaching strategies for stress management, impulse control, goal-setting, and time management.	Teachers should explicitly teach and model strategies for managing emotions, impulses, and behaviors, such as deep breathing, positive self-talk, and goal-setting.	Students with good self-management skills can better focus and persist in the face of challenges, manage stress and anxiety, and make responsible choices.
Social Awareness	This involves understanding the perspectives of others, showing empathy, and appreciating diversity.	Social awareness can be scaffolded in a classroom through cooperative learning activities, role-playing exercises, and discussions about different cultures and backgrounds.	Teachers should expose students to diverse perspectives and cultures and facilitate discussions and activities that promote empathy, respect, and understanding of others.	Students with strong social awareness are likelier to build positive relationships, collaborate effectively, and contribute to an inclusive and supportive classroom environment.

(Continued)

(Continued)

SOCIAL-EMOTIONAL LEARNING COMPONENTS	WHAT DOES IT MEAN AND INCLUDE?	HOW DO YOU SCAFFOLD IT?	WHAT SHOULD YOU KEEP IN MIND?	WHAT STUDENT IMPACT SHOULD YOU EXPECT?
Relationship Skills	This encompasses establishing and maintaining healthy relationships, communicating effectively, and resolving conflicts.	Relationship skills can be scaffolded in a classroom through cooperative group work, conflict resolution activities, and practicing active listening and effective communication.	Teachers should create opportunities for students to practice active listening, effective communication, conflict resolution, and teamwork through cooperative learning activities and group projects.	Students with well-developed relationship skills are better equipped to navigate social situations, resolve conflicts constructively, and build and maintain positive relationships with peers and adults.
Responsible Decision-Making	This involves making ethical and constructive choices about personal behavior and social interactions.	Responsible decision-making can be scaffolded in a classroom through case studies, moral dilemmas, and discussions about the consequences of actions.	Teachers should engage students in critical thinking and ethical reasoning through case studies, moral dilemmas, and discussions about the consequences of actions.	Students with strong decision-making skills are more likely to make responsible choices, consider the well-being of others, and contribute positively to their communities.

online resources Available for download at https://companion.corwin.com/courses/NineDimensionsofScaffoldingforMLs

WHAT IS SCAFFOLDING SOCIAL-EMOTIONAL LEARNING?

Scaffolding for social-emotional learning is the process of providing structured support and guidance to students to help them build and strengthen relationships, develop social skills, and respond to instructional and noninstructional environments with emotional relevance. It involves creating a nurturing class environment, modeling ideal social behaviors, identifying expectations, practicing the use of specific tools and strategies, and gradually transferring responsibility to students for accountability. By scaffolding for social-emotional learning, students are supported to manage their emotions, build strong relationships with teachers and peers, and make responsible decisions.

Social-emotional learning is typically integrated into the school curriculum, often taught explicitly in lessons, and embedded in various programs and activities promoted through a positive school climate and supportive interactions between students, teachers, and the wider school community. Social-emotional learning centers on developing a range of skills and competencies related to understanding and managing emotions, building positive relationships, reducing stress, and making responsible decisions.

FROM RESEARCH TO PRACTICE

Programs focusing on social-emotional learning, from preschool through high school, are most beneficial when they are intentionally designed, planned, and implemented in ongoing, systemic ways (Berman et al., 2018); Collaborative for Academic, Social, and Emotional Learning, 2017; Jones & Kahn, 2017; Weissberg et al., 2015). Students who receive social-emotional education tend to have improved academic performance, better social relationships, and increased emotional well-being. They are also better equipped to handle challenges and succeed in various aspects of their lives, from school to work and personal relationships.

Reflect on the following:

What is your experience with social-emotional learning*? What strategies or tools do you employ to create a supportive and inclusive classroom environment? How do you tailor* social-emotional learning *to meet the diverse needs of your students? Have you witnessed its positive impact on student well-being? What indicators do you use to measure students' progress in* social-emotional learning*?*

____

____

____

____

WHY IS SOCIAL-EMOTIONAL SCAFFOLDING IMPORTANT FOR MULTILINGUAL LEARNERS?

Learning a new or additional language can be a challenging and sometimes frustrating experience. Social-emotional learning supports multilingual learners' mental health and well-being as they learn to manage their emotions, reduce stress, and improve their ability to focus on the complex language acquisition tasks, literacy development, and content attainment through emotional regulation.

Some multilingual learners must make cultural adjustments as they develop competence in a new language and acclimate to a new school and environment. They often come from diverse backgrounds, and social-emotional learning may help them navigate their new environment's social and cultural nuances, fostering a sense of belonging and inclusion. In turn, students learn to better cope with the stress of language acquisition and cultural adaptation.

Research has shown that a strong sense of belonging can significantly impact student success. In our previous work, we have noted:

> Students who feel connected and develop a sense of belonging have a better chance of succeeding—they are more apt to attend school regularly, are more attentive to their schoolwork, and are more likely to graduate as well as further their education beyond high school. The nurturing relationships that our students need are grounded in perspectives that embrace positive attitudes and beliefs, cultural and linguistic competence, an understanding of the needs and experiences of students, and an understanding of the school environment. (Honigsfeld et al., 2021, p. 81)

Communication is critical for helping students feel safe and connected, which is vital for multilingual learners as they work to improve their language skills and interact with peers and teachers. Social-emotional learning promotes empathy, inclusion, and understanding of others. Multilingual learners often face prejudice or bias, and social-emotional learning can help create a more inclusive and accepting learning environment. Multilingual learners also can become more culturally competent and valued in an increasingly diverse and interconnected world.

HOW DOES SCAFFOLDING FOR SOCIAL-EMOTIONAL LEARNING SPECIFICALLY RELATE TO MULTILINGUAL LEARNERS' NEEDS?

Multilingual learners may experience challenges to their self-esteem and identity as they adapt to a new environment, develop language, and honor their culture while adapting to the world around them. Social-emotional competence can provide tools for resolving conflicts and misunderstandings due to language and cultural differences. It helps students develop a positive self-identity and an in-depth awareness of others as well.

New experiences and life changes can be emotionally taxing, and multilingual learners need to build resilience to overcome the challenges and setbacks they might face more effectively. Social-emotional skills are interconnected with cognitive development. Developing social-emotional learning competencies can enhance cognitive functions, which in turn can improve language acquisition and academic performance. Multilingual learners who have well-developed social-emotional skills often perform better academically. These skills improve their ability to remain focused on their studies, set goals, and persist in facing challenges.

WHAT TEACHERS SAY ABOUT SCAFFOLDING SOCIAL-EMOTIONAL LEARNING

During my undergraduate studies, I had the privilege of interning at a grant-funded literacy program for multilingual learners called Opening Word. During my time teaching in the program, I remember quickly learning how engaged the students became when they were given the opportunity to share their stories. They loved showing me photos from their native countries and telling me about their families. Many students never spoke aloud to answer questions about what we were studying, but they would talk nonstop during lunch periods about their personal experiences. Once I recognized this, I made a conscious effort to frequently ask them questions about themselves during class time to create a safe, engaging learning environment. I soon discovered that prioritizing their feelings and emotions created more opportunities for them to engage in authentic spoken language in English. For this reason, social-emotional scaffolding became a part of my daily instruction. One way I would implement this scaffolding approach is through quick check ins to begin class (see Figure 8.3).

FIGURE 8.3 ● Mental Health Check-In Form

Source: Natalie Pecoraro. Used with permission.

Students would be prompted with the above check-in chart at the beginning of class to determine their feelings before each lesson. This process allows students to connect with their emotions, fostering a sense of self-awareness and readiness for learning. By having students connect with their emotions, they are more likely to feel valued and understood, creating a supportive environment for continued participation.

Another way I would implement social-emotional scaffolding is through community building. I would encourage students to pick a nearby location, perhaps a local library, to meet outside of class time to work on provided activity books or other assignments of their choice together. As an incentive, I would offer extra credit as a reward for working collaboratively. I would also join them to assist students with any challenges they may have in a less formal learning environment. I would document all the wonderful work created at the library and publish or showcase it in some way for the whole learning community to view and appreciate.

Lastly, setting individual intentions for learning would be a beneficial tool for each student to create personalized goals. It would help to motivate students and support monitoring their own progress. Goal setting would also assist me with designing lessons that meet individual needs. An example of a goal-sheet I would have my students complete before the beginning of a new unit of study can be seen in Figure 8.4.

—Natalie Pecoraro, ESOL teacher, Opening Word, Amityville, New York

FIGURE 8.4 ● Goal Setting Form

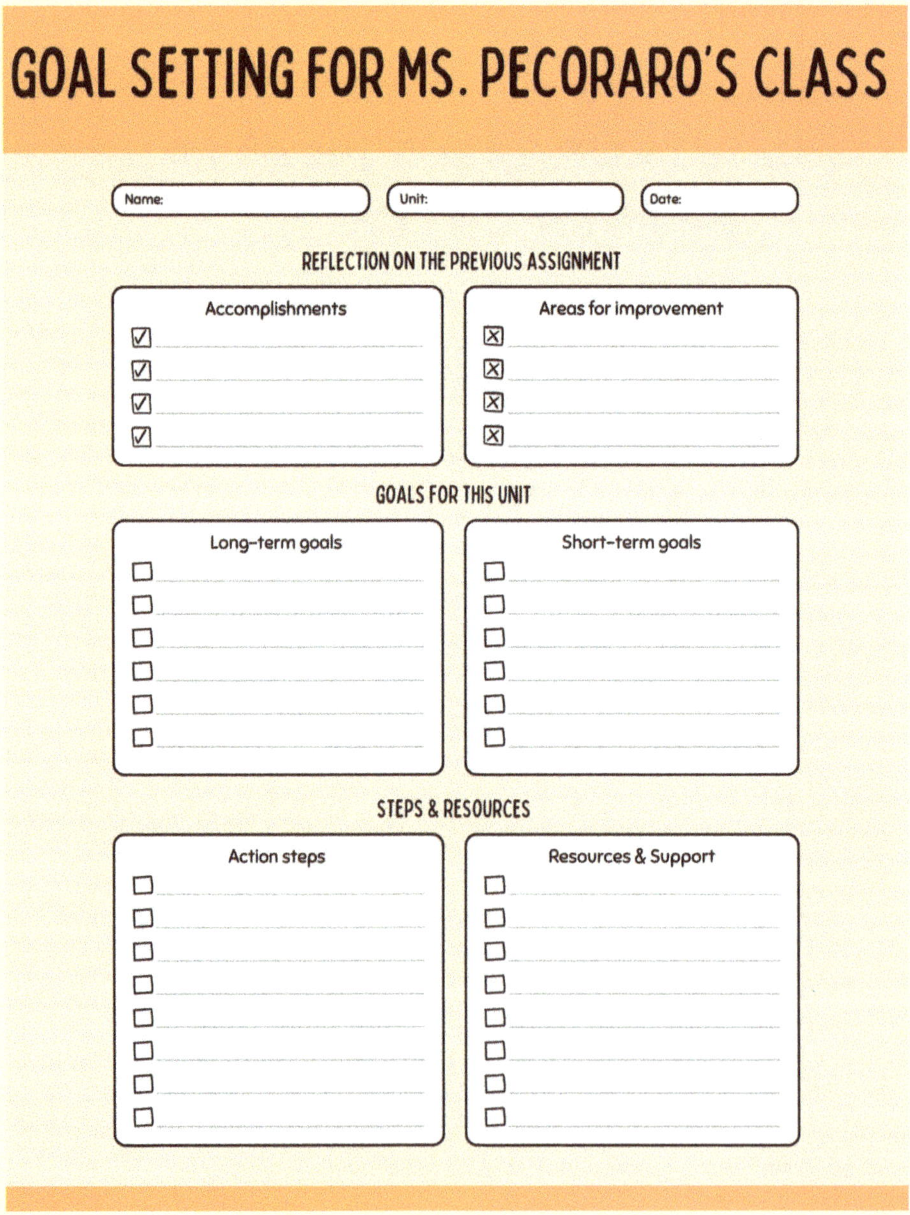

GOAL SETTING FOR MS. PECORARO'S CLASS

Name: | Unit: | Date:

REFLECTION ON THE PREVIOUS ASSIGNMENT

Accomplishments | Areas for improvement

GOALS FOR THIS UNIT

Long-term goals | Short-term goals

STEPS & RESOURCES

Action steps | Resources & Support

Source: Natalie Pecoraro. Used with permission.

GETTING STARTED WITH SCAFFOLDING FOR SOCIAL-EMOTIONAL LEARNING

It is crucial to use opportunities to address multilingual learners' individual social-emotional needs to foster their academic engagement and sense of belonging in the classroom. To incorporate social-emotional learning strategies, tools, and techniques with ELD, consider establishing specific routines to check in with students or embed strategies directly in the context of your teaching:

- ***Fostering peer-to-peer collaboration through activities that focus on teamwork:*** Intentionally divide students into small groups or pairs, note key talking points in writing with sentence starters/stems for students to utilize during the activity, incorporate techniques for students to actively listen and use authentic language, and assign roles and responsibilities within the group to hold students accountable.
- ***Encouraging building life-long skills:*** Develop activities that incorporate problem-solving, promote communication between students, and incorporate flexibility and choice in how students complete activities.
- ***Supporting self-development:*** Create learning experiences for students to focus on time management and self-reflection; encourage students to develop their own viewpoints and engage and learn from others' perspectives; model planning and help them create, plan for, and set goals.
- ***Providing opportunities for students to develop stamina:*** Actively engage in activities that support perseverance, self-regulation, and a growth mindset.

Beyond school, multilingual learners need a toolbox of skills to help them navigate life and be more engaged in their new language environments. To implement social-emotional learning beyond the classroom, we also offer you some ideas about implementing social-emotional learning schoolwide. Here are some ideas to enhance and extend classroom practices:

- Incorporate safe spaces throughout the school and allow students to access them throughout the school day when needed or encouraged to address issues such as cultural disorientation, isolation, anxiety, and fear.
- Implement a student government body to support conflict resolution. Students learn to resolve conflicts peacefully and negotiate effectively to avoid aggression and engage in constructive problem-solving.
- Foster community and civic engagement. Encourage students to be active citizens who feel responsible and empathetic towards themselves, their peers, and the broader community.

TEACHING PRACTICES

Social-emotional scaffolds are supportive strategies that help students develop and apply crucial life skills alongside academic learning. By integrating these scaffolds into daily instruction, educators can create a nurturing environment that fosters emotional intelligence, self-awareness, and positive relationships among students. These scaffolds not only enhance students' social-emotional competencies but also contribute to improved academic performance, classroom behavior, and overall well-being. The following practices align each component of the CASEL framework with a specific scaffolding approach. For each component, we present a scaffolding strategy tailored for classrooms with multilingual learners, outline its benefits, and provide a concrete example of its implementation. This approach demonstrates how to effectively integrate social-emotional learning into instruction for diverse language learners.

WHAT TEACHERS SAY ABOUT SCAFFOLDING SOCIAL-EMOTIONAL LEARNING

Students do not learn from teachers that they cannot trust. I make myself relatable to them and build a relationship with them first before focusing on instruction. Students are the opposite of blank slates, and as teachers, we need to pick their brains and bridge their interests and lives with instruction daily. Students are ready to learn when they feel affirmed, heard, and loved.

—Yulissa Gutierrez, instructional coach, Oklahoma City, Oklahoma

SCAFFOLDING FOR SOCIAL-EMOTIONAL LEARNING PRACTICE #1: BUILDING SELF-AWARENESS

Building Self-Awareness, the first of the core competencies of social-emotional learning, involves helping students develop a deep understanding of their own emotions, thoughts, values, and experiences. This practice encourages students to recognize their strengths and limitations, develop a growth mindset, and maintain a well-grounded sense of self-confidence. Through self-awareness activities, students learn to identify and label their feelings accurately, understand how their emotions influence their behavior, and recognize the impact their actions have on others. This foundational skill sets the stage for all other aspects of social and emotional development.

ADVANTAGES OF THIS PRACTICE

When students have time to reflect, they become more aware of their emotions and how they impact their daily actions and interactions with others. They become more empowered, which enables them to manage their feelings and behaviors more effectively. This daily practice helps students build their self-confidence strengthening their problem-solving and decision-making skills through self-regulation and monitoring. It can improve their motivation, engagement, and resilience.

EXAMPLE: DAILY CHECK-IN JOURNAL

One powerful way to develop this self-awareness is through daily writing, which provides a day-to-day routine for students, allowing them to connect with their thoughts and feelings while also providing information that may help the teacher engage with them on a nonacademic level. Teachers may consider a weekly protocol with each day dedicated to a specific writing activity.

Using a black-and-white notebook or an electronic journal, have students engage in completing writing prompts that tap into their social-emotional frame of mind. Students can include drawings, images, emojis, and colorful designs in electronic journals, videos, audio recordings, and links in their journal entries, enriching their reflections. Provide specific time daily—at the beginning, mid-way point, or end of the class session or day—so that students can reflect on their own well-being, anchor themselves for learning, and identify any social-emotional needs.

Here is a suggested framework for structuring daily activities throughout the week:

- **Mindful Monday:** Present students with a mindful activity to start or end their day.
    - **Strategy: Color and Shape Check-In**
      Ask students to close their eyes for a moment and think about a shape and a color that represent how they are feeling. When ready, direct students to open their eyes, draw the shape and fill it in with the color that matches the image in their minds. If they want to include some words, phrases, or sentences to their entries, they should feel free to do so.
- **Toolkit Tuesday:** Provide students with a simple strategy they can use to calm themselves when they feel anxious or overexcited.

- **Strategy: Palm circling**
  Have students take their right hand and face the palm up to the ceiling. Have them use their left hand, palm side down, to rub the hand in counterclockwise circles lightly. Give them about 20-30 seconds to do this. Have them write the strategy and explain how it makes them feel.

- **Wild Wednesday:** Give students a choice of which prompt they will use when they write in their journal.
  - **Strategy: Writer's Choice**
    Provide a list of different journal prompts students may select from. Here are a few to consider:
    - Describe a time when you felt proud of yourself.
    - What was a challenge you faced in the last 2 weeks? How did you face the challenge? What was the outcome?
    - If you were on a stranded island, identify one song, favorite object, or luxury item you would bring with you and why.
    - Write about a person you admire. Describe the person and tell why.
    - Describe a favorite memory and why it is special to you.
- **Thoughtful Thursday:** Ask students to reflect on their feedback from a teacher or a peer.
  - **Strategy: Mirror Moments**
    Think about the feedback you have received from another person about your work, actions, talents, or relationships, and respond to one of the following prompts:
    - Identify one part that made you think more about your work, actions, talents, or relationships. Describe your feelings and identify what you learned from it.
    - Identify something that made you feel good about your work, actions, talents, or relationships. Describe your feelings and identify what you learned from it.
    - Think about a time someone gave you feedback to improve your work, actions, talents, or relationships. Tell how this feedback may have influenced you.
- **Feel Free Friday:** Give students the "freedom" to choose how they will complete their journal activity.
  - **Strategy: Freedom Pages**
    Provide students with a choice board with options to express a personal event or feeling they experienced during the week. They may write about it, tell others about it in a video, or creatively express themselves in another artistic way (drawing, using media tools, or creating a musical expression). This idea gives students permission to be themselves and control how they share it.

SCAFFOLDING FOR SOCIAL-EMOTIONAL LEARNING PRACTICE #2: EXPANDING SELF-MANAGEMENT

Self-management encompasses the ability to effectively regulate one's emotions, thoughts, and behaviors across different situations. This multifaceted competency includes managing stress, controlling impulses, maintaining motivation, and working toward personal and academic goals. When students develop strong self-management skills, they learn to delay gratification, cope with frustration, and persist through challenges. This involves practical strategies such as using coping mechanisms when faced with difficult emotions, organizing their time and materials effectively, and developing study habits that align with their learning goals. Moreover, self-management extends to the ability to monitor one's progress, adjust strategies when needed, and maintain focus despite distractions. Students with well-developed self-management skills are better equipped to handle academic pressures, navigate social relationships, and maintain emotional balance in various situations, ultimately leading to greater success both in and out of the classroom.

ADVANTAGES OF USING THIS PRACTICE

Self-management practices require minimal planning while offering flexibility in implementation across various group sizes, including individual students, small groups, and the entire class. For educators, it serves as an effective means to gauge the classroom atmosphere. When tensions escalate, or specific situations emerge, it allows for a seamless transition from academic activities to calming exercises. These practices not only help students develop self-awareness and emotional regulation skills but also equip them with strategies to manage stress and control impulsive behaviors. Ultimately, this tool empowers students to better navigate their emotions and responses to their environment.

EXAMPLE: DEEP BREATHING EXERCISES

This type of activity impacts students' behavioral regulation and ability to engage in learning, as well as reduces stress and anxiety. Deep breathing exercises can be embedded into various activities throughout the day or week. Let's explore techniques you can use with your students:

- **Mindful Moment:** Have students find a comfortable position (at their desk or somewhere else in the room) and gently close their eyes. Direct them to focus on a specific word (example: *CALM*) that you have pre-selected and displayed on the board. Ask them to breathe in slowly for a count of 5-4-3-2-1 and continue to focus on the word *CALM*. If other thoughts come into their minds, gently guide them to push them away and continue to focus on the word *CALM*. Ask them to exhale slowly for a count of 5-4-3-2-1. Continue this exercise for 3 to 5 minutes. When the time is up, ask students to gently open their eyes and debrief with them about how they feel. Explain to them that they can use this strategy when they feel nervous, anxious, or overexcited about something. You can accompany this exercise with calming images displayed on an interactive whiteboard and relaxing music.

- **Flower and Candle:** During this exercise, students will breathe in through their nose to smell the flowers (or a scent they enjoy) and breathe out through their mouth to blow out a candle. Ask students to find a comfortable place to sit and pretend there is a string pulling their head up to the ceiling, making them stretch their backs so they are sitting straight. Ask students to gently close their eyes and breathe in the smell of their favorite scent and breathe out of their mouth to blow out a candle. Ask them to repeat this exercise 3 to 5 times or more if necessary.
  (Adapted from Downey & Basile, 2024.)

SCAFFOLDING FOR SOCIAL-EMOTIONAL LEARNING PRACTICE #3: BUILDING SOCIAL AWARENESS

Building social awareness involves developing a student's ability to empathize with others from diverse backgrounds and cultures, understand social norms for behavior, and recognize support systems within their families, schools, and communities. Through this practice, students learn to identify and acknowledge others' emotions, respect different viewpoints and appreciate both similarities and differences among people. The development of social awareness helps students recognize how their actions affect others, understand power dynamics in social situations, and identify resources for support when needed. Teachers can cultivate these skills through structured activities that encourage perspective-taking, cultural appreciation, and community engagement, helping students become more thoughtful and considerate members of their broader social world.

ADVANTAGES OF THIS PRACTICE

This daily practice provides a consistent and predictable start to the day, which can significantly reduce anxiety and foster an increased sense of belonging. Daily check-ins give multilingual learners the opportunity to engage in low-stakes English language practice, encouraging the use of common phrases and expressions while expanding their emotional vocabulary in context. It enhances their listening comprehension skills as they practice understanding their peers and teachers while supporting cultural integration and awareness. It also strengthens the teacher-student relationship by giving them insights into the emotional states and potential concerns multilingual learners may face, enabling them to better understand and address their unique needs. Students typically become more comfortable and confident in their environment when they participate in a morning protocol, which sets the overall tone for the day.

EXAMPLE: MORNING CHECK-IN

Introduce a morning protocol that helps gauge the emotional and physical needs of the students as they enter the classroom or get started for the day. These activities may differ for elementary and secondary students. Consider these developmentally appropriate practices:

- Elementary Classrooms: As the teacher welcomes students into the classroom, allow the students to select how they will check in with the teacher to start their day. Provide a check-in schedule with an outline of the process for students to follow and a list of protocols to choose from each day. To scaffold this practice, include a visual display of emotional emojis and corresponding words and sentence frames (*I feel . . . or today, I feel . . .*) to support verbal language development. For newcomers, consider including a physical check-in, which may include a hug, high five, or a quick spin. This allows them to participate and become more comfortable with the routine.
- Secondary Classrooms: To create a more supportive classroom, consider implementing a short Student Well-being Survey (see Figure 8.5) to gather actionable social-emotional learning data while encouraging student self-reflection. This survey may be implemented monthly to get a pulse on the dynamics of the classroom.

FIGURE 8.5 ● Thriving Minds Questionnaire

Directions: Your responses are anonymous. Please answer honestly—there are no right or wrong answers.

Part 1: General Well-Being: Please rate how much you agree with each statement on a scale of 1-5.

	STRONGLY DISAGREE	DISAGREE	NEITHER AGREE NOR DISAGREE	AGREE	STRONGLY AGREE
I feel like I belong in this class					
I can be myself around my classmates					

(Continued)

(Continued)

	STRONGLY DISAGREE	DISAGREE	NEITHER AGREE NOR DISAGREE	AGREE	STRONGLY AGREE
I know at least one person in the class					
I can turn to a teacher or friend if I need help					
I feel comfortable participating in class discussions					
I believe my voice and opinions matter in this class					

Part 2: Learning Environment: Please complete these sentences.

Something that helps me learn best in this class is...
Something that makes it hard for me to learn in this class is...
When I'm struggling with coursework, I usually...

Part 3: Peer Connections: Think about your interactions with classmates over the past week.

Please rate your interactions:

	VERY CONNECTED	SOMEWHAT CONNECTED	NEUTRAL	SOMEWHAT DISCONNECTED	VERY DISCONNECTED
How connected do you feel to your classmates?					

Please respond to the question:

What is one thing that would help you feel more connected to your peers?	

Part 4: Open Reflection

- What's one thing you're proud of accomplishing in this class recently?

  ____

  ____

- Is there anything else you'd like your teacher to know?

  ____

  ____

Thank you for sharing your thoughts. Your feedback helps create a better learning environment for everyone.

online resources Available for download at https://companion.corwin.com/courses/NineDimensionsofScaffoldingforMLs

SCAFFOLDING FOR SOCIAL-EMOTIONAL LEARNING PRACTICE #4: ENHANCING RELATIONSHIP SKILLS

Enhancing relationship skills involves teaching students how to communicate clearly, listen actively, cooperate with others, resist inappropriate social pressure, negotiate conflict constructively, and seek help when needed. This practice helps students develop the tools to work collaboratively, resolve disagreements respectfully, and maintain healthy boundaries in their interactions. Through structured activities and guided practice, students learn to read social cues, express their needs appropriately, and respond to others with empathy and understanding. These skills are particularly crucial as students navigate increasingly complex social situations, from classroom partnerships to digital interactions, preparing them for success in school, future careers, and personal relationships.

ADVANTAGES OF THIS PRACTICE

Collaborative problem-solving activities help multilingual learners strengthen their language acquisition skills and build their confidence as they communicate with their peers in a worry-free setting. This activity provides students with authentic opportunities to negotiate a variety of situations and experiences with a peer. Together, they learn to work as a team, identify important elements within the situation, break it down, find solutions, foster negotiation, and resolve conflicts.

EXAMPLE: CONUNDRUM CORNER

Design and create a dedicated classroom space for collaborative problem-solving dedicated to facilitating teamwork, creative thinking, and active learning. This type of activity is nonacademic and supports students as they learn to work with their peers and build relationships through increased and targeted interactions. The Conundrum Corner is a collaborative problem-solving space. It can be added as an additional station activity or group work extension for students as they rotate through different learning experiences. The "conundrum" is an everyday challenge that needs to be solved by a team or pair of students, not an individual. This may be generic and connected to a scenario students may encounter at various grade levels or a specific topic (content) you are working on in the class or to make it more realistic. To illustrate the strategy, consider the following:

- Generic Problem: Consider things going on at school to help you develop a problem students can solve in real time. An example could focus on bullying. Scenario: One of your friends broke their arm. Their closest friends make fun of them and tell them they are ugly now and ask how they can look at themselves in the mirror. The bullying escalates every day. Your friend is starting to feel bad about themself. You notice they are reticent; they start to miss school more often and don't talk with anyone. You want to help. Collaborate to create a plan to help your friend.
- Content-Related Problem: 6th-grade students work on sound topics in their science classroom. The problem: The school auditorium also serves as the gymnasium. When students perform a school play or a concert, the people in the audience have a difficult time hearing the sounds as intended due to the acoustic structure of the room. Task: You are playing an instrument in an upcoming concert. You know your family will not hear how much you have practiced. You and your acoustics team need to fix this and improve it for the future. To do this, create a plan of action to address the problem and the steps needed to ensure the audience can hear the concert. Make sure to identify the problem and prioritize the steps needed to solve it.

SOCIAL-EMOTIONAL SCAFFOLDING PRACTICE #5: GUIDING RESPONSIBLE DECISION-MAKING

In practice, teaching responsible decision-making involves creating opportunities for students to analyze situations from multiple angles, identify potential outcomes, and evaluate the ethical implications of their choices. Teachers facilitate this by presenting real-world scenarios that require students to weigh various factors, consider different perspectives, and articulate their reasoning. Students learn to identify their personal values, recognize how these values influence their choices, and understand how their decisions affect both themselves and their community. Through guided discussions and reflective activities, they practice identifying reliable sources of information, recognizing biases, and considering immediate and long-term consequences. This skill development extends beyond classroom walls, helping students make informed choices about academic challenges, peer relationships, social media use, and personal goals. The ultimate aim is to develop students who can independently assess situations, consider ethical implications, and make decisions that reflect both personal integrity and social responsibility.

ADVANTAGES OF THIS PRACTICE

When students discuss and role-play various scenarios, they learn to recognize the situation, explore different perspectives, have opportunities to agree with ideas or respectively disagree, consider different courses of action, and practice making informed decisions based on responsible choices.

WHAT TEACHERS SAY ABOUT SCAFFOLDING SOCIAL-EMOTIONAL LEARNING

I encourage my students to take risks and embrace the opportunity that they are wrong: "Be right or wrong with conviction!" If students hesitate or offer a tentative answer, I prompt them further, "Say it with conviction!" I believe students need to feel safe making mistakes, and they need to embrace the idea that our most powerful lessons come from the mistakes we make.

—Marni Smith, 5th grade teacher at Park Avenue Elementary School, Auburn Public Schools, Maine

EXAMPLE: SCENARIO SPOTLIGHT

Incorporate time for students to discuss and role-play various scenarios. You may consider using characters that students are reading about, people they have been exposed to throughout their learning, or everyday experiences.

- Dealing with It! Identify a topic that would benefit students to role-play in your class. The idea of *Deal With It* is generic and can be applied to various scenarios.
    - Present students with a scenario for them to address: *A small group of students are verbally intimidating and saying terrible things to a new student in the cafeteria. There are several bystanders watching. One of the bystanders videos the situation while the others just continue to watch.* In this activity, students work together in small groups to (1) discuss the overall scenario; (2) consider the role and perspectives of each participant: the bullies (small group of people), the bullied person, and the bystanders within the scenario; (3) identify and clarify the problem, consequences, and outcomes; and (4) make decisions about how to responsibly *Deal With It*. To scaffold this activity, identify the keywords: bully, victim, bystander, problem, consequences, roles, responsibility, etc. In Table 8.3, see an example of a graphic organizer that breaks down each step in the process. You may also use this activity as a guide to develop your own protocol.

TABLE 8.3 ● *Deal With It* Activity

Describe the scenario:	________ watch a new ____________ get ____________ by a group of people in the ____________________. One __________ videos what is happening and the other bystanders ______________________________________.
Who is involved, and what are they doing?	Bullies: New students: Bystanders:
Problem:	
Consequences:	
Outcomes:	
What is one way to deal with the situation? Explain why this is a responsible decision.	One way to deal with this is... This is a responsible decision because...
What is another way to deal with the situation? Explain why this is a responsible decision.	

Once students complete the activity, consider extending it and encourage them to role play and share how they would deal with it and why they believe it is a responsible decision. Give the class an opportunity to discuss whether they agree or disagree and why. To assess students, provide a peer review checklist (see Table 8.4) to make sure students evidence each step they took throughout the activity and comment about what they liked in the role-playing scenario.

TABLE 8.4 • Peer Review Checklist: *Deal With It* Activity

	YES	NO	WARM FEEDBACK (THINGS YOU LIKE ABOUT THE PRESENTATION)
Describe the scenario:			
Who is involved, and what are they doing?			
Problem:			
Consequences:			
Outcomes:			
What is one way to deal with the situation? Explain why this is a responsible decision.			
Critical Feedback:			

INDEPENDENT LEARNING STRATEGIES FOR STUDENTS

Social-emotional learning naturally aligns with independent learning as it empowers students to understand, monitor, and regulate their own emotional and cognitive processes. When students develop strong social-emotional skills, they become more self-aware learners who can recognize their strengths, challenges, and emotional states that impact their learning. This awareness allows them to actively choose and implement strategies that work best for them, whether it's taking a moment to calm down before a challenging task, breaking down complex assignments into manageable steps, or seeking help when needed.

The true power of social-emotional learning emerges when students internalize these practices and independently incorporate them into their daily routines. For instance, a student might recognize signs of frustration during a difficult math problem and automatically implement a learned breathing technique to regain focus. They might proactively use self-reflection tools before starting a project or independently initiate collaboration with peers when they recognize the need for different perspectives. This self-directed application of social-emotional learning skills creates a positive feedback loop—as students experience success through using these strategies, they become more confident in their ability to navigate challenges, motivating them to continue using and refining these practices. Teachers can support this process by gradually releasing responsibility to students, providing opportunities for them to choose and evaluate their own social-emotional learning strategies, and creating classroom environments where self-reflection and emotional awareness are valued as essential components of the learning process. In Figure 8.6, see an example of a personal check-in tool teachers can implement in their classrooms. We invite you to adapt this tool to your own context.

FIGURE 8.6 ● Personal Check-In Tool

Directions: To help you reflect on your social and emotional skills. Rate yourself honestly—there are no right or wrong answers!

Rate each statement.

I. **Self-Awareness***:* Understanding my emotions, thoughts, and values

	I'M JUST STARTING TO WORK ON THIS	I CAN SOMETIMES DO THIS	I CAN USUALLY DO THIS	I CAN CONSISTENTLY DO THIS, AND HELP OTHERS
I can name the emotions I'm feeling in the moment.				
I understand what triggers my strong emotions.				
I can identify my personal strengths and areas for growth.				
I recognize how my emotions affect my behavior.				
I know when to ask for help and who to ask.				

My Self-Awareness Goal:

____

____

II. **Self-Management:** Managing my emotions and behaviors

	I'M JUST STARTING TO WORK ON THIS	I CAN SOMETIMES DO THIS	I CAN USUALLY DO THIS	I CAN CONSISTENTLY DO THIS, AND HELP OTHERS
I can calm myself down when I'm upset.				

I stay focused on tasks even when things get challenging.				
I make plans and work toward my goals.				
I organize my time and materials well.				
I think before I act or make decisions.				

My Self-Management Goal:

____

____

III. **Social Awareness:** Understanding and empathizing with others

	I'M JUST STARTING TO WORK ON THIS	I CAN SOMETIMES DO THIS	I CAN USUALLY DO THIS	I CAN CONSISTENTLY DO THIS, AND HELP OTHERS
I try to understand how others are feeling.				
I respect people who are different from me.				
I consider other people's perspectives.				
I recognize when someone needs support.				
I understand how my actions affect others.				

(Continued)

My Social Awareness Goal:

____

____

(Continued)

IV. **Relationship Skills:** Building and maintaining healthy relationships

	I'M JUST STARTING TO WORK ON THIS	I CAN SOMETIMES DO THIS	I CAN USUALLY DO THIS	I CAN CONSISTENTLY DO THIS, AND HELP OTHERS
I communicate clearly with others.				
I work well in team situations.				
I listen actively when others are speaking.				
I can resolve conflicts peacefully.				
I know how to be a good friend.				

My Relationship Skills Goal:

____

____

V. **Responsible Decision-Making:** Making caring and constructive choices

	I'M JUST STARTING TO WORK ON THIS	I CAN SOMETIMES DO THIS	I CAN USUALLY DO THIS	I CAN CONSISTENTLY DO THIS, AND HELP OTHERS
I think about consequences before making decisions.				
I consider how my choices affect others.				
I take responsibility for my actions.				
I make decisions based on my values.				
I seek help when facing difficult choices.				

My Responsible Decision-Making Goal:

____

____

Reflection

- Which area is my biggest strength right now? Why?
- Which area would I most like to improve? Why?
- What's one specific step I can take this week to grow in my chosen area?

Remember: Social and emotional skills are like muscles—they get stronger with practice!

online resources Available for download at https://companion.corwin.com/courses/NineDimensionsofScaffoldingforMLs

SUMMARY

This chapter examined strategies for scaffolding social-emotional learning for multilingual learners, using the five components of the CASEL framework. The foundation of effective social-emotional learning scaffolding lies in strong teacher-student relationships. These connections create positive classroom communities and promote overall well-being, helping multilingual learners overcome challenges. With this relational foundation, teachers can seamlessly integrate social-emotional learning principles into their daily practices. Scaffolding social-emotional learning is a comprehensive approach that provides structured support to multilingual learners as they develop self-regulation skills, embrace their cultural identities, and strive for academic success. This holistic approach recognizes that effective learning goes beyond academic instruction by nurturing an individual's emotional, social, and cultural growth. Through structured assistance, social-emotional scaffolding equips multilingual learners with a robust toolbox of strategies to actively engage in various environments while maintaining a strong sense of self and honoring their cultural heritage, empowering them to navigate diverse experiences and challenges.

Questions

To further address your teaching practices and how you address the five elements of CASEL, we invite you to explore these questions:

1. ***Self-awareness:*** How will you create a safe and supportive environment for your multilingual learners? How will you help them express their thoughts, feelings, and experiences?
2. ***Self-management:*** How will you model strategies to help students manage their emotions, impulses, and behaviors?
3. ***Social Awareness:*** How will you expose students to diverse perspectives and cultures? How will you facilitate discussions to promote respect and understanding of others?
4. ***Relationship Skills:*** How will you help students effectively communicate and resolve conflicts? How will you foster collaboration?
5. ***Responsible Decision-Making:*** How will you challenge students to think and reason with moral dilemmas critically?

CHAPTER 9

Interactive Scaffolding

"The process of learning to think, remember, solve problems, and the like originates in and cannot be understood apart from a person's interactions with others and cultural artifacts over time."
(Jennifer Wilfrid and Daniella Molle, 2023, p. 53)

Interactive scaffolding is a teaching method designed to support multilingual learners as they develop both language skills and content knowledge simultaneously while collaborating with others. This approach utilizes dynamic, real-time support strategies within interactive and socially engaging classroom activities. Teachers provide tailored guidance based on students' current language proficiency levels, creating opportunities for meaningful language practice in context-rich situations. Through collaborative discourse, multilingual learners simultaneously develop academic language and deepen content understanding as they share ideas and construct meaning with peers (Huynh, 2021). A key aspect of interactive scaffolding is encouraging students to take risks while using and experimenting with language in a safe, supportive environment. It also promotes their autonomy by helping them understand and take responsibility for their own learning process.

Interactive scaffolding requires teachers to remain responsive and flexible throughout instruction. Rather than following rigid plans, you can continuously adjust your support based on real-time student needs and responses. During lessons, you modify language complexity, task difficulty, and contextual supports as students demonstrate varying levels of understanding. This adaptive approach demands keen observation skills as you assess comprehension and engagement to inform immediate instructional decisions. By maintaining this flexibility, you create personalized learning environments that effectively support both language development and content mastery, meeting your students at their current proficiency levels while pushing them toward greater independence.

Interaction stands as a cornerstone of effective communication, playing a pivotal role in language development, especially for multilingual learners. As students engage with one another and their teachers, they co-create a dynamic environment where language skills are not just taught but actively cultivated through practical use. In a classroom, interactive scaffolding occurs across three key dimensions of classroom interaction, each supporting language development and content mastery in unique ways:

1. **Student Interactions** range from one-on-one peer discussions and partner work to small-group collaborative projects and whole-class collective discussions, creating opportunities for authentic language practice and peer support.
2. **Teacher-Led Interactions** encompass individual conferences and targeted support, small group guided instruction, and whole-class direct teaching and facilitated discussions. These structured interactions allow for differentiated instruction and responsive scaffolding based on student needs.
3. **Interactions With Authentic Audiences** complete the framework, including individual student-expert engagement, small group presentations, and whole-class collaborations with community members and external partners. Together, these varied interaction patterns create multiple opportunities for language practice, academic discourse, and meaningful communication while supporting different learning preferences and proficiency levels.

Interactive learning processes serve as a vital platform for the exchange of ideas, allowing students to articulate their thoughts, voice their opinions, and demonstrate their knowledge and skills in meaningful ways. The beauty of this approach lies in its versatility, as communication in the classroom isn't limited to verbal expression alone. In addition to verbal exchanges, students are encouraged to share ideas through written expression, graphic representations, and visual imagery, which create diverse entry points for participation regardless of language proficiency. This approach not only caters to diverse learning needs but also mirrors the complexity of real-world communication. For multilingual learners, a varied landscape of interaction provides numerous entry points for authentic language use. Rather than relying solely on traditional language instruction, scaffolded environments encourage students to use their full linguistic repertoires across different communication channels. As they engage with content through varied expressions, students naturally reinforce language structures and expand vocabulary while developing deeper conceptual understanding. The result is more intuitive language acquisition embedded within meaningful academic discourse.

WHAT TEACHERS SAY ABOUT INTERACTIVE SCAFFOLDING

Interactive scaffolding creates so many meaningful, dense conversations with my students on every level. Students feel like they are in control of their own learning, and you so often get to see that lightbulb go off in their minds as if, (Aha, wait... I know this!).

—Hannah McGoff, ENL teacher, Oswego, New York

WHO IS IT FOR?

Interactive scaffolding is a versatile approach that benefits a wide range of learners, making it an invaluable tool for creating inclusive and dynamic classrooms. While it is particularly crucial for multilingual learners who need additional support to access content while developing language skills, its benefits extend far beyond this group. Students with diverse learning needs, including those with learning disabilities or subject-specific struggles, find this approach helpful in engaging with challenging material. Interestingly, even advanced learners benefit from interactive scaffolding, as it pushes them to articulate their understanding more clearly and consider different perspectives, thereby deepening their knowledge as well as communicative competence. In an interactive learning environment, students become valuable resources for one another by engaging in dialogue, observing peers' work, and collaborating on ideas and decisions (Qureshi et al., 2023). This approach not only enhances learning but also proves particularly beneficial for students from diverse cultural backgrounds. Through peer interactions, students build a collective knowledge base that enriches classroom understanding and learning. See Figure 9.1 for an example of how Elizabeth Choi's middle school students frequently collaborate to complete a task that requires reading, interaction, and peer support while utilizing visually enhanced resources and text-based manipulatives.

FIGURE 9.1 ● Student Interaction Supports Language and Content Learning

Source: Elizabeth Choi. Used with permission.

Some introverted students seem to find that structured interactive activities provide a comfortable framework for safer participation in class discussions. Moreover, this approach nurtures critical thinking skills across the board, encouraging all students to question, analyze, and build upon each other's ideas. Ultimately, interactive scaffolding supports the development of essential 21st-century skills like communication, problem-solving, teamwork, and adaptability (Fox & McDermott, 2015), making it beneficial for all students regardless of their individual learning profiles or backgrounds.

Here are just a few examples of how interactive and collaborative scaffolds support students at various language proficiency levels:

- They support newcomers when they work with same-language partners as they form bilingual peer bridges.
- They support emerging or developing multilingual learners when they participate in a triad structure.
- They support advanced learners when they collaboratively tackle a task and figure out multiple possible pathways to solve a problem.
- They support English proficient students as they continue to participate in joint meaning-making with peers across all stages of language proficiency.

HOW IS INTERACTIVE SCAFFOLDING USED ACROSS PROGRAM MODELS

Interactive scaffolding is a versatile approach employed across various program models to support diverse learners, particularly multilingual learners, and students with different learning needs. This method leverages peer interaction and structured support to make content accessible while promoting language development and critical thinking skills. It typically involves carefully designed group activities, peer tutoring, and collaborative problem-solving tasks that encourage students to collaborate, share ideas, and support each other's learning.

Implementing interactive scaffolding is a flexible process that can be tailored to the specific program model and the unique needs of the student population. The core principle remains consistent: creating meaningful interaction opportunities that support content learning and language development. Teachers in different settings have the power to adapt this approach, incorporating various levels of language support, content modifications, and peer grouping strategies.

In *general education classes*, teachers implement interaction and collaboration as fundamental components of the learning process, recognizing their power to enhance student engagement, deepen understanding, and develop essential social skills. Throughout the school day, teachers balance whole-class discussions, small group work, and peer-to-peer interactions, ensuring that all students have multiple opportunities to engage in meaningful dialogue and cooperative tasks. They create dynamic learning communities that encourage active participation and mutual support among students from diverse backgrounds and ability levels.

In *integrated co-taught classrooms*, teachers leverage the unique strengths of each teacher. The co-teachers work in tandem to design and facilitate lessons that incorporate various forms of student collaboration, ensuring that activities are accessible and beneficial for all learners. The presence of two or more educators allows for more flexible grouping strategies, targeted support during collaborative tasks, and enhanced monitoring of student interactions. Co-teachers model effective collaboration through their partnership, implement various interactive structures throughout the day and thoughtfully integrate supports and accommodations into collaborative activities. Co-teachers co-create a classroom culture that values diverse perspectives and abilities, encouraging students to learn from and support one another while ensuring that all students can participate fully and meaningfully.

In *stand-alone English language development (ELD) classes*, teachers maximize the use of interaction and collaboration as essential components of language acquisition and proficiency development. These classes are designed to support multilingual learners in developing their language skills across listening, speaking, reading, and writing domains. Teachers create a linguistically rich environment where collaborative activities are carefully structured to maximize opportunities for authentic language use, focusing on academic language and conversational fluency. Teachers design lessons encouraging peer-to-peer interaction, allowing students to negotiate meaning, practice new vocabulary and grammatical structures, and develop their communicative competence. Group work and pair activities are frequently employed to increase students' talking time and provide contexts for meaningful language exchange. The teacher serves as both a language model and a facilitator, guiding students through interactive tasks while providing appropriate scaffolding and feedback. Collaboration in these classes often involves culturally responsive content, drawing on students' diverse backgrounds to enhance engagement and connection to their lived experiences.

In *self-contained or integrated special education classes*, teachers tailor the use of interactive scaffolds to meet the unique needs of students with diverse learning challenges. These educators create a supportive and inclusive environment where collaboration is adapted to accommodate various cognitive, physical, and social-emotional needs. Teachers carefully structure interactive tasks to promote social skills development, communication, and academic growth, ensuring that students can participate meaningfully. Collaboration is often implemented through carefully designed group work, peer tutoring, and differentiated cooperative learning projects to match students' Individualized Education Program (IEP) goals. Teachers employ various assistive technologies and alternative communication methods to facilitate interaction among students with different communication abilities. They model and explicitly teach collaborative skills, breaking down complex social interactions into manageable steps for students who may struggle with social cues or taking turns. In these classes, collaboration extends beyond student-to-student interaction to include partnerships with specialists, paraprofessionals, and therapists who work together to support students' holistic development. Through thoughtful implementation of interactive and collaborative practices, teachers in special education settings foster a classroom community where students learn to support one another, build on each other's strengths, and develop essential life skills that promote independence and social integration.

WHAT TEACHERS SAY ABOUT INTERACTIVE SCAFFOLDING

Interactive scaffolding is especially important for our English Language Learners and also benefits the general education students within the classroom. When I am in general education classrooms, I encourage teachers not to group all of the ENL students together in their seating arrangements, groups for working, or on the carpet.

While this is more difficult for me to have to run around the classroom, it allows the ENL students to have peer language models with English speakers around them for the majority of their day. It also makes the English speakers more concise and descriptive in their own language to help the ENL students they are working with understand the material being discussed. All my ENL students want to be social and have friends, especially in the younger grades. So having a peer model, rather than having to only talk to a teacher or to other ENL students, makes their learning more genuine.

—Sarah Kawzenuk, ENL teacher, Horseheads, New York

WHY IS INTERACTIVE SCAFFOLDING AN IMPORTANT APPROACH TO STUDENT LEARNING?

Interactive scaffolding offers many benefits, encompassing language development, social-emotional growth, and academic engagement. In terms of language development, interactions provide students with increased opportunities for authentic language use, exposing them to diverse language models beyond the teacher and allowing them to practice negotiating meaning in academic or real-world contexts. This authentic practice is crucial for developing communicative competence. Socially and emotionally, peer interactions can significantly reduce anxiety associated with language production, as multilingual learners tend to feel more comfortable engaging in learning with peers. These interactions foster an increased sense of belonging within the classroom community and promote the development of intercultural competence as students learn to navigate diverse perspectives and communication styles. How are students engaged in interactive and collaborative activities?

Consider your own practice, and reflect on how learners participate in the following language-based practices:

- ***Using Authentic Language:*** Authentic language provides real-world context, making language learning more relevant and applicable to students' daily lives and future needs.
    - Does the interaction provide opportunities for multilingual learners to use English as well as their full linguistic repertoires in real, meaningful contexts? If so, how? Do activities help them bridge the gap between classroom learning and real-world communication?
- ***Negotiating Meaning:*** The process of negotiating meaning enhances communication skills and problem-solving abilities and deepens understanding as students learn to clarify, rephrase, and construct meaning collaboratively.
    - How do learners interact with others to clarify misunderstandings and modify their language output? How are activities designed to help students notice gaps in their language knowledge and make adjustments?

- *Feeling Motivated*: Motivation is crucial for sustained effort in language acquisition, driving students to persist through challenges and actively engage in learning opportunities.
    - What motivates students to use language? How do you structure activities to boost student confidence? How do you create a low-anxiety environment for students to be engaged in authentic academic and social language use?
- *Developing Competence With Academic Language*: Academic language is vital for success across subject areas, preparing students to tackle complex academic tasks as well as to be future-ready. Whether they plan to go to college/university or pursue a career through technical education, they will find themselves in professional environments where specialized vocabulary and complex language structures are shared.
    - How are activities structured to build, strengthen, and enhance the acquisition of academic language and content knowledge simultaneously? How are activities designed to help students develop both social and academic proficiency?
- *Developing Oracy:* Building fluency and confidence in speaking is critical for effective communication in academic, social, and professional settings.
    - What opportunities do students have to interact with others to practice their speaking and listening skills? What activities do you incorporate to develop authentic fluency and automaticity in language use?
- *Learning With Peers:* Peer interaction offers diverse language models, cultural perspectives, and collaborative opportunities, enriching the learning experience and fostering a sense of belonging.
    - What types of interactive tasks do students participate in to promote peer-to-peer learning? What opportunities do more English proficient peers have to teach others as a means to reinforce their own learning while also supporting their peers?
- *Engaging With Resources*: Exposure to various materials and a range of formats broadens students' linguistic repertoire and develops their ability to navigate different types of texts and media.
    - What multisensory (visual, auditory, tactile, and kinesthetic) and digital resources do students have access to when collaborating with their peers? How are multimodal approaches utilized to enhance comprehension and retention in collaborative activities?

We hope to have persuaded you that interactive scaffolding practices are essential because they create a rich, supportive environment for language and literacy acquisition. By engaging in scaffolded interactions, multilingual learners can develop not only their language skills but also their confidence, cultural competence, and academic abilities, setting the foundation for long-term success in English-speaking (and multilingual) academic and professional environments.

HOW DOES INTERACTIVE SCAFFOLDING SPECIFICALLY RELATE TO MULTILINGUAL LEARNERS' NEEDS?

Interactive scaffolding addresses multilingual learners' need to develop both academic content knowledge and language skills simultaneously. Through structured peer interactions, students practice language in authentic contexts while accessing grade-level content. These scaffolding techniques create a variety of entry points for participation, regardless of language proficiency, providing students with multiple opportunities to take risks and use language in a range of contexts. Advanced speakers can model academic language, while beginning learners contribute through simplified responses or nonverbal communication. As students work together, they intuitively and intentionally adjust their language use and differentiate support for peers, often explaining concepts in various ways until understanding is reached.

FROM RESEARCH TO PRACTICE

Interactive learning environments create a powerful synergy between engagement, collaboration, and academic achievement. By enabling real-time adaptation of instruction based on student input, these approaches foster active participation and deeper involvement in the learning process (Chan et al., 2019). Furthermore, interactive groups cultivate inclusive conditions that encourage all learners to participate, facilitating collaborative interactions in language learning and raising expectations for student performance (Zubiri-Esnaola et al., 2020). Interactive scaffolding further enhances a productive learning environment by providing structured support tailored to students' needs. The interactive nature of this type of scaffolding not only reinforces understanding but also promotes critical thinking and problem-solving skills as students learn to articulate their thought processes, co-construct meaning with their peers, and support one another's learning journey.

Reflect on the following:

How do you ensure all students, regardless of proficiency level, meaningfully contribute to group work? What tools do you use to enhance student collaboration?

GETTING STARTED WITH INTERACTIVE SCAFFOLDING

Interactive scaffolding is a powerful instructional approach that teachers employ to support diverse learners, particularly multilingual learners, and students with varying academic needs, within carefully structured activities that support language development alongside content learning. This approach combines the benefits of peer interaction with intentionally designed support mechanisms to facilitate language development and content learning. Through explicit instruction, teachers provide step-by-step guidance to engage in interactive activities, ensuring all students understand what is expected of them. Next, we can expect students to develop ownership of interactive and collaborative learning opportunities and embrace the benefits that come with such learning.

ENGAGING STUDENTS

Let's make it a priority to create a supportive classroom environment that encourages risk-taking and values diverse contributions. Starting with simple, structured activities can help students become accustomed to working collaboratively and using scaffolded supports. It is important to explicitly teach collaboration skills, providing clear guidelines for effective interaction. As students gain confidence, teachers can gradually increase the complexity of collaborative tasks and reduce scaffolding as appropriate. There are a variety of ways to engage students through interactive practices, including student-to-student, student-to-teacher, and student-to-authentic audiences in the classroom. (See more about each under Teaching Practices.)

TEACHER'S ROLE

Teachers create learning opportunities where students actively engage with each other and with content while providing targeted assistance to bridge gaps in knowledge or skills. Building on these foundational aspects of interactive scaffolding, consider taking on multiple roles within the classroom, each essential to fostering a learning environment rich with conversation, student interaction, and productive struggle (Dweck, 2006; Streitman, 2024). These roles include:

- ***Model:*** Teachers frequently model how to complete a task, what a completed assignment might look like, how to double-check one's work, and so on. It is a bit more challenging to model interaction and collaboration if you are the only educator in the classroom. The co-teaching partnership is a primary model, with teachers demonstrating authentic collaboration, respectful communication, shared decision-making, and mutual support. Their roles may alternate during instruction from one activity to the next or within an activity. Teachers may build on each other's ideas and explanations while demonstrating productive problem-solving when faced with challenges. They use think-alouds to verbalize collaborative processes, show how to approach group work, offer alternative viewpoints, and provide constructive feedback. Teachers explicitly model academic language use for students, demonstrating how to incorporate content-specific vocabulary and language structures in discussions. If you do not have a co-teacher, try these suggestions with an instructional aide, a paraprofessional, or even a student as your partner. You will be surprised how many of your students want to teach their classmates and model an interactive task with you!

- *Facilitator:* As facilitators, teachers co-create an environment conducive to collaborative learning. They implement thoughtful grouping strategies, balancing language proficiency levels and content knowledge to ensure productive peer interactions. Teachers co-design structured activities that promote meaningful interaction, such as jigsaw readings or peer tutoring, while providing scaffolds such as steps to complete, sentence frames to use, and graphic organizers to make collaboration visible to all learners. They monitor group dynamics, ensuring multilingual learners have opportunities to contribute and feel supported in overcoming learning barriers as they are provided real-time feedback on their progress.
- *Guide:* In their role as guides, teachers start out by providing clear, explicit instructions for collaborative tasks, often using verbal and visual cues to support comprehension. Then they step back as they circulate during group work, offering targeted support to students who need them, clarifying concepts, and encouraging deeper engagement through strategic questioning. Teachers guide students in using language support tools effectively, troubleshoot misconceptions or misunderstandings, and help navigate cultural differences that may arise during collaborations.
- *Reflective Practitioner:* As reflective practitioners, teachers continuously co-evaluate the effectiveness of their strategies for supporting interaction and collaboration. They engage in ongoing assessment of students' language development and content understanding within collaborative contexts. Teachers guide students in reflecting on their collaborative experiences, encouraging them to self-assess their language use and participation. They use these reflections to collaboratively adjust their teaching approaches, refine language supports, and set new goals for enhancing collaborative learning experiences.

Use the reflection tool in Table 9.1 to consider how you implement these roles in the classroom. As suggested before, add your own reflection questions under each category to ensure the applicability of the tool.

TABLE 9.1 ● Teacher Reflection of Interactive Scaffolding

TEACHER ROLES	SAMPLE REFLECTION QUESTIONS
Model	• Are my scaffolding examples clear and purposeful? • Am I using culturally responsive examples? • Do I demonstrate academic language with clear visuals?
Facilitator	• How do I support various proficiency levels and equitable participation? • Are groups structured to leverage home languages and maximize peer learning? • Do I provide appropriate processing time?
Guide	• How do I differentiate scaffolds for varying student needs? • When do I intervene versus let students problem-solve? • Am I gradually releasing responsibility to the students?
Reflective Practitioner	• What evidence shows language development? • How do I adapt (in real-time) based on students' needs and progress? • Where can I enhance collaborative opportunities?

online resources Available for download at https://companion.corwin.com/courses/NineDimensionsofScaffoldingforMLs

STRATEGIC IMPLEMENTATION OF INTERACTIVE SCAFFOLDS

Day-to-day interaction is natural and necessary and happens all the time in and out of the classroom. However, interactive and collaborative scaffolds should be strategically implemented within instruction to ensure multilingual learners engage in productive conversations, learn to negotiate with others in multiple meaningful ways and build the skills they need to communicate effectively in and outside the classroom. Focus on participation, language development, and leveraging students' linguistic gifts, as well as many talents and abilities.

- ***Participation:*** Predictable and consistent opportunities to interact help multilingual learners prepare and participate more comfortably during activities with more confidence. Provide opportunities for all students to participate and interact with peers by:
  - Identifying the roles, responsibilities, and expectations (for each student) when working in pairs or small groups.

        - Tips: Try think-pair-share, Jigsaw reading tasks, and peer interviews, among other similar strategies.
        - It is also beneficial to allow students to select their roles and responsibilities for group work. This helps build autonomy as they make conscious decisions about what they are responsible for.
    - Include daily or weekly routines that encourage student participation and provide structured expectations multilingual learners can rely on.
        - Tips: Embed morning meeting, peer feedback, student-led review sessions, and other predictable structures and routines.
    - Design activities that allow students to interact with each other and the target learning materials through various modes of communication.
        - Tips: Utilize graphic organizers, written responses, digital tools, physical movement, and visual aids.

See Figure 9.2 for an example of a Book Talk Glow and Grow template from Holly Siggins's middle school class in Knoxville, Tennessee.

FIGURE 9.2 • Scaffolded Peer Feedback Form

Name of speaker:

Your name:

Glow:

What is something your classmate did really well?

Grow:

What is something your classmate could work on for next time?

Source: Elizabeth Choi. Used with permission.

online resources Available for download at https://companion.corwin.com/courses/NineDimensionsofScaffoldingforMLs

- ***Language Support:*** Teachers can support multilingual learners and help them interact more effectively in all their languages by providing tools:
    - Co-create sentence frames and conversation starters with your students that also represent the varied proficiency levels to support communication.
        - Tips: Get started with commonly used sentence frames and expand the list based on students' authentic language use: I agree/disagree with . . . because . . . , Can you explain why you think . . . , In my opinion, . . .

- Provide visual supports and word banks (to help students make connections to what they are learning while they engage in conversations.
    - Tips: Co-develop anchor charts with key phrases or academic language, content-specific word walls, and images related to the topic.
- Model expectations, provide opportunities to practice skills in low-stakes settings, and allow students to use all their languages to navigate their learning.
    - Tips: Role-play example conversations, use think-alouds to verbalize thought processes, and provide video clips showcasing effective peer interactions.

- ***Leverage Students' Gifts, Talents, and Unique Abilities:*** Structure activities to allow students at different language proficiency levels to meet and exceed grade-level expectations while strengthening and enhancing their language skills.
    - Design challenging, grade-level tasks that require students to work together to solve complex problems or analyze high-level texts with tiered supports.
        - Tips: Use heterogeneous groups, assign roles to leverage students' strengths, provide annotations for text to support language and clarity of concepts, and encourage the use of home language.
    - Create opportunities for students to teach concepts to each other to promote deep understanding and language development.
        - Tips: Try peer learning using the reciprocal teaching framework; set up jigsaw learning with a student expert; implement peer tutoring with structured guidance; and encourage student-led mini lessons and demonstrations.

TEACHING PRACTICES

Let's continue by exploring various teaching practices that effectively implement this strategy in diverse classroom settings. These practices emphasize the importance of carefully structured activities that provide appropriate levels of challenge and support for students at different proficiency levels. They are designed to create a rich, supportive learning environment where all students can actively engage with their peers, content, and language meaningfully.

When students collaborate with peers through structured discussions, collaborative projects, and meaningful exchanges, they promote both academic growth and language development while building cross-cultural understanding. This type of engagement facilitates collaborative problem-solving, enabling students to tackle complex tasks with the support of their classmates. It also encourages peer teaching and learning, a process that allows students to explain concepts to each other, often using language that is more accessible to their peers. Zhu and colleagues (2024) further emphasize the importance of this practice by explaining that students who teach newly acquired concepts to their peers demonstrate significantly better understanding and retention compared to those who only review the material independently. Educators we have worked with also agree that discussions with peers enhance content understanding because multilingual learners can unpack and process information through dialogue, ask and respond to questions, and hear multiple explanations of complex ideas. There are various ways to incorporate interactive scaffolding, as seen in Table 9.2, which provides an overview of different types of interaction—*peer-to-peer*, *small group*, and *whole class* in which students engage in the classroom.

TABLE 9.2 • *Student-to-Student* Interaction

TYPE OF INTERACTION	PEER-TO-PEER	SMALL GROUP	WHOLE CLASS
What is it?	Two students work together to accomplish a task, complete an activity, or work through a problem.	Three to five students collaborate to complete a task or activity.	The teacher engages with all students simultaneously, requiring participation from the entire class.
Purpose	• To engage in peer teaching and learning • To practice speaking and listening • To build confidence	• To encourage diverse perspectives • To develop collaboration skills • To experience a low-pressure environment • To learn from peers and contribute their own strengths.	• To build class community and consensus • To share diverse ideas • To learn to agree and disagree respectfully • To practice public speaking
Group Structure	• Random pairing • Ability-based pairing • Mixed proficiency pairing	• Mixed-ability/proficiency grouping • Interest-based groups • Task-specific groups	• Flexible seating arrangements (including circular or U-shaped class organization) • Panel discussion • Debate team
Task Structure	• Think-pair-share • Information gap activities • Role-playing dialogues • Peer editing	• Jigsaw activities • Group discussions • Collaborative writing • Problem-solving tasks	• Class debates • Presentations • Whole class discussions • Interactive lectures

To better understand how these teaching practices may be implemented in the classroom, it's helpful to examine specific interaction patterns that support student learning. Let's explore examples of one-to-one, small group, and whole class interactive scaffolding practices.

PRACTICE 1: ONE-TO-ONE INTERACTION

One-to-one interaction in the classroom takes three primary forms, each requiring tailored language scaffolds for multilingual learners. Student-to-student pairings enable focused peer tutoring and collaborative problem-solving where partners can work at their own pace while building communication skills, often benefiting from multilingual word banks and visual supports. Student-to-teacher interactions involve individualized conferences, targeted feedback sessions, and personalized support where teachers can scaffold instruction through guided questions, differentiated sentence frames, and immediate feedback based on language proficiency levels, allowing students to access their full linguistic repertoire. Student-to-authentic audience interactions occur when learners engage individually with community members, experts, or peers from other schools through presentations, interviews, or digital communication supported by pre-taught academic vocabulary, rehearsal opportunities, and culturally responsive communication strategies. All three forms of one-to-one interaction benefit from clear expectations, structured language supports, and opportunities for students to demonstrate understanding through multiple modes of expression.

ADVANTAGES OF THIS PRACTICE

One-to-one interactive scaffolds provide significant advantages for both academic and linguistic development. These personalized interactions allow teachers to precisely target support based on individual student needs, adjusting language complexity and content depth in real-time. Students benefit from immediate feedback, opportunities to clarify understanding, and dedicated practice time with language in authentic contexts. For multilingual learners specifically, one-to-one scaffolding creates a low-anxiety environment where they can take linguistic risks, receive targeted pronunciation feedback, and build confidence in using academic language. This individualized attention also enables teachers to better understand students' cultural and linguistic assets, incorporating these strengths into instruction while identifying specific areas for growth. Through these focused interactions, teachers can more effectively monitor progress, adjust supports gradually, and celebrate small wins that might go unnoticed in whole-group settings.

EXAMPLE #1: PARTNER TALK

Student-to-student interaction provides multilingual learners with authentic opportunities to practice language in a low-stakes environment with peers. Turn-and-talk activities create structured opportunities for peer-to-peer learning through focused, brief discussions that support both language development and content understanding. When students engage in these quick conversational exchanges, they use academic language in a low-stakes environment while clarifying their thinking and building communication skills. Through carefully designed prompts and clear discussion protocols, students take turns sharing ideas, asking questions, and building on each other's responses.

In the following example, Turn and Taco (a fun way to rename the Turn and Talk strategy), Alexis Tucker, ELD teacher in Stapleton Elementary School at Framingham Public Schools in Massachusetts, uses the FIESTA protocol she created to incorporate her school slogan: "Let's taco [talk] 'bout our learning!," into a daily routine. She displays the anchor chart, as shown in Figure 9.3, to activate academic conversations and uses the following protocol with students:

FIESTA Protocol for Turn and Taco (Turn and Talk) Academic Conversations:

To Activate the Academic Conversation:

Teacher says: *"Are you FIESTA ready? Facing your partner, interruptions away, make eye contact, sentence frame bookmarks in hand, and ask clarifying questions. Are you FIESTA ready?"*

Students respond: *"Ready to turn and taco!"*

(*Students engage in academic conversation*)

To Consolidate Knowledge:

Teacher says: *"S-a-l-s-a, salsa, salsa look this way!"*

Students respond: *"Salsa, salsa, look your way!"*

(*Teachers and students share out consolidated information from turn and talks*)

FIGURE 9.3 ● Anchor Chart to Support the Fiesta Protocol

Source: Alexis Tucker. Used with permission.

EXAMPLE #2: TEACHER-TO-STUDENT STRATEGY: COMPREHENSION CHECK

Teachers can provide personalized attention and support tailored to student's specific needs in a one-to-one, student-to-teacher setting, enabling in-depth discussions, conferencing time, targeted feedback, and individualized support. During these focused interactions, teachers can assess comprehension more closely, address misconceptions, model academic language, clarify vocabulary, and adjust questioning complexity while building student confidence. These individual exchanges create a low-pressure environment where teachers can observe both content comprehension and language development, providing immediate, differentiated feedback and strategic scaffolding, including primary language support when appropriate. Through this personalized approach, teachers can build stronger relationships with students, understand their unique strengths and challenges, identify specific areas for growth, adjust instruction accordingly, and create a supportive environment for both academic and linguistic development that helps students bridge understanding between languages while developing critical reading comprehension skills. Here are examples of several one-on-one reading comprehension checks:

- To Get Started with a Conference:
  - Begin by having the student summarize the text's main points
  - Use leveled questions moving from literal to inferential understanding: "What happened when . . . ?" "Why do you think the character . . . ?" "How does this connect to . . . ?"
- To Offer Scaffolded Supports:
  - Provide sentence frames: "The main idea is . . ." "I think this means . . ."
  - Use a graphic organizer to track key details
  - Reference text evidence together: "Let's look back at page . . ."
- To Check for Understanding:
  - Ask the student to explain unclear portions in their own words: "I noticed this part seemed challenging—could you tell me in your own way what you think it means . . ."
  - Model a think-aloud for challenging sections: "Let me share my thinking process for this section—when I read this part, I first . . ." Note specific vocabulary or concepts needing clarification (with visuals): "Let's create a visual to help us understand . . ."
- To Document Progress:
  - Record student's comprehension strengths: "I love how you really understood when you . . ."
  - Note areas needing additional support: "Let's mark the spots where we can grow stronger together, like . . ."
  - Plan targeted instruction for the next conference: "Next time we meet, we can work more on . . ."

This focused interaction allows teachers to provide immediate feedback and adjust support based on individual needs.

EXAMPLE #3: AUTHENTIC INTERVIEW

Student-to-authentic audience interaction provides multilingual learners with purposeful opportunities to develop their unique voices and use academic language in real-world contexts beyond the classroom. These structured interactions, such as conducting interviews with community members, writing to community leaders, maintaining personal portfolios, or presenting to industry professionals, allow students to practice professional communication while receiving personalized feedback from real-world audiences. When engaging with external audiences like veterans sharing their service experiences or professionals discussing their careers, students must employ active listening, precise questioning, and thoughtful follow-up responses, which helps them refine their language use and build confidence in authentic communication. Through these meaningful exchanges, students not only develop essential interview and communication skills but also experience the immediate relevance of their language learning while fostering cross-cultural understanding and personal responsibility.

A student can engage in a structured interview with a local veteran or professional following these steps:

Pre-Interview Preparation:

- Research the person's background
- Create question stems: "What inspired you to . . ." "Could you describe a time when . . ." "How did you overcome . . ."
- Practice with sentence frames: "I'm curious about . . ." "Could you tell me more about . . ."

Participation During the Interview:

- Begin with an introduction script: "Thank you for sharing your experiences with me. I'm especially interested in learning about . . ."
- Use active listening strategies and follow-up questions
- Take notes using a graphic organizer
- Record (with permission) for accuracy

Follow-Up Activities:

- Write a thank you note highlighting key learning
- Create a presentation or written piece sharing insights
- Share interview highlights with classmates

Remember to provide multilingual learners with vocabulary support, appropriate images, sentence stems, and rehearsal opportunities before the interview.

PRACTICE # 2: SMALL GROUP INTERACTIONS

Small group interaction encompasses three key configurations that support academic and linguistic development in distinct ways. Student teams work collaboratively on tasks, projects, or discussions with clear roles and language supports like sentence frames and word banks, allowing peers to scaffold each other's learning while practicing language in a supportive environment. Teacher-to-small group instruction enables targeted support through guided reading, station rotations, content discussions, or language development activities, creating a balance between individual attention and peer collaboration where teachers can provide immediate feedback, model academic language, and adjust scaffolds based on the group's collective needs. Small group-to-authentic audience interactions involve teams presenting to community members, conducting group interviews, or collaborating with external partners on projects like business pitches to entrepreneurs or service-learning initiatives, supported by pre-taught vocabulary, rehearsal opportunities, and structured discussion protocols. Across all configurations, teachers should strategically group students to leverage language abilities, provide visual supports, encourage primary language use when beneficial, and establish clear routines for group work that promote both content mastery and language development while allowing teachers to observe group dynamics, assess collaborative skills, and provide real-time feedback on both academic content and interaction skills.

ADVANTAGES OF THIS PRACTICE

Small group interaction practices offer multiple advantages for student learning and development. This format creates intimate learning spaces where students feel more comfortable taking risks with language and content, while receiving immediate peer and teacher support. The smaller setting enables teachers to provide targeted instruction, closely monitor understanding, and adjust scaffolding in real-time based on observed needs.

Students have more opportunities to actively participate compared to whole-class settings, leading to increased language production and deeper engagement with academic concepts. The flexible nature of small groups also allows teachers to group students differently based on language proficiency, content knowledge, or specific learning objectives.

For multilingual learners specifically, small groups provide a low-anxiety environment for practicing academic language, receiving immediate feedback, and building confidence through successful interactions. When working with authentic audiences, the shared responsibility within small groups reduces individual pressure while maintaining high expectations for authentic communication and collaboration. This structured yet supportive approach helps students develop both academic skills and essential interpersonal competencies needed for success.

EXAMPLE # 1: STATION ROTATION

Student team interaction creates collaborative spaces where multilingual learners can practice language while working toward shared academic goals with structured support from peers. Within teams, students take on different roles that allow them to contribute meaningfully regardless of their language proficiency level, building confidence through success in group tasks. These small group settings provide frequent opportunities for negotiating meaning, clarifying understanding, and developing both social and academic language through authentic interaction. Teams also foster a supportive learning environment where students can take linguistic risks, learn from peers' diverse language models, and develop cross-cultural communication skills essential for academic success.

Exploring complex topics requires multiple entry points and varied learning approaches to build student understanding. In the following example, see how Lindsay Manzella, English as an additional language (EAL) teacher at NIST International School in Bangkok, Thailand, designed a station rotation to explore the complex topic of how food is distributed through the food supply chain (from producer to the processor to the retailer to the consumer) while money moves from consumer to producer. The six stations included a variety of resources, including a range of modalities from videos to print-based and digital texts, as well as graphic representations of concepts. Table 9.3 explains what the students do at each station and what they write on their record sheets after the tasks are completed. The station rotation ends with a whole-class wrap-up activity, also scaffolded for student success.

TABLE 9.3 ● Food Supply Chain Station Rotation

STATION	WHAT STUDENTS DO AT THE STATION	WHAT THEY WRITE ON THEIR RECORD SHEET
1. The Food Chain	Watch the video and draw a food chain as Michael Polan describes it.	Sketch of food chain
2. Food Chain Problems	Put the paper slips in order of the food production process. Answer one question and discuss how it might affect consumers.	Write the chosen question and describe how it affects consumers
3. Jobs In Food Production	Write the jobs that people might do at each stage in the food chain	List at least two jobs at each stage
4. Shorten Your Food Chain	Discuss what percentage* of each of the four types of food chains the groups' families use. * For example 5% Home garden 10% Farmer's Market 60% Supermarket 25% Food Delivery Service	Write percentages on the lines Answer the question as a group—How does a shorter food chain help people and the environment?
5. Food Moves from the Farmer to the Consumer and Money Moves from the Consumer to the Producer	Read and discuss an article on the discrepancy between how much farmers make and how much consumers pay for agricultural products.	Give an example and explain their answer with one fact from the resources at the station.
6. Food Supply Chain and flow of money, product, and information	Watch a video and draw the food supply chain including -5 steps of the chain -the direction product flows -the direction money flows -the flow of information	Sketch the food supply chain and list the requirements

WHOLE CLASS WRAP-UP
Each station was about the food production chain but each station looked at it from a different angle (jobs, problems, flow of money and product, etc.). In your notebook, write "Today's Takeaway" for this lesson. We understand that . . .

Source: Lindsay Manzella. Used with permission.

EXAMPLE #2: JIGSAW EXPERTS

Teacher-to-small group interaction enables focused language and content support tailored to the collective needs of students. In these small settings, teachers can provide intensive scaffolding through guided practice, targeted vocabulary development, and immediate feedback that addresses common language challenges shared by the group. These interactions allow teachers to closely monitor comprehension, adjust language complexity in real time, and create low-anxiety environments where students feel comfortable taking linguistic risks. Teachers can also leverage the group dynamic to foster peer support, model academic discourse patterns, and gradually release responsibility as students build confidence in using new language structures.

The *Jigsaw Experts strategy* promotes collaborative learning, develops reading comprehension skills, and encourages peer teaching across diverse ability levels and language proficiencies. This example begins by dividing the class into heterogeneous home groups of 4–5 students, ensuring a mix of language proficiency levels and academic strengths. Each group member receives a different section of a longer text or different but related texts on a common theme.

Students then regroup into expert groups, where all those with the same text section come together. In these expert groups, students collaboratively read and analyze their assigned text, using scaffolds such as graphic organizers or guiding questions. Multilingual learners may be paired with peers and will be strategically placed in expert groups to provide language support. The expert groups then prepare to teach their section to their home group, providing differentiated supports such as sentence frames and visual aids for those who need them.

After preparation, students return to their original home groups and take turns teaching their expert section. Each student is responsible for ensuring their group understands their part. The activity culminates in a whole-class synthesis, where the teacher *facilitates* a discussion to connect all parts of the text or theme. Strategies like a gallery walk or collaborative mind mapping can be used to visualize these connections.

Throughout the process, scaffolding and support are provided through tiered texts, language support tools, and technology aids. Teachers serve as *guides* to offer targeted support during group work. Assessment is conducted through observational checklists, peer and self-assessment rubrics, and a final individual assessment to check comprehension of the entire text.

KEEP THIS IN MIND

Flexible grouping in interactive scaffolding deliberately organizes students into dynamic learning partnerships based on language proficiency, content knowledge, and learning objectives. Teachers strategically pair students to create opportunities for peer teaching, language development, and content mastery while ensuring all students experience both expert and learner roles. This approach integrates students' cultural and linguistic assets, allowing them to leverage their full linguistic repertoire during collaborative tasks. Teachers design activities that promote both academic discourse and social interaction, creating natural opportunities for language practice.

This approach requires ongoing assessment and adjustment as teachers monitor group effectiveness and student progress. Groups remain fluid, allowing for regular reconfiguration based on activity goals, observed interactions, and emerging student needs. Teachers maintain clear documentation of successful grouping strategies while continuously gathering data to inform future combinations. Effective implementation includes establishing clear routines for group transitions, teaching explicit collaboration strategies, and developing systems for tracking student interactions across different grouping configurations. Regular reflection on grouping patterns ensures equitable access to varied learning experiences.

Flexible grouping creates a rich, interactive learning environment that supports the academic and linguistic development of all students, particularly benefiting multilingual learners through authentic peer interaction, varied partnerships, and the development of leadership skills across proficiency levels. This practice promotes active engagement, ensuring every student has a role and responsibility, and builds confidence by allowing students to be "experts" in their assigned role, providing for differentiation, and enhancing comprehension. This model naturally differentiates instruction while building students' confidence, cultural awareness, and collaborative capabilities—essential skills for academic and professional success.

EXAMPLE #3: DIVERSE TEAM PROBLEM-BASED LEARNING (DT-PBL)

When students engage with authentic audiences to solve real-world problems, they develop both academic and professional skills through meaningful collaboration. Small group interactions create supportive environments where students can develop communication strategies, build independence, and tackle complex challenges through structured yet authentic exchanges with external partners and community members. These purposeful exchanges motivate learners to refine their language use and develop strategic communication skills while working toward shared goals. The collective nature of group work creates a supportive environment where students can take risks, leverage diverse perspectives, and build confidence through authentic problem-solving, as explained in the *DT-PBL* strategy example.

The *DT-PBL* strategy is designed for students to solve real-world problems collaboratively while developing language skills, content knowledge, and critical thinking abilities. To implement this practice, follow these steps:

1. ***Define an Authentic Problem***: Invite students to generate a complex, real-world problem relevant to the curriculum and students' lives. For example, how can we reduce food waste in our school cafeteria, or how can we help our local community reduce its carbon footprint over the next year?
2. ***Form Diverse Teams:*** Create heterogeneous groups of 4–5 students, ensuring a mix of language proficiencies, academic strengths, and backgrounds. Assign each student a role based on their strengths or interests (e.g., researcher, data analyst, community liaison, environmental specialist, etc.).
3. ***Gather Information and Research:*** Students work within their expert roles to gather relevant information. Provide differentiated resources (with varied Lexile levels, graphic or visual representation of topics, and videos with closed captioning in home language and English) and scaffolds that are multimodal and multidimensional.
4. ***Engage in Collaborative Problem-Solving:*** Teams share their expert knowledge and brainstorm solutions. To support communication, encourage the use of graphic organizers and visual thinking tools like mind maps or concept boards.
5. ***Develop a Solution Plan:*** Groups refine their ideas and develop a detailed solution plan. Scaffold this step by providing templates with sentence starters, images to generate ideas, or guided questions to support responses.
6. ***Prepare a Joint Presentation:*** Teams prepare to present their solutions to an authentic audience (e.g., school administration and local community members). Assign roles (or have students select their roles) that allow each student to contribute based on their strengths. Scaffold this information by providing, or better yet, co-constructing presentation frames:
    - The topic of our presentation is ________________.
    - In the first part, we give a few basic definitions. In the next section, we will explain _____. In part three, we are going to show ________________.
    - The area of a circle is equivalent to ____________________.
    - The _____ is longer than the ________________.

- In our experiment, varying the amounts of ___________ impacted the reaction.

7. ***Showcase Solutions:*** Host a showcase where teams present their solutions. Invite feedback from the audience to make the experience more authentic. Scaffold this by allowing students to choose how they "showcase" their work (i.e., posters, digital presentations, or newsletters).
8. ***Reflect and Evaluate:*** Guide students through individual and group reflections on the process, their learning, and the effectiveness of their collaboration. Scaffold this by implementing language buddies to pair multilingual learners with more proficient English speakers.

PRACTICE #3: WHOLE CLASS INTERACTION

Whole group interaction involves three distinct configurations that support multilingual learners through carefully scaffolded participation structures. When students work as an entire class, they engage in shared discussions, problem-solving, or projects where teachers implement strategies like think-pair-share, structured talk moves, and visual supports to ensure all students can contribute regardless of language proficiency. Teacher-to-whole group instruction includes direct teaching, modeling, and facilitated discussions where teachers use comprehensible input strategies, multimedia supports, and differentiated questioning techniques while maintaining high expectations and addressing common misconceptions, allowing students to listen to varied language models and observe different interaction styles. Whole group-to-authentic audience interactions occur when the class collectively presents to external audiences, participates in school-wide events or competitions, takes virtual field trips with other schools, or collaborates on large-scale projects like community fundraisers, supported by clear role assignments, rehearsal opportunities, and differentiated participation structures that create a sense of collective purpose and achievement while exposing students to a broad range of perspectives and feedback. Across all whole group configurations, teachers should incorporate wait time, sentence frames at various proficiency levels, strategic use of primary language supports, and multiple modes of expression to ensure equitable participation and language development for all students while fostering a strong sense of classroom community.

Crystal Hafner, librarian at Park Avenue Elementary School, creates an SOP (Standard Operational Procedure) with her students during the first weeks of school. The poster in Figure 9.4 remains on display so all students know what is expected when they come to the rug to listen to a story or participate in whole group instruction.

FIGURE 9.4 ● Co-Created, Illustrated Classroom Norms

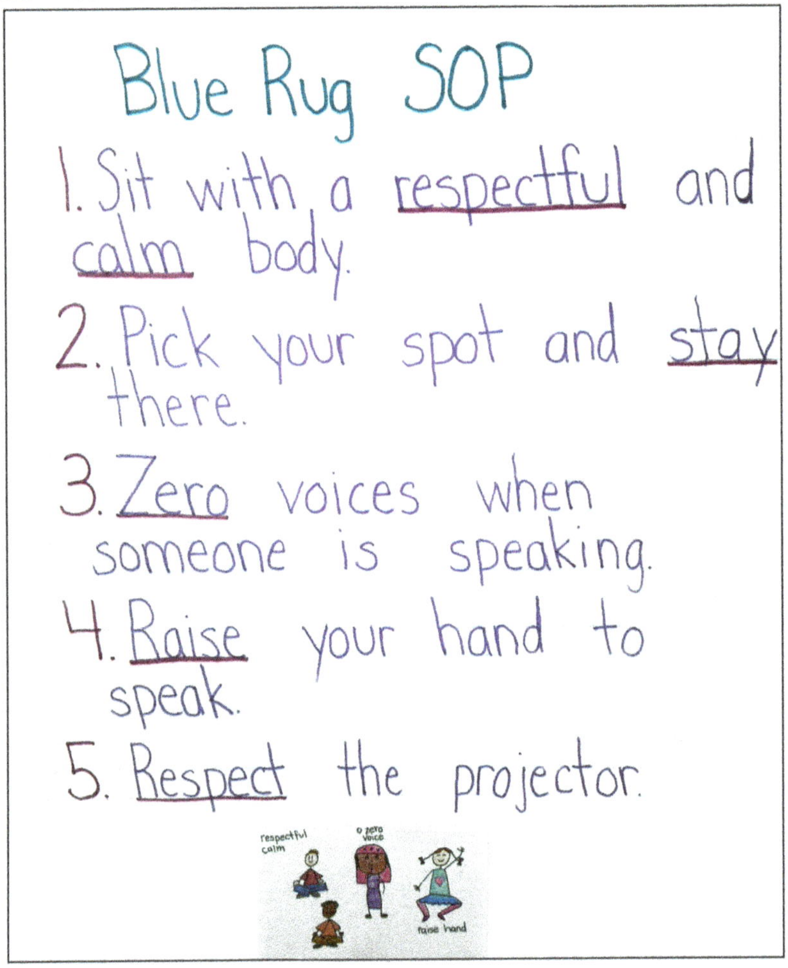

Source: Crystal Hafner. Used with permission.

ADVANTAGES OF THIS PRACTICE

Whole group interaction practices offer several key advantages for multilingual learners and classroom community development. This approach creates shared learning experiences where students benefit from multiple language models, diverse perspectives, and collective problem-solving while building a supportive classroom culture. For multilingual learners specifically, whole group settings provide opportunities to observe various levels of academic language use, participate at their comfort level, and develop confidence through structured participation routines.

The practice supports efficient delivery of content while ensuring consistent messaging and expectations for all students. Teachers can implement scaffolds that benefit the entire class, such as visual supports, gestures, and multilevel sentence frames, creating an inclusive environment where language learning is normalized. These shared experiences also foster cross-cultural understanding and peer support networks, essential for both academic success and social-emotional development. This collaborative approach helps build classroom unity, celebrates diverse contributions, and provides authentic contexts for language development across all proficiency levels.

EXAMPLE #1: READER'S THEATER

Working as a whole group provides multilingual learners with opportunities to observe and participate in rich academic discussions while benefiting from multiple language models at various proficiency levels. During these collective interactions, students engage with shared content through structured participation routines like reader's theater that support both language development and content understanding.

Implementing Reader's Theater provides students the opportunity to read and write story scripts, and as a result, develop ownership of language to build reading fluency, expression, and comprehension while performing skits without the pressure of memorizing text. Students read and reread an assigned script or one that they developed, usually in collaboration with their teacher, using common fables, fairytales, narratives, or even informational texts. They perform these plays in small groups but do not learn their parts by heart (even though with much rehearsal or practice, it could happen); instead, they read them and enhance their performances with voice inflection, tone, and perhaps with a minimal number of props and costumes.

Reader's Theater can be adapted to suit the needs and abilities of students at any grade level, including students who are in middle and high school settings. Although the fundamentals of Reader's Theater remain the same, there are often differences in the types of texts selected and the objectives for its use. Students at the secondary level may be provided with choices for the roles they select, engage in longer, more complex performances, or be encouraged to creatively adapt scripts for increased engagement. Here are some suggestions to prepare for Reader's Theater:

- Begin by selecting a story script that is appropriate for your student's age and grade level, duplicate it, and distribute one to each student.
- Read the script to the students aloud and ask them to read the script with you chorally.
- Next, divide the class in half and have each group read the character parts alternately.
- Further divide students into small groups and assign each one a part (or have students self-select the parts they prefer). Have students practice their parts both as individuals and as a team.
- Invite students to perform for the class.

When students have an idea, assign a different script to each group. Have students practice reading their scripts in their groups. This reading format helps students develop their fluency, pronunciation, intonation, and expressiveness. Additionally, scripts may be altered to accommodate various reading levels so that all students can participate. Depending upon their age and readiness, students may begin to write their own scripts based on stories they enjoy or experiences they have had. After some further rehearsing, you may consider inviting other classes and parents to a special performance of the stories.

Reader's Theater may be considered an effective interactive scaffolding opportunity because it invites students to rehearse scripts, practice interacting with each other, and performing short, manageable skits without having to commit lengthy text to memory. As an extension, you can invite your students to start developing their own Reader's Theater scripts to develop even more ownership of the language and the interaction that takes place between and among students during the activity. (Revisit Chapter 5 for more on Reader's Theater.)

EXAMPLE #2: SOCRATIC SEMINAR

Socratic seminars transform whole-class discussions into dynamic exchanges where teachers guide students through deeper analysis and critical thinking using strategic questioning techniques. In this structured format, teachers facilitate thoughtful dialogue about texts or topics while students build on each other's ideas, supporting both content understanding and academic language development.

The teacher's role shifts from direct instruction to skilled facilitation, using carefully crafted questions to probe student thinking, encourage multiple perspectives, and deepen comprehension. Through intentional scaffolding such as discussion stems, pre-taught vocabulary, and visual supports, all students, particularly multilingual learners, can actively participate in these rich academic conversations while developing essential analytical and communication skills. For multilingual learners, teachers can scaffold by providing differentiated response frames based on language proficiency, allowing brief partner talks for language rehearsal, and encouraging the strategic use of home language resources to support full participation in these academic discussions. In Claggett Creek Middle School of Salem-Kaizer Schools in Oregon, Rachel Cutter and Cierra LaBounty coteach their ELA classes and frequently engage their students in a mini-Socratic seminar. See Figure 9.5 for an example of how scaffolded prompts support student participation as they explore their ideas about animals in captivity.

FIGURE 9.5 ● Scaffolding a Mini-Socratic Seminar

Mini - Socratic Seminar

EQ: **Is it ethical to keep animals in captivity?**

Sentence Frames to use during the discussion *Use evidence from the article or videos as much as possible!

- ★ In my opinion ____ because ____.
- ★ Based on what it says in paragraph __, __________.
- ★ From my perspective _____ because _____.
- ★ To build off of what ___ said, I think ___ because ___.

Agree:

- ★ **I agree with your opinion because ___ and ___.**
- ★ **That was a great point because ___.**

Disagree:

- ★ **I heard what you said, however ____.**
- ★ **I respectfully disagree because ____.**

Source: Rachel Cutter and Cierra LaBounty. Used with permission.

EXAMPLE #3: VIRTUAL FIELD TRIPS

The *virtual field trip* is an innovative teaching practice that promotes interaction and collaboration while engaging students in an immersive, digitally enhanced learning experience that engages students with people in the outside world. Consider the following virtual field trip example that explores ecosystems across the globe. This trip begins by dividing the class into multiple heterogeneous groups, each assigned a different global ecosystem to explore. Students collaboratively research and plan their virtual journey, using digital resources to create an itinerary of key "stops" in their assigned ecosystem. The heart of the experience involves groups embarking on virtual explorations using virtual reality (VR) platforms or 360° videos, with students taking turns as "tour guides" to describe their observations to peers. Throughout the virtual trip, students work together to collect and analyze data on flora, fauna, climate, and human impact, using collaborative online tools to organize their findings (see Figure 9.6 we created to scaffold student research).

FIGURE 9.6 • Virtual Ecosystem Explorer

Location	

Flora (a__________ species)	Images (include pictures of each)

Fauna (a__________ species)	Images (include pictures of each)

Climate	What is the temperature? The temperature is ... What are the participation patterns? Other information:

HUMAN IMPACT
The impact on humans is...

ADDITIONAL OBSERVATIONS
I noticed...

The practice then facilitates cross-ecosystem comparisons by regrouping students to share insights from different ecosystems, fostering a broader understanding of global environmental diversity. Groups reconvene to create multimedia presentations about their assigned ecosystems, shared in a class-wide virtual symposium. This culminating event encourages questions and discussions, deepening understanding across all studied ecosystems. The experience concludes with guided reflection on the learning journey and exploration of real-world applications, connecting the virtual experience to global environmental issues. (Look back to Chapter 7 more on VR used as a digital scaffolding tool.)

KEEP THIS IN MIND

In-the-Moment interactive scaffolds may be carefully crafted or spontaneously implemented into any of the above examples. When students need support as they interact with others, consider some quick ways to implement ready-to-go strategies that can be seamlessly integrated into any lesson at any time, with minimal preparation, enhancing student engagement and support. Visual aids, such as impromptu graphic organizers or quick sketches on the board, can structure thoughts and support understanding, as well as help guide student responses as they collaborate. Teachers can spontaneously assign roles within groups for collaborative work to ensure equal participation. Digital tools like shared online documents or virtual sticky notes can be utilized for real-time collaboration and idea sharing. Even simple gestures, like asking students to show agreement with thumbs up/down, can serve as instant scaffolds. By having a repertoire of these flexible strategies at their disposal, teachers can readily adapt their lessons to include interactive and collaborative elements that support all learners, regardless of the content or context of the lesson.

In-the-Moment scaffolds provide teachers with practical, easily implemented strategies for incorporating interactive and collaborative scaffolds into their lessons with minimal preparation. They provide a toolkit of readily available techniques that teachers can use to enhance engagement and support for all learners at a moment's notice. Refer to Table 9.4 for spontaneous scaffolding tools that can support students at the moment they need them.

TABLE 9.4 • Quick, *In-the-Moment* Interactive Scaffolding

STRATEGY	DESCRIPTION
Quick Draw	Students think about a topic individually, rapidly sketch their learning and discuss with a partner to collaboratively refine their ideas, then share synthesized insights with the class while partners provide supporting details or examples.
Whisper Partners	Regularly check for understanding and provide clarification as needed by having students pair up with a partner and check with one another to make sure they are on track (see Figure 9.7 for an example of this strategy).
Productive Wait Time	Allow extra time for students to process questions and formulate responses by capturing their thoughts as brief notes, then partner them to collaboratively refine and expand their initial ideas into complete, well-structured responses.
Gestures and TPR (Total Physical Response)	Use body language to reinforce learning by teaching and mirroring gestures in pairs or groups while speaking target vocabulary or acting out concepts.
Questioning Technique	Use a variety of question types, from simple yes/no to more complex open-ended questions, and have students collaborate to build on each other's responses through guided discussion and peer elaboration.

FIGURE 9.7 • Scaffolded Guidance for Whisper Partners

Source: Elizabeth Choi. Used with permission.

INDEPENDENT LEARNING STRATEGIES

To maximize the benefits of interactive scaffolds, empower students to take ownership of their learning process, effectively engage with peers, and make the most of supportive structures provided by teachers. When students regularly assess their understanding and participation, they become apt at identifying areas for improvement and setting specific learning goals. This self-awareness helps them engage more purposefully in collaborative activities. Encourage students to decide which learning activities best suit their learning needs within the collaborative framework. Foster a mindset of active learning so students can take initiative in their education, seek out resources, and proactively engage with the material and their peers. Students should feel comfortable asking for clarification from peers or teachers when they do not understand something, promoting a culture of autonomy, curiosity, and continuous learning.

Interactive learning enhances collaboration and improves learning outcomes (Qureshi et al., 2023), especially when students are faced with complex expectations such as negotiating task completion, navigating group dynamics, and creating equitable participation in group work. When teachers provide choices, models, and examples for students on how to interact and collaborate with each other, they help strengthen student autonomy. Multilingual learners benefit from having routines established for group work, engaging in individual and shared reflection on how effective their collaboration was, and planning cooperative learning activities while promoting consistency and efficiency in their learning process. See Figure 9.8 for an example of a collaborative choice board we created for a research project to explore their assigned state in an upper elementary classroom.

FIGURE 9.8 ● Collaborative Research Project Choice Board

Directions: You and your partner have been assigned a state within the United States to explore. Please work together to research your state online and learn more about it. Select one (1) activity from each row to complete together.

Row 1	Design a colorful visitor's guide highlighting key attractions.	Build a digital showcase of top state destinations.	Produce a short video spotlighting state features.
Row 2	Compose a catchy state facts song or poem.	Create a local guide sharing hidden gems and must-see spots.	Research and present how your state has changed over time.
Row 3	Construct a physical relief map showing geography and cities.	Design a series of commemorative state postcards.	Propose your own creative project (with teacher approval).

SUMMARY

Interactive scaffolding helps all students learn effectively while supporting language development. Through structured peer interactions and differentiated supports like sentence frames and visuals, multilingual learners access grade-level content while building language skills. As students progress, scaffolds are gradually removed, creating an inclusive environment where peers learn from each other while developing cultural awareness. Cognitive and social processes may play a role in interactive activities (i.e., collaboratively reading a science lab activity and corresponding text and then explaining it to others) and improve students' learning outcomes, causing greater and more complex brain activity (Zhu et al., 2024). Interactive scaffolding supports language acquisition for multilingual learners and enriches the learning experience for all students, creating a more inclusive and effective educational environment.

Questions

1. What are the key elements of interactive scaffolding, and why are they essential for multilingual learners?
2. How do interactive scaffolding practices prepare students for real-world collaboration?
3. Which of the interactive scaffolding strategies presented in this chapter have you found to most effectively support collaboration in both content and language development in your classroom?
4. What is an example of an interactive strategy you currently use or would like to implement? What scaffolds will work best with this strategy?

CHAPTER 10

Environmental Scaffolding

> *"To serve English Learners, American classrooms need a coherent way of connecting the diverse contexts that have an impact on these students' education and a generative understanding of both scaffolding and nonlinear nature of language development."*
> *Aída Walqui and Mary Schmida, 2023, p. 38*

In our final chapter, we complete our scaffolding blueprint for multilingual learners by uncovering the power to scaffold the very spaces where learning takes place. In our previous chapters, we invited you to consider some innovative ideas about scaffolded learning. In this chapter, we continue to explore more unique aspects of scaffolding for multilingual learners by examining our classrooms and school environments and how they may be reimagined to create more inclusive and inspiring learning spaces for all students.

It is commonly understood that different types of instruction require adjustments to learning spaces—seating arrangements, various class configurations for individual and group work, or access to appropriate tools—print, digital, or otherwise—for students to complete specified tasks. Equally important is the notion that classrooms and schools ought to be inviting places and offer all students not only a sense of belonging, comfort, and care but also opportunities to stimulate engagement, exploration of ideas, and autonomy. As important as it is for students to see themselves in the curriculum they are learning, it is equally important for them to be able to see themselves as a part of a learning community—one that is reinforced by the thoughtful design and use of spaces throughout the school.

Environmental scaffolding requires the thoughtful and intentional structuring of physical learning spaces specially engineered to support students' understanding, engagement, and achievement. It also involves the fostering of classroom and school climates where high expectations are maintained for all students. This approach entails creating learning environments that meet the varied linguistic needs of multilingual learners and encourages autonomy using multilingual, print-rich displays that reflect the cultural and linguistic diversity of students in classrooms and greater school spaces—hallways, offices, cafeterias, gymnasiums, playgrounds, and so on. Figure 10.1 is an example of a teacher-made bilingual poster in a first-grade bilingual class representing the numbers in Mandarin (courtesy of Nancy Weng).

FIGURE 10.1 • Counting in Mandarin—Grade 1

Source: Nancy Weng. Used with permission.

WHO IS IT FOR?

Environmental scaffolding provides instructional resources that support a wide range of learners at varied levels of English language proficiency. Additionally, it can also support designs for innovative classroom spaces that invite all students to better focus and feel safe and comfortable, thereby meeting personal learning preferences. Along with students from culturally and linguistically diverse backgrounds, environmental scaffolding is beneficial to students with disabilities, students with autism, and students with attention and executive functioning challenges.

HOW IS ENVIRONMENTAL SCAFFOLDING USED ACROSS PROGRAM MODELS?

In classroom settings, environmental scaffolding supports instruction for multilingual learners in general education, co-taught, and integrated English language development (ELD) classes as follows:

- In *general education classes*, welcoming class environments are created that promote diverse perspectives, incorporate culturally responsive classroom management strategies, and create opportunities to build a positive class culture. Maintaining high expectations and incorporating student identities into class instruction support all students' success.
- In *co-taught classes*, teaching partners work together to develop print-rich classrooms to immerse students in a literacy-rich environment that is incorporated into daily instruction. Anchor charts, word walls, student work samples, and so on invite students to be self-directed learners and support the completion of literacy tasks.
- In *standalone ELD classes*, it is critical that there is sufficient space and resources for students to engage in language and literacy development activities and practice all four language domains—listening, speaking, reading, and writing—as well as engage with multimedia and technology that can support students' exploration of language through aural, visual, tactual, and kinesthetic means.
- In *self-contained or integrated special education classes with dually identified multilingual learners*, quiet zones support focus for those easily overwhelmed, while minimizing distracting displays aids attention. Movement-friendly areas accommodate students needing physical breaks. A well-structured, flexible layout ensures all learners can access materials, engage meaningfully, and thrive in an environment that balances comfort and support.

In the larger school context, environmental scaffolding can support the navigation of the school through multilingual signage and information and provide resources that promote diverse voices and cultures. It can promote the creation of collaborative learning areas within the school for teacher and student teamwork, communication, and peer-to-peer support. These common learning spaces may include breakout rooms equipped with technology and resources to facilitate group work, discussions, and project-based learning. To further environmental scaffolding, professional learning for teachers might include implementing principles of Universal Design for Learning (UDL)—a framework to create equitable and inclusive learning environments—to address the diverse needs of all learners (see https://udlguidelines.cast.org/ for the updated UDL guidelines 3.0).

FROM RESEARCH TO PRACTICE

In a recent publication, Margo Gottlieb (2023) firmly advocates for not just multilingualism but multiliteracies to be the norm and shares an example of how to set up *multimodal exploration stations* for the students to explore learning in multiple ways in a supportive classroom environment:

(1) 'let's express ourselves' with art supplies, writing tools, recording devices, computers and tablets, audio versions of bilingual books, puppets, props; (2) 'let's solve problems,' with abacuses, puzzles, blocks, plastic shapes, letter and word magnets, whiteboards; and (3) 'let's get moving' with music, traffic signs, a large floor map, different modes of transportation, and board games. (p. 3)

Reflect on the following:

How do exploration stations support the development of multiliteracies and multilingualism in diverse classrooms? How does this type of learning environment encourage self-regulation?

How might cultural considerations influence the design of materials and activities for these exploration stations? How can teachers assess student engagement and learning outcomes in a classroom with exploration stations?

WHAT TEACHERS SAY ABOUT ENVIRONMENTAL SCAFFOLDING

Designing class environments depends obviously on the language level of my students. I do integrate my instruction with a lot of grade-level classes so I'm always discussing things with my co-teachers, and we're always looking for what are some supports that we can give our multilingual learners so that, number one, the content is accessible, and they're able to show what they learned about the content with the proper scaffolds, for example, anchor charts and other graphic organizers.

—Maria Neckonoff, English as a new language (ENL) teacher, Valley Stream, New York

WHY IS ENVIRONMENTAL SCAFFOLDING AN IMPORTANT APPROACH TO STUDENT LEARNING?

Environmental scaffolding supports students' physical, emotional, linguistic, and academic needs, creating learning spaces in which all students can better engage in the learning process. Physical spaces can bolster student learning by offering opportunities to access multimedia aids, provide for hands-on activities, and create rich, interactive, highly engaging classrooms. Environmental scaffolding can also promote inclusivity by ensuring that learning is accessible and meaningful to all students. It can enhance peer-to-peer collaboration, support students in managing anxiety and stress, and facilitate instruction to provide varied and appropriate resources that cater to students' individual learning needs.

Consider how physical spaces promote active learning and increase language and literacy development through flexible seating arrangements. For example, cluster seating, desks arranged in small groups, can promote collaboration and group work among students. Other examples of seating arrangements include round table seating, paired seating, and collaborative learning stations. Having multiple classroom configurations can facilitate the completion of various tasks and group projects. See Figures 10.2 for an example of an alternative seating arrangement.

FIGURE 10.2 ● A Colorful and Comfortable Space for Team Discussions

Environmental scaffolding can support student independence and self-reliance. It can create opportunities for students to problem-solve and complete complex tasks and individual writing projects when there are organized, print-rich learning spaces. Resources such as teacher-made charts that are co-created with students, interactive word walls, step-by-step illustrated guidance documents, reference materials, and digital tools made available for language and literacy support can drive student independence and ownership when combined with areas in the classroom for quiet and focused work.

Creating classroom spaces that are conducive to learning also requires a reduction in disruptions through a multifaceted approach from establishing clear expectations to consistent routines that provide structure and remove uncertainty. Effective classroom management techniques include using hand signals or other nonverbal cues—signs, flashing lights, chimes, count-down clocks, and other objects and materials—to communicate wants and needs from teacher to student or vice versa. For example, students might use three poker chips to indicate specific needs to a teacher during a writing assignment—green for all is well, yellow to ask a question, or red for needing additional support. Active supervision and timely interventions make for safe, secure, and comfortable class environments.

Of equal importance, school climate impacts students' overall relationships with peers, teachers, staff, and administrators within the school which has a great influence on conditions for learning as well as can support physical and emotional safety. School climate is particularly critical to ensure high expectations for students' academic success, respect for cultural differences, and the development of trusting and caring relationships for their security and well-being.

HOW DOES ENVIRONMENTAL SCAFFOLDING SPECIFICALLY RELATE TO MULTILINGUAL LEARNERS' NEEDS?

Environmental scaffolding plays a crucial role in supporting multilingual learners by:

- shaping the physical spaces where students learn,
- creating a nurturing and inspiring learning context,
- establishing the rules of engagement within all learning spaces, and
- fostering a system of beliefs and actions that promote equity and inclusion.

These four elements are vital for the development of positive classroom and school cultures that meaningfully impact multilingual learners' language acquisition and literacy growth as well as support their academic, social, and emotional development. Table 10.1 identifies how each of these aspects relate specifically to multilingual learners.

TABLE 10.1 • Environmental Scaffolding to Support Multilingual Learners

KEY ELEMENTS	ESSENTIAL COMPONENTS	INSTRUCTIONAL STRATEGIES
Physical Spaces	Language-rich environments	Equip classrooms and greater school spaces with multilingual resources for students to access information while reinforcing language and literacy skills.
	Seating arrangements and workspaces	Design classrooms with flexible seating and designate learning spaces for individual and group work as well as student-teacher conferencing.
	Technology integration	Provide access to language learning tools, multimedia, and multilingual resources to engage learners in content and support language needs.
Inspiring Learning Context	Motivation	Make the learning environment inviting and inspiring with ample

(Continued)

(Continued)

KEY ELEMENTS	ESSENTIAL COMPONENTS	INSTRUCTIONAL STRATEGIES
		student input into the classroom design.
	Ownership	Make sure students' interests and passions are captured in a dynamic learning environment.
Rules of Engagement	Clear communication	Jointly create and visually represent classroom rules and responsibilities in multilingual formats; consistently guide students to meet agreed upon norms.
	Classroom management	Implement strategies to accommodate the cultural and linguistic diversity of students; employ clear communication to reduce misunderstandings.
	Collaboration	Encourage peer collaboration to build language facility through social interaction and home language use; design group work with specific roles to foster engagement.
Fostering a System of Beliefs and Actions	High expectations	Affirm the potential of all multilingual learners to succeed and value their individual capabilities; empower students through equitable instructional practices.
	Cultural responsiveness	Value the cultural and linguistic experiences and abilities of multilingual learners bring with them; validate and celebrate student identities to enrich learning for all.
	Professional development	Foster a culture of continuous learning by collaborating with other educators; explore topics such as language learning, cultural competence, and inclusive teaching strategies to support multilingual learners.

online resources Available for download at https://companion.corwin.com/courses/NineDimensionsofScaffoldingforMLs

By carefully crafting physical learning spaces, ensuring an inspiring environment, clearly setting the rules of engagement jointly with students, and continually advocating for a system of beliefs that foster equity and inclusion for multilingual learners, environmental scaffolding will be one practice, among others, that can be used to support all students to thrive academically, socially, and emotionally.

FROM RESEARCH TO PRACTICE

In a study focused on the learning success of multilingual learners, Benjamin Nwokedi (2023) concluded, "The classroom environment plays a pivotal role in the academic performance and engagement of students, particularly in the realm of English language learning" (p. 191). The study revealed the following:

- A well-organized classroom and flexible seating arrangements can not only create an atmosphere conducive to learning, but it can also ensure that multilingual learners are better able to access needed resources, interact with others, and proceed with clarity to focus on and complete tasks.
- The social dynamics within the classroom, including interactions between teachers and students as well as among peers, greatly influence students' motivation and engagement. Positive relationships foster a sense of belonging and support students' active participation.
- The teaching methods and assessment practices used in the classroom are central to the learning process of multilingual learners, leading to improved outcomes and a more enjoyable learning experience.

Simply stated, when the learning environment is supportive, it can enhance language acquisition. When students feel encouraged and valued, they become engaged, active learners. Conversely, a poorly designed classroom can hinder language learning by creating barriers to understanding and communication. Therefore, it is essential to consider the classroom environment as a powerful tool to support multilingual learners.

Reflect on the following:

Consider the importance of creating physical classroom spaces that support all students. How can you ensure your classroom is physically conducive for multilingual learners? How might your classroom design support students' language acquisition, provide resources, and encourage peer-to-peer interaction?

Think about the ways you build a sense of community and belonging in your classroom. What strategies might you use to foster positive social interactions between teachers, students, and their peers? What types of conversations and discussions with students might promote a classroom culture that better engages multilingual learners?

Reflect on your employment of instructional strategies that support and enhance the use of language and literacy skills as well as how you create equitable assessments to evaluate student progress. Which teaching methods and assessment practices have you found to be most effective? What specific needs do your multilingual learners have and how might you address these needs through adjusting the classroom environment?

(Continued)

(Continued)

____

____

____

____

GETTING STARTED WITH ENVIRONMENTAL SCAFFOLDING

Imagine that you are a multilingual learner walking through the school where you work for the very first time. What might you see and hear that would make you feel welcomed and give you a sense that it is a place where you belong? Are there visual cues such as maps to help you navigate the school? Is there signage in multiple languages? Do decorative displays feature people who look like you? Do you hear your home language being spoken? When students see signs and labels throughout the school and in their classrooms in multiple languages, when they see displays that feature people from diverse backgrounds, and when they hear teachers, staff, or other students speaking their home languages, they feel valued, respected, and supported. Among many others, these elements of environmental scaffolding are crucial steps in creating a welcoming and affirming place where all students can learn. Mary Sandoval, ENL instructional coach and multilingual learner literacy and language specialist, shared with us how impactful walking through the hallways of Shenendehowa High School and seeing the flag of her own country of origin was for her as a newly hired educator in the school district. When flags representing students' home countries are displayed in the hallways of the high school, they serve as a reminder and celebration of student diversity (see Figure 10.3).

A powerful way to get started with environmental scaffolding is to do a walkabout and conduct a visual and auditory audit of your classroom as well as the school to ensure that the learning environment is inclusive and supportive of multilingual learners. Consider the checklist in Figure 10.4 as a guide to approach this task.

FIGURE 10.3 ● Hallway With Flags Representing the Members of the School Community

Source: Mary Sandoval. Used with permission.

FIGURE 10.4 ● Getting Started: Environmental Scaffolding Classroom Audit Checklist

- ☐ The seating arrangements allow for peer-to-peer interaction.
- ☐ Co-constructed anchor charts guide peer-to-peer interactions.
- ☐ Seating for multilingual learners ensures they have a clear line of sight to the teacher, other students, and instructional material displayed throughout the room.
- ☐ Posters, charts, and other visual aids clearly support the academic, linguistic, and literacy needs of multilingual learners.
- ☐ Multilingual labels are strategically placed throughout the room.
- ☐ Displays represent the diverse nature of the student body.

(Continued)

(Continued)

- ☐ Print material is available in multiple languages, whenever possible.
- ☐ Libraries and curriculum materials contain culturally diverse content.
- ☐ Technology tools are easily accessible and readily available for students to support their language, literacy, and information needs.

online resources Available for download at https://companion.corwin.com/courses/NineDimensionsofScaffoldingforMLs

TEACHING PRACTICES

Creating environments that support diverse linguistic and cultural backgrounds while promoting academic growth of multilingual learners involves scaffolding classroom and greater school settings to adapt learning spaces that not only makes content accessible and engaging but also provides opportunities for language and literacy growth. Incorporating culturally responsive materials, leveraging visual supports that aid in learning, and balancing rigor with support can encourage students to reach their highest potential. To this end, we offer three broad-based environmental scaffolds which are (1) maintaining high expectations for all students, (2) providing print-rich and literacy-rich environments, and (3) creating safe, comfortable, and productive learning spaces.

ENVIRONMENTAL SCAFFOLDING PRACTICE #1: HIGH EXPECTATIONS FOR ALL STUDENTS

A growing body of research suggests that teacher expectations significantly influence student achievement, highlighting the profound effect of teachers' beliefs on student outcomes (Harlin, Sirota, & Bailey, 2009; Rubie-Davies, 2017). Yet, having high expectations requires more than a set of beliefs about how all children can learn; it requires actionable steps to have them firmly established to make a meaningful impact on students.

Teachers trained in high-expectation practices know how to build positive relationships with their students. They also establish clear expectations, encourage peer-to-peer collaboration, enable students to cultivate their autonomy, and ensure all students engage in complex, challenging tasks that promote their growth in language, literacy, and academics. Conversely, teachers with low expectations often use practices such as maintaining ability groupings, asking closed-ended questions during discussions, focusing on test preparation, or using a one-size-fits-all approach to teaching that limit student development.

Focusing primarily on the achievement gap between multilingual learners and their English-proficient peers can skew teachers' perceptions and limit their ability to maintain high expectations for all their students. For this reason, the focus should shift from what's wrong with students to what's wrong with the way they are being taught. Sometimes, just being classified as a student learning English can lead some educators to have lower expectations of their abilities. By shifting the focus from the achievement gap to the strengths and potentials of multilingual learners, more equitable and supportive learning environments can be created that foster high expectations and create optimal learning conditions.

Embracing high expectations for all students requires that you celebrate the growth and progress of multilingual learners even when they have yet to meet grade-level standards. The recognition of such successes is critical for students to maintain their motivation to learn and believe in their abilities. By celebrating the success of all students, you help to create an environment where effort and improvement are valued as much as final outcomes. By focusing on short-term progress, multilingual learners are better able to develop and maintain their resilience.

ADVANTAGES OF THIS PRACTICE

When teachers establish and maintain high expectations for multilingual learners, they can greatly and meaningfully enhance the learning experiences and academic outcomes for students. High expectation practices incorporate a gamut of strategies including the following:

- Connecting with each student on a personal level
- Explicit learning intentions and success criteria
- Flexible grouping
- Peer collaboration in mixed-ability groupings
- Discussions with open-ended questions
- Celebration of student effort
- Student autonomy
- Rigorous instruction for all students
- Multiple opportunities for feedback

When these strategies are integrated into what teachers routinely do, they create a classroom environment in which learning language and content is consistently supported. Students benefit from advanced comprehension, increased engagement, amplified confidence, and overall better academic performance.

EXAMPLE #1: DIALOGUE JOURNALS: GETTING TO KNOW YOUR STUDENTS

The use of dialogue journals with multilingual learners is a powerful strategy that supports teachers to create personal connections with their students. These journals are written conversations between students and teachers using a standard notebook that is passed back and forth between them at specified intervals. Variations of the strategy can be implemented using online resources such as email exchanges, Google slides, speech-to-text apps, audio journals, and so on. Dialogue journals support students to express themselves in English without the stress and concern of having their work corrected for grammar, spelling, or mechanics. The emphasis on this type of journal writing is for both teacher and student to share their personal experiences with one another to build a stronger relationship while giving students a meaningful context to hone their English language skills.

To initiate the use of dialogue journals, consider the following steps:

- Introduce the idea to students and carefully explain its purpose—a safe space for students to communicate anything they wish.
- Emphasize the purpose of the journal—to openly communicate with one another; writing will not be corrected or graded.
- Distribute notebooks or display the online platform that will be used for journal entries; present and examine together possible models of journal writing.
- Set clear expectations such as the length of journal entries and what they may contain including drawings, photos, emojis, and so on.
- Create a schedule for students to complete and submit their journal entries—stagger the due dates for journals throughout the week to allow yourself time to respond and return each of them within a few days.

Responses to students should be thoughtful and personal as well as relate directly to the contents of students' entries. Keep in mind to avoid correcting student work. Instead, consider modeling good writing by reiterating what the student has written in each response, thereby demonstrating appropriate language use. To get things started, it may be helpful to suggest a writing prompt to guide students' initial responses. Remember to provide feedback and ask questions to continue the conversation and keep students motivated.

There are many benefits to using dialogue journals with multilingual learners. They not only provide a way for teachers to get to know their students, but they also offer a means for low stakes writing that can reduce students' reluctance to engage in written work and further support their fluency and facility in English. Finally, dialogue journals can create a bridge between students and create a caring, nurturing learning environment. (Look back to Chapter 3 for an example of a dialogue journal presented in a different context.)

EXAMPLE #2: MIXED ABILITY GROUPINGS

Although it may appear logical to group multilingual learners together to offer additional support, foster home language use, and incorporate further scaffolding to help them complete assigned tasks, mixed-ability groupings can offer all these opportunities as well as promote high expectations, rigorous instruction, and an inclusive environment where all students feel they belong. Grouping students with varying levels of English proficiency and academic abilities encourages peer-to-peer collaboration, social interactions, and authentic language use. By grouping students strategically and assigning roles or responsibilities students rely on each other's strengths to develop a deeper understanding of content and language learning. Inspired by Kagan and Kagan (2015), some examples of activities with mixed-ability groupings are as follows:

- Jigsaw activities: A learning task is divided into several parts with each student in the group individually becoming an "expert" in one of the parts. In turn, students teach others in their group what they learned.
- Think-Pair-Share-Square: After individually thinking about a question or problem, students first discuss their thoughts with a partner, then share their ideas with another pair to form a group of four (square).
- Reciprocal teaching: students take turns within a group to lead discussions using four key ideas—summarizing, questioning, clarifying, and predicting—thereby guiding the group to engage in discussions.
- Three-step interview: pairs of students take turns to interview each other using a specific set of questions. After the interviews, they join another pair of students to share what they have learned.
- Station rotations: Several learning stations are created related to the same topic with mixed-ability groups rotating through each of them. These stations can include interactive learning games, technology and research, problem solving, manipulatives, and reflecting on one's learning.

It is critical to prepare for any type of group work with students. First, you need to know your students—their language proficiency, home languages, literacy levels, content knowledge, interests, talents, and overall dispositions. Next, form heterogeneous groups that balance students' language abilities, academic strengths, and social skills. Model expectations of effective group work and offer examples of respectful peer-to-peer communication. The use of wall charts or printed table tent cards with questions and sentence stems for responses can further support the use of appropriate language.

Create group activities that initially focus on developing students' social interactions using brief open-ended tasks that help them to practice working in teams and meeting set expectations. Assign roles for each student within the group—leader, timekeeper, recorder, and so on, to ensure all students remain engaged. Monitor group progress by circulating the room and offering support and immediate feedback. Encourage students to reflect on the value of working in mixed-ability groupings and to discuss what they have learned from one another during a whole class debrief following group work.

Various types of group work can positively change the learning environment, and in particular, mixed-ability grouping can clearly transform how multilingual learners experience classroom instruction. Group work fosters collaboration, and mixed-ability grouping promotes the use of English as a common language for engagement. It allows students to learn from one another and exposes all learners to different cultural perspectives. Mixed-ability grouping fosters a sense of belonging and creates a classroom environment that is an inclusive community and a dynamic space for interactive learning. Emily Smyth, ELE (English Learner Education) instructor and Nick Villani, biology instructor at Greater Lowell Technical High School, where they co-create a highly interactive and supportive learning environment by scaffolding the steps of engaging in partner talks as outlined below, and modeling the task as co-teachers, and utilizing a digital anchor chart guide the academic conversation (see Figure 10.5).

FIGURE 10.5 ● Scaffolded Partner Talk Exchange

Example Partner Talk

How to Make a Protein Partner A	**How to Make a Protein Partner B**
A ____________ is sent to a ________________ that a ____________ is needed in the body. This is the **start** of **transcription**. ________________ occurs ____________ the ______________. **DNA** lives in the **nucleus** of a **cell**. **DNA** is the **blueprint** for living things.	A **signal** is sent to a **cell** that a **protein** is needed in the body. This is the ____________ of ________________. **Transcription** occurs **inside** the **nucleus**. ________ lives in the ________ of a ____________. ____________ is the ____________ for living things.

Partner Talk Steps:

1. Students are paired up.
2. Student A and Student B receive the same text but with different content words missing.
3. Students take turns reading their complete sentences to help their partner fill in their blanks. (It ends up alternating between students.)
4. One major rule is that students CANNOT look at their partner's paper. The word must be verbally communicated to their partner, by saying the word and/or spelling it.
5. Then, students record themselves choral reading the passage. Alternatively, they could read it in front of the class if you are using different texts among pairs.

Source: Emily Smyth and Nick Villani. Used with permission.

EXAMPLE #3: EXPLICIT LEARNING INTENTIONS AND SUCCESS CRITERIA

Over the course of our careers as teachers, in-service and preservice teacher educators, coaches, and researchers, we have had the privilege of visiting the classrooms of many different educators—from student teachers to veteran educators. We have frequently noticed that some teachers, at the onset of lessons, eliminate reviewing learning intentions, goals, or objectives beyond just posting, stating, or reading them, overlook checking for students' understanding about what they are supposed to learn, and do not identify and review how students are going to learn what has been planned. Explicit step-by-step instructions coupled with clear learning intentions and detailed success criteria are important ways to scaffold learning for multilingual learners to ensure they can access complex learning, competently perform tasks, and complete classwork as expected.

To support students in understanding what they are going to learn and how they are going to learn it, there needs to be a clear identification of what the expectations are for learning and a breakdown of tasks into manageable steps using language that students can understand. Clarity and comprehensibility are key factors in supporting multilingual learners' overall success by making the learning process more accessible. For this reason, written directions, visual aids, modeling, and demonstrations in addition to verbal instructions further enhance comprehension and ensure task completion. In addition, success criteria provide specific, measurable outcomes to reduce ambiguity, set clear expectations, minimize confusion, and improve students' ability to achieve. These practices are critical in creating an inclusive learning environment where multilingual learners can grow their language, literacy, and academics alongside their peers.

Consider the following aspects of providing overall clarity and comprehensibility:

- **Focused learning intentions**: Use student-centered goals that focus on students' active role in the learning process to promote student buy-in, engagement, and autonomy. Consider developing "I can . . ." statements to set a clear understanding of specific student goals for the lesson and to foster student responsibility for their own learning. Examples of learning intentions using the novel *Maniac Magee* as follows:
    - I can explain how the story shows the difference between truth and legends in Maniac Magee.
    - I can write a clear and organized paragraph about what Maniac Magee teaches about truth and legends.
    - I can support my ideas with examples from the text.

- **Clear success criteria:** Create a step-by-step road map of what successful learning looks like for students. Break down learning intentions into clear, actionable steps so that students confidently work toward meeting the goals that have been set. Consider co-constructing success criteria with your students so that they gain a deeper understanding and take ownership of their work by doing the following:
    - Engage students in whole class, pairs, and team discussions about what successful completion of the learning intentions or goals will resemble. Ask questions such as, "How will we know when we have accurately and effectively completed our tasks?"
    - Brainstorm and list specific criteria that will identify their work as successfully meeting the set goals. Guide students to think about certain aspects of their work using targeted questions such as, "How might we use evidence as criteria for our work?"
    - Adapt the list of agreed upon success criteria into "I will . . ." statements such as, "I will use evidence from the text to support my responses."
    - Review and reflect on the complete set of success criteria.

Figure 10.6 is an example of a set of success criteria inspired by a similar anchor chart in Claudia Leon, middle school ENL teacher's anchor chart.

FIGURE 10.6 • Success Criteria Anchor Chart

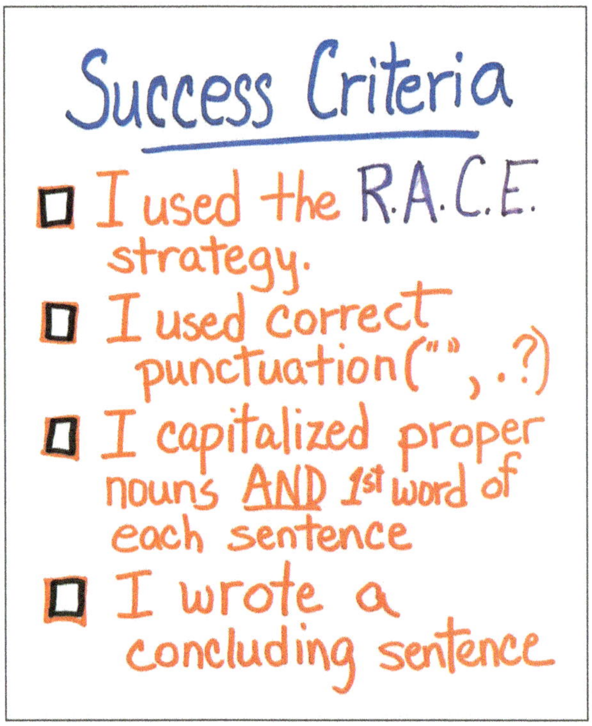

Source: Claudia Leon. Used with permission.

- **Language development support:** Support students to recognize quality work as well as help them develop the use of appropriate vocabulary and grammar by analyzing writing exemplars and student samples. Discuss various models of written responses to strengthen students' understanding and encourage them to meet expectations. Promote students' use of modeled pieces of writing to develop their own responses. Consider engaging students in a shared writing activity using a strategy such as R.A.C.E. which typically stands for: **R**estate the prompt, **A**nswer the question, **C**ite the evidence, and **E**xplain your thinking. Figure 10.7 is an example of providing language development support using the RACE strategy from Claudia Leon's classroom.

FIGURE 10.7 • R.A.C.E. Strategy

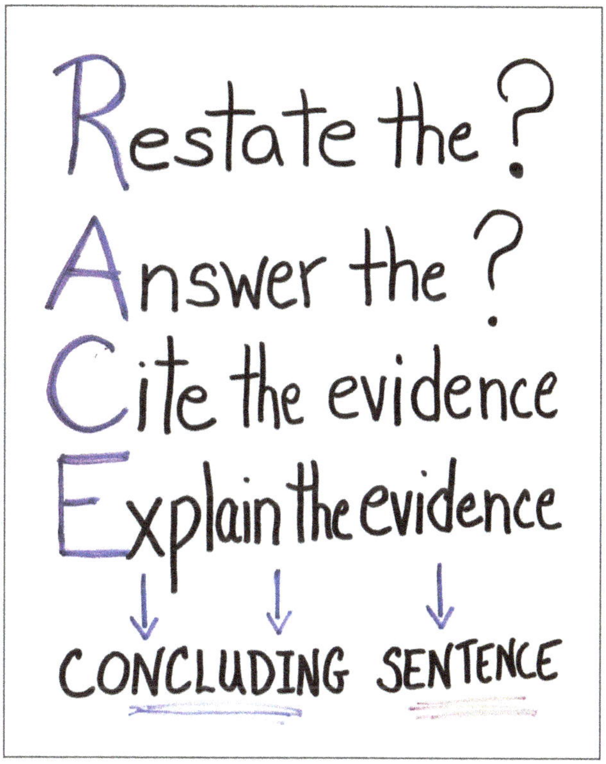

Source: Claudia Leon. Used with permission.

Providing multilingual learners with learning intentions and success criteria fosters high expectations, an inclusive learning environment, and empowers students to achieve their full potential. Better yet, whenever possible, co-create them with your students to enhance their metacognitive and metalinguistic awareness as well as their agency and autonomy as learners. Incorporating these practices creates a structured learning environment where students can build their confidence and remain focused and motivated.

OVERCOMING CHALLENGES TO MAINTAIN HIGH EXPECTATIONS FOR ALL STUDENTS

Setting expectations for student learning can be a bit tricky. Not all students will meet grade-level objectives at the same time or in the same way. Multilingual learners, for example, have a wide range of abilities, with some being ready to meet content-area learning benchmarks while others need greater support and additional time to develop the language and literacy skills needed to comprehend material, apply what they have learned, and demonstrate their understanding. For this reason, expectations of students' abilities and the belief that all students can learn may readily shift, even unconsciously, to lower expectations for certain students. Other factors that may limit maintaining high expectations include limited time and resources, class management difficulties, and external pressures relating to accountability, further hindering the support students need to reach their full potential.

KEEP THIS IN MIND

Expectations should be high, but also clear and achievable. Providing well-defined learning intentions and success criteria help students understand what is expected of them and how they can succeed. Setting high expectations challenges students to reach their full potential, but it is equally important to ensure that these expectations are clearly communicated and attainable.

ENVIRONMENTAL SCAFFOLDING PRACTICE #2 PRINT-RICH AND LITERACY-RICH ENVIRONMENTS

One thing we surmise most teachers enjoy is visiting other teachers' classrooms because we most certainly do! We have found that so much can be learned from observing how others organize materials, display information, arrange furniture, promote inclusivity, and create a welcoming space for student learning. A key aspect for designing learning environments for multilingual learners is to provide print-rich and literacy-rich surroundings within the classroom that promote language acquisition and the ability to engage in the productive use of English.

Language-rich classrooms are designed to clearly support students' academic, language, and literacy development. Printed displays guide students to complete tasks, reinforce key information, help with vocabulary, spelling, and the use of appropriate sentence structures, as well as scaffold overall learning. Displayed materials are not just colorful decorations, but are meaningfully used in lessons, frequently referenced during instruction, and updated regularly to support students' needs. Every piece of print serves as a potential learning tool.

Print-rich environments for learning connect with students' lived experiences and reflect their varied backgrounds and cultural and linguistic diversity. Multilingual displays, photographs reflecting diverse people and communities, and a variety of literature that mirrors students' cultures create classroom environments that are inviting for multilingual learners and validate their identities. These resources foster a sense of belonging and promote cross-cultural understanding, making the classroom a more inclusive space for everyone.

Text-rich learning spaces provide opportunities for multilingual learners to take charge of their own learning. It empowers students to work independently to problem-solve, craft their own responses, learn new vocabulary, and review key concepts. By offering a variety of accessible resources, students are better able to refer to tools that support their understanding, allowing them to navigate challenges on their own. Such learning environments not only foster independence but also guide students to take risks and deepen their comprehension through their own efforts.

ADVANTAGES OF THIS PRACTICE

The presence of print-rich learning spaces offers multilingual learners consistent exposure to language in various contexts—labels, charts, displays, and so on—providing a constant source of vocabulary, language chunks, visual representations of complex texts, even some essential grammar structures to support language learning continuously. Additionally, text-rich environments create opportunities for multilingual learners to see how language is applied in real-world contexts, especially when material is curriculum related, deepening student understanding of how words are strung together and used to relay more complex concepts.

Print-rich classrooms offer several advantages for teachers as well. These resources are easily accomplished and can be done with minimal cost and materials. Most should be co-developed with students, while some might be readily stored and reused, whether kept as hard copies or in digital formats that can be reproduced when needed. Print-rich environments also provide for classroom management giving students accessible information that readily scaffolds learning, fosters independence, and promotes confidence.

EXAMPLE #1: INTERACTIVE WORD WALLS

The traditional use of Word Walls is often seen in early elementary classrooms for teaching sight words by building a printed, alphabetically organized wall of words that are visible and accessible to all students. High-frequency words—those that beginning readers and writers need to know and that often lack predictable spelling patterns—make up about half of the words placed on Word Walls, creating a resource that is beneficial for all children developing early literacy skills. Each week, four or five words are selected to continually build the wall. Daily activities—where students read, write, chant, clap, find, or play interactive games using the Word Wall—provide students with consistent exposure to the spelling, meaning, and use of each word. Figure 10.8 is an example of a commonly featured word wall for an elementary class displayed on a bulletin board.

FIGURE 10.8 ● Elementary Class Word Wall

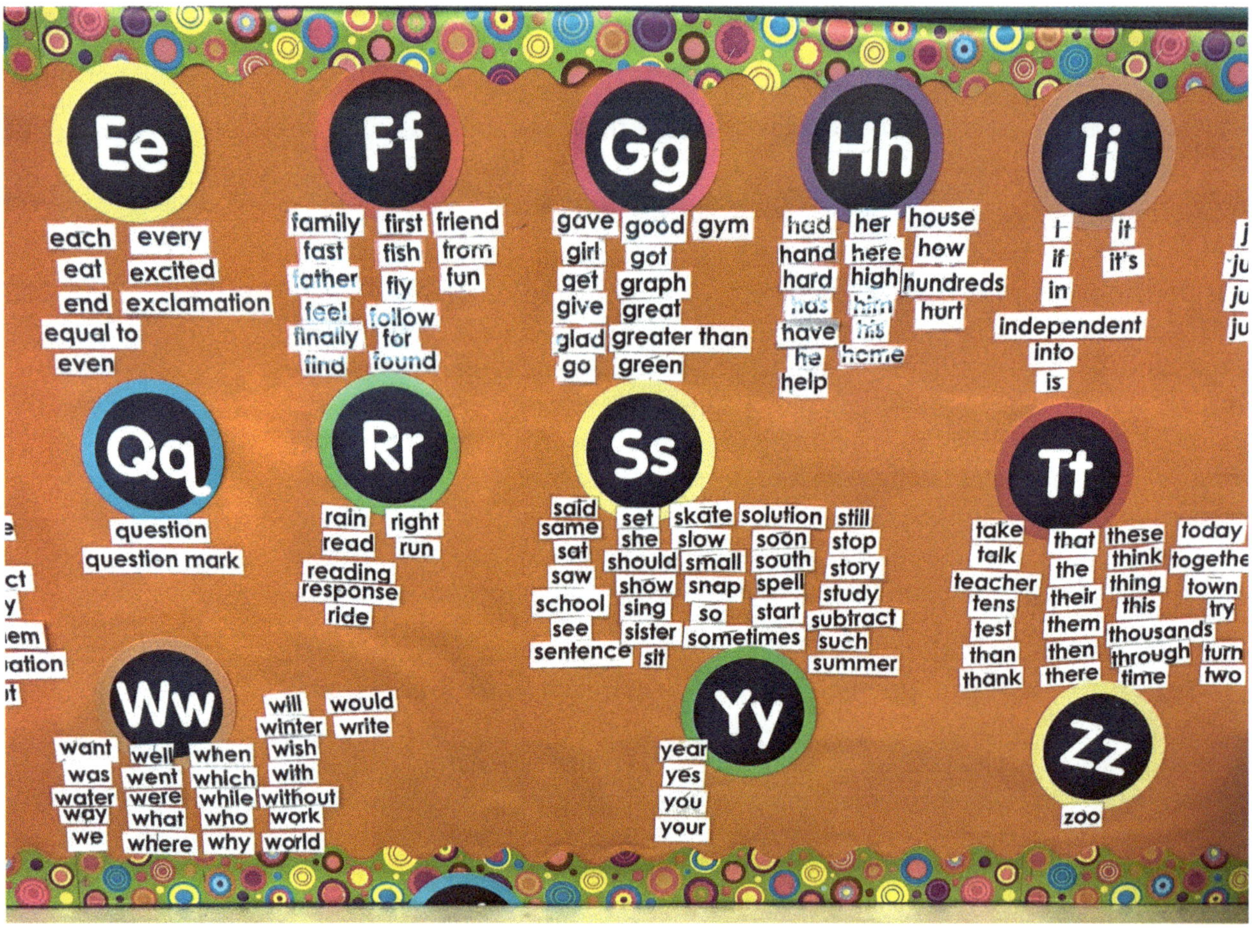

In upper elementary and secondary classrooms, Word Walls can serve as an effective tool for reinforcing vocabulary, particularly subject-specific language and frequently used words in writing. Due to the demands of content-area learning, older students benefit from seeing key vocabulary organized by themes, units of study, or topics relevant to different subjects such as science, social studies, math, or literature. These walls often highlight important concepts and offer a visual reference during writing assignments or discussions. Word Walls should be frequently integrated into lessons by having students interact with the words through games, discussions, self-assessment and other quizzes, or writing prompts. We also encourage involving your students in creating, enhancing, and revising the Word Wall so they develop ownership both of complex academic language and the physical space designated to vocabulary development. Figure 10.9 illustrates how a teacher and students co-created a Word Wall using index cards.

FIGURE 10.9 ● Co-Created Word Wall of Verbs Students Selected From Their Reading

WHAT TEACHERS SAY ABOUT ENVIRONMENTAL SCAFFOLDING

In my current stand-alone classroom where I teach newcomers, I don't really have a Word Wall due to lack of space. However, students do have portable or individual Word Walls or vocabulary lists pertaining to the content they are learning. Also, depending on their level of language proficiency, they have personal dictionaries, and we keep adding words to it as we're building vocabulary so that they can access it during their writing.

—Maria Neckonoff, ENL teacher, Valley Stream, New York

A digital Word Wall can also be substituted for a traditional one, as it frequently happens in Holly Ellis, middle school ESL teacher's classroom in Fort Bend ISD in Texas (see Table 10.2 for a multilingual digital Word Wall in English, French, Arabic, and Vietnamese also containing select illustrations).

TABLE 10.2 • An Illustrated Multilingual Digital Word Wall

Photography	Fotografía	التصوير	Nhiếp ảnh
Learn	Aprender	يتعلم	Học
Camera	cámara	كاميرا	Máy ảnh
Carry	llevar	احمل	mang, thừa nhận
Backpack	mochila	حقيبة ظهر	balo
Photograph	fotografía	تصوير	ảnh chụp
Film	película	فيلم	phim ảnh
Study	estudiar	دراسة	nghiên cứu

Source: Holly Ellis. Used with permission.

Sources: istock.com/kool99, istock.com/yaom, istock.com/finwal, istock.com/Clovera, and istock.com/m-imagephotography

EXAMPLE #2: CO-CONSTRUCTED GRAPHIC ORGANIZERS

Graphic organizers play a critical role in creating print-rich learning spaces for multilingual learners by providing structured, visual representations of information that make academic content and language development more accessible. These tools help students better understand complex concepts by reducing the amount of text that is used to present critical information, thereby promoting better comprehension. Graphic organizers enhance visual processing skills while they also reinforce key vocabulary and phrases, encourage students to brainstorm and connect ideas, facilitate deeper understanding, and aid in language acquisition. They also engage students by encouraging authentic language use and fostering a sense of ownership of student learning when they are collaboratively constructed. Table 10.3 identifies some examples of graphic organizers and how they are used in print-rich classrooms to support multilingual learners.

TABLE 10.3 • Graphic Organizers Used in Print-Rich Classrooms

GRAPHIC ORGANIZER	DESCRIPTION	HOW IT SUPPORTS MULTILINGUAL LEARNERS
Venn Diagram	Contains overlapping circles to compare and contrast two or more things	Supports the analysis and evaluation of the similarities and differences between ideas, concepts, or texts
Concept Map	Organizes information using a central subject and connecting related ideas to that subject	Promotes idea sharing and reinforces comprehension through connected information using various map forms—linear, hierarchical, cyclical, or sequential.
Flowchart	Represents a sequence of steps in a process or a series of events	Visually breaks down complex tasks or events into manageable steps, making the information logical and clear.
KWL Chart	Arranges information to identify what students KNOW, WANT to know, and have LEARNED.	Guides inquiry-based learning and supports language development by framing questions and answers in a structured way.
Frayer Model	Defines a word or concept through its meaning, characteristics, examples, and non-examples	Fosters a deeper understanding of words and concepts through definition, description, and differentiation.

online resources Available for download at https://companion.corwin.com/courses/NineDimensionsofScaffoldingforMLs

Overall, graphic organizers contribute to inclusive and supportive learning spaces, making language and content more accessible for multilingual learners. (Look back at Chapter 6 for further discussion and examples of graphic organizers.)

EXAMPLE #3: CLASSROOM LIBRARIES AND REFERENCE MATERIALS

Class libraries and reference materials can be game changers for your multilingual learners, especially in middle and high school. These resources give students access to a variety of texts that not only build their exposure to information and rich, engaging literature but also connect to their interests and build their facility with language.

The class library can be a place where students explore topics that matter to them, whether it's fiction, biographies, or subject-specific materials that tie into what is being taught. It should also include culturally relevant, multilingual books and materials that reflect the backgrounds of students, helping them to feel represented and as valued members of the class.

As an alarming trend, printed books and materials have gone by the wayside and have been replaced with digital resources. Unlike online content that often needs students to search for a particular topic to find information, printed material can be skimmed and scanned for new and interesting topics to explore. Hard copies of various types of text can open doors to places where students have yet to know about or even imagine.

For multilingual learners, having easy access to printed materials like bilingual dictionaries or visual encyclopedias are critical, especially when their families are in earlier stages of their acculturation to the United States and do not have an extensive family library of books. Class libraries and other print-based tools help students establish or expand their literary lives, build vocabulary, reinforce key concepts, and gain confidence in navigating both language and content. Ultimately, investing in a thoughtful collection of books and resources can engage and empower all students. Figure 10.10 illustrates a class library combined with a welcoming reading nook.

OVERCOMING CHALLENGES USING THIS PRACTICE

Some teachers don't have the luxury of having their own classrooms. The lack of space, particularly in middle and high schools, has resulted in several teachers sharing the same room. For this reason, creating a print-rich learning environment requires intentional collaboration and planning among teachers to carve out specific areas to display essential

FIGURE 10.10 ● Combination Class Library and Reading Nook

print materials—think anchor charts, word walls, or student work—that cater to your diverse learners needs. Thoughtful consideration and respectful use of available wall space as well as rotating displays based on subjects or units can maximize limited space and ensure relevant content is visible. When sharing space for print material is not feasible, consider using portable, flexible tools like tri-fold boards, hanging charts, pocket charts, or digital displays that can provide students with the support they need without permanently occupying wall space. Use bins, folders, or table space for word banks, sentence starters, and reference guides, so students can easily grab what they need for independent work.

KEEP THIS IN MIND

We have only touched the surface of the ways print resources can be made available to students to scaffold learning in text-rich environments. Labeling class items, displaying sentence frames and starters, using multiple languages in class displays, and exhibiting student work, among others, collectively create supportive, linguistically rich learning spaces that promote language development and literacy for all students. We encourage you to invite your students to help prioritize what should occupy the available wall space.

ENVIRONMENTAL SCAFFOLDING PRACTICE #3: CREATING SAFE, COMFORTABLE, AND PRODUCTIVE LEARNING SPACES

Tailoring physical learning spaces and providing support for students' emotional well-being is an essential part of scaffolding the environment for multilingual learners. A classroom that is designed to meet diverse learning demands and preferences not only fosters students to feel productive and make academic progress but also promotes their stability and sense of belonging, enabling them to engage more fully in learning (see Chapter 9 for more on social-emotional scaffolding).

Through considerable conversations and targeted discussions with students as well as thoughtful actions, the class environment can be transformed for multilingual learners into a place where they no longer feel like visitors but learn and thrive. Before initiating any changes to the class environment, first consider the areas of the classroom that might align to student preferences for safety, comfort, and productivity. Next, bring those ideas to life by setting up learning spaces where every student feels seen and supported. Consider how students might transition from one learning space to another, or when students might actively choose their seating each day, based on how they feel most comfortable. By moving from ideas into tangible actions, and through a bit of trial and error, learning spaces can be readily transformed, serve as environmental scaffolds, and lead to impactful outcomes.

To bolster any anticipated changes to the learning environment, classroom management strategies need to be in place. Establishing clear norms and expectations allows students to know the parameters for using various places set for learning. Using a collaborative approach to setting expectations encourages students to express their preferences and needs, which, in turn, will foster a sense of community where everyone feels heard and respected. When students have a say in shaping their classroom experiences, it helps build trust and emotional safety. Figure 10.11 illustrates a classroom space for learning that requires set parameters for its use.

Comfort is physical while safety is emotional. Physically, the arrangement of furniture, access to resources, and the overall aesthetic of the classroom can significantly impact how comfortable students feel. On the emotional side, creating a supportive environment where students can share their experiences and challenges is vital. Emotional safety includes encouraging open dialogue, celebrating multilingualism and cultural diversity, and providing support mechanisms for feedback, guidance, and encouragement. Ultimately, when both physical comfort and emotional safety are prioritized, students are more likely to engage deeply with their learning and develop a sense of belonging.

FIGURE 10.11 • Personal Learning Nooks for Quiet Reading

ADVANTAGES OF THIS PRACTICE

Imagine walking into a classroom where students feel safe, comfortable, and ready to learn. The room is warm and inviting, with flexible seating options—bean bags in one corner, desks in small groups, and a couple of soft armchairs situated near a bookcase filled with colorful resources and materials in different languages. Teacher-made charts with key vocabulary, photographic representations of content, and student work are displayed, making the space feel stimulating and inclusive. In this type of classroom, most students are eager to participate, encouraged to take risks, and they possibly attempt to use new words or ask questions because they know it's okay to make mistakes. Because materials are organized and easy to access, students feel supported without being overwhelmed. These kinds of learning environments are a tremendous advantage for multilingual learners. They give students the space and support to thrive, no matter their language level.

EXAMPLE #1: SPACES FOR EMOTIONAL SAFETY

An interesting turn of events in recent years has led teachers to focus more on emotionally safe learning spaces for fostering student success, especially for multilingual learners. The growing number of classrooms becoming more culturally and linguistically diverse has prompted educators to adopt more inclusive practices and create learning spaces where all students feel valued and understood. This shift in practice acknowledges that emotional factors play a crucial role in learning, especially for those navigating multiple languages and cultures.

There are several key strategies for scaffolding a safe and secure environment for multilingual learners:

- **Multilingual signage.** Using multilingual signage in the classroom and throughout the school can make learning and community spaces more accessible and inviting to students and their families. The display of multiple languages demonstrates that all language knowledge is not only valued but welcome, and students need not leave a vital piece of their identity home when they attend school. In primary schools, consider labeling everyday objects, learning areas, and public spaces in school (e.g., bathrooms, cafeterias, nurse's office) in students' home languages alongside English. In secondary schools, displaying posters with quotes or inspirational messages in multiple languages can foster students' sense of belonging. See Figure 10.12 for an example of a district-wide effort to show support for multilingual learners in North St. Paul, Minnesota, in five languages (English, Spanish, Hmong, Arabic, and Somali).

FIGURE 10.12 • Multilingual Sign Spotted Across School District 622 in Minnesota

- **Culturally diverse images.** Displaying images of people from different cultural backgrounds can create a welcoming atmosphere for students

and their families when they see themselves represented and reflected in the learning community. Affirming cultural identities in this way can open doors for all stakeholders within school communities to accept differences, to develop positive relationships, and to build trust. This type of endeavor for inclusivity also sends a strong message that diversity is valued and celebrated within the school. In both elementary and secondary schools, displaying images of people from various backgrounds might include historical figures and modern-day leaders from various fields. Consider how these displays might promote a variety of perspectives that represent the diversity in the school.

- **Co-construction of behavioral norms and instructional routines.** Create a set of co-constructed class rules with students, setting clear norms and expectations for behavior. By enacting a mutually agreed upon set of rules, students are more likely to feel a sense of ownership of the rules that are set as well as a personal responsibility to follow them. In primary grades, establishing rules with students might involve a brainstorming session in which rules are suggested and agreed upon such as being kind to one another and keeping quiet when the teacher is speaking. In secondary classrooms, students might collaboratively create a code of conduct that emphasizes respecting each other, maintaining academic integrity, and participating in class constructively.

WHAT TEACHERS SAY ABOUT ENVIRONMENTAL SCAFFOLDING

Source: Melissa Dishart and Kristen Budich. Used with permission.

Reggie was born out of our extreme frustration with cellphones in the classroom. Kristen would use her hand to lovingly bark at students and/or grab phones in a way to depersonalize any punitive action. For the holidays last year, I bought Kristen a puppet to make her hand motions even funnier and friendlier for the kids. It turned into a joyful practice that we use to laugh together and allow students to laugh at us. Before long, the students are in on the joke. Reggie *was named after the dreaded ELA Regents exam, but we bring him out in the classroom anytime we need to infuse a little more fun.*

—Melissa Dishart and Kristen Budich, Ossining High School co-teachers

- **Teacher collaboration.** When teachers and paraprofessionals share a classroom, maintaining a safe and comfortable environment for multilingual learners requires consistent communication among the adults in the room, clear role definition and coordination of efforts, and shared cultural awareness and sensitivity including understanding the linguistic and cultural backgrounds of the multilingual learners in their class. Whether you co-teach or merely share the classroom with colleagues during the school day (especially in a high school context), some important conversations must take place. Co-teachers must collaborate to ensure they are aligned on student expectations, instructional strategies, and classroom norms. Regular check-ins and planning time help establish mutual respect, reliance, and foster a cohesive dynamic among teachers, creating an atmosphere where all students feel safe and supported and both teachers have full "ownership" of the classroom.

WHAT TEACHERS SAY ABOUT ENVIRONMENTAL SCAFFOLDING

In my school, there is a strong push for culturally responsive teaching. There's a big welcome sign on my classroom door with clip art of children from all different cultures. Classroom libraries are more reflective of different cultures as well. We have a large Muslim population, and there are chapter books in my 5th grade classes that feature a book series by Rick Riordan (author of the Percy Jackson series), whose main character, Aru Shah, is a Muslim girl. So, there's a big push for diverse classroom libraries, so book wise, different cultures are represented in what students read. We even have a halal menu for our cafeteria offerings. The district is also translating a lot more documents, and they have a multilingual language line for parent-teacher conferences or any communication we use with parents that translates information, making the school community more accessible.

—Maria Neckonoff, ENL teacher, Valley Stream, New York

EXAMPLE #2: SPACES FOR PHYSICAL COMFORT

Student comfort, a critical element of the learning environment, can significantly impact academic outcomes. It can be influenced by thoughtfully shaping various aspects of classroom and school design. When students feel physically comfortable, they are less distracted, allowing them to better concentrate on instruction. There are several factors that contribute to students' physical comfort (Eggebrecht-Weinschreider, 2020) which include:

- The quality of light in the room
- The levels of sound and the perception of noise

- The amount of warmness or coolness
- The seating arrangements to support learning
- The perception of personal space
- Student ownership of the learning environment
- Visual diversity

These elements work together to create a comfortable and inviting atmosphere where students can thrive.

Designing classrooms for student comfort has a particularly positive impact on multilingual learners. A well-designed environment reduces student stress to better support more complex cognitive tasks. For multilingual learners, these tasks include processing new vocabulary, decoding unfamiliar text structures, and understanding academic content simultaneously. When multilingual learners feel more physically secure, they often yield better outcomes.

To start, consider how to redesign classrooms to meet students' needs by offering flexible seating. Provide a range of seating options like bean bags, floor cushions, carpets, or group tables, to give students the choice of what works best for them. Some students may prefer working alone quietly while others will truly make great strides in collaborative workspaces. Figure 10.13 illustrates how productive students can be when they can choose less formal areas for seating.

FIGURE 10.13 • Carpeting Offers Some Students a More Comfortable Workspace

Along with the seating, take into account the lighting, the levels of sound, and the temperature in the classroom. Adjust the lighting, vary the sound, and regulate the levels of warmth and coolness to the best of your ability according to students' preferences. Some pupils may prefer bright light while others get more comfort from the softer lighting provided by floor lamps and such. As for sound, some students thrive in the bustling clamor of a classroom filled with activity—people talking, moving around, working together, or playing music while others benefit from noise-cancelling headphones to minimize perceived noise distractions. Finally, consider how warm or cool the class might be. Overly heated classrooms can put students to sleep while not enough warmth can send students running for their jackets and coats, a distraction that does not lend itself to students being productive.

All in all, reflect on every designated learning space in the classroom to determine if each can provide comfort and support for student learning. Consider how a corner of the room can be set up for individuals to read quietly or how an area selected as a quiet zone might be established. These spaces contrast with others that might be designed to focus on group and/or exploratory learning.

EXAMPLE #3: PRODUCTIVE LEARNING SPACES: MEETING STUDENTS' LEARNING PREFERENCES

There are countless ways to meet students' individual learning preferences, and some of those ways include altering the class environment. Earlier in this chapter, we discussed print-rich classrooms, and how incorporating visual supports, such as anchor charts, graphic organizers, and word walls, help to meet students' individual needs.

In addition to visual supports, providing accessible technology is another way to support students' learning. Ensuring student access to tools like translation apps, language learning software, or tablets helps bridge gaps in understanding and fosters independence. A tech station equipped with headphones and charging stations, for instance, can create an efficient and supportive learning environment.

Lastly, give students ownership of the classroom space by involving them in setting it up to promote engagement and belonging. Allow them to help arrange desks, make decisions about how and where to display their work, or organize materials so they are readily accessible. This involvement can help to ensure that the classroom environment reflects their needs and preferences. Additionally, paying attention to students' perceptions of personal space is crucial. Some students may need more room to feel comfortable and secure, while others might thrive in closer, more collaborative class configurations. Thoughtful attention to personal comfort and ownership contributes to a positive, inclusive learning atmosphere where students are more likely to engage and be content.

OVERCOMING CHALLENGES USING THIS PRACTICE

Designing learning spaces where students feel safe, comfortable, and therefore productive is no easy task. It requires thoughtful planning, consideration of the physical space available, and knowing how to create an atmosphere that fosters security and belonging. Unfortunately, there are sometimes challenges and limitations that are beyond any one teacher's control. First and foremost are budget constraints that may not allow for the purchase of needed materials, technology, furniture, carpeting, lighting, and so on, to create a classroom for optimum student learning. Next are the limitations set by the physical space, including the size and layout, of the room, which may make it difficult to achieve separate zones for quiet areas and group work and thereby miss the mark meeting students' learning preferences. Physical space limitations might also bring about issues with material organization and storage, making resources less accessible or nonexistent. Noise levels may also be difficult to control depending upon the location of the classroom and the use of school spaces that surround it. Although teachers have the power to adapt and innovate with the resources they have at hand, ensuring that their classrooms remain spaces where students can feel safe, valued, and ready to learn is a test of their resilience, creativity, and commitment to meeting the diverse needs of every learner.

KEEP THIS IN MIND

Teachers can always take creative steps to maximize the potential of their learning spaces. By making small adjustments, such as rearranging furniture, incorporating visual displays, or establishing routines that promote focus, teachers can support both the comfort and productivity of their students.

WHAT TEACHERS SAY ABOUT ENVIRONMENTAL SCAFFOLDING

My ideal class environment for multilingual learners would have multiple tables where students can work in groups to collaborate with each other, and there would be a space for kids to explore using hands-on activities. And there'd be lots of books! I would create a print-rich environment with a variety of learning spaces to support language development. For example, I would have a large word wall that we add to regularly, as well as a second word wall focused on shades of meaning to help students expand their vocabulary and use more precise words. I believe vocabulary is one of the most important aspects of language learning because it gives students access to reading, writing, and content knowledge. I would also include opportunities for students to explore word parts, such as prefixes and sufixes, to deepen their understanding of language.

—Maria Neckonoff, ENL teacher, Valley Stream, New York

INDEPENDENT LEARNING STRATEGIES FOR STUDENTS

Whether or not you are an avid fan of project-based learning, we see an opportunity here for your students to engage in some interior design projects. Students might work in small groups to offer input or perhaps even completely redesign your classroom environment. If this might be too comprehensive an endeavor, you can open a suggestion box and invite your students to anonymously leave comments about the classroom environment and share their ideas for improvement. You might be surprised by how many observations and insights your students want you to consider! Consider the 4 Cs framework we developed for nurturing student input and independence related to environmental scaffolding in Table 10.4.

TABLE 10.4 ● The 4 Cs Framework for Student Independence

KEY ELEMENTS	WHY DOES IT MATTER	WHAT IT MIGHT LOOK LIKE
Communication	Students must be able to share if they experience discomfort or feel unsafe.	Educators have an open-door policy and regularly invite student conversations.
Choice	Students must have some control over their "home away from home"—their classroom environment and must be able to make responsible choices.	Students are regularly given the option to choose their seating arrangements for select learning activities.
Creativity	Students' talents and gifts must be recognized and nurtured in multiple ways.	Classroom space celebrates student work, such as designated wall space for student creations.
Collaboration	Students must understand that there are lots of diverse ideas and needs within a classroom community.	Students collaborate with classmates to contribute to enhancing the classroom environment to be more conducive to learning for all.

WHAT TEACHERS SAY ABOUT ENVIRONMENTAL SCAFFOLDING

As I reflect on the importance of how a classroom is arranged for learning, and how it might support students with diverse learning needs, I think that the physical environment profoundly influences students' educational experiences. I have observed in my class just how a well-structured classroom can foster safety and a sense of belonging while accommodating students with varied learning preferences and needs. For example, the creation of distinct learning spaces in the classroom has encouraged students to collaborate with one another, complete independent work without distraction, and participate in hands-on activities, thereby enhancing their engagement, support, and enjoyment.

Flexible seating options stand out as a vital aspect of classroom design. Allowing students to choose from various seating arrangements such as bean bags, couches, carpets and traditional chairs enables them to find their preferred level of comfort, which, in turn, helps students to focus and remain on task. Classroom arrangements, like seating choices, foster student autonomy and empower them to take ownership of their learning journeys. Moreover, the intentional organization and positioning of materials and displays reinforces a commitment to inclusivity. By incorporating resources that reflect diverse cultural and linguistic backgrounds, every student feels acknowledged and valued. This practice not only promotes a sense of belonging but also enriches the classroom experience for all students by incorporating varied perspectives.

Maintaining a well-organized classroom with clear labeling not only prevents clutter but also teaches students valuable skills in responsibility and independence while supporting the building of language and literacy skills. When students recognize where materials belong and relate their accompanying labels to spoken words, they are better able to take charge of their class environment and their own learning. Ultimately, I think an effective classroom arrangement is a celebration of each student's uniqueness that nurtures an inclusive atmosphere where all learners thrive. Each element—seating, organization, and displays—play a crucial role in creating a supportive educational space.

—Yonique Benn, special education teacher, Baldwin, New York

SUMMARY

In this chapter, we uncovered the transformative power of reimagining learning spaces for multilingual learners. We explored how each classroom and school can be designed to create inclusive, engaging environments where high expectations for every learner is its cornerstone. We reviewed how creating print-rich environments for scaffolded learning are essential for the engagement of multilingual learners. By ensuring student access to relevant resources, all students are better able to see themselves in the curriculum as well as can take charge of their own learning. Equally important is for attention to be paid in creating safe and comfortable learning spaces through thoughtful designs that keep students' learning preferences in mind. Environmental scaffolding for multilingual learners highlights the necessity of structuring physical learning spaces to support each student's overall understanding, engagement, language acquisition, and academic achievement.

Questions

1. How can creating a print-rich environment with visual supports, such as word walls and graphic organizers, help multilingual learners better access and engage with content?
2. To what extent do flexible seating arrangements address the diverse learning preferences of multilingual learners, and how can their effectiveness be assessed?
3. How can educators effectively integrate students' cultural backgrounds and languages into classroom environments while balancing the academic needs of multilingual learners with those of their monolingual peers?
4. What specific environmental factors, such as noise levels or lighting quality, have the greatest impact on multilingual learners' focus and academic success, and how can these factors be mitigated to create an optimal learning space?

References

Adachi, B., & Cho, H. (2024, November 18). Cross-linguistic transfer: Practical strategies for supporting English learners [Conference session]. In *2024 Dakota TESOL Conference*. ND.

Alvarez, J. (2010). *In the time of the butterflies*. Algonquin Books.

American Library Association. (2022). *2022 ALSC graphic novels lists*. https://www.ala.org/alsc/publications-resources/book-lists/graphicnovels2022

Anderson, E. F. (2015). Engaging and effective strategies for English language learners. In D. Sisk (Ed.), *Accelerating and extending literacy for diverse students* (pp. 66–83). Rowman & Littlefield.

Anderson, J., & La Rocca, W. (2017). *Patterns of power: Inviting young writers into the conventions of language, Grades 1–5*. Stenhouse.

Anderson, J., Leech, T., & Clark, M. (2021). *Patterns of power: Inviting adolescent writers into the conventions of language, Grades 6–8*. Stenhouse.

Anderson, L. W., & Krathwohl, D. R. (Eds.). (2001). *A taxonomy for learning, teaching, and assessing: A revision of Bloom's Taxonomy of educational objectives*. Allyn & Bacon.

Bambrick-Santoyo, P. A., Settles, A., & Worrell, J. (2013). *Great habits, great readers: A practical guide to K–4 reading in light of the Common Core*. Jossey-Bass.

Beck, I. L., McKeown, M. G., & Kucan, L. (2002). *Bringing words to life: Robust vocabulary instruction*. Guilford.

Berman, S., Chaffee, S., & Sarmiento, J. (2018). *The practice base for how we learn: Supporting students' social, emotional, and academic development—Consensus statements of practice from the Council of Distinguished Educators*. National Commission on Social, Emotional, and Academic Development, The Aspen Institute.

Blackburn, B. (2008). *Rigor is not a four-letter word*. Routledge.

Blackburn, B. (2025). *Scaffolding for success*. Routledge.

Bloom, B. S. (1956). *Taxonomy of educational objectives: The classification of educational goals*. David McKay.

Boblett, N. (2012). Scaffolding: Defining the metaphor. *Teachers College, Columbia University Working Papers in TESOL & Applied Linguistics*, *12*(2), 1–16.

Bruner, J. S. (1978). The role of dialogue in language acquisition. In A. Sinclair, R. Jarvella, & W. J. M. Levelt (Eds.), *The child's conception of language* (pp. 241–256). Springer-Verlag.

Bunch, G. C. (2013). Pedagogical language knowledge: Preparing mainstream teachers for English learners in the new standards era. *Review of Research in Education*, *37*, 298–341.

Bunch, G. C., & Martin, D. (2021). From "academic language" to the "language of ideas": A disciplinary perspective on using language in K–12 settings. *Language and Education*, *35*(6), 539–556.

Burhan-Horasanlı, E. (2022). Digital social reading: Exploring multilingual graduate students' academic discourse socialization in online platforms. *Linguistics and Education*, *71*, e101099.

Burkins, J., & Yaris, K. (2013). *Top ten themes of IRA Convention 2013*. www.burkinsandyaris.com/top-ten-themes-of-ira-convention-2013

Cappello, M., & Walker, N. T. (2016). Visual thinking strategies: Teachers' reflections on closely reading complex visual texts within the disciplines. *The Reading Teacher*, *70*(3), 317–325.

CAST. (2024). *Universal design for learning (UDL)*. https://udlguidelines.cast.org/

Chan, S. C. H., Wan, C. L. J., & Ko, S. (2019). Interactivity, active collaborative learning, and learning performance: The moderating role of perceived fun by using personal response systems. *The International Journal of Management Education*, *17*(1), 94–102.

Clark, J. M., & Paivio, A. (1991). Dual coding theory and education. *Education Psychology Review*, *3*(3), 149–210.

Collaborative for Academic, Social, and Emotional Learning (CASEL). (n.d.). *Fundamentals of SEL*. https://casel.org/fundamentals-of-sel/

Cooper, A. (2012). *10 tips for teaching English-language learners: Tools and techniques for better instruction*. https://www.edutopia.org/blog/teaching-english-language-learners-ayanna-cooper

Craddock, A. (2021). Let's give them something to talk about.... *Science and Children*, *59*(1), 47–53.

Dalton, B. (2012). Multimodal composition and the Common Core State Standards. *The Reading Teacher*, 66(4), 333–339.

de Oliveira, L. C., & Westerlund, R. (Eds.). (2023). *Scaffolding for multilingual learners in elementary and secondary schools*. Routledge.

de Oliveira, L. C., & Westerlund, R. (2023). Scaffolding for multilingual learners. In L. C. de Oliveira, & R. Westerlund (Eds.), *Scaffolding for multilingual learners in elementary and secondary schools* (pp. 1–6). Routledge.

Diamantopoulou, S., & Ørevik, S. (Eds.). (2022). *Multimodality in English language learning*. Routledge.

Dove, M. G., & Honigsfeld, A. (2013). *Common core for the not-so-common learner, Grades K–5: English language arts strategies*. Corwin.

Downey, M., & Basile, A. (n.d.). *Mandala collections texts: Smell the rose, blow out the candle: Mindful breathing practice K–5*. https://texts.mandala.library.virginia.edu/text/smell-rose-blow-out-candle-mindful-breathing-practice-k-5

Dubinsky, J. M., & Hamid, A. A. (2024). The neuroscience of active learning and direct instruction. *Neuroscience & Biobehavioral Reviews*, 163, e-105737.

Dubois, D., Cance, C., Coler, M., Paté, A., & Guastavino, C. (2021). *Sensory experiences: Exploring meaning and the senses*. John Benjamins.

Dweck, C. (2006). *Mindset: The new psychology of success*. Random House.

Eggebrecht-Weinschreider, C. (2020). *Comfort is critical for student success: Here are 3 simple factors to consider*. https://spaces4learning.com/articles/2020/05/25/comfort-is-critical-for-student-success.-here-are-3-simple-factors-to-consider.aspx

Fendick, F. (1990). *The correlation between teacher clarity or communication and student achievement gain: A meta-analysis*. https://www.proquest.com/openview/c32e5bd99c5fed2f57cec49cfde13851/1?pq-origsite=gscholar&cbl=18750&diss=y

Ferlazzo, L., & Sypnieski, K. H. (2022). *The ESL/ELL teacher's survival guide: Ready-to-use strategies, tools, and activities for teaching all levels* (2nd ed.). Jossey-Bass.

Fernandes, M. A., Wammes, J. D., & Meade, M. E. (2018). The surprisingly powerful influence of drawing on memory. *Current Directions in Psychological Science*, 27(5), 302–308.

Fernández-Fontecha, A., O'Halloran, K. L., Wignell, P., & Tan, S. (2020). Scaffolding CLIL in the science classroom via visual thinking: A systemic functional multimodal approach. *Linguistics and Education*, 55, e-100788.

Fisher, D., & Frey, N. (2021). *Better learning through structured teaching: A framework for the gradual release of responsibility* (3rd ed.). ASCD.

Fisher, D., Frey, N., & Akhavan, N. (2020). *This is balanced literacy: Grades K–6*. Corwin.

Fisher, D., Frey, N., & Almarode, J. (2023, June 1). *Supporting learners in where they go next in their learning: Back-end scaffolding*. Corwin Connect. https://corwin-connect.com/2023/06/supporting-learners-in-where-they-go-next-in-their-learning-back-end-scaffolding/

Fisher, D., Frey, N., Hattie, J., & Thayre, M. (2017). *Teaching literacy in the visible learning classroom: Grades 6–12*. Corwin.

Flores, N. (2020). From academic language to language architecture: Challenging raciolinguistic ideologies in research and practice. *Theory Into Practice*, 59(1), 22–31.

Ford, S., & Ford, S. (2014). *K.I.M. (Key Word + Important Information + Memory Device) vocabulary strategy*. https://helpingeducateothers.wordpress.com/2014/06/23/k-i-m-key-word-important-information-memory-device-vocabulary-strategy/

Fox, S., & McDermott, C. (2015). The role of 21st century skills in two rural regional areas of public education. *Journal for Leadership and Instruction*, 14(2), 26–30.

Francis, E. M. (2022). *Deconstructing depth of knowledge: A method and model for deeper teaching and learning*. Solution Tree Press.

Freeman, D., & Freeman, Y. (2007). *English language learners: The essential guide*. Scholastic.

Frey, N., Fisher, D., & Almarode, J. (2023). *How scaffolding works: A playbook for supporting and releasing responsibility to students*. Corwin.

García, O., & Solorza, C. R. (2021). Academic language and the minoritization of U.S. bilingual Latinx students. *Language and Education*, 35(6), 505–521.

García, O., & Wei, L. (2014). *Translanguaging: Language, bilingualism and education*. Springer.

Gibbons, P. (2015). *Scaffolding language scaffolding learning: Teaching English language learners in the mainstream classroom*. Heinemann.

Gonzalez, V. (2020). *Sketchnoting with students: The why and how*. https://seidlitzblog.org/2020/02/26/sketchnoting-with-students-the-why-and-how/

Gottlieb, M. (2023). Right from the start: Enriching learning experiences for multilingual learners through multiliteracies. *Center for Applied Linguistics*.

Grapin, S. (2019). Multimodality in the new content standards era: Implications for English learners. *TESOL Quarterly*, 53(1), 30–55.

Green, J. D., & Dillard, B. (2021). Scaffolding the scaffold: Creating graphic organizers to support your students' learning. *Transformative Dialogues: Teaching and Learning Journal*, 14(2), 61–74.

Halliday, M. A. K. (Ed.). (1980/2004). *The language of early childhood*. Continuum.

Hammond, J. (2023). Scaffolding: Implications for equity for diverse learners in mainstream classes. In L. C. de Oliveira & R. Westerlund (Eds.), *Scaffolding for multilingual learners in elementary and secondary schools* (pp. 9–28). Routledge.

Hammond, J., Cranitch, M., & Black, S. (2018). *Classrooms of possibility: Working with students from refugee backgrounds in mainstream classes*. NSW Government. https://app.education.nsw.gov.au/serap/ResearchRecord/Summary?id=46

Hammond, Z. (2015). *3 tips for making any lesson more culturally responsive*. https://www.cultofpedagogy.com/culturally-responsive-teaching-strategies/

Harlin, R., Sirota, E., & Bailey, L. (2009). Review of research: The impact of teachers' expectations on diverse learners' academic outcomes. *Childhood Education*, 85(4), 253–256.

Hesse, K. (1999). *Come on, rain!*. Scholastic.

Hill, J., & Flynn, K. (2008). Asking the right questions. *National Staff Development Council*, 29(1), 46–52.

Honigsfeld, A., & Cohan, A. (2024). *Collaboration for multilingual learners with exceptionalities: We share the students*. Corwin.

Honigsfeld, A., & Dove, M. G. (2022). *Co-Planning: Five essential practices to integrate curriculum and instruction for English Learners*. Corwin.

Honigsfeld, A., Dove, M. G., Cohan, A., & McDermott Goldman, C. (2021). *From equity insights to action: Critical strategies for teaching multilingual learners*. Corwin.

Huynh, T. (2021). *#34. Three types of scaffolding: There's a scaffold for that—ELL strategies*. https://tankhuynh.com/scaffolding-instruction/

Ironside, N. (2024). What I heard from my students about mental health—And what helps. *Educational Leadership*, 81(5), 26–31.

James, S. (1997). *Leon and Bob*. Candlewick.

Jocius, R. (2020). The CLICK model: Scaffolding multimodal composing for academic purposes. *Language Arts*, 97(3), 146–158.

Jones, S. M., & Kahn, J. (2017). The evidence base for how we learn: Supporting students' social, emotional, and academic development. In *Consensus statements of evidence from the Council of Distinguished Scientists*. Aspen Institute.

Jones, L., Smith, S. L., & Durham, C. (2022). Teachers as digital composers: Designing digital jumpstarts to scaffold for emerging bilingual learners. *Computers and Education*, *189*, e-104592.

Kafka, F. (1915/2010). *Metamorphosis*. Tribeca Books.

Kagan, S., & Kagan, M. (2015). *Kagan cooperative learning*. Kagan Cooperative Learning.

Krashen, S. (1982). *Principles and practice and language acquisition*. Pergamon Press.

Krashen, S. D. (1988). *Second language acquisition and second language learning*. Prentice-Hall International.

Kress, G. (2010). *Multimodality. A social semiotic approach to contemporary communication*. Routledge.

Ladson-Billings, G. (2021). I'm here for the hard re-set: Post pandemic pedagogy to preserve our culture. *Equity & Excellence in Education*, 54(1), 68–78.

Maldonado Rodríguez, L. A., & Krause, G. (2020). Flowing with the translanguaging corriente: Juntos engaging with and making sense of mathematics. *Teaching for Excellence and Equity in Mathematics*, 11(2), 17–25.

Masoumi, D., Bourbour, M., & Lindqvist, G. (2023). Mapping children's actions in the scaffolding process using interactive whiteboard. *Early Childhood Education*, 52, 1209–1220.

Mayer, R. E. (2005). *The Cambridge handbook of multimedia learning*. Cambridge University Press.

McKenzie, J. (1999). *Scaffolding for success*. http://fno.org/dec99/scaffold.html

Michaels, S., & O'Connor, C. (2015). Conceptualizing talk moves as tools: Professional development approaches for academically productive discussions. In L. B. Resnick, C. S. C. Asterhan, & S. N. Clarke (Eds.), *Socializing intelligence through academic talk and dialogue* (pp. 332–347). American Educational Research Association.

Michaels, S., O'Connor, M. C., & Hall, M. W. (with Resnick, L. B.). (2010). *Accountable talk: Classroom conversation that works (Version 3.1)*. University of Pittsburgh.

Michaels, S., O'Connor, M. C., & Hall, M. W. (with Resnick, L. B.). (2016). *Accountable talk sourcebook: For classroom conversations that work*. University of Pittsburgh.

Model Teaching. (2022). How to use the Frayer Model in your classroom. https://www.modelteaching.com/education-articles/teaching-strategies/how-to-use-the-frayer-model-in-your-classroom

National Center for Education Evaluation at IES. (2021). *Promoting Alternative THinking Strategies (PATHS®) Intervention Report*. https://ies.ed.gov/ncee/WWC/Docs/InterventionReports/wwc_SLE_PATHS_IR_mar2021.pdf

New York Times Learning Network. (n.d.). *What's going on in this picture?* https://www.nytimes.com/column/learning-whats-going-on-in-this-picture

Nordmeyer, J., Boals, T., MacDonald, R., & Westerlund, R. (2021). What does equity really mean for multilingual learners? *Educational Leadership*, 78(6), 60–65.

Nwokedi, B. (2023). Influence of classroom environment on the academic performance of students in English language. *International Journal of Advance Social Sciences and Education*, 1(4), 191–198.

Pacheco, M. B., Daniel, S. M., Pray, L. C., & Jiménez, R. T. (2019). Translingual practice, strategic participation, and meaning-making. *Journal of Literacy Research*, 51(1), 75–99.

Pacheco-Guffrey, H. (2021). Cultivating digital literacy. *Science and Children*, 58(5), 10–13.

Pearson, P. D., & Gallagher, M. C. (1983). The gradual release of responsibility model of instruction. *Contemporary Educational Psychology*, 8(1), 112–123.

Prasannakumar, S. (2018). Improving working memory in science learning through effective multisensory integration. *International Journal of Mind, Brain, & Cognition*, 9(1–2), 83–89.

Pritchard, R., & O'Hara, S. (2016). Framing the teaching of academic language to English learners: A Delphi study of expert consensus. *TESOL Quarterly*, 51(2), 418–428.

Quillen, K., & Thomas, S. (2015). Drawing-to-Learn: A framework for using drawings to promote model-based reasoning in biology. *CBE—Life Sciences Education*, 14, 1–16.

Qureshi, M. A., Khaskheli, A., Qureshi, J. A., Raza, S. A., & Yousufi, S. Q. (2023). Factors affecting students' learning performance through collaborative learning and engagement. *Interactive Learning Environments*, 31(4), 2371–2391.

Randall, B. (2023). *Has the Endangered Species Act saved species from extinction?*. https://www.snexplores.org/article/has-endangered-species-act-saved-species-from-extinction

Ray, K. (2023). *Here is what research says about screen time and school-aged kids*. https://edtechmagazine.com/k12/article/2023/01/heres-what-research-says-about-screen-time-and-school-aged-kids

Reading Rockets. (2023). *Concept maps*. https://www.readingrockets.org/classroom/classroom-strategies/concept-maps

Riordan, R. (2005). *The lightning thief*. Hyperion Books for Children.

Ritchhart, R. (2015). *Creating cultures of thinking: The 8 forces we must master to truly transform our schools*. John Wiley and Sons.

Roskos, K. A., Tabors, P. O., & Lenhart, L. A. (2009). *Oral language and early literacy in preschool: Talking, reading, and writing*. International Reading Association.

Rowe, M. B. (1972). Wait time and rewards as instructional variables, their influence on language, logic, and fate control: Part one—wait time. *Journal of Research in Science Teaching*, 9(2), 81–94.

Rubie-Davies, C. M. (2017). *Teacher expectations in education*. Routledge.

Rubin, H., Estrada, L., & Honigsfeld, A. (2022). *Digital-age teaching for English learners: A guide to equitable learning for all students* (2nd ed.). Corwin.

Salisu, A., & Ransom, E. N. (2014). The role of modeling towards impacting quality education. *International Letters of Social and Humanistic Sciences*, 32, 54–61.

Scholastic (2023). *Top graphic novels that encourage students to read*. https://www.scholastic.com/teachers/teaching-tools/book-lists/top-graphic-novels-for-reluctant-readers.html

Schroeder, N. L., Nesbit, J. C., Anguiano, C. J., & Adesope, O. O. (2018). Studying and constructing concept maps: A meta-analysis. *Educational Psychology Review*, 30(2), 431–455.

Seidlitz, J., Rogers, M., & Lara, M. (2024). QSSSA: The essential method for structuring conversations in all classrooms. *Seidlitz Education*.

Shi, J., Cheung, A. C. K., & Ni, A. (2022). The effectiveness of Promoting Alternative Thinking Strategies program: A meta-analysis. *Frontiers in Psychology*, 13, 1030572.

Si, Q., Hodges, T. S., & Coleman, J. M. (2022). Multimodal literacies classroom instruction for K–12 students: A review of research. *Literacy Research and Instruction*, 61(3), 276–297.

Singer, T. W. (2025). *Accelerating language and literacy: The flip-to guide to multilingual learner excellence in the core* (2nd ed). Corwin.

Sova, S. (2024). *Reigniting the joy of reading with book tastings*. https://www.edutopia.org/video/reigniting-reading-joy-book-tastings

Steinbeck, J. (1993, reissue ed.). *Of mice and men. Penguin Books*.

Streitman, K. N. (2024). Crafting a professional teacher learner through models of learning and positive psychological coaching tools. *Argumentum*, 20, 420–437.

Sundar, K. (2022). Concept mapping: A powerful tool for learning. *American Educator*, 46(1), 40–47.

Sweller, J. (2010). The Cognitive Load Theory and educational psychology. *Learning and Instruction*, 20(3), 241–245.

Symons, C., & Bian, Y. (2022). Exploring a linguistic orientation to facilitating refugee-background youth's meaning-making with texts: A self-study. *Linguistics and Education*, 70, e-101031.

Terada, Y. (2019). *The science of drawing and memory*. https://www.edutopia.org/article/science-drawing-and-memory

Vasinda, S., & Pilgrim, J. (2022). Technology supports in the UDL framework: Removable scaffolds or permanent new literacies? *Reading Research Quarterly*, 58(1), 44–58.

Victoria State Government (2018). *Literacy teaching toolkit: Multimodal literacy*. https://www.education.

vic.gov.au/school/teachers/teachingresources/discipline/english/literacy/readingviewing/Pages/litfocusmultimodal.aspx

Walsh, J. A. (2022). *Questioning for formative feedback: Meaningful dialogue to improve learning*. ASCD.

Walqui, A., & van Lier, L. (2010). *Scaffolding the academic success of adolescent English language learners*. WestEd.

Walqui, A., & Schmida, M. (2023). Reconceptualizing scaffolding for English learners: An ecological/sociocultural perspective. In L. C. de Oliveira & R. Westerlund (Eds.), *Scaffolding for multilingual learners in elementary and secondary schools* (pp. 29–47). Routledge.

Wang, C., Chen, K., & Lin, Y. (2018). The impact of graphic scaffolding on student knowledge acquisition in a computer programming course. *International Journal of Information and Education Technology*, *8*(3), 232–237.

Weissberg, R. P., Durlak, J. A., Domitrovich, C. E., & Gullotta, T. P. (2015). Social and emotional learning: Past, present, and future. In J. A. Durlak, C. E. Domitrovich, R. P. Weissberg, & T. P. Gullotta (Eds.), *Handbook of social and emotional learning: Research and practice* (pp. 3–19). Guilford Press.

WIDA. (2020). *WIDA English language development standards framework, 2020 edition: Kindergarten—Grade 12*. https://wida.wisc.edu/sites/default/files/resource/WIDA-ELD-Standards-Framework-2020.pdf

Wilfrid, J., & Molle, D. (2023). Scaffolding multilingual learners' equitable participation in disciplinary learning: A discussion of concepts and tools. In L. C. de Oliveira, & R. Westerlund (Eds.), *Scaffolding for multilingual learners in elementary and secondary schools* (pp. 48–62). Routledge.

Wolfe, P. (2001). *Brain matters: Translating research into classroom practice*. ASCD.

Wood, W. (2019). *Good habits, bad habits: The science of making positive changes that stick*. Farrar, Straus and Giroux.

Xu, N., & Valdez, V. E. (2023). Introducing translanguaging as pedagogy: Unpacking preservice ESL teachers' language ideologies and practices. In A. Esmail, A. Pitre, A. Duhon-Ross McCallum, J. Blakely, & H. P. Baptiste (Eds.), *Literacy, vocabulary, and acculturation: A critical education triangle for English language learners* (pp. 93–100). Rowman & Littlefield.

Yale Center for Emotional Intelligence (YCEI). (n.d.). *Ruler*. https://medicine.yale.edu/childstudy/services/community-and-schools-programs/center-for-emotional-intelligence/ruler

Yeung, A. S., Lau, A. S., & Cheung, A. C. K. (2017). Graphic scaffolding for English language learning. *Educational Technology Research and Development*, *65*(5), 1025–1039.

Zhu, W., Wang, F., Mayer, R. E., & Liu, T. (2024). Effects of explaining a science lesson to others or to oneself: A cognitive neuroscience approach. *Learning and Instruction*, *91*, 1–11.

Zike, D. (1992). Big book of books. *Dinah-Might Adventures*.

Zissou, R. (2019). *I had to run for my life*. https://junior.scholastic.com/issues/2019-20/090219/i-had-to-run-for-my-life.html?language=english#1010L

Zubiri-Esnaola, H., Vidu, A., Rios-Gonzalez, O., & Morla-Folch, T. (2020). Inclusivity, participation and collaboration: Learning in interactive groups. *Educational Research*, *62*(2), 162–180.

Zull, J. E. (2002). *The art of changing the brain: Enriching the practice of teaching by exploring the biology of learning*. Routledge.

Zwiers, J. (2014). *Building academic language: Meeting Common Core Standards across disciplines, Grades 5–12*. Jossey-Bass.

Zwiers, J. (2019). *Next steps with academic conversations: New ideas for improving learning with classroom talk*. Stenhouse.

Zwiers, J., & Crawford, M. (2009). How to start academic conversations. *Educational Leadership*, *66*(7), 70–73.

Index

CORWIN

To help every educator
help every student

We believe that every single student deserves a great education

We believe that knowing our impact is both a privilege and a responsibility

We believe that a fair, stable, and thriving society is built on education

PROFESSIONAL LEARNING SINCE 1990

Solutions YOU WANT | **Experts** YOU TRUST | **Results** YOU NEED

INSTITUTES

Corwin Institutes provide regional and virtual events where educators collaborate with peers and learn from industry experts. Prepare to be recharged and motivated!

corwin.com/institutes

ON-SITE PROFESSIONAL LEARNING

Corwin on-site PD is delivered through high-energy keynotes, practical workshops, and custom coaching services designed to support knowledge development and implementation.

www.corwin.com/pd

VIRTUAL PROFESSIONAL LEARNING

Our virtual PD combines live expert facilitation with the flexibility of anytime, anywhere professional learning. See the power of intentionally designed virtual PD.

www.corwin.com/virtualworkshops

CORWIN ONLINE

Online learning designed to engage, inform, challenge, and inspire. Our courses offer practical, classroom-focused instruction that will meet your continuing education needs and enhance your practice.

www.corwinonline.com

PLSN209A8

Visit www.corwin.com

CORWIN

ACO 365867